BRADMAN IN WISDEN

EDITED BY GRAEME WRIGHT

Hardie Grant Books

Published in 2008 by arrangement with John Wisden & Co Ltd
by Hardie Grant Books
85 High Street
Prahran, Victoria 3181, Australia
www.hardiegrant.com.au

Wisden is a registered trademark of John Wisden & Co Ltd

Bradman in Wisden is an updated edition of *Wisden on Bradman*,
which was originally published in 1998.

National Library of Australia Cataloguing-in-Publication data:
Wright, Graeme (editor)
   Bradman in Wisden : 100th birthday edition. 1st edition
   (Bradman in Wisden : one hundredth birthday edition)
   ISBN 978 1 74066 632 9 (hbk)
   1. Bradman, Donald, Sir, 1908-2001
   2. Wisden Cricketers' Almanack
   3. Cricket–Australia–History–20th century
   4. Cricket players–Australia–Biography
796.358092

Jacket and text design by Luke Causby, Blue Cork
Typeset by Nathan Hayward
Printed and bound in Australia by Griffin Press

10 9 8 7 6 5 4 3 2 1

Photo credits: The Bradman Museum, Bowral: pp. 2, 28, 34, 56, 62, 68, 84, 106, 125, 143, 181,
192, 203, 218, 225, 254, 268, 277, 300, 306, 315, 323, 335, 343, 368; Cricket NSW library: pp. 50,
130; Hulton Archive/Getty Images: pp. 20, 24, 38, 74, 80, 90, 102, 110, 152, 247.

CONTENTS

MAN OF THE PEOPLE

REFLECTIONS

SEASON BY SEASON 1927–1949

INTRODUCTION

WHEN NINETEEN-YEAR-OLD Don Bradman hit a hundred on his first-class debut, for New South Wales against South Australia in December 1927, *Wisden Cricketers' Almanack* was well established as cricket's book of record. By the time he retired from first-class cricket in 1949, Sir Donald Bradman, as he now was, had rewritten many of the game's records and his name was indelibly inked in *Wisden* for all time. Almost sixty years later, on the centenary of his birth on August 27, 1908, he still headed the career averages for Test Matches (99.94) and first-class cricket (95.14). In Tests he led the qualifiers by 21.80 runs per innings; in *Wisden*'s first-class list there was no-one within 23 points of him.

Of the twenty-four batsmen in the 2008 *Wisden* with 100 or more hundreds to their name, Bradman is the only one not to have played county cricket in England and he took approximately half as many innings to reach his 100th hundred as the next fastest, Denis Compton (295 to 552). It almost goes without saying that he was the first non-English cricketer to attain this milestone. He has more double-hundreds (37) and triple-hundreds (6) than anyone else. For almost thirty years his unbeaten 452 for New South Wales against Queensland was the world record individual score. Only two men have passed it since. And so the list goes on. Most double-hundreds in a season (6 in 1930), most hundreds on a tour of England (13 in 1938). The pages that follow proclaim landmarks passed as regularly as the passing of time. For unlike Napoleon, an earlier conqueror of fields at home and abroad, Bradman never did have to confront his 'burnt-out hour'.

This is what *Wisden* does so well. It encapsulates cricket's past. The match reports capture the essence of Bradman's playing days; the essays give substance to the figures by offering a more rounded portrait of the cricketer who dominated his game for two decades as few men have dominated any sport at any time. They tell us something of the character and temperament of the batsman to whom scoring centuries was not a pastime but a career. His hundreds came at an average of one for every three times he batted, and newspapers, not surprisingly, labelled him 'the century-maker' and 'the run-machine'. 'Bradmanesque' entered the language to describe values of high proportions.

Crowds flocked to see him bat. To borrow from Neville Cardus, they came to see him 'knock solemnity to smithereens', and many left the ground as soon as he was out. When he toured England, as he did four times, county secretaries would seek an assurance that Bradman would play, such was the effect his presence had on gate receipts.

When Glamorgan played the Australians in 1930, Dai Davies, the county's off-break bowler, could not believe his ears when his captain, Maurice Turnbull, took him off just after he'd almost bowled Bradman late on the opening day, Saturday. He pleaded in vain for another chance, promising Turnbull that he'd get Bradman out in his next over. 'That's what we don't want,' replied Turnbull, only too aware of the people who would come to watch Bradman bat on the Bank Holiday Monday. And indeed, Glamorgan's small profit at the end of the season owed everything to the receipts from that game.

While past *Wisden*s recount the crowds and the runs and the records, what they do not do is take the readers beyond the cricketer. We see nothing of the family man or the successful businessman. Bradman was a stockbroker and later held directorships in many Australian companies. Nor do we see what it was, beyond the run-scoring, that made him both a hero of his time and a legendary figure in Australian life.

R. L. (Bob) Arrowsmith, who was *Wisden*'s principal obituary writer from 1975 to 1987, held the view that what a man does off the field had nothing to do with *Wisden*. 'A man may be a horrible piece of work,' he said, 'but at the same time get on all right in the cricket world.' *Autres temps, autres moeurs.*

Not that Bradman was a horrible piece of work. Far from it. But the Arrowsmith way of thinking does give an indication of why contemporary *Wisden*s concerned themselves only with the cricketer, rather than putting him within the context of his times. When Don Bradman returned from England in 1930, Australia having regained the Ashes thanks in major measure to his 131 at Trent Bridge, 254 at Lord's, 334 at Headingley and 232 at The Oval, he was greeted with unparalleled adulation. And it was more than those scores that counted. His youth and genius caught the mood of an age that was looking to its young men and women to build a new way for Australia. At the same time his modest manner and his strict moral upbringing were in tune with a society not yet ready to abandon the established codes of conduct. Even so, as some well-publicised conflicts with the Australian cricket establishment illustrated, he was always prepared to fight his corner. No respecter of position for position's sake, Bradman was in that respect an Australian's Australian.

That was why England's Bodyline tactics in 1932-33 struck so deeply at the core of the nation. Devised and implemented to stop Bradman from making his match-winning centuries, it was a negative philosophy born of defeatism. It was alien to the tenets of sportsmanship, and it cut Australians as surely as 'the bloodsuckers of the Bank of England', with their policy of calling in British loans just when Australia was struggling through the Depression years. Its employment by the patrician Jardine was interpreted as a symbol of Britain's determination to keep Australia under her dominion. In that series Bradman transcended the cricket field and entered the consciousness of the young nation. He became Australia.

In compiling this anthology, I was amused at the way *Wisden Cricketers' Almanack* gave 'England' or the 'MCC Team' pride of place in the heading of its match reports of games in Australia. The convention these days is to name the home side first, and indeed when the Australians toured England, the home team did come first. From this distance in time it seems a small point, but it reflects the mindset of Empire, whether that mindset was conscious or subconscious. The mother country took precedence over the former colony.

Sir Donald Bradman's knighthood in the 1949 New Year Honours recognised his services to cricket; his investiture in 1979 as a Companion of the Order of Australia honoured a life dedicated to the game. Among the many appointments he held, he was from 1960 to 1963 and again from 1969 to 1972 the Chairman of the Australian Cricket Board – the first Test cricketer to hold this post. He endeavoured, he said, to encourage all that was best for the development of cricket.

Yet for all the endless intrusions that accompany fame and public office, Sir Donald remained a humble and private man. He was extremely fortunate in his marriage to Jessie Menzies, a childhood friend, describing their life together as 'the greatest partnership of my life'. Even so, their happiness did not pass untainted by sadness, as one line in *Wisden* does record. In 1936 Bradman withdrew from South Australia's first match against the MCC touring team following the death of their first child, a son, within two days of his birth. How this affected him we are not told. *Wisden* tells us simply that, 'After a disappointing start [to the Test series], he had an aggregate of 810 runs ...' *Autres temps, autres moeurs.*

However, just as times and manners change, so too *Wisden*. What happens off the field has become as much part of a cricketer's repertory as his or her deeds on it. Even when playing days are little more than a dream of fields, the prurient reader gets to scratch around.

So it has been with Sir Donald Bradman. Among the obituaries and feature articles that followed his death were those that delved beyond the great cricketer in search of a human face to the man, maybe with a hope that the human face would reveal some fallibility that made Bradman more like other poor mortals. More like ourselves, in fact. As if it mattered.

Bradman never wanted to be a national icon; if anything he went out of his way to avoid it. And yet the mythology, the iconolatry and the iconoclasm all found their ready subscribers. Do they tell us any more about Bradman, or do they say more about the writers; more perhaps about Australia itself? That search for the man behind the myth can also be a search for a truth, and one truth behind the Bradman myth is that it belongs to an Australia connected to its past, rather than one in touch with its present, let alone its future. Indeed, questioning the myth can be the healthy response of an Australia confident in itself and its future. The need for the Bradman myth no longer applies in an Australia able to assert its own identity as a nation. Countries change just as times and manners change.

Not that dismantling the myth in any way diminishes Bradman the man and Bradman the cricketer. As the following pages make clear, Sir Donald Bradman remains a one-off, the outstanding batsman of his generation and his century, a great Australian. He doesn't have to be an icon.

Graeme Wright

EDITOR'S NOTE

THIS ANTHOLOGY WAS FIRST PUBLISHED in 1998 as *Wisden on Bradman* on the occasion of Sir Donald Bradman's ninetieth birthday and has been revised and updated to mark the centenary of his birth. The essays and match reports come from *Wisden* publications ranging from 1929 to 2008. Naturally, over those years, styles and fashions changed, and so for the purpose of this book I have tried to be typographically consistent, even though it has meant changing a style used in the source. I have also added commas in years when it seemed *Wisden* had a moratorium on them.

Where inconsistency remains is in the initials of players. These remain as they appeared in *Wisden* at the time, so that D. Bradman needed a year before his upgrading to D. G. Bradman and Stan McCabe, for example, had to go through a tour of England before his 'J' was recognised. Only when an incorrect initial could lead to the wrong conclusion that there were two players of a certain surname, rather than one, or the wrong initials suggested a different player altogether, has the original version been amended. Nor have retrospectively corrected scores been adjusted. This anthology is not intended as an addition to the game's impressive statistical library. It is simply a celebration of a great cricketer.

Match reports have been abridged to concentrate on Bradman without, I trust, losing the flavour of *Wisden*. Where *Wisden* did not publish a scorecard, but gave only a 'potted' score, the teams and fuller summarised scores are given. In the few instances when one of Bradman's first-class games did not appear in *Wisden*, a similar method is used, with square brackets placed around the heading to show it was not taken from *Wisden*.

The numbers to the right of each first-class match denote the number of the match and innings played by Bradman. For example, the numbers

6 (11, 12) denote that this was the sixth game and the eleventh and twelfth innings of his first-class career. His Test Matches have been numbered similarly on a separate line.

Ray Webster's two magisterial volumes, *First-Class Cricket in Australia*, and the Association of Cricket Statisticians' *Who's Who of Cricketers* have been invaluable reference works in compiling this anthology. A useful ready-reckoner has been *D. G. Bradman*, compiled by Derek Lodge for the Famous Cricketers Series published by the Association of Cricket Statisticians and Historians.

In kindly consenting to his father's articles being republished in this edition, Sir Donald's son, John Bradman, remarked that his father 'was forever dipping into *Wisden*, which he held in high regard as a unique and trusted record and which gave him a great deal of pleasure throughout his life'. He recalled how Sir Donald would enjoy taking a *Wisden* from his set and leafing through the pages before citing from it, as if to say, 'There you are, it's in *Wisden*.' Just as *Wisden* readers around the world do regularly, in fact.

SIR DONALD BRADMAN, AC, 1908–2001

Fans flock to lay a hand on Bradman after his record-breaking 334 at Headingley, 1930.

SIR DONALD BRADMAN, AC, 1908–2001

BY ERIC MIDWINTER

The obituary of Sir Donald Bradman, which appeared in the 2002 Wisden Cricketers' Almanack, *was written by Eric Midwinter, a social historian whose work includes the theatre and soccer as well as cricket. He was Editor of the* MCC Cricket Annual *from 1997 to 2006.*

SIR DONALD GEORGE BRADMAN, AC, the most effective batsman in cricket's history, died in Adelaide on February 25, 2001, at the age of ninety-two, having been ill with pneumonia. He was born on August 27, 1908, with Australia, as a nation-state, but seven years old; twenty-two years later, he had become and would remain its most illustrious citizen. A legion of obituarists recorded and analysed his skills, and such was his impact on the game and on society that some of their analogues – Winston Churchill, Jack Kennedy, Shakespeare, Diana, Princess of Wales, the Pope – did not appear unduly extravagant.

Family and Other Background

Donald Bradman was the youngest of the five children of George and Emily Bradman. His father, a farmer and carpenter, was the son of Charles Bradman, who emigrated from East Anglia in 1852. Born at Cootamundra in the south-east corner of New South Wales, the young Don lived for three years on a farm at nearby Yeo Yeo, whereupon the family moved to Bowral, some seventy miles from Sydney and now the home of the Bradman Museum and Trust. It was here that the legendary practice with golf ball and single stump was undertaken, employing the brick stand of the family water tank. A bright, quick-witted scholar, an adept pianist and active in several sports, he attended primary and intermediate high school, leaving at fourteen to work in the Percy Westbrook estate agency. During his early cricketing career, he was involved, perhaps a little reluctantly, with sports goods promotion and journalism. Among his writings are four books, *Don Bradman's Book* (1930), *My Cricketing Life* (1938), *Farewell to Cricket* (1950) and a crystal-clear manual of instruction, *The Art of Cricket* (1958).

Later he would become a stockbroker with the Harry Hodgetts company in Adelaide, going on to establish his own successful stockbroking and investment concern, Don Bradman and Co., from which he retired in 1954. Over the next decades he took up directorships in a number of businesses and, having taken to golf with a will, was a long-time member of the Kooyonga Golf Club, near Adelaide. He was a strenuous worker in the field of cricket administration, serving six years as Chairman of the Australian Cricket Board of Control (1960–63 and 1969–72), the first Test cricketer to hold this post, as a Selector from 1936 to 1971 (apart from the 1952-53 season, when his son was ill) and, unflaggingly, as a member of the South Australia Cricket Association committee from 1935-36 to 1985-86. He did his best to offer sensible counsel on such issues as throwing, the South African ban and the Packer crisis, and he remained an unrepentant advocate of a reversion to the back-foot no-ball ruling.

In 1920, Don Bradman met Jessie Menzies of Glenquarry and, as schoolchildren, they became firm friends, eventually marrying at St Paul's Church, Burwood, Sydney on April 30, 1932. A vibrant and attractive brunette, Jessie Bradman provided him with a close and stable relationship over sixty-five years until her death, after severe illnesses, in 1997. Some have suggested that she was his only close ally, at once his solace and his occasional good-natured goad. Having lost a baby in 1936, the Bradmans had two children, John, born in 1939, and Shirley, born in 1941. So acute did John Bradman find the stress of being his father's son that he adopted the name of Bradsen in 1972, but to his father's pleasure he reverted to the family name in 2000. Bradman himself remained a warily private figure, prepared to take on arduous sporting and managerial tasks but flinching a trifle at limelight or unwarranted intrusion.

In the later part of his life, he lived in the fashionable Kensington Park district of Adelaide. He was knighted in 1949 and appointed a Companion of the Order of Australia in 1979. Following a private funeral – his family politely refused the accolade of a state funeral – a public memorial service was held in St Peter's Cathedral, Adelaide on March 25, 2001, with the proceedings shown on giant screens at the Adelaide Oval. On October 18, in the presence of family members and sixty privately invited guests, his ashes were spread at the Bradman Oval in Bowral.

Cricket: the Early Years

In 1920-21, the twelve-year-old Bradman scored 115 not out, his first century, for Bowral High School against Mittagong School and when, a season later, one of the Bowral club first team failed to turn up, Bradman, their scorer, played instead and made 37 not out. It was his first game with adults. After a convincingly successful flirtation with tennis, he settled down at seventeen to cricket and, in 1925-26, scored 234 for Bowral against Wingello, for whom Bill O'Reilly was bowling. He joined the St George club in Sydney for the 1926-27 season and made 110 on debut against Petersham, having adjusted seamlessly from dirt pitch to coir matting to turf. In December 1927, he made his first-class debut at Adelaide for New South Wales against South Australia and, not long past his nineteenth birthday, made 118.

Such marked achievement led to Test selection a year later, but, as Australia were trounced by England at Brisbane by 675 runs on a sticky wicket alien to his youthful experience, he made only 18 and one and was dropped for the first and last time in his international career. Returning for the Third Test at Melbourne, he scored 79 and 112 amid tumultuous scenes as the crowd recognised the emergence of a genius and a likely upturn in Australian cricketing fortunes. They were not disappointed: Bradman hit another century at the MCG in the Fifth Test as Australia ended a run of five straight defeats by England. Between these hundreds he completed a marathon 340 not out against Victoria at Sydney; the following year, again at the SCG, he established a world first-class individual record of 452 not out in New South Wales's second innings against Queensland. Almost three-quarters of a century later, it remained the highest innings by an Australian and in Australia.

His introduction into the international arena was crowned by an astonishing first tour of England in 1930, when he assembled what remains the record sum for a series: 974 runs, with an average of 139.14, in the five Tests. This included 334 at Leeds, his highest Test score and then the highest such score ever, an innings watched by the young Len Hutton, who observed how carefully Bradman found the spaces between the fielders. But it was the 254 in his first Test at Lord's that Bradman considered his perfect innings, in that every shot, including the one when he was out, was exact in its technical assessment and operation. That fabled summer he made 2,960 first-class runs, with 1,000 before the end of May, and eleven centuries in all matches. At the more material level there was a gift of £1,000, worth something like forty times as much today, from the soap magnate, Arthur Whitelaw, which indicated that, although he was an amateur, his cricket was the serious key to Bradman's livelihood.

The West Indians were his next victims when they toured Australia in 1930-31, with 447 more Test runs flowing from his quicksilver blade. There was national dismay when he was tempted by Accrington to play as its professional in Lancashire League cricket, but a counter-offer of newspaper, radio and promotional work kept him true to his Australian roots. Against South Africa in 1931-32 he achieved his highest seasonal Test average of 201.50 from 806 runs in five innings; his four centuries included 299 not out at Adelaide. Throughout these years, he was also scoring regularly and fruitfully in club and Sheffield Shield cricket, similarly able to sustain his concentration and acumen without undue stress.

Cricket: the Middle Years

Then came the notorious Bodyline series against England, though before it started, on his return from touring North America with Arthur Mailey's team, he became involved in a dispute with the Australian Board over his journalistic activities. That was resolved, but he still missed the First Test of 1932-33 through illness. Bill Bowes bowled him first ball in the Second, but he responded well with 103 not out in the second innings, his only hundred of that controversial rubber. Douglas Jardine, the autocratic English captain, employed intimidating leg-theory bowling, with Harold Larwood, along with Bill Bowes and Bill Voce, delivering short-pitched balls at high speed to a packed on-side field. There is little doubt that this ruthless campaign arose from an English despair over Bradman's ascendancy. His riposte was to shift leg-wards and rap the ball through an almost deserted off side, rather after the fashion of J. T. Tyldesley's murderous approach to leg-spin bowling. England won the battle but lost the war, for Jardine's tactics were condemned as unsporting and perilous. There were unfriendly exchanges and diplomatic ramifications, followed by changes in the Laws of Cricket to restrict on-side field placements. Bradman's average was pared to 56.57 for the series and it is worth noting that this was considered a measure of containment.

The rancour of the Bodyline series lingered but there was a substantive element of reconciliation on the 1934 tour of England, when Australia regained the Ashes. After a comparatively tentative beginning to the tour, Bradman scored 304 in the Headingley Test, followed by 244 at The Oval, where he shared a record second-wicket stand of 451 with Bill Ponsford, still the best in Ashes matches. Such heavy scoring sent his average for the series soaring to 94.75 from 758 runs, and he made 2,020 runs in that English summer. However, his health, which had for a year or so been troublesome, became critical when he fell victim to acute appendicitis. The cricketing world held its breath until he recovered, but it was a year before he played first-class matches again.

In pursuit of his business concerns, he moved to Adelaide and commenced playing for South Australia in 1935-36. Having scored a century on his last appearance for New South Wales, at Sydney in 1934, he marked his first Shield match for his new team with 117 against his old State, and captained South Australia to their first title since 1926-27. He made the sixth and last of his triple-hundreds, 369, against Tasmania at the end of the season, giving him an aggregate of 1,173 runs at 130.33, and the following season, when MCC toured under Gubby Allen, he was appointed captain of Australia. After an uneasy baptism, with two lost Tests, he rallied in characteristic fashion and saved the Ashes with spirited knocks of 270 at Melbourne (putting on 346 for the sixth wicket with Jack Fingleton after reversing Australia's batting order to counter a rain-affected pitch), 212 at Adelaide and 169, again at Melbourne. He averaged 90 from 810 runs in the series, and huge crowds cheered him on in noisy admiration.

Visiting England in 1938, he began excellently with 1,000 runs by the end of May in an amazing seven innings, and overall he scored 2,429 on the tour, with thirteen hundreds. In the Tests he hit centuries at Nottingham, Lord's and Leeds and enjoyed an average of 108.50, although his exploits were overshadowed by Hutton's monumental endeavour in the final Test when he accumulated 364 to eclipse Bradman's Ashes record. Undaunted, Bradman launched into his own domestic season, 1938-39, with a stream of six consecutive centuries to equal C. B. Fry's mark from 1901, and he ended it with a phenomenal average of 153.16 from seven innings in seven games. Soon war came to rob him of opportunities to add to his laurels and statisticians may only muse over what his record might have been.

Cricket: the Later Years

Weary bowlers and knowledgeable critics, who had assured their readers and listeners that his genius lay in sharp eyesight, were doubtless bemused to find that, when examined during his military service, Bradman's eyes were below average, a condition ascribed to his run-down condition. Next, an excruciating back problem led him to be invalided out of the Army in June 1941. It took him a long time to recover, and he was further dogged by the financial and legal troubles of his business patron, Harry Hodgetts, a situation that led Bradman to establish his own brokerage.

Thus there were question marks over both the fitness and availability of the now thirty-seven-year-old Bradman for post-war cricket. After deciding to play on, he had an uncomfortable start to the 1946-47 MCC tour. In the First Test at Brisbane he had laboured over 28 runs when he was 'caught' at second slip by Jack Ikin, the premier close-in fielder of his day and a chevalier among sportsmen. To Wally Hammond's chagrin, both Bradman and, more crucially, the umpire believed it was a bump ball; Bradman eschewed his ring-rustiness and flourished in what Neville Cardus termed a 'Lazarus' innings of 187. In the next match, at Sydney, chiefly in a partnership of 405 with Sid Barnes, he scored 234, and went on to total 680 runs at an average of 97.14 for the series, a calamitous one for England.

The touring Indian party of 1947-48 was treated to even greater exercises in dominance, with Bradman notching 715 runs for an average of 178.75. It was also against these visitors, for an Australian XI at Sydney, that he completed his 100th century, all done and dusted in 295 innings. He was the first non-English batsman to reach this target, as well as the quickest to the mark before or since.

In 1948, he led the famed 'Invincibles', a team acknowledged by many commentators as the finest international combine ever fielded, on their unbeaten tour of England. Carping voices might have hoped for a spin bowler of the uppermost rank to complete that 'ministry of all the talents', but by and large the claim remains a fair one. Bradman himself made 2,428 runs at an average of 89.92, celebrating his fortieth birthday with 150 against the Gentlemen in his adieu to Lord's, while in the Tests he scored 508 runs (72.57), including 173 not out at Headingley to help speed the Australians to a winning total of 404 for three on the final day. In the final Test at The Oval, however, Eric Hollies bowled him second ball for 'the most famous duck in history' when, to cite perhaps the best-known cricket statistic, he required only four runs to preserve an overall Test average of 100.

Apart from three more first-class games in the 1948-49 season, including a valedictory century, that was, from the straightforward cricketing angle, that. An adequate compendium of his figures is difficult to draft. The awe and majesty of this exceptional sportsman did lie more in his serial acquisition of runs than in the manner of his doing. Others might be prettier or more regal (although it would be unfair to hint that he was unattractive to watch, such was the balance and command of his technique), but none could keep the scoreboards rattling so peremptorily.

In the broadest of brush-strokes, he totalled 28,067 first-class runs in 234 matches and 338 innings at an average of 95.14 including 117 centuries, thirty-seven of them double-centuries. In sixty-two Sheffield Shield games, he averaged 110.19 from 8,926 runs, with thirty-six hundreds. Of his twenty-nine Test hundreds, there were twelve doubles including the triples at Leeds in 1930 and 1934. Within those parameters may be traced 1,000 intricacies of mathematical astonishment, but in the end they all subscribe to one fundamental truth: that a man who scores a century every 2.88 innings and a double-century every 9.13 has perfected a skill beyond normal imagining.

The Cricketer

The numbers are mightily persuasive. Donald Bradman is assuredly the most efficacious batsman cricket has known. There may be mutterings about this or that batsman emulating him on damp wickets, but they scarcely affect the outcome, and it should be recalled that Bradman played all his first-class cricket in Australia or England and none, for example, on the subcontinent, where he might have found conditions to his especial liking. Another discussion relates to the alterations in the game that might have tempered his run-getting, but these, too, may be exaggerated. Cricket has not witnessed much basic change since, about the turn of the 20th century, its institutional construct and principal techniques had been rounded and developed. What Bradman might have lost on the swings of more consistently agile fielding, defensive field placements and dilatory over-rates, he might have gained on the roundabouts of shortened boundaries, less varied attacks and improved equipment. Visualise him in a limited-overs match, with its restrictions on bowling and fielding.

Of moderate size, some 5 ft 7 in tall, he was a wiry, tireless character who seemed as unpressed at the end of a long, hot day as at its beginning. He walked slowly to the wicket, adjusting his sight to the light, always with a genial smile playing about his lips, and that measured tread was guaranteed to signal to opponents a discouraging assurance. He is said to have picked up the ball quicker than most, yet it was perhaps his ability to move rapidly into position from a stance of serene stillness that was an important key to his mastery.

From that juncture he appeared ready to select shots with deceptive ease and execute them with a frightening dominance, his unusual grip always militating against him lofting the ball. Much has been written of his indomitable powers of concentration. Mortal man cannot begin to understand the degree of composed self-reliance upon which this mental vigour was based. Other cricketers, said C. L. R. James, 'had inhibitions Bradman never knew'. The sole tiny bow to convention lay in his rarely opening the batting, although it seldom seemed to diminish him if a wicket fell immediately and he had to take centre stage. W. G. Grace would have scorned the wasted time of an inferior being permitted to replace him at the top of the order. None the less, no one has matched what Neville Cardus called Bradman's 'cool deliberate murder or spifflication of the bowling'.

He was a single-minded but never a selfish batsman. His compulsion, and it was as fierce in other branches of his life, was the winning of cricket matches, not the self-aggrandisement of personal run-making. Where some cricketers may have felt that making individual runs was the purpose, for Don Bradman it was a means to the end of victory. Thus he recognised that there were two foes. As well as the opposition, there was that proverbial old enemy, time. He therefore conflated two extremes of batsmanship – an unrelenting tenacity in defence and a complementary resolve to score quickly, adhering to the text of the American Civil War general who believed that the spoils went to those 'who get thur fustest with the mostest'.

The Sportsman

Charles Davis, the Melbourne author of *The Best of the Best*, demonstrated with lucid arithmetic what many cricket fans have believed as an item of faith: namely, that Bradman was not only the best cricketer but the best sportsperson of all time. Jack Nicklaus would have had to win twenty-five major golf titles, instead of his eighteen, and Michael Jordan would have had to have increased his average basketball points a game from thirty-two to forty-three to rival the great cricketer. Although the ghost of Sir Donald might occasionally glance over its ethereal shoulder to mark the progress of the phenomenal Tiger Woods, there the mathematical matter rests.

Under the pressure of such attainment, one feels forced to seek counter-arguments. It has been suggested that Bradman rarely played against what, by the statistics of wicket-taking, bowling average and strike-rate, might be regarded as England's top bowlers of all time. One statistician, Peter Hartland, has calculated that W. G. Grace, when aged twenty-five and having scored some 10,000 first-class runs at an average of 61, was at that moment twice as good as any contemporary batsman – a dominance not even Bradman could match. It might be cavilling to recall that Bradman was not a great cricketer but a great batsman. He was an unassuming leg-spinner with a mere thirty-six first-class wickets to his name; a highly competent out-fielder who took 131 catches, plus a solitary stumping; and a hard-nosed, shrewd captain. But this did not make him an all-round cricketer in the Garry Sobers or W.G. mould.

The Legend

The young Australia was struck by three hammer-blows in its first half-century as a nation-state. Its sacrifice in World War One amounted to 14.5 per cent of its mobilised troops. That is 1.2 per cent of the entire population; close to the 1.6 per cent of the British slain. The Depression years brought unemployment to 29 per cent of the labour force, with national income dropping by 30 per cent from 1929 to 1932. Then World War Two brought more perils, including the possibility of Japanese invasion of the Australian mainland. Historians are agreed that, from the late 1920s to the post-war years, Don Bradman acted as a unifier of the nation, a focus for its battered self-belief and damaged social fabric.

Of course, he was not a knowing standard-bearer: he had secular sainthood thrust upon him, which makes the comparison with Churchill, an ambitious seeker after power, a little lavish. Bradman rejected invitations to accept political or diplomatic appointments. As Charles Williams perceptively analysed in *Bradman* (1996), in cricket as well as to some extent in the nation there was a rift in Australia. Reduced crudely to an over-simplified equation, it was Protestant-Masonic, lower middle-class English, monarchical and subdued versus Roman Catholic, working-class Irish, republican and ebullient. Naturally some irritable envy was involved. There is no more telling tale than E. W. Swanton's recollection of the Oval Press box in 1948, with Jack Fingleton and Bill O'Reilly at hazard of strokes as they choked with mirth at Bradman's downfall in his last Test.

That uniformly abused tag of icon may legitimately be applied, however bold the deeds of other heroes, to only two cricketers. In that cricket is transparently a cult, Grace and Bradman played the roles of founder and consolidator. Because of the initial momentum of cricket, W. G., the creature of the railway, the steamship, the telegraph and the popular newspaper, has the wider distinction of being the father of modern sport at large, while The Don, although aided by the wireless, missed out on the expansion, engendered by air travel and satellite television, that has given sport a broader global spread. Indeed, spectator sport is the nearest we have to a *lingua franca*, a common cultural denominator, making a very few persons into meaningful beacons. The great Brazilian footballer, Pelé (number two to Bradman on the Davis scale of earth-shattering sports activity, with a ratio of 3.7 to the cricketer's 4.4), must take some precedence, and Muhammad Ali has to be considered in such a cultural examination.

Bradman is definitely of that tiny ilk – so much so that obituarists who compared him with Shakespeare, Michelangelo and Keats were slightly missing the point that Bradman may not be exclusively captured as part of an elitist, classical culture, but glows as a bright star in the popular constellation. Much as it might offend those who admired Donald Bradman in quasi-religious and high artistic terms, the logical comparisons, outside sport itself, are with the other global art-forms, such as cinema or pop music, coupling him with such names as Charlie Chaplin, Walt Disney and Elvis Presley. As both highly functional craftsman and cultural idol, he was exalted by millions.

D. G. BRADMAN, 1927–49

FIRST-CLASS CAREER AT A GLANCE

Season	M	I	NO	Runs	HI	Avge
1927-28	5	10	1	416	134*	46.22
1928-29	13	24	6	1,690	340*	93.88
1929-30	11	16	2	1,586	452*	113.28
1930	27	36	6	2,960	334	98.66
1930-31	12	18	0	1,422	258	79.00
1931-32	10	13	1	1,403	299*	116.91
1932-33	11	21	2	1,171	238	61.63
1933-34	7	11	2	1,192	253	132.44
1934	22	27	3	2,020	304	84.16
1934-35			(Did not play)			
1935-36	8	9	0	1,173	369	130.33
1936-37	12	19	1	1,552	270	86.22
1937-38	12	18	2	1,437	246	89.91
1938	20	26	5	2,429	278	115.66
1938-39	7	7	1	919	225	153.16
1939-40	9	15	3	1,475	267	122.91
1940-41	2	4	0	18	12	4.50
1945-46	2	3	1	232	112	116.00
1946-47	9	14	1	1,032	234	79.38
1947-48	9	12	2	1,296	201	129.60
1948	23	31	4	2,428	187	89.92
1948-49	3	4	0	216	123	54.00
Totals	234	338	43	28,067	452*	95.14

* Signifies not out.

AGGREGATES

	M	I	NO	Runs	HI	Avge
In Australia	142	216	25	18,147	452*	95.01
In England	92	122	18	9,920	334	95.38
Totals	234	338	43	28,067	452*	95.14

IN TEST MATCHES

	T	I	NO	Runs	HI	Avge
v England	37	63	7	5,028	334	89.78
v India	5	6	2	715	201	178.75
v South Africa	5	5	1	806	299*	201.50
v West Indies	5	6	0	447	223	74.50
Totals	52	80	10	6,996	334	99.94

SUMMARY

	M	I	NO	Runs	HI	Avge
Test Matches	52	80	10	6,996	334	99.94
For Australians in England	73	90	14	7,163	278	94.25
For New South Wales	41	69	10	5,813	452*	98.52
For South Australia	44	63	8	5,753	369	104.60
For Australian XI	14	19	1	1,233	172	68.50
For Other Teams	10	17	0	1,109	225	65.23
Totals	234	338	43	28,067	452*	95.14

HIGHEST INDIVIDUAL SCORES

452*   New South Wales v Queensland, at Sydney 1929-30

369   South Australia v Tasmania, at Adelaide 1935-36

357   South Australia v Victoria, at Melbourne 1935-36

340*   New South Wales v Victoria, at Sydney 1928-29

334   Australia v England, at Leeds 1930

304   Australia v England, at Leeds 1934

RECORDS BY BRADMAN

The only player to score more than 300 runs in an innings six times, he also holds the record for scores over 200 – 37.

The only Australian to score more than 100 hundreds – 117 in all; 76 in Australia and 41 in England.

He scored a hundred on his first appearance in first-class cricket and in his own Testimonial match after announcing retirement.

Two separate hundreds in a match four times. When he retired this was exceeded only by C. B. Fry (5), W. R. Hammond (7) and J. B. Hobbs (6).

He shares with C. B. Fry (1901) and M. J. Procter (1970-71) the record number of hundreds in succession – six.

Most hundreds in a season by an Australian in England – thirteen in 1938.

Most hundreds in an Australian season – eight in 1947-48.

He twice scored more than 1,000 runs before the end of May. No other Australian has accomplished this, and no other cricketer more than once.

Highest aggregate by an Australian in an English season – 2,960 runs in 1930.

Highest aggregate in Australia – 1,690 in 1928-29.

Over 1,000 runs in sixteen seasons, twelve of them in Australia.

The only Australian to exceed 2,000 runs on four English tours.

Most double-hundreds in Australia v England Test Matches – eight.

Highest score in Test Matches in Australia – 299* v South Africa at Adelaide in 1931-32 (superseded by R. M. Cowper, 307 v England, 1965-66, and M. L. Hayden, 380 v Zimbabwe, 2003-04).

Highest aggregate for one series of Tests – 974 in England in 1930.

Second-wicket world record – 451 with W. H. Ponsford against England at The Oval in 1934 (superseded by S. T. Jayasuriya and S. Mahanama, 576, Sri Lanka v India, 1997-98).

Fifth-wicket world record – 405 with S. G. Barnes against England at Sydney in 1946-47.

HUNDREDS – 117

1927-28

118	New South Wales v South Australia, at Adelaide.
134*	New South Wales v Victoria, at Sydney.

1928-29

131 133*	New South Wales v Queensland, at Brisbane.
132*	New South Wales v MCC, at Sydney.
112	Australia v England, at Melbourne.
340*	New South Wales v Victoria, at Sydney.
175	New South Wales v South Australia, at Sydney.
123	Australia v England, at Melbourne.

1929-30

157	New South Wales v MCC, at Sydney.
124 225	Test Trial Match, at Sydney.
452*	New South Wales v Queensland, at Sydney.
139	1930 Australian XI v Tasmania, at Hobart.

1930

236	Australians v Worcestershire, at Worcester.
185*	Australians v Leicestershire, at Leicester.
252*	Australians v Surrey, at The Oval.
191	Australians v Hampshire, at Southampton.
131	Australia v England, at Nottingham.
254	Australia v England, at Lord's.
334	Australia v England, at Leeds.
117	Australians v Somerset, at Taunton.
232	Australia v England, at The Oval.
205*	Australians v Kent, at Canterbury.

1930-31

121   New South Wales v South Australia, at Sydney.

258   New South Wales v South Australia, at Adelaide.

223   Australia v West Indies, at Brisbane.

220   New South Wales v Victoria, at Sydney.

152   Australia v West Indies, at Melbourne.

1931-32

135   New South Wales v South Africans, at Sydney.

226   Australia v South Africa, at Brisbane.

219   New South Wales v South Africans, at Sydney.

112   Australia v South Africa, at Sydney.

167   Australia v South Africa, at Melbourne.

167   New South Wales v Victoria, at Sydney.

299*   Australia v South Africa, at Adelaide.

1932-33

238   New South Wales v Victoria, at Sydney.

157   New South Wales v Victoria, at Melbourne.

103*   Australia v England, at Melbourne.

1933-34

200   New South Wales v Queensland, at Brisbane.

101   V. Y. Richardson's XI v W. M. Woodfull's XI, at Melbourne.

187*   New South Wales v Victoria, at Melbourne.

253   New South Wales v Queensland, at Sydney.

128   New South Wales v Victoria, at Sydney.

1934

206   Australians v Worcestershire, at Worcester.

160   Australians v Middlesex, at Lord's.

140   Australians v Yorkshire, at Sheffield.

304   Australia v England, at Leeds.

244   Australia v England, at The Oval.

149*   Australians v An England XI, at Folkestone.

132   Australians v H. D. G. Leveson Gower's XI, at Scarborough.

1935-36

117   South Australia v New South Wales, at Adelaide.

233   South Australia v Queensland, at Adelaide.

357   South Australia v Victoria, at Melbourne.

369   South Australia v Tasmania, at Adelaide.

1936-37

212   D. G. Bradman's XI v V. Y. Richardson's XI, at Sydney.

192   South Australia v Victoria, at Melbourne.

270   Australia v England, at Melbourne.

212   Australia v England, at Adelaide.

123   South Australia v Queensland, at Brisbane.

169   Australia v England, at Melbourne.

1937-38

101   South Australia v Western Australia, at Adelaide.

246   South Australia v Queensland, at Adelaide.

107 }
113 }   South Australia v Queensland, at Brisbane.

104*   South Australia v New South Wales, at Sydney.

144   1938 Australian XI v Tasmania, at Hobart.

102   1938 Australian XI v Western Australia, at Perth.

1938

258   Australians v Worcestershire, at Worcester.

137   Australians v Cambridge University, at Cambridge.

278   Australians v MCC, at Lord's.

143   Australians v Surrey, at The Oval.

145*   Australians v Hampshire, at Southampton.

144*   Australia v England, at Nottingham.

104   Australians v Gentlemen of England, at Lord's.

101*   Australians v Lancashire, at Manchester.

102*   Australia v England, at Lord's.

135   Australians v Warwickshire, at Birmingham.

144   Australians v Nottinghamshire, at Nottingham.

103   Australia v England, at Leeds.

202   Australians v Somerset, at Taunton.

1938-39

118   D. G. Bradman's XI v K. E. Rigg's XI, at Melbourne.

143   South Australia v New South Wales, at Adelaide.

225   South Australia v Queensland, at Adelaide.

107   South Australia v Victoria, at Melbourne.

186   South Australia v Queensland, at Brisbane.

135*   South Australia v New South Wales, at Sydney.

1939-40

251*   South Australia v New South Wales, at Adelaide.

138   South Australia v Queensland, at Adelaide.

267   South Australia v Victoria, at Melbourne.

209*   South Australia v Western Australia, at Perth.

135   South Australia v Western Australia, at Perth.

1945-46

112   South Australia v Australian Services XI, at Adelaide.

1946-47

106   An Australian XI v MCC, at Melbourne.

119   South Australia v Victoria, at Adelaide.

187   Australia v England, at Brisbane.

234   Australia v England, at Sydney.

1947-48

156   South Australia v India, at Adelaide.

100   South Australia v Victoria, at Adelaide.

172   An Australian XI v India, at Sydney.

185   Australia v India, at Brisbane.

132
127*   } Australia v India, at Melbourne.

201   Australia v India, at Adelaide.

115   1948 Australian XI v Western Australia, at Perth.

1948

107   Australians v Worcestershire, at Worcester.

146   Australians v Surrey, at The Oval.

187   Australians v Essex, at Southend.

109   Australians v Sussex, at Hove.

138   Australia v England, at Nottingham.

128   Australians v Surrey, at The Oval.

173*   Australia v England, at Leeds.

133*   Australians v Lancashire, at Manchester.

150   Australians v Gentlemen of England, at Lord's.

143   Australians v South of England, at Hastings.

153   Australians v H. D. G. Leveson Gower's XI, at Scarborough.

1948-49

123   Bradman Testimonial Match, at Melbourne.

Signifies not out.

VICTOR LUDORUM

CRICKETER OF THE YEAR
BY S. J. SOUTHERTON

GIANT OF THE WISDEN CENTURY
BY NEVILLE CARDUS

CRICKETER OF THE CENTURY
BY JOHN WOODCOCK

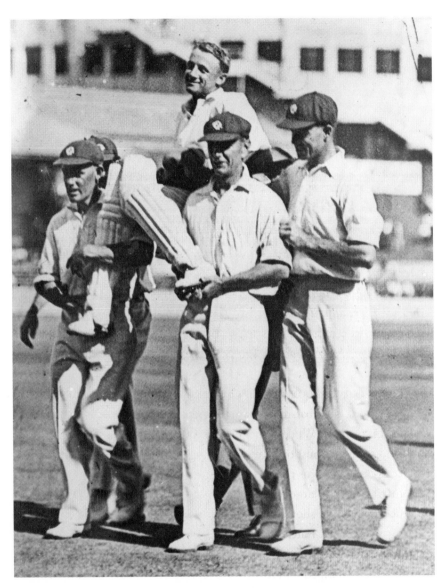

Bradman is chaired by team-mates after his world-record innings of 452 not out for New South Wales against Queensland in January 1930.

CRICKETER
OF THE YEAR

BY S. J. SOUTHERTON

Following his success on his first tour of England, in 1930, Don Bradman was chosen as one of Wisden's Five Cricketers of the Year *in the 1931 Almanack. The other four were his fellow Australian, Clarrie Grimmett, Bev Lyon (Gloucestershire), Ian Peebles (Oxford University, Middlesex and England) and Maurice Turnbull (Glamorgan). Sydney Southerton was a partner in the Cricket Reporting Agency, which for many years was responsible for compiling the Almanack, and he was Editor of the 1934 and 1935 editions of* Wisden.

DONALD GEORGE BRADMAN, coming to England for the first time, met with greater success as a batsman than any other Australian cricketer who has visited this country. When it is considered that he made his first appearance in a big match only just over three years ago – to be exact it was at Adelaide in December 1927 – his rise to the very top of the tree has been phenomenal. Yet in that particular encounter, his first for New South Wales in the Sheffield Shield, he showed clearly he was someone out of the common by scoring 118 and 33. Later on in that season in Australia he put together 73 against South Australia and 134 not out against Victoria and those performances stamped him as a future representative batsman. Sure enough, he got his place in the Australian team a year afterwards when the MCC side, under A. P. F. Chapman, were in that country. He did not justify expectations in a Trial match in October but in the same month he scored 131 and 133 not out against Queensland. Subsequent scores for his State included 71 not out against Victoria, 340 not out in the return with Victoria and 175 against South

Australia. Meanwhile, he had secured a place in the Australia eleven at Brisbane but, dismissed for scores of 18 and one, was passed over for the next Test. It was obvious a bad mistake had been made in leaving him out and, chosen for the third match at Melbourne, he put together 79 and 112. At Adelaide in the Fourth Test, in which England were successful by 12 runs, he scored 40 and 58, being run out in the second innings when he and Bert Oldfield looked like winning the match for Australia, while in the concluding Test Match – the only one in which Australia was successful during that tour – he obtained 123 and 37 not out, being in with Jack Ryder at the finish.

By this time he had, of course, firmly established himself, and it did not need another even more successful season in 1929-30 to make his inclusion in the team for England a certainty. He put together many fine scores in Sheffield Shield matches and at Sydney in the first week in January eclipsed everything else by an astonishing innings of 452 not out for New South Wales against Queensland. This score – the highest individual ever hit in first-class cricket – occupied him only 415 minutes and included forty-nine 4's. A month before this, playing in the Trial match prior to the team for England being selected, he put together for Woodfull's Eleven against Ryder's Eleven 124 and 225, while on the journey to England he hit up 139 against Tasmania. In Sheffield Shield matches that season he averaged over 111, or more than twice as many as any other cricketer in the tournament, with an aggregate of 894 runs.

Already, therefore, he had in a very short space of time accomplished wonders, but his triumphs were far from being at an end, for in England he left further records behind. In the second innings of his first Test Match in this country, at Trent Bridge, he made 131, following that with 254 at Lord's, 334 at Leeds and, after failing at Manchester, putting together 232 at The Oval. With his big innings at Leeds he beat the record individual score in Test Matches between England and Australia which had stood since 1903-04 to the credit of R. E. Foster, with 287 at Sydney. Without a not out to help him, an aggregate of 974 runs in seven innings gave him an average of over 139 for the five Test Matches, and in the course of the summer he altogether played eleven three-figure innings for his side, six of these being over 200.

Just as they did during the last tour of the Englishmen in Australia, so, at the present time, opinions differ as to the merit of Bradman's abilities, judged purely from the standpoint of the highest batsmanship. Certain good judges aver that his footwork is correct; others contend the reverse is the case. Both are right. For a fast, true wicket his footwork, if not on quite such a high plane as that of Charles Macartney, is wonderfully good. When the ball is turning, however, there are limitations to Bradman's skill. As was observed by those who saw him on a turning wicket at Brisbane and on one nothing like so vicious at Old Trafford last summer, this young batsman still has something to learn in the matter of playing a correct offensive or defensive stroke with the conditions in favour of the bowler. Still, as a run-getter, he stands alone. He does not favour the forward method of defence, much preferring to go halfway or entirely back. His scoring strokes are many and varied. He can turn to leg and cut with delightful accuracy, but above all he is a superb driver. One very pronounced feature of his batting is that he rarely lifts the ball, and as he showed English spectators so frequently last season, and particularly against England at Lord's, he will send two consecutive and similar deliveries in different directions. In grace of style he may not be a Trumper or a Macartney but his performances speak for themselves. Over and above his batting he is a magnificent field and, like all Australians, a beautiful thrower. Occasionally he has met with success as a bowler, but while his powers as a run-getter remain with him there is no need for him to cultivate the other side of the game.

Bradman first learned his cricket in pick-up matches at the Bowral Intermediate High School, and when he went to Sydney in 1926 at the invitation of the State Selectors for a practice at the nets he was a somewhat uncouth, uncultured batsman. Still, he made 37 in a Trial match and then played in the Southern Districts country team. He reached first-grade cricket in Sydney for the St George club in 1926 and, as has already been told, proceeded thence into the New South Wales eleven. After he left school, where he was entirely self-taught in batting, he played for the Bowral club and, with scores of 234 and 300, had an aggregate of 1,318 and an average of 109. In the one match he played for them in 1926-27 he scored 320 not out. Not yet twenty-three, Bradman should have years of cricket in front of him and, judging by what he has already accomplished, there would seem to be no limit to his possibilities.

Bradman poses for photographers in the wake of his world-record 452 not out against Queensland in 1929-30.

GIANT OF THE WISDEN CENTURY

BY NEVILLE CARDUS

The 1963 Wisden *was the 100th annual edition and among the special features commissioned to commemorate this landmark was 'Six Giants of the Wisden Century'. In response to the Editor's request, Neville Cardus (later Sir Neville) delivered 'appreciations' of the six he considered to be great cricketers of the past 100 years. His selections were S. F. Barnes, Sir Donald Bradman, W. G. Grace, Sir Jack Hobbs, Tom Richardson and Victor Trumper.*

SIR DONALD BRADMAN (hereinafter to be named Bradman or The Don) must be called the most masterful and prolific maker of runs the game has so far known. He was, in short, a great batsman. Critics have argued that he was mechanical. So is a majestically flying aeroplane. The difference between Bradman and, say, Victor Trumper as batsmen was in fact the difference between an aeroplane and a swallow in flight. But it is nonsense to say that Bradman's batsmanship was without personality or character, or nature, or that it was in the slightest anonymous. He had a terrifically dynamic style. It was thrilling to see him gathering together his energy at the last second to hook, a stroke somehow reminding me of a boxer's swinging stunning 'right'.

Like all great players, he made his strokes very late. He didn't move at all until the ball was on him; then the brilliant technique shot forth concentrated energy – and the axe fell. All the strokes were at his command. After he had appeared almost for the first time in an Australian State match, J. V. Ryder, Australian captain, was asked, 'How does this young

Bradman bat?' And Ryder, a man of few but eloquent words, replied, 'He belts the hell out of everything he can reach.'

Bradman's achievements stagger the imagination. Moreover, I think he knew at the time that he was about to do these extraordinary things; for he planned everything. No cricketer has had a quicker, shrewder brain than Bradman's. At Leeds in 1934, Australia bowled England out on a beautiful turf for 200. Then, at the afternoon's fall, Australia lost three wickets for 39. That evening Bradman cancelled dinner with me, saying he was going to bed early as, next day, it would be necessary for him to score 200 'at least!' I reminded him that on his previous Test appearance at Leeds, in 1930, he had scored 334. 'The law of averages is against you pulling off another big score here tomorrow in a Test,' I said. He replied, 'I don't believe in the law of averages.' Next day he set about scoring 304.

The extraordinary point of his innings is that, until this Leeds Test, Bradman had battled in the rubber with a certain lack of concentration, as though the effects of the Jardine–Larwood Bodyline assaults on him of 1932-33 were still shaking him. At Nottingham and Lord's, he played fast bowling with a rhetorical slash, a quite wild impetuosity. Now, at Leeds, in a serious hour for Australia, he could summon back at one call the old cool, premeditated craft and foresight.

I asked him once, in Melbourne, to give me some idea of how he did it all. 'Every ball for me is the first ball,' then, he added, taking away my breath, 'and I never think there's a possibility of anybody getting me out.'

The critics say he couldn't bat on a turning pitch. Hedley Verity held the opposite opinion – from experience. It is a fact, though, that The Don seemed occasionally not to face up to a 'sticky' pitch, *on principle*. He argued that wickets should be covered from rain, especially in his own country. It wasn't fair that a side should bat in perfect run-getting conditions one day. Then next day the other side could be trapped on a spitting pitch.

Bradman had all the attributes needed to cope with the spinning, kicking ball – swift feet, and an eye rapid and comprehensive. Against Larwood's devastating Bodyline attack, dangerous to breastbone and skull, Bradman in the Tests scored 396 runs, average 56.57. Jardine reduced his powers temporarily by half; but no other mortal batsman could have coped with Larwood as Bradman coped with him. In spite of Larwood's velocity and menace – seven fieldsmen on the leg or on side –

Bradman was driving or punching, to the vacant off side, bowling coming like lightning from a spot on or outside the leg stump, often rising shoulder high.

He first came to England in 1930, twenty-one years old. He began at Worcester with 236 in four and a half hours, twenty-eight boundaries. To Leicester he proceeded, to score 185 not out. Then, on the soft wicket v Yorkshire, he scored 78. And a newspaper placard announced, 'Bradman fails'. It was in 1930 that he exhibited, I think, the most wonderful batsmanship of his life, when during the Lord's Test Match he came to the wicket after Ponsford had got out. In two hours and forty minutes before half-past six, he cut, drove and hooked the England attack to the tune of 155. J.C. White, the untouchable, was brought on immediately to keep The Don quiet. White's first ball, a good length, was slapped to the on boundary, near the clock at the Nursery. Bradman leapt yards out of his crease; and the crack of his bat sent the Lord's pigeons flying in affrighted circles.

Nobody ever saw Bradman show mercy to a loose ball. If he went on the defensive, there was good reason. At Trent Bridge, in 1938, Australia followed on after they had scored 411 in response to England's 658 for eight (declared). McCabe made history with a marvellous and gallant 232. But the pitch grew dusty and the closing day had a severe ordeal waiting for Bradman. Early that day Bradman wrote home to his wife, Jessie, telling her that a job of work had to be done, but, he guessed, all would have turned out well for Australia long before his letter reached her. Bradman then set forth to Trent Bridge and saved the day by batting nearly six hours.

Never, as I say, did he play with sterile negation. He was a Test cricketer of our contemporary temper, realistic and without cant. He reacted to the environment in which he found himself. He hadn't to play, as Trumper was obliged to play, in this country, in games limited to three days. If he didn't throw his wicket away, as Trumper frequently did on reaching his hundred, the reason was that he played in a different economy of the game than Trumper ever knew. If and when Bradman stayed at the wicket all day he not only put his team in a position pretty secure from defeat but into a position from which the Australian bowlers could attack, with time to bring in victory; also he was holding the crowd in thrall.

He was a born batsman, out of a remote part of his beloved Australia, never coached academically; consequently he was free to give rein to his innate and rare gifts. He was born, too, with a good brain. Nobody has excelled Bradman's 'cricket sense', his intuitions and understanding. He must be counted among Australia's cleverest, most closely calculating cricket captains.

After he had scored a triple-century on a warm day at Leeds in 1930, he came from the field apparently cool, no sign of perspiration, not a buckle out of place, flannels immaculate, and, as the crowd roared him home, he seemed withdrawn and impersonal. People said that he lacked emotion. Maybe he was content to be the cause of 'emotion' in others – in bowlers, for example. Personally I have found in Sir Donald plenty of friendliness and humour. But, then, I was never called on to bowl or play cricket against him! Discussing him entirely from the point of view of a writer on the game, I am happy to say that he was for me a constant spur to ideas. A newspaper column couldn't contain him. He was, as far as a cricketer can be, a genius.

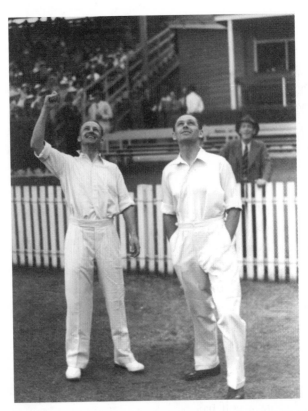

Bradman tossing up with Gubby Allen at Brisbane in 1936-37, his first match as Australia's captain. He never lost a Test in which he won the toss: this time Allen called correctly and England won handsomely.

CRICKETER OF THE CENTURY

BY JOHN WOODCOCK

For the 2000 Wisden, *The Millennium Edition, Editor Matthew Engel invited an electorate of 100 cricketers, writers, historians and observers from the nine Test-playing countries to choose Five Cricketers of the 20th century. All named Sir Donald Bradman. The other four were Sir Garfield Sobers (90 votes), Sir Jack Hobbs (30), Shane Warne (27) and Sir Vivian Richards (25). The Bradman profile was written by John Woodcock, Cricket Correspondent of* The Times *from 1954 to 1987 and Editor of* Wisden Cricketers' Almanack *from 1980 to 1986.*

'HE'S OUT.' To the thousands who read them, whether they were interested in cricket or not, the two words blazoned across the London evening newspaper placards could have meant only one thing: somewhere, someone had managed to dismiss Don Bradman, of itself a lifelong claim to fame.

Sir Donald George Bradman was, without any question, the greatest phenomenon in the history of cricket, indeed in the history of all ball games. To start with, he had a deep and undying love of cricket, as well, of course, as exceptional natural ability. It was always said he could have become a champion at squash or tennis or golf or billiards, had he preferred them to cricket. The fact that, as a boy, he sharpened his reflexes and developed his strokes by hitting a golf ball with a cricket stump as it rebounded off a water tank attests to his eye, fleetness of foot and, even when young, his rare powers of concentration.

Bradman himself was of the opinion that there were other batsmen, contemporaries of his, who had the talent to be just as prolific as he was but lacked the concentration. Stan McCabe, who needed a particular challenge to bring the best out of him, was no doubt one of them. 'I wish I could bat like that,' Bradman's assessment of McCabe's 232 in the Trent Bridge Test of 1938, must stand with W.G.'s 'Give me Arthur [Shrewsbury]', when asked to name the best batsman he had played with, as the grandest tribute ever paid by one great cricketer to another.

So, with the concentration and the commitment and the calculation and the certainty that were synonymous with Bradman, went a less obvious but no less telling humility. He sought privacy and attracted adulation.

How did anyone ever get him out? The two bowlers to do it most often, if sometimes at horrendous cost, were both spinners – Clarrie Grimmett, who had ten such coups to his credit with leg-breaks and googlies, and Hedley Verity, who also had ten, eight of them for England. Is there anything, I wonder, to be deduced from this? Both, for example, had a flattish trajectory, which may have deterred Bradman from jumping out to drive, something he was always looking to do. Grimmett was not, in fact, the only wrist-spinner to make the great man seem, at times, almost mortal. Bill O'Reilly was another – Bradman called him the finest and therefore, presumably, the most testing bowler he played against – as were Ian Peebles and Walter Robins; and it was with a googly that Eric Hollies bowled him for a duck in his last Test innings, at The Oval in 1948, when he was within four runs of averaging 100 in Test cricket. Perhaps, very occasionally, he did have trouble reading wrist-spin; but that, after all, is its devious purpose.

By his own unique standards, Bradman was discomfited by Bodyline, the shameless method of attack which Douglas Jardine employed to depose him in Australia in 1932-33. Discomfited, yes – but he still averaged 56.57 in the Test series. If there really is a blemish on his amazing record it is, I suppose, the absence of a significant innings on one of those 'sticky dogs' of old, when the ball was hissing and cavorting under a hot sun following heavy rain. This is not to say he couldn't have played one, but that on the big occasion, when the chance arose, he never did.

His dominance on all other occasions was absolute. R. C. Robertson-Glasgow called The Don 'that rarest of Nature's creatures, a genius with an eye for business'. He could be 250 not out and yet still scampering the first run to third man or long leg with a view to inducing a fielding error.

Batsmen of today would be amazed had they seen it, and better cricketers for having done so. It may be apocryphal, but if, to a well-wisher, he did describe his 309 not out on the first day of the Headingley Test of 1930 as 'a nice bit of practice for tomorrow', he could easily have meant it. He knew as well as anyone, though, that with so much more emphasis being placed on containment and so many fewer overs being bowled, his 309 of seventy years ago would be nearer 209 today. Which makes it all the more fortuitous that he played when he did, and, by doing so, had the chance to renew a nation and reinvent a game. His fame, like W. G.'s, will never fade.

FAREWELL TO CRICKET

Sir Donald Bradman's *Farewell to Cricket* is simultaneously more than it appears and less than Sir Donald's admirers would claim. First of all, the book must be seen in relation to its author's position. As potential 'news', anything The Don writes which accuses or 'reveals' will be a five days' wonder. I am convinced that he wanted no sensation: certainly little or no publicity was necessary to sell the book in large numbers. He did, however, I feel, wish to adjust many past differences, for this book is not for nothing called *Farewell to Cricket*. All the old dissensions, all his detractors' grounds for fault-finding during Bradman's cricket career, are dealt with and explained by Bradman in the light of his views and experience. Without the extravagance of his supporters, he has stated his own case and adduced sufficient reason to make it good. All this and a faithful record of the author's mighty cricketing achievements are here. On the other hand, this is not a great book: ability to score centuries in Test Matches is no more a guarantee of ability to write a great book than the ability to write a great book is the guarantee of power to score a century in a Test. I am, however, convinced that Sir Donald Bradman himself wrote this book – which is more than most famous cricketers can say of the books which bear their names. Sir Donald Bradman was never an easy man to know, but behind the words of this book the careful reader may catch glimpses of him, as I believe, in the round. If only for that reason, this account of a great career will not be forgotten.

From 'Cricket Books, 1950', by John Arlott

AS SOME SAW HIM

AN AUSTRALIAN VIEW
BY H. V. EVATT

BUSINESS-CRICKETER
BY R. C. ROBERTSON-GLASGOW

A PERSONAL RECOLLECTION
BY E. W. SWANTON

Bradman with his fiancée Jessie Menzies in the back garden of the Bradman house, Bowral, c1931. He would later describe their marriage as 'the most important partnership of my life'.

AN AUSTRALIAN VIEW

BY THE HON. JUSTICE HERBERT V. EVATT

This article appeared in the 1938 edition of Wisden. *In 1930 'Doc' Evatt had become the youngest ever justice of the High Court of Australia. He was Attorney-General and Minister for External Affairs in the Labor government in the 1940s and President of the UN General Assembly in 1948–49.*

IN 1937, D. G. BRADMAN completed ten years of first-class cricket. During that period many of his batting performances have been unprecedented. He has broken one record after another and already, in actual achievement, he has far surpassed the performances of all other batsmen of Australia. There is an easy-going tendency to discount the significance of cricket records and averages, and in some circumstances they may be misleading. But, in the long run, the records may lead irresistibly to certain conclusions, and in Bradman's case they prove beyond doubt that he is one of the very greatest batsmen of all time, possessing the faculty of doing his best on the most important occasions.

Bradman's figures are necessarily silent as to important aspects of his batting. At times the speed of his scoring has been phenomenal. For instance, his world-record score of 452 was made in 415 minutes. Typical of his brilliant hitting in Sheffield Shield cricket was the 238 in 195 minutes obtained for New South Wales against Victoria in 1932. His record Test score of 334 at Leeds in 1930 was made in 381 minutes. In 1934, at Folkestone he hit Freeman for 30 runs in an over. At Scarborough in the same season he scored 132 in ninety minutes. In 1931-32, in a second-class fixture at Blackheath, New South Wales, Bradman and Wendell Bill scored 102 runs in three eight-ball overs, Bradman obtaining 100 out of the 102. He hit ten 6's and nine 4's including 40 from one over. His total for the innings was 256, including fourteen 6's and twenty-nine 4's.

Whatever the original limitations of his stroke repertoire, Bradman has become the master of every stroke in the game. But the outstanding quality of his batting skill is that he employs it functionally, ever adjusting it to the task in hand. In England in 1934, when he was fighting against the onset of illness, some of the critics declared that he had degenerated into a mere slogger. But he rose to the great occasions of the Fourth and Fifth Tests. Undoubtedly his big partnerships with Bill Ponsford in those two games accentuated his illness, and the operation he subsequently underwent prevented his playing cricket again until 1935-36. He then captained South Australia to its first Sheffield Shield championship since 1926-27. Most recently, what I have called the functional character of his batting has been shown during his three great Test centuries against the last England side. Characteristic of Bradman's in-cricket is his perfect running between wickets and his shepherding of younger players during critical periods of an innings. Moreover, the team value of his performances is also evidenced by the fact that they have frequently synchronised with partnerships during which Bradman's partner has also batted with remarkable success.

Indeed, the team value of his mammoth scores has been immense. His innings have ensured not only practical freedom from the risk of defeat, but very often actual victory. Throughout his Sheffield Shield cricket career, the four-and-a-third-day or the four-day time limit has been in force. It was Bradman who first appreciated the increased importance of the time factor in such matches. He also perceived that, even in limitless Test Matches, and certainly in Tests subject to a time limit, quick scoring must usually be of enormous advantage to his side. Thus, both in Australia and England, Bradman has always endeavoured to accelerate the rate of scoring during the course of the day's cricket, a practice which few batsmen of modern times have adopted.

During the period of Bradman's career, the treatment of international cricket by the 'popular' Press has often added to the responsibilities of the players; and in Bradman's case, praise and blame have sometimes succeeded each other with bewildering rapidity. Fortunately, his character has enabled him to concentrate all his attentions upon the game itself. Further, he has vindicated the opinions of many that he would be a great success as captain, and it now seems certain that he will captain Australia for some time to come.

I cannot part with the subject of this sketch without expressing gratitude for the infinite pleasure which Bradman's batting has given to all cricket lovers. Unique as his record is, it cannot adequately describe his cricketing genius. Despite all his honours, Donald Bradman is still as modest and unassuming as the young country lad who came to Sydney in 1927 intent upon success in the greatest of all games.

Bradman the business-cricketer turns up for work.

BUSINESS-CRICKETER
BY R. C. ROBERTSON-GLASGOW

Affectionately known as 'Crusoe', Robertson-Glasgow played against Don Bradman in 1930 for An England XI at Folkestone. Principally a bowler, although a useful batsman as well, he played for Oxford University and Somerset before going on to write widely and entertainingly about cricket. He became Cricket Correspondent of the Morning Post *in 1933 and during World War Two wrote the 'Notes on the Season' for* Wisden. *This article appeared in the 1949 Almanack to mark Bradman's retirement.*

DON BRADMAN will bat no more against England, and two contrary feelings dispute within us: relief, that our bowlers will no longer be oppressed by this phenomenon; regret, that a miracle has been removed from among us. So must ancient Italy have felt when she heard of the death of Hannibal.

For sheer fame, Dr W. G. Grace and Don Bradman stand apart from all other cricketers – apart, indeed, from all other games-players. The villagers used to crowd to their doors when W. G. and his beard drove through their little main street. Bradman, on his visits to England, could never live the life of a private citizen. He couldn't stroll from his hotel to post a letter or buy a collar-stud. The mob wouldn't let him. There had to be a car waiting with engine running, and he would plunge into it, like a cork from a bottle. When cricket was on, Bradman had no private life. He paid for his greatness, and the payment left some mark. The informal occasion, the casual conversation, the chance and happy acquaintance, these were very rarely for him, and his life was that of something between an Emperor and an Ambassador. Yet, for all that, there remained something of that boy who, thirty years before, had knocked a ball or ball-like object about in the backyard of a small house in New South Wales. He never lost a certain primitive and elemental 'cheekiness', and mingled, as it were, with his exact and scientific calculations, there was the immortal impudence of the *gamin*.

But, above all, Bradman was a business-cricketer. About his batting there was to be no style for style's sake. If there was to be any charm, that was for the spectator to find or miss. It was not Bradman's concern. His aim was the making of runs, and he made them in staggering and ceaseless profusion. He seemed to have eliminated error, to have perfected the mechanism of stroke. Others before him had come near to doing this; but Bradman did it without abating the temperature of his attack. No other batsman, surely, has ever been able to score so fast while at the same time avoiding risk. He was, as near as a man batting may be, the flawless engine. There were critics who found surfeit in watching him. Man, by his nature, cannot bear perfection in his fellow. The very fact that something is being done which had been believed to be impossible goads and irritates. It is but a short step from annoyance to envy, and Bradman has never been free from envy's attacks. So, when, first in 1930, he reeled off the centuries, single, double and treble, there were those who compared him unfavourably with other great ones – Trumper, Ranjitsinhji, Hobbs, Macartney. And Bradman's answer was more runs. Others, perhaps, *could* have made them, but they didn't. No one before had ever been quite so fit, quite so ruthless.

It was a coolly considered policy. Cricket was not to be his hobby, his off-hours delight. It was to be his life and his living. He did not mean to be just one of the stars, but the sun itself. Never was such ambition achieved and sustained. Never was the limelight directed so unwaveringly on one man in one game. To set such a standard was unique. To keep it was a miracle.

When Bradman next came to England, in 1934, there were now certain qualifications. He was found to be incomplete against the great left-hand bowler, Hedley Verity, on a sticky wicket. At Lord's, in the Second Test, he lost his head, if one may use such a phrase of such a master of calculation and coolness. Perhaps it was attributable to his uncertain health. But too much emphasis has been laid on this failure. Verity himself did not agree with the popular generalisation that Bradman 'couldn't play on the bad ones'. And he knew. But it should be said that, with the exception of

Larwood in Australia during the 1932-33 tour, Verity was the one bowler who battled with Bradman on something like level terms, even on the truest of pitches. Besides this failure at Lord's in 1934, another man, one of his own team, contributed to some dimming of the Bradman glory. That was W. H. Ponsford, of Victoria. He was playing in his last Test series against England. Most of his records, once seemingly unassailable, had been stolen by Bradman; but now Ponsford, one of the greatest players of spin bowling that ever batted, ran level with his rival, and actually beat him in the matter of Test average by a decimal point.

Already Bradman had proved his power to live on a pinnacle of success. Now, against G. O. Allen's team in Australia, 1936-37, he was to show that he could return from failure. He started downright badly, and the vultures that await the fall of the great hovered expectantly. But he disappointed them, and, by the end of the tour, he was once more the authentic Bradman. In 1938, his third visit to England, he came as captain. Henceforward, in Tests, except for one innings of 234 at Sydney, he was to deal in single centuries only. It was a concession to old man Time.

Where does Bradman stand as a captain? Such a question opens the way to opinions which, even when gathered from those who played with him from day to day, cannot be reduced to any certain conclusion. On the field he was superb. He had seen and weighed it all. Shrewd and tough, he was not likely to waste anything in dreams or mercy. No one ever saw Bradman not attending. Cricket, to one who made and kept his way from hard beginnings, was a business, not a pastime.

He made mistakes. He took only three regular bowlers on to the field for the last Test at The Oval in 1938. For him, as for Australia, the match was a disaster. Bradman, when bowling, fell and injured his leg. England scored 903 for seven wickets; Hutton 364. Both these totals [were] Test records. Bradman was unable to bat, and Australia lost by the record margin of an innings and 579. How different from the scene of ten years later, when Lindwall went through the England batting like a steam drill. But, all in all, Bradman was the supreme tactician.

On the personal side, his success was more doubtful. Great captaincy begins off the field. True leadership springs from affection even more than from respect. Bradman certainly earned the respect. But, by his very nature, he was bound to have admirers rather than friends. Stripped to the truth, he was a solitary man with a solitary aim. It was what the man did rather than what he was that invited obedience. There are humorously affectionate stories about most great cricketers; intimate, if somewhat apocryphal tales about them. But there are no funny stories about The Don. No one ever laughed about Bradman. He was no laughing matter.

During World War Two, disturbing rumours reached England about his health; and, whatever truth there may have been in them, certainly the England team under W. R. Hammond found Bradman uncommonly near to being a sick man. But, happily, he recovered. So did his batting. Not without luck, surely earned, he first groped, then rushed, his way back to normal.

There followed his last visit as a Test cricketer to England. As a batsman he no longer flamed high above his fellows. He was now no more than a very fine player, and it was arguable that both S. G. Barnes and A. R. Morris were stronger factors in the quelling of bowlers. But Bradman's fame, if possible, increased. Next to Winston Churchill, he was the most celebrated man in England during the summer of 1948. His appearances throughout the country were like one continuous farewell matinée. At last his batting showed human fallibility. Often, especially at the start of the innings, he played where the ball wasn't, and spectators rubbed their eyes. But such a treasury of skill could spare some gold and still be rich. He scored 138 against England at Nottingham, and, when it much mattered, 173 not out at Leeds. Most important of all, he steered Australia through some troubled waters and never grounded on the rocks. Returning home, he received the first knighthood ever given to a playing cricketer.

Bradman's place as a batsman is among the few who have been blessed with genius. He was the most wonderful run-scorer that the game has yet known, and no batsman in our own time has so highly excited expectation and so rarely disappointed it.

A PERSONAL RECOLLECTION

BY E. W. SWANTON

Jim Swanton followed Don Bradman's progression from his first appearance at Worcester in April 1930 through his four tours of England and MCC's first post-war tour of Australia. After Bradman's retirement in 1949 they developed a friendship and maintained a correspondence that lasted until Swanton's death in January 2000. Written in 1996, this recollection was commissioned to appear in Wisden *after Bradman's death and did so in the 2002 Almanack.*

IN ESTIMATING DON BRADMAN'S cricket and his personality, one is confronted by a dichotomy between public acclaim and private qualification. Whereas his batting in the English summer of 1930 lifted him swiftly to a pinnacle of achievement beyond compare, he was simultaneously imprisoned by fame to a degree he could not readily accept. His own country, a young nation in search of home-grown idols, found in him something of a reluctant hero.

His impact on the English scene always remained clear in the memory, for in 1930 I was in my early years as a cricket writer, and the Lord's Test that summer was the first I reported. My late-April impression at Worcester was of a dapper little man, well-sweatered against the cold, nimble of foot, amazingly quick between the wickets, tirelessly ticking up 236 runs at almost a run a minute. So his batting continued throughout the tour: prolific, almost chanceless, an ever-growing monument to concentration and fitness. By mid-July the image of a phenomenon without parallel was clear to see. The command performance that hoisted him to a status of his own was without doubt his 254 at Lord's. At half-past three of a sunny Saturday afternoon, with Australia 162 for no wicket in answer to England's 425, King George V in grey bowler hat, with walking stick and buttonhole, inspected the teams lined at the Pavilion gate. Fifth ball afterwards, Ponsford was caught at slip by Hammond off White and in came the twenty-one-year-old from Bowral. He was not normally a spectacular starter, but now he moved swiftly out to his first ball and hit it on the full up to the Nursery seats. As White had pinned down the Australians with marvellous skill in 1928-29, this was a strategic blow as well as the opening stroke of his first 50 in 45 minutes. At close of play The Don was 155 not out, scored at exactly a run a minute. On the Monday, and more sedately, he completed what he always rated his finest innings — despite what came next.

His 309 not out on the first day of the Third Test at Headingley not only beat R. E. Foster's 287 at Sydney, hitherto the highest in England–Australia Tests, but also was 95 runs more than anyone (Foster, again) had scored in a day's Test cricket. It commenced with a hundred before lunch. By chance, I shared a cab back to the Queen's Hotel in Leeds that evening with two or three of the Australians and so had an insight into The Don's relationship with the rest of the team. 'Now we'll be good for a drink from the little beggar,' was the comment, but no such luck. At the hotel desk there he was, asking that a pot of tea be brought to his room. I cannot claim to have known him then, but it is well established that he showed no inclination for the company off the field of his colleagues. He was teetotal, a young country boy in a touring party most of whom were not only older but came from the more sophisticated background of the city. Yet, while he did not put his hand in his pocket or in any way court popularity with them, he was alive from the first to the financial opportunities that fame was bringing. Depression was deep in Australia. His ambition was to achieve a degree of security that would enable him to marry his childhood friend, Jessie Menzies.

What turned the coolness of most of his fellow-players to indignation and worse was the decision of his employers, the Sydney sports goods firm of Mick Simmons, to transport their celebrity from Perth to Sydney by rail and air, ahead of the team who continued their homeward journey by ship. Australia had found a hero beyond all imagination, and his arrival in turn at Adelaide, Melbourne and Sydney brought scenes of utmost hysteria. The

Don found himself enveloped in mayoral welcomes, presentations and dinners that had been arranged to greet the team, whose feelings, as they trailed unheralded in his wake, can be easily imagined. It meant nothing to them that in every impromptu speech The Don paid warm tribute to his captain, Billy Woodfull, and to the team. He has always stressed in his writings how embarrassing he found this triumphal cavalcade; apart from the embarrassment, the episode permanently damaged relationships with his contemporaries.

When I next encountered The Don, on the Australian tour of 1934, contact between the countries had been scarred by Bodyline, from which he emerged toughened mentally but with his playing reputation almost unscathed. He was the appointed vice-captain, clearly in line for the succession, but his recuperation from a critical operation for appendicitis and peritonitis after the tour kept him out of cricket for a year. Vic Richardson took the Australians to South Africa in 1935-36, and when Don was promoted to the captaincy, for the 1936-37 tour of G. O. Allen's side, he knew that several under his command would have preferred playing for the popular, outgoing Richardson.

This element, headed by Bill O'Reilly and Jack Fingleton, was still with him in the side he brought to England in 1938. The bowling in support of O'Reilly was too weak for Australia to do better than halve the rubber, but with thirteen hundreds in twenty-six innings – one every other! – the captain could well be said to have led by example, until he broke his ankle at The Oval. What richer irony could be imagined than, after congratulating Len Hutton on surpassing his record 334, Bradman should turn his ankle over in the deep bowling-mark dug by O'Reilly? My belief is that he did not have an Australian side solidly behind him until after those two Irish-Australians retired.

Don Bradman's war is an unhappy chapter in his life, not only because he suffered a health breakdown that culminated in his being invalided out of the armed forces after twelve months. His transfer from the RAAF, in which he volunteered as an observer, to a physical-training job in the Army soon became the subject of criticism. The MCC party were made aware of this feeling on arriving in Australia in 1946-47. On the face of it, he had opted to exchange a non-commissioned combatant role for one carrying a commission supposedly behind the lines, although his unit was shortly due overseas. In fact, The Don had privately sought the advice of Lord Gowrie, the Governor-General, who, he told me, strongly advised him to accept the Army offer. His lordship should have known his Australians better.

The Don Bradman who emerged after the war was a more mature citizen with a broader vision than one had known before. His handling of an almost unfledged Test side earned their friendship as well as their admiration. On a personal level, once one had gained his trust he was the most reliable and understanding of friends. He was quick to see the benefit to the game of co-operation with a responsible Press when the fourteen correspondents who accompanied MCC to Australia in 1946-47 formed the Cricket Writers' Club. It was thanks to his influence, as a member of the Australian Board of Control – inclined in the past to hold the Press very much at arm's length – that our club's invitation to the 1948 Australians enabled us to stage their first dinner engagement of the tour; incidentally, it was about the first post-war cricket dinner possible under food rationing. In the presence of the recently married Prince Philip, whose first cricket occasion this certainly was, Don Bradman made a speech rich in sentiment and humour, expressive of shared perils and the renewed fellowship of cricket. It was the speech of a statesman which the nation heard in full because the BBC held back the nine o'clock news.

After his retirement, Don retained a perpetual personal involvement in the game, as administrator, Selector, author and journalist. He had two spells as Chairman of the Australian Cricket Board and served it almost continuously for thirty years. There is no book of its kind to beat his *The Art of Cricket*, and his commentaries on the England–Australia series of 1953 and 1956 for the *Daily Mail* were models of their kind. His only other visits to England were to the historic ICC meeting of 1960 on the throwing crisis, and for a charity dinner for the benefit of the Lord's Taverners Fund in 1974.

The Don's influence behind the scenes in the matter of suspect actions was never made public. Convinced by filmed evidence of its seriousness – 'the most complex problem I have known in cricket because it was not a matter of fact but of opinion' – he went along with the dubious decision that, for the visit of Australia to England in 1961, there should be a moratorium for the first few weeks on throwing. But he returned to Australia with a personal solution in mind. He obtained from the State captains a confidential list of suspects and was able to see to it that none of them was selected. *Finis*. As to the Lord's Taverners dinner, he was assured that his presence would produce a £10,000 windfall. It did: there were 900 present, he spoke brilliantly, and he had spent the previous day signing every individual menu. The Don never gave less than 100 per cent.

Nor, as the years went by, did he decline help to any organisation or individual who solicited it. Forewords flowed from his pen, and every personal letter was answered by return post in his own hand. The healthy evolution of cricket depends on old players giving their services to the game in any of the ways open to them. Sir Donald Bradman left the field at the peak of his fame: yet in a sense he never retired, for his experience, his intellect and his time were always at cricket's disposal.

THE ART OF CRICKET

The Art of Cricket, by Sir Donald Bradman, has already, in the few months of its life, established itself as a classic of the game. Sir Donald clearly bent himself to the task of writing it with that single-minded concentration which raised his batting to such sustained heights. He indulges no literary excesses, but impressively – and quite characteristically – employs words with precision, undeterred by theories of style from using the same word a second time on the heels of the first when, in fact, that word is the only one which perfectly suits his purpose. Superficially, *The Art of Cricket* is a book of instruction: to the interested reader, however, it becomes much more than that. It is a reflection of the author's approach to the game and a careful gathering of his thinking about it, presented with superbly chosen illustrations. So it becomes the nearest approach yet achieved to an epitome of cricket. That the chapters on batting, fielding and captaincy should be illuminating was to be expected: that those on bowling should be so profound is a measure of the great batsman's study of his adversaries. To the younger reader this must be an impressively revealing study: while, at the other pole of play, it is hard to believe that even a Test cricketer could read it without profit. It has been said that Sir Donald, in his cricket, allied to his physical gifts that type of genius which Carlyle described as 'an infinite capacity for taking pains'. Those who never saw Bradman bat can be convinced of that second quality in him by reading his book.

From 'Cricket Books, 1958', by John Arlott

BRADMAN ON CRICKET

CRICKET AT THE CROSSROADS

WHITHER CRICKET NOW?

THE STATE OF THE GAME

THE THROWING TRUCE

Bradman making a characteristically aggressive front-foot drive during a Sheffield Shield game, 1930.

CRICKET AT
THE CROSSROADS

'This year,' Wilfrid H. Brookes wrote in his Editor's Preface to the 1939 Wisden, 'I have been favoured with articles by several well-known cricket personalities. Mr Don Bradman readily agreed to help and his views on important points of present-day cricket are sure to prove of widespread interest.' The previous year, 1938, Bradman had captained the Australians on their tour of England and, with his century in Australia's victory at Leeds, had helped ensure that they retained the Ashes.

THE EDITOR OF WISDEN has honoured me by asking for a contribution from my pen. He has left the subject of the article to me, but in doing so has helpfully made suggestions regarding various phases of cricket which are today the cause of much discussion. As I looked through those suggestions, I conceived the title of this article. It is intended to convey a meaning but not to be misunderstood.

No matter how much we love cricket and desire to regard it as a friendly pastime we cannot possibly disassociate its future, at least in the first-class category, from the cold, hard facts of finance. Nor can we blind ourselves to the fact that at this very moment public support for cricket (possibly excepting Test cricket, around which there is special glamour) suggests either that cricket is becoming less attractive or other forms of entertainment are gaining ground. It is a state of affairs calling for very serious consideration from player and legislator alike.

I am all in favour of 'hastening slowly' and have admired the peaceful but purposeful way in which cricket has for so long been administered in England.

Nevertheless, I cannot help feeling that with the quickening of modern tempo, the more Americanised trend which is demanding speed, action and entertainment value, it behoves all of us to realise we are the custodians of the welfare of cricket and must guard its future even more zealously than its present.

No matter what we may desire individually, we cannot arrest nor impede the tenor of everyday life whether it be in business or sport. With such thoughts uppermost in my mind, my reflections are intended to convey the impressions gleaned by an Australian who will naturally view things from a slightly different angle from the average Englishman. Also my opinions are based upon experience in the middle allied to contact with administrative officers and the public.

Duration of Test Matches

One of the most debated subjects at the moment is whether Test Matches should be limited or played out. Considerable colour has been lent to this particular aspect of cricket because of the remarkable happenings at The Oval last August. I have always held the opinion that it is futile to expect Australian teams to travel many thousands of miles to compete in a series of matches for the Ashes, and yet play under conditions which allow quite a big possibility of one match deciding the rubber, especially when that result may depend entirely on the weather and be inconsistent with the degree of skill otherwise displayed. But I rather doubt whether the big issue is limited or played-out Tests. I think the first consideration is the mental outlook of the individual who can, if he chooses, spoil any game by his interpretation of its character. And secondly, would it not be a better game if, by virtue of rules and conditions, the possibility of a match extending beyond three or four days became extremely improbable?

If these problems were attended to, maybe the other one would disappear. At least, I think it very largely would. There can be no doubt that in recent years changes have taken place in the methods adopted for preparing certain English wickets. The popular term used for the latest and questionable method is 'doping the wicket'. From my experience on this tour and discussions with people who are in a position to know, I am satisfied that some groundsmen can, and do, 'dope' their wickets. The effect is to produce an absolutely dead and lifeless wicket, useless to any type of bowler and not conducive to strokeplay by the batsman.

It is imperative that we should have wickets which are true and not dangerous (fiery wickets produce a crop of accidents, rob batsmen of confidence and drive them into less dangerous sports), but let them be reasonably natural and amenable to some fair degree of wear, not the sort upon which the world's best spin bowlers can't turn the ball an inch until the pitch is three days old. This difficulty with wickets mainly applies to Test Matches. County matches are usually played on wickets offering some degree of equality, whilst practice wickets on most English grounds receive so little consideration that one has virtually no chance of getting real practice except in the middle. The scales are not evenly balanced, and the question of wickets needs serious consideration.

A prominent English international, writing in the daily Press, declared, 'Give me another half hour of Leeds and let me forget The Oval.' He probably conveys in that statement the innermost thoughts of the majority of the players and the public. I agree with him, if I may add 1934 and 1938 after 'The Oval'. I do that to ensure that my concurrence will not be misconstrued. At The Oval in 1934 we Australians accomplished approximately what England did in 1938, so that I have experienced both winning and losing under those conditions. People left The Oval tired of watching the unequal fight. They did it when Ponsford and I were batting in 1934. They did it when Hutton and Hardstaff were batting in 1938. Not so at Leeds. The match was one succession of thrills. People fought to get into the ground, not out of it. Their hearts beat frantically with excitement, mine along with the rest of them. Did anyone think of that curse of modern cricket – batting averages? No! It was the game which mattered. Australia won. She nearly lost and if she had it would have been a greater game still. It was stirring, exhilarating cricket. There wasn't time to think of timeless Tests at Leeds.

Views on LBW

I believe the time is imminent when another change in the LBW Law should be made. When our forefathers devised this beautiful game, I have no doubt they intended it to remain a contest between bat and ball. But evidently, to use the words of an eminent politician, 'they didn't make it clear', and the practice of pad obstruction eventually reached such proportions that it became necessary to legislate against the use of pads.

Irrespective of where the batsman's pads or feet are, I believe that if a ball is pitched in a line between wicket and wicket or on the off side of the wicket and would have hit the stumps but is prevented from doing so by part of the batsman's person (provided the ball has not first touched his bat or hand) the bowler is entitled to be rewarded. Under the existing Law, that part of the batsman's person which is struck by the ball *must be between wicket and wicket*. Those last six words afford the batsman too much latitude.

An experiment could be tried with my suggestion similar to the experiment tried before the last alteration. I am confident that it would result in further reducing huge scores, increasing off-side shots, brightening the play and reducing the effectiveness of the purely defensive 'rabbit'. The leg side may have to be considered in later years, but it would possibly be too drastic a step to alter both sides at once. Just prior to the introduction of the last alteration in the LBW rule, there was a great deal of adverse comment about it. I then stated that these hypothetical ills would be found to disappear in practice. They did – and they would do so again.

The Over and the Toss

An experiment is going to be made with the eight-ball over. It has been used in Australia for years, has proved a great success and saved a tremendous amount of time. The only people who can reasonably object to it are the fast bowlers. Whilst their claims may be reasonable, we must consider the welfare of the game itself before any of its component parts. And in any event, if the authorities consider that fast bowlers are going to be unjustly handicapped, there may be other ways of assisting them, such as by allowing a new ball earlier than after the scoring of 200 runs as at present.

We very frequently hear a suggestion that the old method of tossing should be dispensed with. If any person has grounds for objection, surely it is I, after my 1938 experiences, but, on the contrary, I favour retention of the present method. To enable one captain to know in advance which team would have the choice of batting would pave the way to so many undesirable possibilities that I do not think it worthwhile discussing.

A Plea for Modern Scoreboards

I do, however, counsel very urgently the need of up-to-date scoring- boards of the Australian type at your principal grounds. I have just been reading an article in an English publication by a well-known writer. He was describing the happenings in an important match at Lord's. After telling of a glorious innings by a young player, he wrote, 'I had no idea of his identity – there were no scorecards about at the time.'

Such a state of affairs to an Australian enthusiast is hard to comprehend. I am well aware of the forceful argument regarding the revenue produced from selling scorecards, but I submit that 10,000 spectators who do not need scorecards to tell them what is happening are going to be a happier and more virile advertisement for the game than 8,000 who do. Cricket needs to retain its present followers and to gain new ones. Modern scoring-boards would be a big help, and any temporary loss would be recouped eventually through the turnstiles.

THERE ARE MANY other factors upon which I could enlarge, such as playing hours, the number of matches, and so on. They are sure to form a basis for future debate and argument, but their importance is, for the present at any rate, subservient to other problems. Whether my suggestions prove practicable or otherwise, time alone will tell. They are at least submitted in an honest endeavour to assist in ensuring that the game we all cherish so much will be enjoyed by future generations no less than our own.

I doubt if a happier series of Test Matches than the 1938 series has been played and I am quite sure the administrators of England and Australia are more closely united now than ever before. To me, therefore, it seems an appropriate time to try to achieve a greater measure of uniformity of opinion upon current cricket problems.

Net practice, as well as time in the middle, was an important component of Bradman's successful return to Test cricket after World War Two.

WHITHER
CRICKET NOW?

'I am especially pleased that Sir Donald Bradman is among the contributors,' the Editor, John Woodcock, wrote in his Preface to the 1986 edition of Wisden. *'His only previous article for the Almanack, in 1939, was headed* Cricket at the Crossroads. *He chose that title himself (as he did this), saying that it was "intended to convey a meaning but not to be misunderstood". It was written after what he felt had been a singularly happy series of Test Matches between England and Australia. Last summer's, also between England and Australia, was the same; but it is now another world we live in, as the great batsman observes.'*

AT THE REQUEST of the Editor I wrote a short piece for the 1939 *Wisden*. My main theme then was a plea for cricket to adapt itself to the quickening tempo of modern life, for administrators to consider ways of speeding up the game, to provide more modern scoreboards (especially in England), to face up to financial problems, and so on. Little did I appreciate at the time what a revolution would engulf cricket before another fifty years had passed.

The great stadiums of Sydney and Melbourne now display huge electronic scoreboards costing millions of dollars and giving a wealth of information to the spectators. The enormous electric light towers turn night into day at the flick of a switch. That, in turn, demands the use of a white ball, and to satisfy the television and marketing moguls the players turn out in a variety of coloured outfits. The whole scene stirs up human emotions ranging from those of a largely new and young audience (more liberally sprinkled with females than of yore), who yell and scream their support, to those of the dyed-in-the-wool lovers of Test cricket, who yearn for more peaceful, bygone days. As with so many things, it becomes well-nigh impossible to bring about a reconciliation between the opposing attitudes.

But where does the truth lie and what about the future?

Despite my deep feeling for the traditional game, and my conviction that a vast majority of players and the public still regard Test cricket as the supreme contest, we must accept that we live in a new era. If Sir Neville Cardus were alive today, I can well imagine how eloquently he would bemoan the huge attendances at pop concerts compared with the lack of support for opera or a Beethoven evening. But I am sure he would also admit that, irrespective of the quality of the music or the musicians, the public are primarily interested in entertainment. Perhaps he would throw in his well-known reference to an eagle, no matter how beautiful in flight, being no match for the Concorde. I am satisfied that one-day cricket, especially day/night cricket, is here to stay. If there is a threat to the survival of the game of cricket, that threat lies in the first-class arena, and it behoves the administrators to understand the challenge and face up to it.

I confess to a love for both types of game. Nothing can match the continuous cut and thrust of a Test Match, where the advantage see-saws and the result is unpredictable to the last ball. I can't imagine any sporting event being more exciting than the tied Test between West Indies and Australia. It wasn't only the finish. Here you had two teams of great players, led by imaginative and intelligent captains determined from the first ball to pursue victory by adhering to the principles upon which the game was founded. The match had spin and speed, superb batting and fielding; every facet of the game was manifested as both sides strove for victory.

It starkly revealed the Achilles' heel of the limited-overs match, namely the premium placed on defensive bowling and negative and defensive field-placing. One can get bored to death watching countless singles being taken when even the world's fastest bowler may be operating with no slips and five men on the boundary.

But let me turn to the good things about one-day cricket. It rids the game of the unutterable bore who thinks occupancy of the crease and his own personal aggrandisement are all that matter. It demands fieldsmen of great speed and agility with good throwing arms. The standard of fielding at all levels of cricket has undoubtedly been lifted. Running between the wickets, too, has taken on a new dimension. Risks must be taken to maintain the essential run-rate. Umpires are put under enormous pressure, having to adjudicate frequently on split-second issues: to their credit, I believe they have responded in a very positive manner and improved their standards.

Inevitably one sees the odd umpiring mistake, graphically portrayed by the modern marvel of the instant replay on television. With this new aid available, I should see no loss of face or pride if umpires were to agree, when in doubt about a decision, to seek arbitration from 'the box'. This could never apply to LBW, but for run-outs, and, on odd occasions, for stumpings or a disputed catch, it would seem logical.

My first-class playing career began in 1927, and having watched first-class cricket in 1921 I have seen as observer, player or administrator all the great players of the last sixty-five years. Indeed, I can probably claim to span seventy-five years because many of the 1920-21 players also played before the Great War. It is still absolutely fascinating to me to watch and compare players of different generations.

How often I was asked in 1985 whether Clive Lloyd's West Indians were the best team of all time! Unhesitatingly I replied that they were the best fielding combination I have seen. But no matter how competent their batting, bowling and fielding, they were so reliant on fast bowlers that they became out of balance on a slow, turning pitch. In addition, the batting became vulnerable, which was proved in Sydney when Australia's two spinners, Murray Bennett and Bob Holland, tore the heart out of the West Indian batting to win a convincing victory for Australia. And without detracting from the skill of Bennett and Holland, it was clear to any knowledgeable observer that they were not of the quality of Bill O'Reilly and Clarrie Grimmett. To me these facts are indisputable and tend to place matters in their proper perspective. Australia's victory confirmed my view that my 1948 side was the best I ever saw, with Lloyd's 1984-85 team and Warwick Armstrong's 1920-21 Australian side not far behind. And my reading of history causes me to think Joe Darling's 1902 Australians were perhaps equal to any.

Many cricket enthusiasts claim that the one-day game has brought in its wake a decline in batting technique. This may have some validity, but it is not necessarily true. People get confused between a normal mode of play and the essential improvisation needed to circumvent defensive fields. Vivian Richards and Lloyd are marvellous examples of batsmen capable of coping quite adequately in both types of cricket without sacrificing any basic soundness of technique. The main difference in their one-day attitude has been a willingness to take the risk of lofting the ball over fieldsmen's heads. I doubt if modern players in general cut or pull quite as well as some of their forebears did, but I attribute this largely to the ultra-heavy bats they use. These hinder shots other than those of the perpendicular kind, such as the drive.

Undeniably the limited-overs game caters for a plethora of fast and medium-pace bowlers who tend to bowl just short of a length. In general it discourages, in fact it almost tolls the knell of, the slow leg-spinner. But here again one must acclaim the marvellous leg-spin bowling of the young Indian, Laxman Sivaramakrishnan, who proved against the best batting in the world in Sydney and Melbourne early in 1985 that he could bowl his ten-overs stint, get wickets, and still be economical. I don't doubt that O'Reilly, Grimmett, Benaud, Verity and others would have done the same. So perhaps, after all, the game is highlighting the fact that *top-quality* spinners can and will survive any challenge.

An interesting facet of the limited-overs game is the general rule governing bouncers. It unquestionably controls them in a sensible and practical way, and is a rule which I believe should be adopted in all grades of cricket without delay. It clearly reveals the way experimental laws could be used in one-day games to ascertain their effectiveness and/or desirability in first-class matches.

I also believe we have now reached the stage when some limitation in the length of a bowler's run-up is warranted. It would be the first and most logical step towards speeding up the over-rate. In Australia that magnificent player, Malcolm Marshall (excluding Frank Tyson, the fastest bowler I have seen since Harold Larwood), has repeatedly shown us that a short run-up is sufficient to generate maximum speed.

The money now being paid to players has spawned professionalism beyond anything dreamed of fifty years ago. With so much money at stake I doubt if the modern professionals enjoy their cricket as much as did the players who were financially independent of the game and played purely for the love of it. Perhaps, too, monetary reward is responsible for some of the theatrical performances and even bad manners occasionally portrayed in recent years on the field. Happily I feel this unhealthy phase is on the wane, as players understand that good sportsmanship and keen competitiveness are not incompatible.

Whither Cricket Now?

Most people agree that too much cricket was played during the Australian summer of 1984-85, owing to the Melbourne anniversary tournament being added to the schedule. It highlighted the need to strike a proper balance between one-day games and normal first-class matches. The attendances at Sheffield Shield matches were adversely affected. Indeed, the mounting losses on Shield games, now amounting to hundreds of thousands of dollars annually, constitute the most seemingly intractable problem confronting Australian cricket today. We need the Shield to produce Test cricketers, but can receipts from sponsorship, television rights etc, continue to make up the losses?

Lovers of cricket will find in the pages of *Wisden* plenty of evidence that cricket has had its problems for a century past. Things have not changed much. Problems are still there – they are just different. It remains for players and administrators to accept the challenge to keep cricket alive and vibrant, and not to shrink from the decisions needed to ensure that end.

Bradman (left) with HRH The Duke of Edinburgh and Middlesex, and English cricketer Denis Compton at the Cricket Writers Club dinner for the Australian team, April 1948.

THE STATE
OF THE GAME

For the July 1993 edition of Wisden Cricket Monthly, *Sir Donald Bradman,
then in his eighty-fifth year, recalled in some detail his two earlier articles for*
Wisden *and discussed other matters that he felt merited consideration by cricket's
administrators. What follows are extracts from that wide-ranging article.*

THIS TIME [writing in *Wisden* 1986] I harked back to my 1938 views and
commended [certain] changes, not least the innovative floodlighting of
main grounds and the use of a white ball – thereby providing a marvellous
night-time spectacle. I see no reason why we can't have Test and Sheffield
Shield matches played under lights. I'm sure spectators would love them,
and any technical disabilities could be overcome. Some players question
such a move, but they are professionals, are paid substantial fees, and it is
their province to provide the entertainment the public demands and to
generate the finances required to support the structure of modern cricket.

It is interesting to see that in 1986 I advocated the use of a third umpire
or instant replay to determine close run-out decisions. Where facilities are
available, what possible objection can there be to making sure a decision is
correct? Instead of creating dissatisfaction, it seems to have generated
enthusiasm, and in the few seconds required to give a verdict there is
mounting and appreciative excitement.

I find myself very torn over the issue of so-called neutral umpires. Firstly
the title is a misnomer. *Ipso facto* it bears the stigma that local umpires are
biased. To me it is totally illogical that when England play Australia at Lord's

there shall not be an English umpire – even though he be the best in the world. Also, how can a country like Australia build up the competence of her umpires if they can't be used in Tests at home? I know the intention is fine and the appearance of neutrality is a plus. And if the two countries concerned agree on having independent umpires, let their wishes be met. But I can't bring myself to believe it should be mandatory.

I conclude with two comments. I still believe the eight-ball over is better than six. It may be unpopular with fast bowlers and with the television stations, but it would be good for cricket.

Secondly, I remain convinced that the front-foot no-ball Law is a disaster. England introduced the rule despite opposition from Australia. It has been a dismal failure. I don't think MCC realises the depth of opposition to this rule by the general public, and also by most players and by a large number of umpires. It was introduced mainly to control a mere handful of draggers. That they could be controlled by a disc system in association with the back-foot rule which gave satisfaction for upwards of 200 years was proven beyond all doubt in Australia – by me in England in 1948 as Australian captain and similarly by Richie Benaud in 1961.

The front-foot Law places an intolerable burden on umpires, who inevitably make mistakes in LBW and caught-behind decisions as a result of it. Sir George (Gubby) Allen was one of those who originally advocated changing to the front-foot Law, but shortly before he died Gubby admitted to me that he now realised it had been an abject failure and he wanted to revert to the back foot.

THE THROWING TRUCE

In his obituary tribute to Sir George Allen in the 1990 Wisden, *Sir Donald recalled the part their long-standing friendship played in helping to resolve the contentious issue of throwing.*

ALTHOUGH THAT [THE 1936-37 SERIES] ended our contests on the field of play, Gubby's life and mine continued to follow similar paths in that we both made our livelihoods out of stock and sharebroking, and that we both dedicated ourselves to cricket administration, an area which presented significant differences of opinion between England and Australia. The culmination of these differences came just before the proposed Australian tour of England in 1961 over the vexed question of what constituted a fair delivery. Enormous publicity had been given to the bowling actions of certain Australians, and the situation of virtually trial by the media became well nigh intolerable – so much so that [Australian Chairman] Bill Dowling and I were despatched to England by air for consultations with our English counterparts.

In essence the problem was thrown into the laps of [MCC President] Harry Altham and Gubby Allen, representing England, and Bill Dowling and myself, representing Australia. There were very frank exchanges of views and much argument, but in the end the measures adopted, which brought an end to the crisis, became possible only because both Gubby and I had implicit faith in the integrity of each other. The final outcome was an agreement for a 'throwing truce' during the first five weeks of the 1961 season (of which I was the instigator) and the drafting of a new Law concerning a 'fair' delivery, for which Gubby became responsible. History shows that our method of buying time proved of immense value.

SIR DONALD BRADMAN – A BIOGRAPHY

Published to coincide with the Great Man's seventieth birthday, Irving Rosenwater's book is a remarkable tribute to one of cricket's most illustrious subjects – The Don. It is, as were Bradman's runs, prolific. There are 399 pages of text (he might just as well have made it 400 – Bradman would have), half a dozen pages of statistics and a comprehensive index of eleven pages – 416 in all. This is, of course, not the first book on Bradman, nor the first serious study of him. B. J. Wakley did that in *Bradman The Great*. But Mr Rosenwater's is a different type of study. As he says, he avoids the relentless day by day description of every Test Match in which Bradman took part. He is clearly an admirer of Bradman, and if he intends to brush aside any criticism of him at one time or other, he does so with most convincing evidence, making his points as succinctly and powerfully as any advocate would. To choose any particular passage to quote from a book of this length is a testing exercise. I suppose (Mr Rosenwater does, too) that if one is thinking of a comparison for Bradman's deep scientific appreciation of the game in the pages of English cricket history, the man would be C. B. Fry, that amazing athlete and academic. I quote part of a letter from C.B. to Don Bradman:

> You have added so much to the novelty and complexity of strokeplay as well as to the standard and size of individual scores. I see that some of my supporters argue that I had stronger bowling to play, but I don't go anything on that, because it is easier to make a mistake against bad bowling than good. If one can really bat, the better the bowling, the better one plays, don't you think?

I am sure that, at the end of it all, Irving Rosenwater will harbour one regret – that he never saw the subject he has chronicled with such painstaking research and affection at the high noon of his career as a cricketer, in full, flowing action.

From 'Cricket Books, 1978', by Gordon Ross

SERVING
THE GAME

SIR DONALD BRADMAN – SELECTOR
BY IRVING ROSENWATER

THIN-SKINNED, WARM-HEARTED
BY DOUG INSOLE

Bradman with adoring schoolboys at the Adelaide Oval, 1958.

SIR DONALD
BRADMAN – SELECTOR

BY IRVING ROSENWATER

Irving Rosenwater's Sir Donald Bradman: A Biography *won the Cricket Society Literary Award in 1978. His other works include co-authorship of* England v Australia, *and he was the scorer for BBC TV in England and Channel 9 in Australia. This article appeared in the 1972* Wisden.

'SELECTORSHIP – A FASCINATING JOB REALLY, DESPITE ITS COMPLEXITIES'
Sir Donald Bradman in 1958.

ONE ASPECT OF the career of Sir Donald Bradman that seems to have escaped the myriad of writers who have penned their multitude of words on him is his role as a Selector. As both a State Selector and a Test Selector, Sir Donald gave a span of service which, in terms of years, far exceeded his playing career. Indeed, more than half his life has been spent as a South Australian and Test Selector, and though he had shed both roles by the start of the recent Australian season, at the age of sixty-three he is by no means old as Selectors go. Jack Ryder was still selecting Sheffield Shield sides for Victoria and Test sides for Australia as an octogenarian.

Sir Donald announced his retirement from Test selectorship on February 9, 1971, shortly after the side for the final Test against England had been chosen. He had been chairman of the panel for the 1970-71 series, as well as for many series before that. His announcement gave family and business pressures, as well as 'health problems', as the reason for his

69

retirement. Richie Benaud, who made his Test debut in 1951-52 when Sir Donald was a Selector, declared in the Melbourne *Herald*, 'Sir Donald was easily the best Selector I came across in the game anywhere in the world, not just in Australia.' The shrewd judgment of Sir Donald, backed by an unparalleled career as a player, was undoubtedly a potent factor in the general success of Australian sides over the last thirty-five years.

The appointment of Bradman as a Test Selector, just a few days after his twenty-eighth birthday in 1936, was to some extent fortuitous, for although he was generally expected to be made captain by the Australian Board for the Tests against G. O. Allen's side, the vacant position on the selection committee, to which Bradman was appointed, arose only through the death on June 11, 1936, of Dr C. E. Dolling, who happened to be the South Australian representative. Dr Dolling had been both a State and Test Selector and a good enough batsman to have scored 140 for South Australia in his first innings against an English side, in 1907-08. A prominent member of the medical profession, he suffered a sudden seizure in his surgery in Adelaide and died about an hour later, aged only forty-nine. He was a man of sound judgment and very straight in his methods, and Bradman's own tribute to him at the time said that he was 'a wise and tactful administrator, and that, as a Selector, he enjoyed the confidence of everybody'. Those same qualities Bradman himself sought to display on behalf of Australian cricket.

The three Australian Selectors for the 1936-37 series against England were appointed by the Australian Board at their meeting in Adelaide on September 10, 1936. Bradman was the only newcomer, to join E. A. Dwyer (NSW) and W. J. Johnson (Victoria), and he accepted the position, as he later said, 'with some reservations'. There had never been – and still has not been – a younger Selector appointed by the Board. In pre-Board days, however, both Joe Darling and S. E. Gregory had also been twenty-eight when they were two of the Selectors of the 1899 side for England, and W. Bruce was the same age when he helped to select the 1893 team.

At the time of his appointment Bradman had already had one season's experience as a State Selector for South Australia, having commenced those duties when he transferred to Adelaide from New South Wales and assumed the State captaincy for the 1935-36 season. He was to remain a South Australian and Test Selector until he temporarily retired from both positions (owing to the illness of his son, John) before the 1952-53 season.

He took no part in selecting Australia's sides that summer against the visiting South Africans or South Australia's Shield teams, his place in both roles being taken by Phil Ridings, who had succeeded Bradman as captain of South Australia four years before. Likewise, Sir Donald had no hand in the selection of the 1953 Australian team in England (whose tour he covered as a special writer), but in the autumn of 1953 he was restored to the South Australian selection committee, and before the arrival of MCC in 1954-55 he was back as a Test Selector. Before the start of the 1970-71 season Sir Donald retired as a State Selector for health reasons, but continued for the season at national level. Before the season was over he decided not to stand for election in either capacity in the future.

For South Australia in Sheffield Shield matches, Sir Donald Bradman was a Selector in twenty-eight seasons in all, twenty-three of them after the war. In that period his State won the Shield only four times (including twice when he was captain), though it is strange that for the two seasons that he stood down, 1952-53 and 1970-71, South Australia emerged winners. In the twenty-eight seasons involved, South Australia finished first four times; second five times; third (or joint-third) seven times; fourth three times; and fifth nine times. The only seasons they were undefeated were in 1935-36 and 1938-39, both under Bradman's captaincy.

It is at Test level, of course, that a Selector's record is always more interesting, though a Selector, naturally, is always one of a team. The normal method in Australia, ever since the formation of the Board, has been to appoint three Selectors, both for home series and for choosing overseas sides. The only exception to this was in the 1928-29 series, when there were four Selectors. Unlike the situation in England, the Australian Board never appoints a formal chairman. There has in fact never been any official record of such a position, and when, before the 1928-29 selection panel was appointed, opinion was obtained by the Board whether it had constitutional power to appoint a Chairman of Selectors, it was advised that the Board had no such power. The Selectors have in fact always arranged the chairman among themselves – and it seems that they have never been required to report to the Board who has been so appointed. Sir Donald Bradman acted in the capacity of chairman on all occasions that he served since World War Two, though the position was an unofficial one.

It is astonishing to consider that Sir Donald has been involved in the selection of very nearly half of all Australia's Test sides from 1877 to date.

Add to those the matches in which he played before becoming a Selector, and his personal involvement in his country's Tests extends to 55 per cent of all matches – a prodigious record, considering that Test cricket was already half a century old before he made his first-class (let alone his Test) debut.

The full record of Australia in Test cricket for the matches in which Sir Donald was one of the Selectors is as follows:

Played	Won by Australia	Lost by Australia	Drawn	Tied
151	68	32	50	1

Thus, in these games, Australia lost an average of one in five Tests, though immediately after the war she had a wonderful (and at that time a record) run of twenty-five matches without defeat. Four successive losses to South Africa in 1969-70 somewhat spoiled the average.

In terms of Test sides that have left Australia, Sir Donald was jointly responsible for fourteen – from the 1938 team to England to the 1969-70 team to India and South Africa, with the sole exception of Lindsay Hassett's side to England in 1953. These fourteen teams played altogether in twenty series away from Australia (including on three occasions a solitary Test) and, of their eighty Tests against all countries, lost less than a quarter – virtually the same record that home Australian teams experienced in the same period. In addition, Sir Donald was one of the Selectors for the five Australian sides that visited New Zealand, without playing Tests, under W. A. Brown in 1949-50, I. D. Craig in 1956-57 and 1959-60, L. E. Favell in 1966-67, and S. C. Trimble in 1969-70. On all these selection committees, Sir Donald served with the regular Test Selectors of the time, except that in 1949-50 E. A. Dwyer (NSW) acted as manager of the Australian team to South Africa and his place as Selector for the New Zealand tour was taken by A. Vincent (NSW).

Altogether, the selection committees on which Sir Donald served were responsible for sending into the field 114 Australian Test players, including twenty who were chosen for but a solitary Test. Charges of State rivalry and favouritism have often been levelled against Australian administrators (and Selectors in particular), but in fact the strongest States have had the strongest representation in Australian sides, and Sir Donald's own State of South Australia can hardly be said to be favoured in the distribution. South Australia has had a Test Selector since the Board Selectors first functioned, in the 1907-08 season, though in exactly the same way that, on figures, South Australia emerges as the third strongest of the Sheffield Shield sides, so she comes third in the table of Test representation. The 114 players have been chosen from the five Sheffield Shield States as follows: Victoria 38, New South Wales 31, South Australia 21, Queensland 13 and Western Australia 11. In cases of dual affiliation, the State recorded is that for which the player was playing when first chosen for a Test.

It is often said that Australia introduces fewer players into the Test arena than England, and that it is more difficult to get out of an Australian side than into it. In the course of the seventy Tests played between England and Australia during Sir Donald's tenure as a Test Selector, ninety-nine Australian players (including Sir Donald himself) took the field, while the number who appeared for England was 111 – so the difference was not all that great. Sir Donald of course was merely one of a team as a Selector, and he did not always have the decisive voice, despite the aura that has evolved over the years that his influence was such that the last word was automatically – and emphatically – his. Through a dozen years of his term, from 1954-55, he was one of a triumvirate together with Jack Ryder (Victoria) and Dudley Seddon (NSW) – though he also served for lesser periods with E. A. Dwyer (NSW), W. J. Johnson (Victoria), R. N. Harvey (NSW) and S. J. E. Loxton (Victoria) – and we may never know to what extent Sir Donald himself instigated, concurred or was overruled in such talking-points as the omission of Grimmett and Tallon in 1938, Miller and O'Neill to South Africa in 1949 and 1957 respectively, Simpson to Pakistan and India in 1959, and Walters to the West Indies in 1965. Perhaps the shroud of history is best left undisturbed in such instances.

From now on, for better or for worse, Australian Test selection will proceed without the thoughts of Sir Donald Bradman. His involvement with the game outside the Selectors' room will doubtless remain as intense, profound and invaluable as hitherto – it would be a pity, and a major loss, if it were otherwise. In recent years the time involved in selectorial duties, coupled with the necessary absences from home and business, have made things for him increasingly difficult to manage. Sir Donald himself has estimated that he spent 'about eight years' away from home during his period as a Test Selector – a voluntary act of adherence to cricket that sometimes gets submerged in the charisma of brilliance of the Bradman career. 'Selectors,' said Sir Donald once, 'are very conscientious people who are in the unenviable position of not being able to make public their views or policy.' In a moment of candour on another occasion he said, 'When I was Australian XI captain and Selector, I was castigated more than once for the omission of a certain man when in fact I fought for his inclusion. But those details can't be published. I simply mention them in the hope that the difficulties of selection committees may be more fully understood.' Mr S. C. Griffith, Secretary of MCC, expressed the view in 1971 that 'Sir Donald must be one of the most able and highly respected Test Selectors in the history of the game'. Few will cavil at that. Sir Donald Bradman, Selector, will assuredly hold a place of high significance in the history of Australian cricket.

Bradman in 1938: his ability to move rapidly into position from a stance of serene stillness was the key to his supremacy at the crease.

THIN-SKINNED,
WARM-HEARTED
BY DOUG INSOLE

Doug Insole played in nine Tests for England in the 1950s, and was subsequently
an England Selector, Chairman of the Test and County Cricket Board, Manager
of the England sides that toured Australia in 1978-79 and 1982-83, and President
of MCC. This appreciation appeared in the 2008 edition of Wisden.

ALTHOUGH I HAD MET DON BRADMAN on previous tours, my first real
conversation with him was at Harrogate in 1956, when Walter Robins
invited me to join them at dinner during the Leeds Test Match in which I
was playing – though you'd hardly know it. Don was writing about the
series for the *Daily Mail*, and I had recently been elected to the MCC
Committee and to their Cricket Committee. I have never been sure
whether the great man saw the occasion as an opportunity to instil into this
young whippersnapper of a Pom his ideas about how cricket should move
forward, but as a two-hour teach-in it was a remarkable experience. Not a
smile, not a quip, hardly a bite to eat. Just a relentless appraisal of the LBW
Law, restricted leg-side fields, over-rates, player behaviour and so on. I was
immensely impressed, if not always in agreement.

We next met in 1960 at White's Club in London. England's tour of
Australia in 1958-59 had been tainted by the throwing controversy, and
The Don had come to England to meet Gubby Allen and to sort out the
problem prior to the Australians' tour of England in 1961. I was invited to
attend the meeting, presumably to provide comic relief, and listened
spellbound to a session of verbal sparring until The Don indicated that the

only practical way of resolving the matter was not to pick 'chuckers', and so relieve the umpires of the task of calling them. It was a bold suggestion, which eliminated the need for any major change of law, and Don said he would sell it to his fellow administrators of Australian cricket. I drove Don back to the Waldorf that evening and we got to talking about mutual acquaintances in the game, finding that our opinions were very similar.

Thereafter we corresponded regularly for about forty years, although to my great regret I did not keep the early letters. In 1965, when England had just begun their tour of Australia, he told me that Ken Barrington had batted in one innings like 'a snail with rheumatism' and in the next he tore the bowling apart, which was a curious mixture. Absolutely right.

It was during this tour that I first visited Australia, met Don's wife Jessie, and was entertained at the family home in Adelaide. Jessie was simply delightful and it was amazing to see how much more relaxed Don was when she was there. She had a gentle and effective way of calming Don down and of correcting him if she disagreed with his version of events. From then on I made regular visits to Australia because, apart from my cricket commitments, I worked for several companies with major commercial interests out there, and I saw quite a lot of the Bradman family away from the cricket environment.

I soon came to realise that The Don had a very thin skin and that he was easily hurt by criticism, often responding in a manner that must have delighted editors anxious to keep the pot boiling. In particular, he resented the 'sniping' of Jack Fingleton and Bill O'Reilly. On one occasion he wrote that he had spent seven years away from home on cricket matters, that he had served as administrator and Selector without being paid a cent, that his opinions had been unbiased if not always right, and his conscience was clear. I somehow felt it a pity that at ninety years of age he found it necessary to justify himself to me, of all people, in that way.

When the Packer situation arose, Don was so reluctant to raise his head above the parapet that there was even a suspicion among Australians that he was not opposed to the new way of things. I know his reluctance to speak out disappointed some of his colleagues on the Board, and there is no doubt he was apprehensive about legal action if he put his feelings into words. He was, however, in no way reluctant to offer his advice to me, as Chairman of the English Board, and told me that while Australia had a contract to see out their tour of England in 1977, England had the chance to take a clear stand by making an example of their Packer players.

As the years went by, Don became less inclined to attend cricket matches because of the constant demand for autographs, photographs and so on. He nevertheless watched everything that came on television, and his judgment remained spot on. In 1992, he wrote that Australia seemed to have some fine young batsmen and the seventeen-year-old Ponting was as good as he had seen for years. As early as 1994 he wrote that Warne was the best slow spinner in history – O'Reilly being in a unique slow-medium class of his own. I asked regularly over the years who were the fastest bowlers he had seen, and his view remained constant: Tyson, Larwood and Thomson.

On a personal level, Don could be very compassionate. His letters during a tough couple of years when I lost a daughter in an air accident and my wife after a long illness were very moving, as were his reflections on his own family traumas over the years. He loved England and counted a number of Englishmen as close and true friends – among them Gubby Allen, Walter Robins, the Bedsers and Colin Cowdrey. His cricketing philosophy resembled in many ways that of the old English amateur. Above all, respect for authority and, in particular, the umpires. If he could have changed one thing in cricket it would have been the front-foot no-ball rule, which he looked upon as a disaster – a matter on which we were poles apart.

I valued his friendship enormously and looked forward eagerly to visiting him or receiving his letters, which were packed with news, incident, and opinions. He loved his golf, and at the age of ninety-plus was still getting round under his age. He must have been one of the dodgiest drivers of a car in South Australia, and his sense of humour was more sledgehammer than rapier. But there is no doubt in my mind that as player and administrator Don was the most influential figure in world cricket in the 20th century.

BRADMAN THE GREAT

Bradman The Great, by B. J. Wakley, is an unusual book; clearly a labour of love, it might have been thought more suited to a limited edition than for the general public. Yet it is a highly desirable item for the cricket collector, for Sir Donald Bradman's admirers – of whom there must be many – and for those who relish patiently compiled and well-made books. It includes a description of every season, every series, every one of the 234 matches and every innings in which Bradman played during his first-class cricketing career. Its appendix includes quite unusual statistics and analyses of his cricket: 48,595 runs (including extras) were added while Bradman was at the wicket, of which he scored 28,067 (57 per cent). Australia never lost a Test in which he won the toss. 'He never made "spectacles", though he twice made two noughts in successive innings in different matches (in 1931-32 and 1936-37); of his sixteen "ducks" twelve were in the first innings and four in the second, but he only batted in the second innings after making nought in the first on seven occasions, making 13, 103, 82, 97, 6, 12 and 56 respectively.' He made 25.47 per cent of the runs scored by sides in which he batted. These items give some impression of the style and content of a 317-page book more elaborate than any previously devoted to any cricketer – even W. G. Grace.

From 'Cricket Books, 1959', by John Arlott

MAN OF
THE PEOPLE

NATIVE HERO
BY MICHAEL DAVIE

SIR DONALD™
BY GIDEON HAIGH

BRADMAN AND THE BRITISH
BY RICHARD HOLT

BEYOND THE LEGEND
BY GIDEON HAIGH

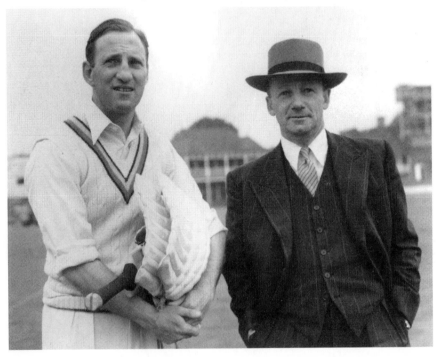

England captain Len Hutton and Sir Donald Bradman at Trent Bridge before the start of the 1953 Ashes series, which Sir Donald covered as a correspondent for the *Daily Mail*. At the time Hutton's 364 in 1938 and Bradman's 334 in 1930 were the highest individual scores in Australia v England Tests.

NATIVE HERO

BY MICHAEL DAVIE

Journalist and biographer Michael Davie was Editor of the Melbourne Age *and a former cricket correspondent of the* Observer *in London. This article appeared in the April 2001 edition of* Wisden Cricket Monthly.

ADULATION IS NOT an Australian attribute. Cutting down tall poppies is a national pastime. Yet at the time of his death, the reputation of Sir Donald Bradman stood higher in his own country than it had upon his retirement in 1949. For fifty years he was the object of greater sustained interest than any other Australian of his era, including the long-serving Prime Minister, Sir Robert Menzies, and possibly any other Australian ever, including the celebrated outlaw, Ned Kelly. A Bradman Museum flourished in Bowral; a section of the State Library in Adelaide was turned into a shrine containing fifty-one volumes of Bradman's scrapbooks and other memorabilia.

Other countries have produced sporting geniuses; other countries have been passionate about sport. But Australia is obsessed by sport, encouraged ever since the middle of the 19th century by politicians and headmasters who saw that it could play an important part in the emerging Australian culture and the making of a new nation. Bradman acquired heroic status because he unwittingly tied together sport and nationalism. He was the first sportsman whose successes were seen by his fellow citizens as successes not simply for him, his team and his particular sport, but for his country. This identification is commonplace everywhere now, in an era when a poor Olympic performance is regarded as a national failure. But it was not that way between 1928 and 1934, when Bradman was establishing his mastery and being hoisted on to the pedestal from which he has never been dislodged.

Consider first the point made by the *Oxford Companion to Australian Sport*: 'Australians have always set great store on the heroes and heroines who have defeated another country.' Now consider the context of Bradman's first appearances on the national stage in 1928, remembering that – at that time – the population of the mother country was just over forty-eight million and the population of Australia was just under seven million. David versus Goliath. In 1928, what is known in Australia as the Great Depression was just beginning. Wool and wheat prices were falling; unemployment figures were rising. Australia, as one commentator put it, was 'floating on a sea of British loans' – and the London bankers were getting nervous. In the first days of 1929 Bradman made his first Test century, and he did so against the strongest team to represent England abroad. England won the series with ease, which is part of the reason why the emergence of the 'Boy from Bowral' was greeted with special rapture and anticipation.

That year, 1929, was the year of the Wall Street crash. It had disastrous results for Australia. At the same time, amid social and industrial unrest, the country found itself forced to pay back London bond-holders at the expense of Australian wage-earners. Before the Depression, Australians had been encouraged to see their continent as a future United States, with a comparable population. But the Depression shattered their pride, as the country slid into fear and hopelessness. In Bradman alone, and his demonstrable superiority to any Englishman, could they take comfort. Politicians might fail them but Bradman never did. He began 1930 by scoring a world-record 452 not out for New South Wales against Queensland at Sydney, and in England several months later he tore into the English bowlers with a record-breaking savagery never before seen on a cricket field.

Two years later Jack Lang, the demagogic Labor premier of New South Wales (Bradman's then State), drew up a plan to default on payments to London and was consequently thrown out of office by the unilateral action of the English State Governor, Sir Philip Game. The action began just as Douglas Jardine started to ponder the Bodyline campaign of 1932-33, aimed at countering the Bradman threat. Bradman was restricted to an average of 56.57, but in Australia not a dent was made in his public reputation. His admirers were right: in England in 1934 he dominated again, with a first-class average of 84. His position in the Australian pantheon was unassailable.

No one doubted his genius: the figures spoke for themselves. But other players – Hobbs, Trumper, Archie Jackson – had been almost as talented. What was truly different about Bradman was his single-minded determination and self-belief. Jack Fingleton played in four series with him and was probably his harshest critic. Noting Bradman's aloofness, both from his colleagues and from well-wishers, Fingleton added in mitigation that if he had not been so aloof he probably would not have become a world-beater.

That Bradman was a hard competitor was known when he retired. But the full complexity of his nature was not revealed until after his retirement. He did not exactly become a recluse, because he continued to dominate Australian cricket as an administrator. But invitations to the Bradman household were rare and his public appearances rationed. At the Adelaide Oval, his arrivals and departures were organised and guarded. His golf partners were drawn from the Adelaide establishment, or from socially acceptable visiting Englishmen. Such interviews as he gave were granted only to interviewers he trusted not to ask difficult questions. Exchanges with his English friends were invariably confined to cricket.

Oddly, given his oft-repeated desire to maintain the popularity and spirit of cricket, he did not exercise his power as beneficially as he might have done. He said there had been no sledging in his day and he would have sacked any player who tried it. Yet sledging in its modern form, the continuous verbal abuse of opposing batsmen, became popular under Ian Chappell, who was born and raised in Adelaide under Bradman's nose. A public reproof of Chappell by Bradman would have stopped the practice.

Similarly, opponents of Kerry Packer's World Series Cricket were disappointed that Bradman's role in the crisis was played behind closed doors – if he played any part at all. Surely, they thought, he could not approve of the furtive way in which established Australian Test players threw in their lot with Packer? Yet he offered not one word of criticism.

When Bradman retired, Arthur Mailey, the great leg-spin and googly bowler, called him an enigma. 'While he gives the impression of avoiding the spotlight,' Mailey said, 'he is sensibly conscious and perhaps appreciative of its power.' He added, 'Bradman never made the mistake, common to many, of thinking that personal popularity is more potent than success.'

Both these remarks help explain the way Bradman conducted his life. When criticised, he made another hundred. He disliked criticism, which was one reason why he avoided the Press. During the throwing controversy on England's 1958-59 tour, I buttonholed him in the lobby of the Menzies Hotel in Melbourne. I was covering the tour for the *Observer* and considered, like everyone else with two eyes, that Ian Meckiff was a chucker. Later, in 1960, Bradman said throwing was 'the most complex question I have known in cricket', because two people of goodwill could, quite genuinely, take opposite sides. It was hard to believe there could be two views about Meckiff. Yet Bradman, though a Selector, did nothing to address the problem. Perhaps he was not prepared to be thought to be giving in to England's complaints.

In reply to my question in the Menzies Hotel, he stepped into the lift – one of the old-fashioned kind with an open, iron-latticed gate – pushed the button and, as he ascended, rapped out in his high voice, 'No comment!' I was left to contemplate his vanishing trousers. It was a typical Bradman performance.

With the great man's death, more about him will no doubt emerge – the documents and files written by him when he was an administrator, for instance. But we may be sure that nothing will affect his standing. He is a legend, and that's that.

Bradman plays a late cut through slips in the Second Test at Lord's, 1948. This was his last Test match on the famous ground.

SIR DONALD™

BY GIDEON HAIGH

Gideon Haigh is an award-winning author and journalist who edited Wisden
Cricketers' Almanack Australia *from 1999 to 2001. This article appeared in*
Wisden Cricket Monthly, *September 1998, on the occasion of Sir Donald
Bradman's ninetieth birthday.*

THE AUSTRALIAN SPORTING PUBLIC is notoriously fickle, bestowing and
withdrawing devotion in a blink, apt to forget even the firmest of favourites
within a few years of retirement. Yet the flame of Sir Donald Bradman,
seven decades since he first made headlines, has never burned brighter. No
public appearances are expected for his ninetieth birthday: almost a year
after the passing of his beloved wife, Jessie, Bradman finds them strenuous.
But his continued health will be the subject of front-page encomiums, and
feature in evening television bulletins: an annual vigil for some years now.
Whatever the tribulations of state, the cricket-fancying Prime Minister,
John Howard, will convey congratulations.

Never mind that the youngest people with clear recollection of Bradman
the batsman are nudging sixty themselves, for his feats appear to be growing
larger, not smaller, as they recede into antiquity. In the last decade, the cricket-
industrial complex has produced a trove of books, memorabilia albums,
videos, audio tapes, stamps, plates, prints and other collectables carrying the
Bradman imprimatur, while the museum bearing his name at Bowral
continues to derive a tidy income from licensing it to coins, breakfast cereals
and sporting goods. Sir Donald Bradman has become Sir Donald Brandname.

Mention 'The Don' in Australia and no one mistakes it for a reference to *The Godfather*. Little bits of his legend can be found everywhere. Australian state capitals boast twenty-two thoroughfares named in Bradman's honour (Victor Trumper has eight). Australians corresponding with the Australian Broadcasting Corporation do so to PO Box No. 9994, Bradman's totemic Test batting average. A newspaper poll [in 1997] found that Bradman was the Australian most respondents wanted to light the flame at the 2000 Olympics.

In some respects, however, Bradman himself has been supplanted in importance by Bradmyth. The idea of him is at least as important as the reality. It is odd, but not really surprising, that the best biography of Bradman was written by an Englishman: Irving Rosenwater's superb *Sir Donald Bradman*. And, despite the recent proliferation of Bric-a-Bradman, no one anywhere has tangibly added to the sum of human knowledge about The Don in twenty years. The most recent Bradman biography, Lord Williams's *Bradman: An Australian Hero* (1996), is a case in point: of 428 footnotes, 244 referred to four titles, two of them previous Bradman biographies.

It may justly be asked what more of the Bradman saga begs understanding. The Greatest Story Ever Bowled To is so beguiling as it is: uncoached boy from the bush rises on merit, plays for honour and glory, puts Poms to flight, becomes an intimate of sovereigns and statesmen, retires Cincinnatus-like to his unostentatious suburban home. But turning Bradman into Mr 99.94 is a little like reducing Einstein to Mr $E=mc^2$. Read most Bradmanarama and you'd be forgiven for thinking that his Test innings were the sum of him. His family is invisible. Precious little exists about Bradman's three decades as an administrator. There is next to nothing about his extensive business career. And no one, I think, has ever grasped what is perhaps most extraordinary about Bradman: his singularity as a man as well as a cricketer. For the great irony of his beatification is that he never was an acme of Australian-ness.

For most Australian boys, for instance, participation in sport is a rite of passage, an important aspect of socialisation. Yet if Bradman developed close cricketing pals in his Bowral boyhood, they kept remarkably schtum afterwards. The rudimentary game with paling bat and kerosene tin wicket in some urban thoroughfare is one of Australian cricket's cosiest images: think of Ray Lindwall and his cobbers playing in Hurstville's Hudson Street, trying to catch the eye of Bill O'Reilly as that canny old soul walked by; or of the brothers Harvey playing their fraternal Tests behind the family's Argyle Street terrace in Fitzroy. Bradman's contribution to the lore of juvenile cricket, by contrast, is one of solitary auto-didacticism, his water-tank training ritual with golf ball and stump.

That carapace hardened as Bradman reached cricketing maturity, and set him still further apart. Where the archetypal Australian male is hearty and sanguine, priding himself on good fellowship, hospitality and ability to hold his alcohol, Bradman was private, reserved, fragile of physique and teetotal. Where the traditional Australian work ethic has been to do just enough to get by, Bradman was a virtuoso who set his own standards and allowed nothing to impede their attainment.

Australia in the late 1920s, moreover, was not a country that seemed likely to foster an abundance of remarkable men. It was a small subsidiary of empire, with an ethnically and culturally homogenous population of six million. Even that big bridge was still to come. There were extremes of wealth and poverty, but social mobility was constrained both by economic hardship and the prevailing belief in an underlying social equality. Writing of Australia in 1928, the year of Bradman's Test debut, the American critic, Hartley Grattan, was amazed by the vehemence of this latter faith. 'Australia is perhaps the last stronghold of egalitarian democracy ... The aggressive insistence on the worth and unique importance of the common man seems to me to be one of the fundamental Australian characteristics.' As D. H. Lawrence described it in his novel of 1920s Australia, *Kangaroo*, 'Each individual seems to feel himself pledged to put himself aside, to keep himself at least half out of count. The whole geniality is based on a sort of code of "You put yourself aside, and I'll put myself aside." This is done with a watchful will: a sort of duel.' Bradman, however, was not 'a common man', and he assuredly did not 'put himself aside'. In the words of Ben Bennison, who collaborated with the twenty-one-year-old on *Don Bradman's Book*, 'He set out and meant to be king ... To the last ounce he knew his value, not only as a cricketer but as a man.'

The times may have been ripe for such individual aspiration. Certainly, Bradman's benefactors on Australia's 1930 tour of England had no difficulty singling him out for gifts and gratuities. And nothing before or since has paralleled the Caesar-like triumph that Bradman's employers, the sports-goods store Mick Simmons Ltd, organised for him when the team returned to Australia, where he travelled independently of his team and was plied with public subscriptions and prizes in Perth, Adelaide, Melbourne, Goulburn and Sydney. It was the beginning of a career in which Bradman showed conspicuous aptitude for parlaying his athletic talent into commercial reward. At a time when Australian industry lurked behind perhaps the highest tariff barriers on earth, Bradman was the quintessential disciple of the free market.

No dispute that Bradman deserved every penny and more. No question of undue rapacity either. As that felicitous phrasemaker Ray Robinson once expressed it, The Don did not so much chase money as overhaul it. Equally, however, Bradman's approach betokens an elitism uncharacteristic of Australia at the time, and a quality that few today would willingly volunteer as a national hallmark. It was this impregnable self-estimation – not arrogance, but a remarkable awareness of his entitlements – that distanced Bradman from his peers. Some criticisms of The Don by his playing contemporaries were undoubtedly actuated by jealousy but, all the same, he seems to have been incapable of the sort of gesture that might have put comrades at their ease.

The philosophy of Bradman's playing career emerged again in his approach to administration and selection. Biographers have served Bradman poorly by glossing over his years in officialdom. His strength and scruples over more than three decades were exemplary; the foremost master of the game became its staunchest servant. But he largely missed the secular shift toward the professionalisation of sport in the late 1960s and early '70s. His attitude remained that, if a player was good enough, he could profit from the game through other avenues. This does not seem a response of one who understood the struggles of others less blessed.

Discussing the rise of World Series Cricket, he told Williams in January 1995 he 'accepted that cricket had to become professional'. Yet, as Dr Bob Stewart comments in his work on the commercial and cultural development of post-war Australian cricket, *I Heard It On the Radio, I Saw It On the Television*, cricket wages declined markedly in real terms during the period that Bradman was Australian cricket's *éminence grise*. When he quit as a player, the home Test fee was seven times the average weekly wage. A quarter of a century later it was twice the average weekly wage. Ian Chappell opined in his *The Cutting Edge* that the pervasiveness of Bradman's attitude to player pay within the Australian Cricket Board 'contributed to the success World Series Cricket officials had when … they approached Australian players with a contract.'

Perhaps these paradoxes of the Bradman myth relate something about the complex Australian attitude to sport. As Australian social commentator Donald Horne once put it, 'It is only in sport that many Australians express those approaches to life that are un-Australian if expressed any other way.' But, as Bradman enters his tenth decade fit for both commodification and canonisation, two questions seem worth asking, with apologies to C. L. R. James.

First: what do they know of Bradman who only cricket know? Surely it's possible in writing about someone who has lived ninety years to do something more than prattle on endlessly about the fifteen or so of them he spent in flannels – recirculating the same stories, the same banal and blinkered visions – and bring some new perspectives and insights. Second: what do they know of cricket who only Bradman know? A generation has now grown up in Australia that regards cricket history as 6,996 and all that. Where are the home-grown biographies of Charlie Macartney, Warwick Armstrong, Bill Woodfull, Bill Ponsford, Lindsay Hassett, Keith Miller, Neil Harvey, Alan Davidson, Richie Benaud, Bob Simpson, even Ian Chappell and Dennis Lillee, plus sundry others one could name? Such is the lava flow from the Bradman volcano, they are unlikely to see daylight.

So enough with the obeisances already. Yes, Bradman at ninety is a legend worth saluting. But as the American journalist, Walter Lippman, once said, 'When all think alike, none are thinking.'

Worcestershire captain Allan White flips the coin, Bradman calls and the 1948
Australians embark on the tour that will lead to their being labelled 'the Invincibles'.

BRADMAN AND THE BRITISH

BY RICHARD HOLT

Richard Holt is the author of Sport and the British, *and at the time this article appeared in the 2002* Wisden *he was research professor at the International Centre for Sports History and Culture at De Montfort University in Leicester.*

BATTING STATISTICS put Sir Donald Bradman in a league of his own. Yet his records, his scoring speed, even his double and triple Test hundreds do not alone explain his special relationship with the British public. Runs were a necessary but not a sufficient condition of Bradman's heroic status in Britain. His batting explains the awe and admiration in which he was held. But it does not explain the remarkable affection of the British public for a man who, as the *Daily Mail* observed in 1930, 'was a menace to English cricket'.

His four tours of England gave the public enough time to get to know him – and for many to see him – but not enough to tire of him or take him for granted. In 1948, he was said to be the best known public figure after King George VI and Churchill. Presenting him with a replica of the Warwick Vase, donated by public subscription to its Bradman Fund, the *People* claimed Bradman had been 'honoured in a way that no other overseas sportsman has enjoyed'. This adulation spread beyond the heartlands of English cricket, spanning social classes and generations, cutting across the regions and nations of Great Britain. He played his last competitive matches on tour in Scotland and was asked for his autograph twenty-five times on a short walk in Aberdeen.

Why did the British public come to *like* Bradman so much? Being an Australian of English descent was an advantage. Bradman's career also happened to coincide with the inter-war boom in radio broadcasting and the rise of the cinema newsreel. The Press, especially mass circulation 'Sundays' such as the *People* and the *News of the World*, whose joint circulation reached thirty million by the time Bradman retired, gave extensive coverage to Test cricket, especially the Australian tours. His first autobiography, *My Cricketing Life*, was serialised in the *News of the World* in 1938. Never had so much been known by so many about so few, as Churchill might have said when he bumped into Bradman at Victoria Station in 1934 and had the *Daily Mail* photograph the two of them shaking hands.

For all its subsequent warmth, the British relationship with Bradman got off to a cool start. His assault on England and the English counties in 1930 left the public awe-struck and a little resentful. This was not just a matter of his treatment of the local bowlers. His natural reticence and puritan instincts irritated his own team and the English public after his record Test innings of 334. Twenty years later, he was still wondering if he was expected to parade through the streets of Leeds. The Press had mistaken his youthful shyness for petulance. It took time for him to realise that he needed, and lacked, the common touch.

When Bradman next appeared in England in 1934, it was in the wake of the Bodyline tour of 1932-33. By then, the English public and MCC were having second thoughts about the tactics of physical intimidation employed by Jardine to stop Bradman. England had not emerged well out of their bowling war. Shared values of sportsmanship were more important than winning at all costs; there was an unspoken guilt of which Bradman was the chief beneficiary. He had, moreover, stood up well to the battering – he still had the highest average for the series – and emerged from it with some dignity. J. M. Kilburn caught the new public enthusiasm for Bradman, which was especially strong in Yorkshire, 'The crowd raced to the pavilion and made a lane halfway to the wicket.' As he went in, 'there was a silence of suspense; a murmur of, "He's here," swelling to a roar of welcome'. He went on to score 304.

That summer of 1934 was the turning-point in Bradman's relationship with the British. Fair play was part of the national self-image, and it would have been perverse and petty to deny Bradman his laurels. Then fate intervened. At the end of the series he was rushed into hospital with peritonitis. For a day or two his life was in danger. The public suddenly saw this remarkable run-making machine in a new light as a young man with a new bride, whose dash from Sydney to Perth to get the first boat caught the popular imagination. The *Daily Mail*, one of Britain's biggest-selling newspapers, kept up the bulletins from his bedside, reporting The Don wisecracking with the nurses: 'What's the score? Is it over 100?' To general relief he not only recovered quickly but had also shown the first signs of a sense of humour. He spent a pleasant time in England convalescing with his wife. 'Don and Jessie', as they were now affectionately known, fell in love with the English countryside. 'Nothing in the world ever appealed to me more than England as nature made her,' he wrote later of that time; and nothing could have pleased [Prime Minister] Stanley Baldwin and the majority of Englishmen more.

Bradman began to apply the same meticulous thoroughness to answering the thousands of letters he received that he took to his batting. He was captain for the next tour of England in 1938, and this gave him a new and much wider public platform. Cricket captains were expected to be sporting ambassadors, attending endless public functions and making polite speeches. Bradman, the plain country boy turned stockbroker, had to learn the etiquette of representing his country in the 'mother country'. In fact, Bradman mastered the art of being a gentleman so well that some of his Australian team-mates never forgave him. His new gentility, however, went down very well in Britain.

History, too, was running his way. Anglo-Australian relations had sunk to a low ebb in the early 1930s, but by 1938 both countries were anxious to reinforce the imperial bond in the face of mounting international tension. Britain feared Germany; Australia feared Germany's new ally, Japan. Bradman was a firm believer in the British Empire; he was a Protestant, a Freemason, an imperialist and a conservative who strongly opposed what he saw as the anti-British tendency of Irish Catholics in Australian cricket. Indeed, Bradman's bitter dispute with Bill O'Reilly, Jack Fingleton and others did him no harm in England. Britain saw the best side of Bradman. His integrity, his respect for the monarchy, his generosity when Len Hutton broke his record in the final Test at The Oval in 1938 were music to the British ear. As a captain, he endorsed the values of sportsmanship – 'the very essence of this great game' as he later wrote in *The Art of Cricket* – which had a profound resonance with a broad swathe of the British public.

World War Two strengthened a bond that was already strong. Hence when Bradman arrived for his final series in 1948, Britain rolled out the red carpet. R. C. Robertson-Glasgow set the tone. 'We want him to do well,' he chirped, 'we feel we have a share in him.' And he did do well. The Australians were unbeaten. Bradman's was a triumphal progress to Balmoral, 'cherishing the friendly, homely manner' of the royal family. Getting a duck in his final innings against England and missing his century Test average by a decimal point oddly enhanced his status. When he received his knighthood, he was suitably modest, claiming he saw it as 'the medium through which England's appreciation of what Australian cricket had meant to the British Empire' could be expressed.

The knighthood also holds the key to another aspect of his appeal. Like the bulk of the British, he believed in both meritocracy *and* deference. He respected hierarchy so long as talent was properly recognised. Like Hobbs and Sutcliffe, Woolley and Compton, Bradman's own life reflected a wider pattern of upward mobility. 'I could not help thinking that this knighthood was a sporting example to the world of true democracy,' he wrote in *A Farewell to Cricket*, adding that 'the same opportunity exists for every Australian boy'. To the middle classes, Donald Bradman, batsman and stockbroker, stood for suburban virtue rewarded. To the working man, his blend of virtuosity and grit struck a chord, especially in the North, where his professionalism was more appreciated than in the South. Physically he was slight, with the deceptive frailty of that other great sporting hero of the time, footballer Stanley Matthews. Bradman was treated like an honorary Northerner and was 'greeted like an emperor by the crowd' at Headingley in 1948. On retirement he was made an honorary member of both Lancashire and Yorkshire.

'If statistics were the last word in cricket it would be easy to prove that Donald George Bradman was the greatest cricketer who ever lived,' *The Times* wrote in a farewell leader, adding tartly, 'happily they are not'. And there were still a few reservations around the Long Room at Lord's about 'the little robot under the green peaked cap'. Where was the fun, the bravura or the classicism in Bradman? Yet even his few critics had to admit that 'no one has contributed more to the game'. *The Times* closed on an elegiac note, imagining a future 'Australian batsman ... piling up a century' – a Steve Waugh perhaps – while 'old stagers who watch him will be able, however finely he plays, to murmur, "Ah, but you should have seen Bradman."'

BEYOND THE LEGEND

BY GIDEON HAIGH

This article appeared in the 2002 edition of Wisden Cricketers' Almanack.

THE STORY OF Sir Donald Bradman always involved more than cricket – more even than sport. One can only marvel at the statistics, and the one batting average that nobody need ever look up. Yet, in its degree and duration, especially in Australia, Bradman's renown is as much a source of wonder: he was, as Pope wrote of Cromwell, 'damned to everlasting fame'. Few figures, sporting or otherwise, have remained an object of reverence for more than half a century after the deeds that formed the basis of their reputation. But with Bradman's death in 2001 comes a question: what difference will it make to his legend now that, for the first time, it has obtained a life independent of his corporeal existence?

On the face of it, the answer appears to be: not much. In Australia, the Bradman story detached from the Bradman reality some time ago, taking on the qualities of myth. In the 1990s, in particular, a sort of cultural elision turned Bradman from great batsman to great man: by Prime Minister John Howard's lights, 'the greatest living Australian', elevated not merely by his feats but by 'the quality of the man himself'. Inspired by Bradman, Howard claimed, Australians could make 'any dream come true', and 'not just in cricket but in life'. This was a new experience for Australians. Poet and critic Max Harris once declared that 'the Australian world is peopled by good blokes and bastards, but not heroes'. Yet, by the end of his life Bradman was not merely a 'hero'; he had also been, in effect, retrofitted as a 'good bloke' – that peculiarly Australian formulation implying, essentially, someone like everybody else.

Why this happened can only be conjectured. Perhaps it was the self-image as a sports-loving nation to which Australians cling with such tenacity. Perhaps it was part of the recrudescence of Australian conservatism (it's hard to imagine Howard's republican predecessor, Paul Keating, singling Bradman out as 'the greatest living Australian'; indeed, perhaps that partly accounts for his electoral failure). It may be as simple as Bradman keeping his head while all about him were losing theirs. He avoided the public eye, courted no controversies and scorned fame's usual accoutrements. It would be an exaggeration to describe him as an outstanding citizen, at least as this is commonly understood: he was not a conspicuous philanthropist or supporter of causes, and the duty to which he devoted himself most diligently was simply being Donald Bradman, tirelessly tending his mountainous correspondence and signing perhaps more autographs than anyone in history. But there is no doubt that, standing aloof from modern celebrity culture, he retained a dignity and stature that most public figures sacrifice.

This being the case, it may be that 'the greatest living Australian' segues smoothly into becoming the greatest dead one. But there are reasons against this progression: countries move on, palates jade, reputations are reassessed. There is already something anomalous about Bradman's standing in Australia. National heredity and heritage during his playing career were almost exclusively British; as Dr Greg Manning has noted, Australia's cultural homogeneity in the 1930s and 1940s was a precondition of the Bradman phenomenon. But since the late 1980s, British and old Australian components have accounted for less than half Australia's population. Even the idea of a monolithic Australian mourning of Bradman's death was mostly a media assumption. *The Chaser*, a satirical newspaper, expressed this drolly with a story headlined: 'Woman unmoved by Bradman's death.'

A significant role in the ongoing Bradman story will be played by the Bradman Museum at Bowral. So far the Museum is a success story: a collecting institution for cricket that is largely self-funding, thanks partly to royalties from the Bradman name, worth between a quarter and half a million Australian dollars annually. And for this, Bradman himself can take a deal of credit. It was he, says the Museum's curator, Richard Mulvaney, who 'recognised that the Museum would always have problems getting enough money to do the things it wanted to do', and ten years ago vouchsafed the commercial rights to his name and image.

The Museum's future financial security was consolidated in August 2000 by an unforeseen consequence of the South Australian government's decision to rename an Adelaide thoroughfare in honour of its favourite adopted son. When several businesses in the new Sir Donald Bradman Drive proposed exploiting their location in advertising, the Bradman family sought Government intervention, and the subsequent amendment to Australia's Corporations Law – preventing businesses from registering names that suggested a connection with Bradman where it did not exist – invested The Don with a commercial status previously the preserve of members of the royal family. The amendment has already proved its worth in the relative scarcity of necrodreck in Australia after Bradman's death. In the longer term it should secure for cricket the financial fruits of The Don's legacy, for which the game can be grateful.

Enhanced power over the Bradman franchise sets the Museum challenges. Its charter is to be 'a museum of Australian cricket commemorating Sir Donald Bradman'. The legislation, explicit acknowledgment that Bradman's name is a commodity with commercial value, subtly firms the emphasis on the latter role – something the Museum recognised by signing an agency agreement for the exploitation of the name with a sports management group. To be fair, Mulvaney perceives the dilemma. He is adamant that the Museum will not, in his watch, become a one-man hall of fame. 'While it's in my interest to continue putting Bradman's name forward, we shouldn't take his name out of context. We have to be careful that we don't allow excesses where the name takes on a completely different meaning.'

To how much protection, though, is Bradman entitled? This question was raised in 2001 in an episode involving two letters, from Bradman to Greg Chappell, dating from the World Series Cricket schism in 1977. After defecting to Kerry Packer's enterprise, Chappell found himself *persona non grata* in his adopted state of Queensland, and confided to a *Brisbane Telegraph* journalist some disparagements of the quality of local cricket administrators that Bradman had made to him some years earlier. When these were published, Chappell received a letter of rebuke for what Bradman viewed as a breach of trust. An exchange of correspondence followed in which Bradman enlarged on certain personal philosophies, as well as lamenting the frequent Press misrepresentation to which he had been subject.

These were important artefacts. They evoked both the passion of the moment – for this was a time when tempers in cricket were frayed on all sides – and the personality of the writer. In some respects it is from such flashes of candour that biographies are built; thus Plutarch's famous remark, in his life of Alexander the Great, that 'very often an action of small note, a short saying, or jest, will distinguish a person's real character more than the greatest sieges or the most important battles'. But when the letters were auctioned by Christie's in July 2001, Chappell was roundly censured for another breach of trust, that of Bradman's privacy. An anonymous consortium of businessmen purchased the letters and presented them to Mulvaney at the MCG on what would have been The Don's ninety-third birthday.

Even ignoring the question of whether it is possible to breach the privacy of the dead, it was a curious interlude. It went unremarked, for example, that the letters had previously been quoted from, without protest, in Adrian McGregor's 1985 Chappell biography. And it evinced a disconcerting cultural timidity in Australia, a squeamishness about anything other than the 'approved' version of the Bradman story. In an interview with *Sporting Collector*, Mulvaney was quoted as saying that the Museum 'considered the contents not necessarily to be in the public interest' and that it had 'no option but to keep them private' – which made it sound like an issue of national security. However, in an interview for this article Mulvaney said that the magazine had misrepresented his views: his concern was purely with copyright, which he felt Christie's had breached by reproducing the letters in its catalogue, and he insisted that the Museum had no wish to inhibit study of Bradman material. But when permission was sought to quote from the letters here, Sir Donald's son, John, withheld it; he stated, albeit politely, that this was his present policy on all such enquiries.

One can sympathise with John Bradman's position. No policy will satisfy everyone. Permission for all will invite excess and exploitation; permission for some will smack of favouritism; permission for none will be construed as censorship. Yet attempting to control what is published about Bradman in such a way will carry risks. Revisionists will move in regardless; indeed, they already are. In November 2001, the *Australian* published two articles concerning 'The Don We Never Knew', the work of a foot-slogging journalist, David Nason. One revealed what appeared as vestiges of a family rift between The Don and his Bowral kin, disclosing the view of Bradman's nephew that 'Don Bradman only ever cared about Don

Bradman'; the second examined how the alacrity with which Bradman took over the defunct stockbroking firm of the disgraced Harry Hodgetts antagonised Adelaide's establishment.

What was truly noteworthy about the articles was not that they appeared, but that nothing resembling them had appeared before, that none of Bradman's soi-disant 'biographers' had treated his family and financial lives other than perfunctorily. Indeed, it may be that Bradman's most ardent apologists end up doing him the gravest disservice. Identifying a great sportsman isn't difficult: the criteria are relatively simple. Designating a great man entails rather more than a decree, even prime ministerial; some intellectual and historical contestation must be involved. Credulity invites scepticism – and, unlike trade names, reputations cannot be declared off limits by the wave of a legislative wand.

BRADMAN: THE ILLUSTRATED BIOGRAPHY

Bradman: The Illustrated Biography, by Michael Page, is a weighty volume in the best sense of the word. It is also large: 376 quarto pages with 300 illustrations, all of which are strictly relevant and many of which are published here for the first time. The wrapper and the title page note that this biography has been compiled 'using the private possessions of Sir Donald Bradman' which, as the author's introduction, 'A Note of Thanks', makes clear, may be taken to mean also that Sir Donald provided personal information and, where necessary, guidance. Michael Page, who is English born, settled in Australia in 1952 and is an experienced author of fiction, travel and, most notably, studies of Australian history and social life. He was invited to prepare this book after Sir Donald had declared himself unable to accept Macmillan's request to write his autobiography, but agreed to make his personal records available to Mr Page if he would undertake a biography. He notes that his subject has 'a formidable memory, apparently capable of recalling every ball of every significant match'; as a result he is 'able to feel that the narrative is a totally accurate interpretation of Sir Donald's story and of his attitude towards life.'

His final words of gratitude to Sir Donald are 'for the privilege of knowing one of the great men of our time'. This is not, however, a fulsome book. Indeed, it deliberately avoids sensationalism or extravagance. There have been eleven previous biographical studies of Bradman, those of A. G. Moyes and Irving Rosenwater of appreciable value; while Sir Donald himself has published four books of an autobiographical nature. None, though, is of this stature. It is not an easy read, but it is as near complete as may be; and, in its way, a model of its kind.

From 'Cricket Books, 1983', by John Arlott

REFLECTIONS

THE SUPREMELY PRACTICAL MAN
BY PHILIP DERRIMAN

WHO KNOWS IF HE WAS HAPPY?
BY MIKE COWARD

CAPITALISING ON CRICKET
BY CARL BRIDGE

Bradman on his way to a fourth tour century against Worcestershire, 1948.

THE SUPREMELY PRACTICAL MAN

BY PHILIP DERRIMAN

Philip Derriman is a cricket writer for the Sydney Morning Herald, *an author and from 1990 to 1996 was Editor of the* Australian Cricket Almanac. *The obituary from which this abridged article is taken appeared in the 2001-02 edition of* Wisden Cricketers' Almanack Australia.

IT WAS TO BE EXPECTED after Sir Donald Bradman's death that Australia's newspapers and television channels would out-do themselves with tributes, given his special place in the nation's life, but nobody could have foreseen the extraordinary response to his death in the rest of the cricket world. In England, where Bradman's supremacy as a batsman used to be acknowledged only grudgingly, the obituaries were long and effusive, and more than one writer was prepared to argue that Bradman was unique not merely in cricket but in world sport as a whole. *The Times's* Simon Barnes, for instance, noting that nobody else had dominated his or her sport as Bradman had dominated cricket, wrote that there was a genuine case for declaring Bradman 'the greatest player of any sport that ever plied his trade'.

It was the *degree* of Bradman's superiority, of course, which made, and has kept, him so famous. For an individual to be acknowledged, almost universally, as the best-ever in a sport is rare enough. What sets Bradman apart, though, is not merely that he was the best but that he was so much better than everyone else – that, as the England bowler Bill Bowes once described it, he was 'better from the ankles up'. The scorebooks confirm that he was, and so do the first-hand accounts of those who played with and against him, virtually all of whom, it seems, regarded him as being in a class of his own. Unfortunately, those contemporaries never quite managed to identify the secret of his success. We still do not really know how this small, entirely self-taught cricketer from a country town managed to out-perform all others in the world by a staggering margin. Now that Bradman and most of his contemporaries are gone, perhaps we never will.

Inevitably, Bradman's batting methods have come to be analysed in retrospect. Greg Chappell has taken a special interest in his unusual stance and backlift, believing they may have been the key to his marvellous balance, while in England a coach named Tony Shillinglaw has begun teaching Bradman's technique to young English batsmen. He is convinced that Bradman's 'unorthodox' methods should be accepted as the model for all batsmen to follow. Behind all this is the quite reasonable belief that, to do what he did, Bradman must have tapped some special, hitherto unknown source of performance, both mental and mechanical.

It seems that everyone who played with or against Bradman or who got to know him outside cricket was fascinated by his personality. For good or ill, Bradman was a special character. All who came in contact with him felt he was different, and the essence of that difference was that he seemed to deal with things as they really were and did not allow emotion to affect his judgment of them. He was the supremely practical man. This wasn't a particularly endearing trait, for it could make Bradman seem blunt, inflexible and unfeeling, but it was undoubtedly an important part of the psychology that he applied to his cricket. If he abounded in confidence at the batting crease, it was because he *knew* he had every bowler's measure and was not distracted by baseless self-doubts. As the writer Evan Whitton concluded, he wasn't an enigma, as many have suggested, but actually quite a simple man with 'a remarkable capacity to focus on essentials'.

Nobody in Bradman's day considered him a graceful or stylish batsman, yet the newsreels show he was an exceptionally loose-limbed individual who possessed a wonderful freedom of movement, best exemplified by the ease with which he spun around while playing the pull shot, a favourite stroke, often ending up facing fine leg. When you watch newsreel film of Bradman, the overall impression he creates is one of well-oiled co-ordination – a 'fluidity of movement', as Peter Roebuck described it after watching a television show on Bradman. He looks light, nimble, decisive, balanced, controlled. Then there is the extraordinary abandon with which he moved inside and outside the batting crease. In countless photos he can be seen a metre or more down the pitch, driving on the run. As Jack Fingleton noted, Bradman never hesitated to go down the pitch because he never, ever, counted on missing a ball. It is hard to think of a single photo of any modern batsman in a similar pose.

The post-war Bradman was not nearly as dynamic a batsman as the Bradman of old. Bill O'Reilly wrote that he had lost his killer instinct. Yet he still scored Test centuries almost as often as before – eight of them in his twenty-three post-war Test innings for an average of 105.72. The difference now was that his centuries no longer tended to become double-centuries. The teams he led consisted largely of new, younger players, and it seems Bradman got on better with them than with pre-war players of his own vintage. He finished his international career on a high note in 1948 by leading a powerful Australian team on a tour of England without losing a match. A few months later, in January 1949, he was knighted, and two months after that he bowed out as a player altogether. He did not bow out of cricket, however. He was a member of the Board of Control, later called the Australian Cricket Board, from 1945 to 1980, apart from two years in the late 1940s, and long after that he remained a force in the game, regularly consulted by the administrators in charge. Indeed, he is said to have remained, if reluctantly, influential in the game's affairs until the 1990s.

To the end, Sir Donald guarded his privacy with as much determination as he had once guarded his wicket, invariably refusing requests for interviews and public appearances. On the other hand, he was an active correspondent who willingly exchanged letters even with people he knew only distantly, some of whom were surprised at the candour with which he expressed views on quite contentious matters.

After some initial reservations, Sir Donald supported and took a keen interest in the Bradman Museum at Bowral, whose opening he attended in 1989. It was his last trip to his home town. After he died, it was revealed he had chosen the Museum's environs, close to the oval where he played as a boy for the Bowral XI, as the final resting-place of his ashes.

At the re-dedication of Bradman Oval, Bowral, 1976.

WHO KNOWS IF HE WAS HAPPY?

BY MIKE COWARD

Mike Coward is a journalist and author who writes on cricket for The Australian *newspaper and commentates on radio and television. This article appeared in the April 2001 edition of* Wisden Cricket Monthly*, based on a conversation between the author and WCM Editor Stephen Fay.*

DON BRADMAN was a most exacting man, meticulous to the point of pedantry and accustomed to having his own way. He was not into mateship. That aloofness made him an intimidating figure, but he believed in manners and responsibilities. This meant that he was a scrupulous correspondent, and that he behaved well towards the autograph hunters who sometimes queued outside his front door in Adelaide. 'They are the bane of my bloody life,' he said in an unguarded moment in 1993. But he did not refuse one of them. He never did.

He was, until the end, intensely competitive. Even in his eighties he would come down like a ton of bricks on any bridge partner who made a mistake, and was reluctant to play with them again. But this was a man who was quite willing to correct the Queen when he thought she was in error about the tied Test at Brisbane in 1960-61. It was only his wife, Lady Jessie, who would or could say to him, 'Don't be silly.'

Lady Jessie was the mediator between Sir Don and his son, John, who changed his name to Bradsen in 1972. His daughter, Shirley, who had been born with cerebral palsy, was his favourite. The marriages of both children failed, though John presented Sir Don with two grandchildren – Greta, now aged twenty-one, and Tom, aged nineteen. Lady Jessie had an especially close relationship with John after nursing him through polio as a child, and had much to do with the revival of the relationship between father and son towards the end of her life. In 2000, John decided to revert to the name Bradman, and in the last year of Sir Don's life they spent hours talking together.

Sir Don had been thrilled with the way John handled the memorial service for Lady Jessie at St Peter's Cathedral in Adelaide, and he liked to watch the video of the funeral and memorial services – which included a performance by Greta's *a cappella* group. He was not an emotional man, but he desperately missed Lady Jessie: his muse, his confidante, soul-mate, adviser … everything.

Lady Jessie had been a gardener, who liked to grow orchids and freesias, and Sir Don continued to work in the garden after her death. He took an interest in viticulture, too, and it was a myth that he was a teetotaller. He liked wine and developed a pretty good knowledge of it, with a particular taste for Henschke Hill of Grace shiraz – an excellent South Australian wine. He also liked a brandy and ginger after a round of golf, which he would pay for himself. Sir Don's taste in food was plain – shepherd's pie and bread-and-butter pudding – but so precise was his planning for dinner parties that some of his guests believed that he had committed to memory their preferred food and drink. He and Lady Jessie were generous hosts.

He was conservative by nature in business, politics and cricket, but never predictable, and we do not know what he thought about the republican referendum. About cricket, he was tolerant of change. He reminded opponents of coloured clothing and one-day cricket that the Blues played the Pinks at Sydney in the 19th century, and he never spoke publicly about Packer's World Series Cricket.

I first met him in the 1960s when I wrote about district cricket in Adelaide, and got to know him better in the 1970s when I was chief cricket writer for the *Adelaide Advertiser*. I interviewed him about Bodyline, although he agreed to talk only after the Editor said he could read the article before it was published. He did not like the way the media developed – especially strident tabloid journalism – and he wrote to me in 1989, 'No doubt you find my desire to live a private life free from publicity incompatible with your occupation but, having done more than a fair thing over fifty years, at the age of eighty-one I am as determined as possible to resist further encroachment on [it].' He did not join the fiftieth anniversary celebration of the Invincibles 1948 tour of England. He did not even attend his own ninetieth birthday party.

I never held him in awe; I asked him direct questions and I think he liked that. But I would not presume to say whether he was a happy man. His own contemporaries never made that judgment either. (Bill O'Reilly, who might have done so, always said that history does not look favourably on those who piss on statues.) Assessing Bradman has become the responsibility of my generation, and we are not fully equipped to do so. That is a sadness.

Jack Fingleton and Don Bradman step out along The Strand, London, followed by admiring schoolboys, 1938.

CAPITALISING ON CRICKET

BY CARL BRIDGE

Professor Carl Bridge is Head of the Menzies Centre for Australian Studies at King's College, London. This article appeared in the 2008 Wisden *to mark the centenary of Sir Donald Bradman's birth.*

THE CRICKETER AND CRICKET WRITER, R. C. Robertson-Glasgow, first met the young Donald Bradman at the 1930 Folkestone Cricket Festival and the circumstances of their meeting are instructive for anyone seeking to find out what made Bradman tick. At the time Bradman was twenty-two years old, an Australian batting prodigy breaking records almost daily, the cynosure of every eye. But Bradman was not in the centre of a journalistic scrum or drinking with his mates and admirers in the bar. Robertson-Glasgow found him in the writing-room of his hotel: 'I had rushed into it to dash off some postcard, and, as I addressed it, my eye caught a huge pile of letters; next to them – almost buried *under* them – sat Bradman. He had made his name in cricket … And now, quiet and calculating, he was, he told me, trying to capitalise his success.' Apart from his astonishing cricketing ability, here in a nutshell is the clue to Bradman's remarkable career, through cricket, to stockbroking, to the boardrooms of some of Adelaide's leading companies, back to the highest levels of cricket administration, and finally to legendary status as 'the greatest living Australian'.

The legend, as legends almost inevitably must, has Bradman emerging from humble obscurity in the bush and rising through his natural talents to undreamed-of heights; the reality, as ever, is more complex and more interesting. This legend is the more persistent because Bradman himself promoted it assiduously in his own writing, speeches and interviews over a lifetime, and because it chimes in absolutely with what the average Australian has always wanted to believe.

Bowral, the rather atypical New South Wales country town where Don Bradman grew up, contains other important clues. Nestling in the Southern Highlands some seventy miles south of Sydney at over 2,000 feet, Bowral in Bradman's day was known as 'the sanatorium of the south' for its clean mountain air, its 'English' countryside with its acclimatised European flowers, shrubs and trees, and its enviable reputation as a salubrious retreat for the Sydney rich. The State Governor's summer house was in nearby Sutton Forest. In English terms it was a mini Bath, Cheltenham or Harrogate, a spa town transplanted. Its population at the 1911 census, when Bradman was two, was 2,620. Known for its conservative politics, the town was run by a tight group of professionals and businessmen, all Protestants, many of them Freemasons. There was no radical working-class to speak of, as elsewhere in Australia, since there was no shearing or mining industry there to support it. In other words, it was a town where diligence and deference would be highly rewarded.

According to the legend, Bradman's father was a poor, jobbing bush carpenter whose family was living in a humble weather-board cottage on a small-holding at Yeo Yeo outside Cootamundra when Bradman was born. The legend omits to say that by the time Bradman was a schoolboy in Bowral in the early 1920s, the family owned a substantial three-bedroom, double-brick California bungalow, with characteristic sleep-out verandah, overlooking one of the town's main parks, and his father was a relatively well-off, self-employed builder. The part of Bowral where the Bradmans lived was the preserve of the town's business and professional elite, its shopkeepers, solicitors, headmasters, and successful tradesmen. Bradman's brother became a shopkeeper and farmer, one sister married a dairy farmer of substance, another became a professional piano teacher and the third married an engineer.

Bradman attended the local high school and sang in the choir of the local Anglican church, St Jude's, both of which were almost literally across the park on which he lived, now Bradman Oval. For his singing the young Don received sixpence a service. He left school at the then usual age of fourteen and was employed in a respectable white-collar position as a ledger-keeper in a local real estate agency; a slight, snowy-haired youngster with a good head for figures and a maturity beyond his years. As a teenager he was both scorer for and then, unusually for one so young, the elected honorary secretary of the Bowral Town Cricket Club. As secretary, incidentally, he was assiduous in getting the team's results in the local Press, which of course highlighted his own prodigious batting feats.

In this way, and by word of mouth, Bradman's exploits on the cricket field gained him a reputation in the town and district, and the news soon spread to Sydney. He also excelled at tennis. Indeed, in 1926, it was a toss-up whether he pursued a tennis-playing or a cricketing career. What finally decided the matter for him was an offer from the Sydney grade-cricket club, St George, to pay his rail fares and expenses each week to play in Sydney. The canny Bradman saw the offer as a good commercial proposition. They paid the grand sum of thirty shillings a week when the return train fare was only 8s 6d; so, provided Bradman was prepared to leave Bowral early on Saturday mornings and catch the late train home on the same day, which he invariably did, he could show a handsome profit. He would persist with this long commute for his first season and a half. Bradman's team captain in the Country Week for 1927 was Alan Seiler, who later commented most perceptively that his young charge was 'a silent worker, a deep thinker ... the game was treated by him as a business'.

At the end of 1928, nearly a year after his first-class debut in the Sheffield Shield, Bradman moved to Sydney, where he boarded in Concord West with Mr and Mrs G. H. Pearce (though he later moved to live with St George's secretary, Frank Cush, and his wife at Rockdale when NSWCA residency rules required it). Pearce was an insurance inspector with a connection to the Bowral real estate agency. Bradman worked as company secretary (really office manager) of a branch office that the Bowral agency opened in Sydney to try to cash in on the suburban land boom of the 1920s. Unfortunately for him, however, the boom soon became a bust as the Great Depression began to bite, and the office closed by year's end. His job security in tatters, the young Bradman learned a painful lesson.

Concord West also happened to be close to Burwood where Jessie Menzies and her parents were living. Jessie, his childhood sweetheart from Bowral, was now a clerk with the Commonwealth Bank. Apart from keeping body and soul together, Bradman as a respectable white-collar worker needed to save money to get married. To this end, he accepted a position with Mick

Simmons, Sydney's largest sporting-goods shop, promoting their cricket equipment. As biographer Roland Perry has written, Bradman realised quickly that he 'did not want a career as a store dummy or circus freak', and he sought to diversify his commercial activities.

Bradman's selection for the 1928-29 Test series against the Englishmen introduced him into a new social world. For instance, he attended black-tie dinners at Sydney's finest hotel, the Wentworth, in the presence of the Governor, and along with the rest of the team was given membership of Tattersalls Club in Brisbane while making his Test debut there. But his position depended on his Test batting form, and after scoring 18 and one he was dropped for the Second Test. Recalled at Melbourne he then hit two centuries in the next three Tests. In 1929-30 he made the world-record 452 not out against the hapless Queenslanders in Sydney. As a result of this and other dizzying batting feats he was a household name in Australia by the end of that season.

Bradman's big opportunity came when he was selected for the 1930 Ashes tour of England. Not only would the tour pay £600 for six months' work (at a time when £5 a week was a good wage), but he would write *Don Bradman's Book*, which was serialised in the British and Australian Press. Moreover, by breaking the Test batting record at Leeds, he would win an honorarium of £1,000 from an admirer, British-based Australian soap tycoon Arthur Whitelaw. This money he put straight into Jessie's bank account where it earned more-favourable interest as she was a bank employee, as well as by now his unofficial fiancée. Some of his team-mates bemoaned the fact that the tight-fisted teetotaller did not spend some of the loot in the bar on them, but Bradman was as single-minded in business as he was on the pitch.

The book contract landed Bradman in trouble with the Australian Board of Control when the *Star* newspaper breached Bradman's tour contract by publishing some of his material before the tour had ended. The Board duly fined him £50, but Bradman netted £5,000 from the trip, made up from royalties, endorsements, tour fees and the honorarium.

Bradman's *annus mirabilis* in 1930 established him as a god all over the cricketing world – Bradmania spread apace – but he was especially treasured in Sydney, which boasted its three 'ours': 'our harbour, our bridge and our Bradman'. The great Sydney Harbour Bridge was still under construction in 1930, but its symbolic importance was already established.

A keen and talented amateur pianist, Bradman composed a song, 'Every Day is a Rainbow Day for Me', which was cut as a record by a popular artist, and he declined a film part in Hollywood. This was also the time of the hit song, 'Our Don Bradman'. He had finally saved enough money to marry respectably and keep a wife and family.

The unprecedented success of his 1930 Ashes tour had brought Bradman lucrative offers to turn fully professional and join the Lancashire League. The Accrington club, in particular, had pursued him with a package worth £1,050 per season. This, however, would have taken him out of Australian Test cricket. The Australian Press denounced him – unfairly given the uncertainties of employment during the Depression – for considering 'Blighty boodle' and putting 'pocket before country'. In the meantime, Sydney interests put up a rival package, almost as lucrative, which involved his writing for the *Sun* newspaper under Johnnie Moyes (New South Wales ex-player, Selector and Bradman mentor), broadcasting on radio 2UE and working for F. J. Palmer's department store doing the same sort of promotional work he had done at Mick Simmons. Jessie, who wanted to stay near her family, and no doubt with children in mind, persuaded him to accept the Sydney offer and stay put.

'The most important partnership of my life' began in April 1932 when Don and Jessie were married at St Paul's Anglican Church in solid, lower middle-class Burwood. They then, almost immediately, went on an all-expenses-paid cricketing tour of North America, organised by the great Australian googly bowler and wit, Arthur Mailey, during which The Don was photographed meeting his baseball equivalent, Babe Ruth, at Yankee Stadium in New York. On their return Don and Jessie lived in a flat in North Sydney, which had just been joined to the city by the new bridge.

As Douglas Jardine's Bodyline tourists neared Fremantle, Bradman was once more locked in controversy with the Board, who were bent on refusing to select him unless he renounced his newspaper contract. It was only when Frank Packer, proprietor of the *Sun* (and father of World Series Cricket's Kerry) agreed to a moratorium on Bradman's writing during the Ashes Tests that the Board were satisfied. Oddly, however, Bradman was allowed to continue with his evening broadcasts, presumably because radio was thought to be too ephemeral to matter. This is not the place to rehearse the drama of the Bodyline Tests – the story is too well known – but it should be noted that Bradman and his major antagonist in the Australian Test team,

Jack Fingleton, also a journalist, have both been accused of leaking to the Press the Australian captain Bill Woodfull's famous dressing-room reproach to the England manager, Plum Warner, that 'There are two teams out there. One is trying to play cricket and the other is not.' To their dying days both Fingleton and Bradman denied the allegation. (Fingleton never forgot the incident, and when he thought it was the reason he was not selected for the 1934 Ashes tour he blamed Bradman for not owning up. He would hold a lifelong grudge.) In the Bodyline series, The Don's average was 56.57, half his previous career figure. It still left him Australia's best in the series. That such a dreadful method of attack had to be used at all simply made the Bradman legend the more potent.

It is important to understand something of the political and economic context in Australia of the 1930 and 1932-33 Test series. The Great Depression hit Australia very hard. About a third of the workforce was unemployed and, staggeringly, Gross Domestic Product fell by a quarter. The Bank of England's Sir Otto Niemeyer recommended cost-cutting and a balanced budget to the Australian Federal Government, while at the same time servicing the British bond-holders who held so much of the country's external debt. This was an explosive mixture and Jack Lang, the charismatic populist Labor premier of New South Wales, one of the hardest-hit states, blamed bloated British capitalists for the plight of the unemployed and refused to service the State's debt, choosing to spend the money on welfare. Willy-nilly, Bradman was taken up as the great popular hero on the sporting field who tamed the British lion; he became a great national symbol of hope. Bodyline upset this populist dream – it was a sort of cricketing Gallipoli – but at least Bradman lived to fight another day. Lang, on the other hand, was dismissed from office by the State Governor, an Englishman, and was subsequently defeated at the polls. The irony, of course, was that Bradman was personally an imperial loyalist and far too conservative and respectable to have any truck with the radical nationalist Langites. And he was sufficiently aware not to commit himself either way in public. Nevertheless, for many working-class Australians, he and Lang were mythologised as popular Davids who stood up to the might of the imperial Goliath.

On August 1, 1933, with his customary thoroughness, Bradman sat for and passed at his first attempt and 'with great credit' the New South Wales Umpire's exam. He was motivated in part by his desire to explore ways of countering Bodyline by changing the Laws of the Game, but mostly by his desire for a complete grounding in the game preparatory to his probable assumption of the mantles of State and national captaincy.

Bradman's next move again shows his hard-headedness and pragmatism. Harry Hodgetts, the South Australian representative on the Australian Board, and a stockbroker, lured Bradman to Adelaide with an offer of a training position in his firm and a salary of £500 a year (paid by the South Australian Cricket Association) and a further £200 (from Hodgetts) when not on cricket tours overseas. At twenty-five Bradman had been offered a position that guaranteed security in a professional life beyond cricket, and out of the Sydney limelight. After his illness during the 1934 tour of England (when he was vice-captain) he missed the next domestic season. In 1935-36, he became captain of South Australia, and the following year a national Selector and captain of Australia. Hodgetts had made a shrewd business decision for South Australian cricket: gate receipts for the New South Wales matches at the Sydney Cricket Ground fell by half and those at the Adelaide Oval more than doubled.

Interestingly, Bradman's best friend in English first-class cricket was the Middlesex slow-bowling all-rounder, Walter Robins, who, though a public school boy, claimed he too had come from 'the sticks' and had made his name by his own efforts. Robins was a London insurance broker, and the Bradmans were impressed. They were especially struck by the Robins's well-appointed, two-storeyed house in rural Buckinghamshire. (Another English Test-playing friend, Gubby Allen, had a similar one.) Predictably, the Bradmans built such a house, two storeys with ten rooms, including a billiard room, in leafy Kensington Park in the shadow of Mount Lofty. In such a way could cricket be a social escalator for those with the right talents and energy. In his eyes, at least, Bradman's lifestyle now approximated to that of the English gentleman amateur, though to be more accurate, given the SACA contribution to his wages, he was a shamateur.

As Australian skipper for the 1936-37 and 1938 Ashes contests, Bradman poured balm on the Bodyline wounds, aided by the fact that the English counties had effectively banned the practice and by MCC chosing amenable England captains. Bradman's diplomacy followed in the footsteps of Woodfull's 1934 Australians who had blazed the way. Goodwill and trust were restored and the bonds of Empire, loosened in 1932-33, were tightened once more. The easing of the Depression and the gathering war clouds in Europe and Asia also played their parts in the reconciliation.

There were, however, some internal glitches. Clarrie Grimmett blamed Bradman for his omission from the 1936-37 Australian team, and four Roman Catholic, Irish-Australian larrikins who were members of that team – Fleetwood-Smith, McCabe, O'Brien, and O'Reilly – were carpeted by the Board for lacking full commitment under Bradman's captaincy. (Fingleton, another who fitted that description, escaped censure, perhaps because he had just scored a century.) The four naturally blamed Bradman, who was a Protestant and a Freemason, though not particularly committed to either persuasion. In fact, Bradman did not know about the Board's action until afterwards and he had championed Fleetwood-Smith's inclusion. Moreover, in 1938, Bradman would win a significant victory over the Board when, mid-tour, he negotiated the right for all team members to have their wives with them, and Mrs McCabe, Mrs Fleetwood-Smith and Mrs Bradman joined the tour before its end.

Charles Williams in his biography of Bradman makes too much of this sectarian divide. In fact, many of Bradman's good friends were Catholics, including McCabe and Sylv Phelan, Don's long-time Adelaide golfing partner. Williams also hints, wrongly, at Bradman's supposed membership of a right-wing, militaristic organisation – akin to the British Union of Fascists – via the Illawarra Regiment. Far from being clandestine, the Illawarra Regiment was a regular militia formation that Bradman had no choice but to join, as young men of his age were required under the Government's Compulsory Military Training scheme to enlist. When the Scullin Labor Government ended the scheme in 1929, Bradman resigned soon afterwards.

After the outbreak of war in 1939 Bradman applied to become an airman but ended up, through no fault of his own, as a physical training officer based at Frankston in Victoria. He might eventually have been transferred to active service in the Middle East, but the onset of crippling fibrositis in his back led to his being invalided out of the Army and he went back to stockbroking, playing little cricket for four years. His main patriotic effort was in the Commonwealth Club, raising money for and administering Gowrie Scholarships to pay for the education of the children of servicemen and women.

If the closing of the Sydney real estate agency in 1929 had reminded the Bradmans of the need to be prudent and to have a secure income, the sudden collapse of Hodgetts and Co. in July 1945 came as a bombshell.

Harry Hodgetts had overstretched himself by investing heavily in a hotel complex in Darwin, only to see it bombed by the Japanese, and to make matters worse one of his agents in the outback mining town of Broken Hill had embezzled funds. To cover his shortfall, Hodgetts had fraudulently used £88,884 of his clients' money, and as a result he was gaoled for five years. Bradman was an employee of the firm and not responsible for any of this misbehaviour. Indeed, he himself was owed £726 and was one of 238 unsecured creditors, among them the State Governor and several charities. Bradman found himself jobless overnight. Moving quickly, and having bought a seat on the stock exchange in his own right in 1943, he put up a new shingle outside the offices, Don Bradman and Co. Jessie, with her book-keeping experience, put a great deal of effort into the new enterprise. The Adelaide establishment, however, was put out by the speed of the move. Fellow brokers were upset when they learned that the business would not be put out to general tender and that Bradman had not paid to acquire it. But the official receiver made these decisions, not Bradman. Whatever the truth behind Bradman's foreknowledge or otherwise of Hodgetts's criminal dealings, and we shall probably never know, there were some among the old Adelaide families who were never to forgive the Bradmans for their perceived impropriety, pushiness and opportunism. Many others, however, found it difficult to hold a grudge against a man who was a living legend, even when his feet of clay were showing.

It was touch and go whether Bradman would play Test cricket again post-war, given his age, health and business concerns. Still, he was prevailed upon to captain against Wally Hammond's Englishmen in 1946-47. The First Test in Brisbane contained the notorious Ikin incident, when Ikin apparently caught Bradman in the slips and The Don did not walk, thinking it a bump ball. Hammond and many of his team thought otherwise and the series got off to a grim start. Had Bradman been given out on 28, his score at the time, his indifferent form was likely to have prompted him to retire from cricket then and there. Instead, he went on to make 187. Thank goodness he survived the appeal or he might not have toured England again in 1948.

The 1948 trip, which crowned Bradman's playing career, also marked his apotheosis as a cricketing ambassador. The two countries craved a restoration of normal life after the war – rationing was still in place in

Britain in 1948 – and Bradman's team seemed to show that what people imagined as the halcyon cricketing days before the war had returned. At the end of this perfect tour for Australia – the team were unbeaten throughout – Bradman retired from Test cricket and he was knighted in the New Year's Honours for his services to cricket, the great imperial sport. Stanley Melbourne (later Lord) Bruce, Australia's High Commissioner in London, 1933–45, wrote in a letter to him on his knighthood:

> I see you have modestly said it is really in recognition of the great game for which you have done so much. I regard it as something more than that and as a recognition of the great services you have rendered to inter-imperial relations by your tact and outstanding personality. Pehaps I am better able to appreciate the value of what you have done in this direction, owing to the long period for which I have acted as Australia's representative in Great Britain.

It was even rumoured that Bradman himself might be appointed High Commissioner.

In retirement Bradman continued his stockbroking successfully until 1954, when he sold his business and henceforth devoted his time fully to his various directorships and to cricket administration. He was also a great fundraiser for charity, especially for handicapped children. He wrote two splendid books, his autobiography, *Farewell to Cricket* (1950) and the best coaching manual to date, *The Art of Cricket* (1958). And he was to play his last cricket match ever in 1963 when his great friend, admirer and fellow conservative, Robert Menzies, lured him briefly out of retirement to join his Prime Minister's XI against Ted Dexter's MCC tourists. Virtually to the end, Bradman generously and assiduously signed bats and photographs and answered dozens of letters a day from admirers from all over the cricketing world. In this way he continued to burnish his legend.

Essentially a shy man, Bradman avoided unnecessary publicity even when a player and guarded himself and his family fiercely during his retirement. Personal tragedy and ill-health stalked the Bradmans. Apart from his much-publicised illnesses in 1934 (appendicitis and life-threatening peritonitis) and in the 1940s (crippling fibrositis), the Bradmans had to cope with the infant death of their first son in 1936, the affliction with polio for a year (1952) of their other son, and their only daughter's cerebral palsy. Jessie fought a long battle with cancer before her death in 1997. Don himself died bed-ridden and blind, aged ninety-two.

The rise of republican nationalism in Australia in the 1990s witnessed a desperate rediscovery and rebranding of national icons. For the new generation, Bradman was hailed as 'the greatest living Australian'. In 1996, then Prime Minister John Howard opened the second stage of the Bradman Museum (perhaps better called a secular shrine) at Bowral and two Bradman commemorative stamps and a Bradman $5 coin were issued. Bradman also broke his self-imposed purdah to grant Kerry Packer's Channel 9 TV an exclusive interview, provided Packer paid one million dollars to the Bradman Foundation and Museum. Three more special coins were minted on his death in 2001. He was even seriously suggested, despite his advanced age, for the presidency of the much-anticipated Australian republic in 1999. Astutely, Bradman was consistent in his refusal to say whether he was a monarchist or republican, thus keeping the support of both factions, as national icons perhaps should. Over the years he had been constructed by commentators and his Australian public as a radical nationalist protagonist in the 1930s and as an imperial loyalist in the 1940s. In the 1990s both identities virtually coalesced into a single conservative nationalist narrative. Legend now dictated that he was the most invincible of the Invincibles, as the 1948 tourists were invariably described.

There was nothing of the freewheeling, hard drinking, easy-going, beer-and-a-bet larrikin about Bradman: he was not an archetypal Australian 'mate'. But he did embody another more conservative and less well-known tradition which stressed the equally Australian values of hard work, determination, especially in adversity, individualism, upward social mobility, entrepreneurship, respectability, loyalty, directness and fair but hard play. At root this tradition is Protestant, broadly middle-class and anglophile. The prevailing hagiography does not do Bradman's life and character justice. He needs to be rescued from the naïve nationalist reductionism of the Bradolators, of whichever political stripe.

A more believable Bradman can be seen slowly emerging from the archives: a man who kept much to himself but was an outrageously flamboyant entertainer; a man who was a mercurial mixture of prudence and daring, self-effacement and confidence, self-interest and community mindedness; a man who is a true exemplar of the conservative, hard-edged but enlightened pragmatism of Robert Menzies and John Howard. Backing his own judgment to the full, always calculating the odds, occasionally sailing uncomfortably close to the wind, Bradman made the most of his life's chances, to devastating effect on the cricket field and much more than adequately off it. Whatever emerges from the archives, however, one thing will not change: we Australians will always remain rightly proud of 'our Don', the greatest batsman of them all and, whatever the odd revisionist might unearth, without doubt Australia's greatest son.

SEASON
BY SEASON
1927–1949

1927-28

A young Bradman at the Sydney Cricket Ground, November 1928.

1927-28

Important alterations in the rules of the Sheffield Shield competition were in operation during the season of 1927-28. It was made clear during Queensland's first year in the tournament that, to enable the programme to be adhered to, a time limit was necessary, and the rules were altered to provide that matches should be restricted to four full days and a portion of the fifth day. Moreover, a system of scoring by points was adopted and instead of Queensland and South Australia, as previously, meeting once each year, all the States had to play each other twice. So far as can be judged as the result of one season, the innovations have been beneficial to the game. ...

From 'Cricket in Australia: The Inter-State Matches'

SOUTH AUSTRALIA v NEW SOUTH WALES 1 (1, 2)

Played at Adelaide, December 16, 17, 19, 20, [21, 1927]. A keenly fought match ended in exciting fashion, South Australia, despite some splendid bowling by McNamee, getting home by one wicket. Bradman joined the select band of cricketers who have made a century in their first Sheffield Shield match ...

[The nineteen-year-old Bradman came into the New South Wales team for his first-class debut when Archie Jackson, suffering from a boil on his knee, was named as twelfth man.]

New South Wales

N. E. Phillips b Whitfield	112	–	lbw b Grimmett	11
G. Morgan b Scott	11	–	b Grimmett	34
T. J. E. Andrews c Williams b Grimmett	58	–	b Scott	20
*A. F. Kippax c Alexander b Williams	143	–	c and b Grimmett	0
A. Scanes c Williams b Schneider	44	–	c Whitfield b Grimmett	26
† W. A. Oldfield c Hack b Grimmett	12	–	c Richardson b Grimmett	4
D. Bradman c Williams b Scott	118	–	b Grimmett	33
F. Jordon lbw b Scott	1	–	lbw b Grimmett	0
S. C. Everett st Hack b Grimmett	5	–	c Harris b Scott	8
A. A. Mailey b Scott	0	–	c Schneider b Grimmett	5
R. L. A. McNamee not out	1	–	not out	1
B 2, l-b 5, w 1, n-b 6	14		B 1, l-b 1, w 1, n-b 5	8
	519			**150**

South Australia bowling: *First innings*—Scott 19.6–1–99–4; Whitfield 17–3–43–1; Grimmett 31–1–160–3; Williams 11–0–70–1; Lee 17–1–76–0; Schneider 6–0–39–1; Alexander 3–0–14–0; Johnson 1–0–4–0. *Second innings*—Scott 17–3–46–2; Whitfield 7–1–26–0; Grimmett 21.7–5–57–8; Williams 2–0–13–0.

South Australia

K. J. Schneider, G. W. Harris, *V. Y. Richardson, W. C. Alexander, E. A. Johnson, H. E. P. Whitfield, †A. Hack, P. K. Lee, C. V. Grimmett, J. D. Scott and N. L. Williams.

First innings: 481 (Schneider 108, Harris 77, Richardson 80, Alexander 42, Hack 45, Grimmett 43 not out; Everett three for 92, Mailey three for 143). *Second innings:* Nine for 189 (Alexander 49, Grimmett 32; McNamee five for 53).

Umpires: G. A. Hele and J. J. Quinn

VICTORIA v NEW SOUTH WALES   2 (3, 4)

Played at Melbourne, December 23, 24, 26, 27 [1927]. Victoria won by 222 runs, largely owing to Ponsford and Woodfull, their first-wicket batsmen, but the great performance of the match was that of McNamee of New South Wales, who, tall and of medium pace, took seven wickets for 77 – the finest achievement in bowling during the season. ... Woodfull ... was prompted to close the second Victoria innings – an action in a second innings taken for the first time in the history of the competition.

[By following his 437 against Queensland a week earlier with 202 in Victoria's first innings, Ponsford became the first batsman to score successive double-centuries in Australia.]

Victoria

W. H. Ponsford, *W. M. Woodfull, H. L. Hendry, A. E. V. Hartkopf, J. Scaife, A. E. Liddicut, C. Sindrey, †J. L. Ellis, D. D. Blackie, F. L. Morton and H. Ironmonger.

First innings: 355 (Ponsford 202, Woodfull 99; McNamee seven for 77, Mailey three for 117). *Second innings:* Seven for 386 dec (Ponsford 38, Woodfull 191 not out, Hendry 59, Scaife 54; Everett three for 66).

New South Wales

N. E. Phillips b Ironmonger	26	–	b Morton	4
G. Morgan lbw b Ironmonger	93	–	lbw b Morton	4
T. J. E. Andrews b Ironmonger	110	–	c Hartkopf b Morton	53
*A. F. Kippax lbw b Morton	26	–	lbw b Blackie	35
A. Jackson c Woodfull b Blackie	6	–	lbw b Blackie	16
D. Bradman lbw b Hartkopf	31	–	b Blackie	5
A. Scanes b Ironmonger	3	–	lbw b Blackie	1
†W. A. Oldfield not out	30	–	not out	11
S. C. Everett lbw b Blackie	10	–	c Hendry b Ironmonger	13
A. A. Mailey c Woodfull b Ironmonger	8	–	c and b Blackie	0
R. L. A. McNamee b Blackie	1	–	c Hendry b Blackie	0
B 11, l-b 7, w 1, n-b 4	23		B 4, l-b 4, n-b 2	10
	367			**152**

Victoria bowling: *First innings*—Morton 13–1–41–1; Liddicut 8–1–23–0; Blackie 26.2–3–103–3; Hendry 3–0–17–0; Ironmonger 34–5–108–5; Hartkopf 10–0–52–1. *Second innings*—Morton 10–0–52–3; Blackie 11.6–3–32–6; Ironmonger 12–0–58–1.

Umpires: J. Richards and D. Elder

NEW SOUTH WALES v QUEENSLAND   3 (5, 6)

Played at Sydney, December 31 [1927], January 2, 3, 4, 5 [1928]. Recovering splendidly after following on 417 in arrear, Queensland went very near to victory, New South Wales, with eight second innings wickets down, being 127 behind at the finish. Kippax played his highest innings in first-class cricket ... When New South Wales had to bat again on a pitch damaged by rain, Nothling made a great effort to force a win against time ...

[Queenslanders Rowe and Higgins followed first-ball dismissals in the first innings with centuries in the second innings.]

Bradman in Wisden

New South Wales

N. E. Phillips c Hurwood b Bensted	17	–	lbw b Nothling	29
J. M. Gregory c and b Nothling	63	–	run out	0
T. J. E. Andrews b Hurwood	41	–	b Nothling	11
*A. F. Kippax not out	315	–	c O'Connor b Nothling	9
A. Ratcliffe c O'Connor b Nothling	25	–	b Nothling	0
A. Jackson c O'Connor b Bensted	19	–	c O'Connor b Hurwood	9
G. Morgan c O'Connor b Bensted	121	–	c Gough b Thompson	12
D. Bradman b Gough	0	–	c O'Connor b Nothling	13
†H. S. Love b Rowe	26	–	not out	13
E. O'Brien b Gough	6	–	not out	0
R. L. A. McNamee st O'Connor b Gough	1			
B 2, w 1, n-b 2	5		B 2, l-b 1, n-b 1	4
	639		(eight wkts)	**100**

Queensland bowling: *First innings*—Bensted 27–1–126–3; Hurwood 27–4–118–1; Nothling 28–3–109–2; Gill 8–0–57–0; Thompson 17–1–68–0; Gough 16.5–0–100–3; Rowe 13–1–56–1. *Second innings*—Bensted 2–0–4–0; Hurwood 18–4–40–1; Nothling 21–7–39–5; Gill 1–0–1–0; Thompson 4–1–5–1; Gough 2–1–3–0; Rowe 2–0–4–0.

Queensland

L. L. Gill, L. E. Oxenham, W. Rowe, F. C. Thompson, L. Litster, O. E. Nothling, *†L. P. D. O'Connor, F. J. Gough, R. L. Higgins, E. Bensted and A. C. Hurwood.

First innings: 276 (Litster 82, Nothling 74, O'Connor 37; Phillips four for 26). *Second innings:* 590 (Higgins 179, Bensted 38, Thompson 68, Rowe 147, O'Connor 32, Oxenham 50, Gough 42; Bradman two for 41).

Umpires: A. Williams and S. Parsons

NEW SOUTH WALES v SOUTH AUSTRALIA   4 (7, 8)

Played at Sydney, January 6, 7, 9, 10 [1928]. In this match, Jackson of New South Wales enjoyed the distinction of making two separate hundreds. ... Another important factor in a New South Wales victory by 118 runs was the fast bowling of Nicholls.

New South Wales

H. C. Steele b Scott	14	–	b Scott	5
A. Jackson c McKay b Wall	131	–	b Grimmett	122
T. J. E. Andrews b Wall	44	–	lbw b Scott	2
*A. F. Kippax c Wall b Lee	17	–	lbw b McKay	58
A. Ratcliffe c Richardson b Grimmett	10	–	c Hack b Scott	30
D. Bradman c and b McKay	2	–	st Hack b Grimmett	73
F. Jordan c Alexander b Wall	12	–	b Grimmett	31
C. O. Nicholls b Scott	18	–	st Hack b Grimmett	5
A. A. Mailey st Hack b Grimmett	1	–	b Scott	7
†H. Davidson c Hack b Wall	10	–	b Scott	2
R. L. A. McNamee not out	0	–	not out	4
B 14, l-b 8, w 7, n-b 3	32		B 15, l-b 8, w 3, n-b 3	29
	291			**368**

South Australia bowling: *First innings*—Scott 13–2–57–2; Wall 17–3–51–4; Lee 2–0–15–1; Grimmett 24–1–106–2; McKay 7–0–30–1. *Second innings*—Scott 22.2–2–108–5; Wall 11–2–51–0; Lee 2–0–18–0; Grimmett 26–0–137–4; McKay 1–0–4–0.

South Australia

K. J. Schneider, G. W. Harris, *V. Y. Richardson, A. J. Ryan, †A. Hack, C. V. Grimmett, W. C. Alexander, D.G. McKay, P.K. Lee, J. D. Scott and T. Wall.

First innings: 248 (Ryan 41, Hack 50, Grimmett 54, Alexander 58; Nicholls five for 115, Bradman none for 11). *Second innings:* 293 (Schneider 54, Richardson 86, McKay 40, Lee 30; Nicholls four for 84, Mailey three for 113).

Umpires: G. Borwick and W. Bowes

NEW SOUTH WALES v VICTORIA   5 (9, 10)

Played at Sydney, January 26, 27, 28, 30, 31 [1928]. The return match between these States furnished a new Shield [and Australian] record in the making of eight individual hundreds, and so great was the mastery of the batting that during four and a half days 1,513 runs were scored and only twenty-nine wickets fell.

[The match, which was drawn, 'drew a record attendance of 67,615 people and produced a "gate" of over £4,606'.]

New South Wales

J. M. Gregory lbw b Morton	12	–	c Ryder b a'Beckett	4
A. Jackson c Hendry b a'Beckett	11	–	b Blackie	44
T. J. E. Andrews c and b Morton	4	–	b Blackie	32
*A. F. Kippax b a'Beckett	134	–	b Blackie	42
G. Morgan b Blackie	110	–	c and b Blackie	0
D. Bradman st Ellis b Blackie	7	–	not out	134
N. E. Phillips lbw b a'Beckett	0	–	b Morton	2
†W. A. Oldfield c sub b a'Beckett	101	–	b Blackie	49
C. O. Nicholls b a'Beckett	110	–	c Rigg b Blackie	18
A. A. Mailey b a'Beckett	12	–	not out	11
R. L. A. McNamee not out	8			
B 16, l-b 1, w 1, n-b 6	24		B 9, l-b 4, w 2, n-b 2	17
	533		(eight wkts dec)	**353**

Victoria bowling: *First innings*—Morton 26–0–175–2; a'Beckett 32.6–3–119–6; Blackie 41–10–128–2; Ironmonger 19–4–67–0; Hendry 5–0–20–0. *Second innings*—Morton 12–1–55–1; a'Beckett 17–2–63–1; Blackie 29–2–101–6; Ironmonger 21–2–80–0; Hendry 5–1–12–0; Ponsford 3–0–25–0.

Victoria

*W.M. Woodfull, W.H. Ponsford, H.L. Hendry, J. Ryder, K.L. Rigg, J. Scaife, E.L. a'Beckett, †J.L. Ellis, D.D. Blackie, F.L. Morton and H. Ironmonger.

First innings: 422 (Woodfull 94, Hendry 138, Ryder 106, Scaife 35 not out; Gregory four for 81, Mailey three for 128). *Second innings:* One for 205 (Woodfull 81 not out, Rigg 110 not out; Bradman none for 14).

Umpires: W.G. French and A.C. Jones

1928-29

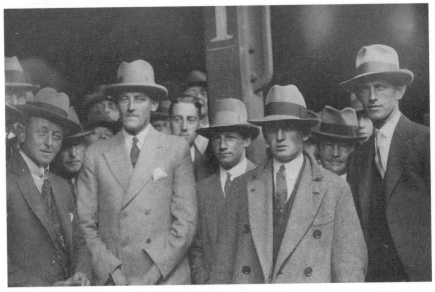

The Australian team that beat England at the MCG in the Fifth Test of the 1928-29 series.

1928-29

New South Wales, going through the season without defeat, carried off the Sheffield Shield; they won three games outright and gained first innings points in the three other matches. Naturally, the competition was overshadowed by the tour of the MCC team, and interest in the contests suffered to some extent through States having to take the field without some of their leading players. This state of things, however, had one good result, as it gave opportunity for younger players to be tried out in the best company, and New South Wales, in wresting the trophy from Victoria, owed much to the success of their colts, notably Bradman, Jackson and Fairfax.

Bradman during the season scored 1,690 runs [24 innings – 13 games] in first-class cricket, thereby setting up a new record [previously 1,534 in 27 innings – 14 games by G. A. Faulkner on South Africa's tour of Australia in 1910-11], and in Sheffield Shield matches averaged 148.33. His 340 not out against Victoria was the highest individual score ever made on the Sydney ground. Moreover, Bradman, making 131 and 133 not out against Queensland at Brisbane, joined the distinguished band of cricketers who have put together two separate centuries in a match. ...

From 'Cricket in Australia: The Inter-State Matches'

[*Note:* On MCC's tour of Australia, W. R. Hammond also passed Faulkner's mark, scoring 1,553 in 18 innings – 13 games.]

AUSTRALIA v REST OF AUSTRALIA   6 (11, 12)
(TEST TRIAL MATCH)

Played at Melbourne, October 19, 20, 22 [1928]. The Trial match gave little help to the Australian Selectors in their task of strengthening the batting for a Test eleven, The Rest failing lamentably at their first attempt and suffering defeat on the third day by an innings and 43 runs. ...

Rest of Australia

G. W. Harris c Oxenham b Gregory	6	–	st Oldfield b Grimmett	51
†L. P. O'Connor b Oxenham	31	–	b Oxenham	0
A. Jackson c Oldfield b Oxenham	18	–	c and b Grimmett	27
C. Kelleway run out	15	–	lbw b Oxenham	26
*V. Y. Richardson c Hendry b Gregory	5	–	b Oxenham	0
D. G. Bradman c Oldfield b Grimmett	14	–	b Oxenham	5
F. C. Thompson st Oldfield b Grimmett	5	–	c Oldfield b Grimmett	20
Dr O. E. Nothling lbw b Grimmett	8	–	not out	62
C. O. Nicholls lbw b Oxenham	0	–	st Oldfield b Grimmett	47
J. D. Scott b Oxenham	0	–	b Oxenham	1
H. Ironmonger not out	2	–	b Oxenham	4
B 1, l-b 5, n-b 1	7		L-b	1
	111			**244**

Australia bowling: *First innings*—Gregory 11–2–26–2; Blackie 17–8–21–0; Oxenham 17.2–9–28–4; Grimmett 11–3–29–3. *Second innings*—Gregory 9–1–34–0; Blackie 9–0–22–0; Oxenham 19.2–2–62–6; Grimmett 19–1–125–4.

Australia

W. H. Ponsford, H. L. Hendry, T. J. E. Andrews, A. Kippax, R. K. Oxenham, J. Scaife, *W. M. Woodfull, J. M. Gregory, C. V. Grimmett, †W. A. Oldfield and D. D. Blackie.

First innings: 398 (Ponsford 79, Hendry 45, Andrews 44, Kippax 34, Gregory 38, Grimmett 43, Oldfield 58; Kelleway three for 72, Bradman one for 36).

Umpires: J. Richards and P. E. Smith

QUEENSLAND v NEW SOUTH WALES   7 (13, 14)

Played at [Exhibition Ground] Brisbane, October 27, 29, 30, 31, November 1 [1928]. If failing to justify expectations in the Test Trial, Bradman batted so brilliantly in the first of the Sheffield Shield matches that he scored a hundred in each innings. In winning by six wickets, after being 76 behind on the first innings, New South Wales owed nearly everything to Bradman and Hooker, the former making 264 for once out and the latter taking ten wickets for less than 12 runs each. ... [In their first innings, New South Wales lost their last six wickets for two runs; in their second, needing 399 to win, an] opening partnership of 121 by Jackson and Loder and a third-wicket stand of 185 by Bradman and Kippax brought victory with plenty of time to spare.

Queensland

R. K. Oxenham, *†L. P. O'Connor, F. J. Gough, W. Rowe, F. C. Thompson, R. Higgins, Dr O. E. Nothling, E. Knowles, E. C. Bensted, P. M. Hornibrook and H. M. Thurlow.

First innings: 324 (O'Connor 72, Gough 67, Higgins 58, Bensted 36 not out; Hooker six for 46, Morgan three for 36). *Second innings:* 322 (Gough 39, Thompson 158 not out, Knowles 30, Higgins 33; Hooker four for 72).

New South Wales

A. Jackson c Hornibrook b Nothling	50	–	c Nothling b Rowe	71
R. Loder b Thurlow	1	–	run out	49
D. G. Bradman c O'Connor b Thurlow	131	–	not out	133
*A. F. Kippax b Thurlow	47	–	c Hornibrook b Rowe	96
G. Morgan lbw b Thurlow	4	–	b Thurlow	6
†H. S. B. Love c O'Connor b Thurlow	5	–	not out	31
C. O. Nicholls b Thurlow	2			
H. Hooker b Oxenham	0			
J. Carter lbw b Oxenham	0			
N. Campbell b Oxenham	0			
R. McNamee not out	0			
L-b 4, n-b 4	8		B 11, l-b 3, n-b 1	15
	248		(four wkts)	**401**

Queensland bowling: *First innings*—Hornibrook 12–2–52–0; Thurlow 15–3–59–6; Oxenham 18.2–3–56–3; Nothling 8–1–22–1; Rowe 5–0–15–0; Bensted 6–0–30–0; Thompson 1–0–6–0. *Second innings*—Hornibrook 20.4–3–62–0; Thurlow 21–2–94–1; Oxenham 29–2–77–0; Nothling 13–0–52–0; Rowe 11–3–45–2; Bensted 9–0–35–0; Thompson 8–3–21–0.

Umpires: J. P. Orr and J. A. Scott

MCC TEAM v NEW SOUTH WALES   8 (15, 16)

Played at Sydney, Friday, Saturday, Monday, Tuesday, November 9, 10, 12, 13 [1928]. The match with New South Wales was … drawn, 1,447 runs being scored while only twenty wickets went down. MCC put together the great total of 734 … [their highest score in first-class matches at the time. The fourth-wicket stand of 333 between Hammond and Hendren] was the highest stand ever made for any wicket against New South Wales. Hendren, having twice driven Bradman over the sight-screen for 6, was caught in the long field off the next ball. … New South Wales lost three wickets for 52 [by stumps on Saturday: the third wicket fell at 38] but on the Monday, Kippax, Bradman and Kelleway played uncommonly well. The first two added 90 for the fourth wicket, while Bradman and Kelleway put on 68. Bradman, who hit to leg and drove very hard, survived two or three appeals for leg-before before Freeman, with whom he was never comfortable, bowled him round his legs. … Following on 385 behind, New South Wales had three men out for 115 soon after lunch on the last day, but no further success fell to the English bowlers, Kippax and Bradman each making a hundred and adding 249 in rather more than two and a half hours. The batting during this time was extremely good, Kippax showing his finest form in cutting and driving and Bradman playing much better than in the first innings.

MCC Team

H. Sutcliffe, Mr D. R. Jardine, E. Tyldesley, W. R. Hammond, E. Hendren, M. Leyland, †L. Ames, *Mr A. P. F. Chapman, M. W. Tate, H. Larwood and A. P. Freeman.

   First innings: Seven for 734 dec (Sutcliffe 67, Jardine 140, Hammond 225, Hendren 167, Leyland 47 not out; Bradman one for 55 off five overs).

New South Wales

G. Morgan b Hammond	1	–	c Ames b Larwood	18
A. Jackson b Tate	4	–	run out	40
T. J. E. Andrews c Chapman b Tate	14	–	b Tate	19
*A. F. Kippax lbw b Hammond	64	–	not out	136
D. G. Bradman b Freeman	87	–	not out	132
C. E. Kelleway not out	93			
J. M. Gregory st Ames b Tate	7			
†W. A. Oldfield c Ames b Freeman	33			
C. O. Nicholls c Jardine b Freeman	26			
H. Hooker c Hammond b Freeman	14			
N. Campbell c Chapman b Freeman	0			
B 3, l-b 3	6		B 14, l-b 5	19
	349		(three wkts)	**364**

MCC Team bowling: *First innings*—Tate 28–3–98–3; Hammond 17–3–64–2; Freeman 37.2–3–136–5; Larwood 4–1–10–0; Leyland 12–1–35–0; *Second innings*—Tate 15–2–36–1; Hammond 15–0–73–0; Freeman 25–3–81–0; Larwood 16–5–33–1; Leyland 12–1–61–0; Jardine 3–0–22–0; Hendren 5–0–21–0; Sutcliffe 4–1–18–0.

Umpires: W. Bowes and A.C. Jones

MCC TEAM v AN AUSTRALIAN XI   9 (17, 18)

Played at Sydney, Friday, Saturday, Monday, Tuesday, November 16, 17, 19, 20 [1928]. In a match of comparatively modest scoring, the MCC gained by eight wickets their first victory of the tour – over an Australian XI drawn, with the exception of Nothling of Queensland, entirely from New South Wales and South Australia. [Victoria felt that the expenses of £1 per day were not sufficient.] Larwood, Tate and White all bowled admirably in dismissing the Australian XI in less than four hours and a half for 231. Andrews gave promise of doing well ... but until Bradman went in, no real resistance was offered to the attack. Bettington, who after some years in England had returned to Australia by the same vessel as that on which the English cricketers travelled, made some good cuts in a useful innings, and in the end Bradman took out his bat after a stay of three hours and twenty minutes. ...

An Australian XI

*V. Y. Richardson b White	24	–	c Geary b Larwood	21
G. W. Harris b Larwood	19	–	b White	56
T. J. E. Andrews b White	39	–	c Hobbs b Geary	25
A. Jackson c Geary b Larwood	14	–	c Duckworth b Tate	61
D. G. Bradman not out	58	–	lbw b Tate	18
G. Morgan c Duckworth b Tate	15	–	b Geary	9
Dr O. E. Nothling c Sutcliffe b White	11	–	not out	29
Dr R. H. Bettington c Hendren b Geary	34	–	b Larwood	8
†W. A. Oldfield c Hendren b Tate	0	–	run out	7
J. D. Scott c Hendren b Larwood	5	–	b Tate	0
H. Hooker c Larwood b Tate	2	–	c Hendren b Geary	1
W	1		B 3, l-b 4, w 1	8
	231			**243**

MCC Team bowling: *First innings*—Larwood 18–1–80–3; Tate 16.7–4–38–3; Geary 13–1–65–1; White 28–8–47–3. *Second innings*—Larwood 19–0–81–2; Tate 22–2–65–3; Geary 14.1–4–42–3; White 19–5–47–1.

MCC Team

J.B. Hobbs, H. Sutcliffe, Mr D.R. Jardine, C.P. Mead, E. Tyldesley, E. Hendren, H. Larwood, M.W. Tate, *Mr J.C. White, G. Geary and †G. Duckworth.

First innings: 357 (Hobbs 58, Sutcliffe 42, Mead 58, Tyldesley 69, Tate 59, Geary 33; Nothling three for 61, Bettington three for 98). *Second innings:* Two for 118 (Hobbs 67 not out, Sutcliffe 31).

Umpires: W.G. French and S. Parsons

ENGLAND v AUSTRALIA
(FIRST TEST MATCH)

10 (19, 20)
1 (1, 2)

Played at [Exhibition Ground] Brisbane, Friday, Saturday, Monday, Tuesday, Wednesday, November 30, December 1, 3, 4, 5 [1928]. Having by now run into first-rate all-round form, England entered upon the opening Test Match with feelings of confidence, but not even the most sanguine member of the team could have anticipated that they would gain a victory by such an astounding margin as that of 675 runs – easily the most pronounced success by runs in the history of Test Matches. ... Australia relied largely upon tried men, Bradman being the one youngster to secure inclusion. On paper, their eleven appeared quite formidable ... All ideas on this point were upset by the damage to Gregory [knee injury] and Kelleway's indisposition [food poisoning]. ...

[In their second innings] Australia's wretched position was made hopeless by heavy rain during the night followed in the morning by bright sunshine. ... The last six wickets – the two invalids being still unable to bat – went down in fifty minutes, Australia being all out for 66. Woodfull, batting splendidly, received no support at all, nearly everyone who joined him hitting out wildly immediately on going in. ...

England

J.B. Hobbs, H. Sutcliffe, C.P. Mead, W.R. Hammond, Mr D.R. Jardine, E. Hendren, *Mr A.P.F. Chapman, M.W. Tate, H. Larwood, Mr J.C. White and †G. Duckworth.

First innings: 521 (Hobbs 49, Sutcliffe 38, Hammond 44, Jardine 35, Hendren 169, Chapman 50, Larwood 70; Gregory three for 142, Grimmett three for 167). *Second innings:* Eight for 342 dec (Sutcliffe 32, Mead 73, Jardine 65 not out, Hendren 45, Larwood 37; Grimmett six for 131).

Australia

W.M. Woodfull c Chapman b Larwood	0	–	not out	30
W.H. Ponsford b Larwood	2	–	c Duckworth b Larwood	6
A.F. Kippax c and b Tate	16	–	c and b Larwood	15
H.L. Hendry lbw b Larwood	30	–	c Larwood b White	6
C.E. Kelleway b Larwood	8	–	absent ill	0
*J. Ryder c Jardine b Larwood	33	–	c Larwood b Tate	1
D.G. Bradman lbw b Tate	18	–	c Chapman b White	1
†W.A. Oldfield lbw b Tate	2	–	c Larwood b Tate	5
C.V. Grimmett not out	7	–	c Chapman b White	1
H. Ironmonger b Larwood	4	–	c Chapman b White	0
J.M. Gregory absent hurt	0	–	absent hurt	0
B 1, l-b 1	2		N-b	1
	122			**66**

England bowling: *First innings*—Larwood 14.4–4–32–6; Tate 21–6–50–3; Hammond 15–5–38–0. *Second innings*—Larwood 7–0–30–2; Tate 11–3–26–2; Hammond 1–0–2–0; White 6.3–2–7–4.

Umpires: D. Elder and G.A. Hele

VICTORIA v NEW SOUTH WALES   11 (21, 22)

Played at Melbourne, December 22, 24, 25, 26, 27 [1928]. Putting on 307 for the last wicket – a world's record – Kippax and Hooker resisted the Victoria attack for more than five hours and were clearly responsible for New South Wales gaining a first innings lead. ... Hooker played fine, defensive cricket while Kippax – at the wickets from late Monday afternoon until after midday on Wednesday – batted with such delightful ease and effect that the whole aspect of the game was altered. ...

Victoria

H.L. Hendry, F. Baring, *J. Ryder, K. Rigg, R. Ellis, J. Scaife, E. a'Beckett, †J.L. Ellis, H.I. Ebeling, W.J. Rayson and H. Ironmonger.

     First innings: 376 (Ryder 175, a'Beckett 113; Hooker three for 100). *Second innings:* Six for 251 dec (Baring 30, a'Beckett 95, Hendry 69 not out; Fairfax three for 45).

New South Wales

A. Jackson c J. Ellis b Ironmonger	19			
A. Fairfax c Ironmonger b a'Beckett	2	–	b R. Ellis	30
T. J. E. Andrews b Hendry	33			
*A. F. Kippax not out	260			
D. G. Bradman b Hendry	1	–	not out	71
C. Kelleway b Hendry	0	–	c a'Beckett b Ironmonger	13
D. Seddon lbw b Ironmonger	0	–	not out	38
†H. S. B. Love lbw b Ebeling	0			
C. O. Nicholls b Ebeling	10			
S. Everett lbw b Ironmonger	20			
H. Hooker c Ryder b a'Beckett	62			
B 5, l-b 6, n-b 2	13		L-b 3, w 1	4
	420		(two wkts)	**156**

Victoria bowling: *First innings*—a'Beckett 29.1–2–92–2; Ebeling 25–1–81–2; Ironmonger 33–4–95–3; Hendry 18–5–58–3; Rayson 7–0–42–0; R. Ellis 10–1–31–0; Baring 5–1–8–0. *Second innings*—a'Beckett 10–3–19–0; Ebeling 4–1–10–0; Ironmonger 8–2–12–1; Rayson 5–0–41–0; R. Ellis 6–1–29–1; Baring 5–0–22–0; Rigg 2–0–19–0.

Umpires: J. Richards and P. E. Smith

ENGLAND v AUSTRALIA   12 (23, 24)
(THIRD TEST MATCH)   2 (3, 4)

Played at Melbourne, Saturday, Monday, Tuesday, Wednesday, Thursday, Friday, Saturday, December 29, 31 [1928], January 1, 2, 3, 4, 5 [1929]. England, having proved successful in the two previous Test games, naturally approached the third with a certain amount of confidence. In the end they won by three wickets, this victory giving them the rubber and the retention of the Ashes. There were many changes of fortune in the course of the great struggle, but scarcely anything in the whole tour approached the long, drawn-out tension of the last innings before the winning hit was made. In ordinary circumstances, little might have been thought of the task of getting 332, but these runs had to be made on a rain-ruined wicket and anybody who knows the Melbourne ground will appreciate the stupendous effort required. ...

     England had the same eleven as Sydney, but Australia made further changes, bringing in Bradman [twelfth man a fortnight earlier in Sydney], a'Beckett and Oxenham for Ponsford, Nothling and Ironmonger. These alterations undoubtedly made Australia a better combination ... Bradman, with two fine displays of batting, showed what a mistake had been made in leaving him out of the second match. ... [He] helped Ryder to put on 64 in less than an hour [after which he] and a'Beckett added 86 ... Bowled by a yorker at 373, Bradman scored well in front of the wicket, hitting nine 4's during his stay of over three hours. ... On the second day 62,259 people witnessed the play, this being a record attendance for one afternoon. ...

When Australia went in a second time, Richardson again failed, and although Woodfull batted uncommonly well and Kippax helped to add 78, there were four wickets down for 143. England then stood in a good position, but Bradman – nearly bowled by White when seven – assisted Woodfull to put on a valuable 58, and subsequently proceeded to make his first hundred in a Test Match. ... There were seven men out for 252, but Oxenham helped to add 93 at a rate of a run a minute before Bradman's innings closed at 345. Bradman batted over four hours, hit eleven 4's and brought off many splendid drives. ...

The total attendance at the match reached 262,467, the receipts being £22,561 18s. The attendance was easily a record.

Australia

W. M. Woodfull c Jardine b Tate	7	–	c Duckworth b Tate	107
V. Y. Richardson c Duckworth b Larwood	3	–	b Larwood	5
H. L. Hendry c Jardine b Larwood	23	–	st Duckworth b White	12
A. F. Kippax c Jardine b Larwood	100	–	b Tate	41
*J. Ryder c Hendren b Tate	112	–	b Geary	5
D. G. Bradman b Hammond	79	–	c Duckworth b Geary	112
†W. A. Oldfield b Geary	3	–	b White	7
E. L. a'Beckett c Duckworth b White	41	–	b White	6
R. K. Oxenham b Geary	15	–	b White	39
C. V. Grimmett c Duckworth b Geary	5	–	not out	4
D. D. Blackie not out	2	–	b White	0
B 4, l-b 3	7		B 6, l-b 7	13
	397			**351**

England bowling: *First innings*—Larwood 37–3–127–3; Tate 46–17–87–2; Geary 31.5–4–83–3; Hammond 8–4–19–1; White 57–30–64–1; Jardine 1–0–10–0. *Second innings*—Larwood 16–3–37–1; Tate 47–15–70–2; Geary 30–4–94–2; Hammond 16–6–30–0; White 56.5–20–107–5.

England

J. B. Hobbs, H. Sutcliffe, W. R. Hammond, *Mr A. P. F. Chapman, E. Hendren, Mr D. R. Jardine, H. Larwood, G. Geary, M. W. Tate, †G. Duckworth and Mr J. C. White.

First innings: 417 (Sutcliffe 58, Hammond 200, Jardine 62; Blackie six for 94). *Second innings:* Seven for 332 (Hobbs 49, Sutcliffe 135, Jardine 33, Hammond 32, Hendren 45).

Umpires: D. Elder and G. A. Hele

SOUTH AUSTRALIA v NEW SOUTH WALES   13 (25, 26)

Played at Adelaide, January 11, 12, 14, 15, 16 [1929]. Narrowly missing the triumph of two separate hundreds, Jackson particularly distinguished himself in a match which New South Wales won by 60 runs.

New South Wales

D. G. Bradman c Grimmett b Wall	5	–	b Wall	2
T. J. E. Andrews b Wall	32	–	c Richardson b Wall	7
*A. F. Kippax lbw b McKay	107	–	b Wall	7
A. Jackson b Grimmett	162	–	c Grimmett b Carlton	90
A. Fairfax c Hone b Grimmett	36	–	c and b Grimmett	20
D. Seddon c Alexander b Carlton	8	–	b Grimmett	0
C. Andrews lbw b Grimmett	1	–	c Pellew b Wall	87
†W. A. Oldfield c Pellew b Carlton	26	–	c and b Grimmett	48
C. O. Nicholls b Carlton	5	–	c Wall b Williams	29
B. A. Cooper b Carlton	9	–	c Wall b Williams	12
N. Morris not out	2	–	not out	0
B 4, l-b 3, n-b 2	9		B 5, l-b 6	11
	402			**313**

South Australia bowling: *First innings*—Wall 22–2–92–2; Carlton 34–6–95–4; Grimmett 37–4–128–3; Williams 8–0–43–0; Pellew 3–1–15–0; McKay 5–0–20–1. *Second innings*—Wall 24–1–78–4; Carlton 21–3–51–1; Grimmett 32–2–105–3; Williams 11.2–0–52–2; McKay 4–0–16–0.

South Australia

G. W. Harris, *V. Y. Richardson, C. E. Pellew, W. C. Alexander, †A. Hack, B. W. Hone, D. G. McKay, N. L. Williams, C. V. Grimmett, T. W. Wall and T. A. Carlton.

First innings: 304 (Hack 34, Hone 35, Grimmett 71 not out, Wall 43; Nicholls three for 63, Fairfax four for 54). *Second innings:* 351 (Harris 42, Alexander 79, McKay 74, sundries 34; Fairfax three for 82, Bradman none for 22).

Umpires: G. A. Hele and A. G. Jenkins

NEW SOUTH WALES v VICTORIA   14 (27)

Played at Sydney, January 24, 25, 26, 28, 29 [1929]. This proved to be the key match of the competition and New South Wales, taking first innings points, made sure of the Sheffield Shield. Of absorbing interest, the cricket was especially notable for the feat of Bradman, who made 340 not out – the highest score by a New South Wales player in Sheffield Shield games and the highest in a first-class match on the Sydney ground. Bradman batted for roughly eight hours and did not give a chance. ... Hooker and Bettington ... bowled with such success that Victoria had to follow on 448 behind. Hooker actually took four wickets with four balls, his victims being Ebeling, Gamble and Ironmonger in one over, and Austen with his next ball – his first in the second innings. ...

New South Wales

A. Jackson b Ironmonger	41	A. Marks c Lansdown b Darling	56
A. Fairfax b Gamble	104	R. H. Bettington c Austen b Darling	40
D. G. Bradman not out	340	J. Fingleton not out	25
*T. J. E. Andrews lbw b Ironmonger	19	B 11, l-b 15, n-b 2	28
S. McCabe b Gamble	60	(six wkts dec)	**713**

†H. L. Davidson, C. O. Nicholls and H. Hooker did not bat.

Victoria bowling: Gamble 29–1–193–2; Ebeling 39–3–142–0; Ironmonger 56–7–220–2; Darling 18–1–77–2; Scaife 2–0–14–0; Austen 1–0–17–0; Onyons 1–0–22–0.

Victoria

B.A. Onyons, E.T. Austen, J. Scaife, L. Darling, W. Reddrop, H.C. Lansdown, T. Bird, *†J.L. Ellis, H.I. Ebeling, H.S. Gamble and H. Ironmonger.

First innings: 265 (Onyons 61, Scaife 42, Darling 37, Reddrop 33; Hooker six for 42, Bettington three for 92). *Second innings:* Seven for 510 (Onyons 131, Scaife 91, Darling 96, Lansdown 48 not out, Bird 63, sundries 41).

Umpires: A.C. Jones and W.H. Bayfield

ENGLAND v AUSTRALIA   15 (28, 29)
(FOURTH TEST MATCH)   3 (5, 6)

Played at Adelaide, Friday, Saturday, Monday, Tuesday, Wednesday, Thursday, Friday, February 1, 2, 4, 5, 6, 7, 8 [1929]. The rubber having been won, the English team had no cause for anxiety beyond the desire to preserve their unbeaten record. Still, they did not exhibit any lack of keenness in the Fourth Test Match which, characterised by very even scoring throughout, had a most exciting finish, England gaining a victory by 12 runs. This success atoned for the defeat on the same ground in the previous tour, when Australia won by 11 runs. England had no reason for changing their eleven, but Australia brought in Jackson for Richardson, the young New South Wales batsman enjoying the distinction of playing a three-figure innings in his first Test Match. Before going further, it is only right to pay a great tribute to his performance. Accomplished, as will be told later, in circumstances calculated to daunt a player of mature experience, it was, in point of style and beauty of execution and strokeplay, the best innings played against the Englishmen during the whole tour. Other achievements made the match memorable. Hammond followed his innings of 251 and 200 at Sydney and Melbourne respectively by making two separate hundreds ... and, above all, White, sending down over 124 overs, obtained thirteen wickets for 256 runs, eight of them in the second innings. ...

Going in on the second day just before half-past three, Australia made a deplorable start, three wickets falling for 19 runs. ... It was then that Jackson revealed his great powers. ... Ryder helped him to add 126, Bradman stayed while 82 were put on, and then 60 more came in fifty minutes before his superb innings ended at 287. ...

[Needing 349 to win, Australia began their second innings on Wednesday evening, scoring 24 without loss] and on Thursday and Friday there came a fight which will long be remembered by those who saw it. ... [When play ended on Thursday] Australia, with six men out for 260, required 89 to win. When, next morning, Bradman and Oxenham carried the score to 308, victory for Australia appeared more than likely. These two had added 50 in sixty-five minutes. At 320, with Bradman run out [for the only time in his Test career], fortunes changed again. Oldfield hit a ball to cover-point, both batsmen dashing for the run, but Hobbs returned like lightning for Duckworth to put the wicket down. Grimmett stayed for half an hour, but left at 336, Tate at short-leg knocking up the ball from a hard hit and bringing off a great catch. Blackie went in amidst tense excitement and carefully played four balls from White. Then came one pitched just a little shorter; Blackie hooked it high into the long field in front of square-leg where Larwood, running a few yards, brought off a fine catch and finished a wonderful struggle.

England

J.B. Hobbs, H. Sutcliffe, W.R. Hammond, Mr D.R. Jardine, E. Hendren, *Mr A.P.F. Chapman, †G. Duckworth, H. Larwood, G. Geary, M.W. Tate and Mr J.C. White.

First innings: 334 (Hobbs 74, Sutcliffe 64, Hammond 119 not out, Chapman 39; Grimmett five for 102). *Second innings:* 383 (Hammond 177, Jardine 98, Tate 47; Oxenham four for 67).

Australia

W. M. Woodfull c Duckworth b Tate	1	– c Geary b White	30
A. Jackson lbw b White	164	– c Duckworth b Geary	36
H. L. Hendry c Duckworth b Larwood	2	– c Tate b White	5
A. F. Kippax b White	3	– c Hendren b White	51
† J. Ryder lbw b White	63	– c and b White	87
D. G. Bradman c Larwood b Tate	40	– run out	58
E. L. a'Beckett b White	36	– c Hammond b White	21
R. K. Oxenham c Chapman b White	15	– c Chapman b White	12
*W. A. Oldfield b Tate	32	– not out	15
C. V. Grimmett b Tate	4	– c Tate b White	9
D. D. Blackie not out	3	– c Larward b White	0
L-b 5, w 1	6	B 9, l-b 3	12
	369		**336**

England bowling: *First innings*—Larwood 37–6–92–1; Tate 42–10–77–4; White 60–16–130–5; Geary 12–3–32–0; Hammond 9–1–32–0. *Second innings*—Larwood 20–4–60–0; Tate 37–9–75–0; White 64.5–21–126–8; Geary 16–2–42–1; Hammond 14–3–21–0.

Umpires: D. Elder and G. A. Hele

MCC TEAM v NEW SOUTH WALES   16 (30)

Played at Sydney, Friday, Saturday, Monday, Tuesday, February 15, 16, 18, 19 [1929]. The return match with New South Wales – like the first, left drawn – was quite spoiled by rain. A very heavy downpour prevented cricket on Friday and the match did not start until three o'clock on Saturday afternoon. Few people, indeed, expected cricket to be possible even then, but the ground made a good recovery. Some of the English team had become scattered, but fortunately they were got together in time. ... More rain came on the Tuesday and, cricket being impossible, the game was at once given up.

New South Wales

A. Jackson lbw b Tate	5	†W. A. Oldfield not out	3
A. Fairfax c Tyldesley b Tate	40	H. Hooker lbw b White	3
T. J. E. Andrews c and b White	2	C. Morris c sub b White	4
*A. F. Kippax c Tate b Geary	17	R. L. McNamee c Mead b White	0
D. G. Bradman c Tyldesley b White	15	B 9, l-b 2	11
A. Marks b Freeman	17		**128**
S. McCabe b Freeman	11		

MCC Team bowling: Tate 10–2–21–2; White 23.5–8–48–5; Geary 9–3–16–1; Freeman 13–3–32–2.

MCC Team

J. B. Hobbs, M. Leyland, E. Tyldesley, C. P. Mead, *Mr A. P. F. Chapman, †L. Ames, M. W. Tate, G. Geary, Mr J. C. White, A. P. Freeman and H. Sutcliffe.

First innings: Four for 144 (Hobbs 39, Tyldesley 68 not out; Fairfax three for 36).

Umpires: W. H. Bayfield and A. C. Jones

NEW SOUTH WALES v SOUTH AUSTRALIA   17 (31, 32)

Played at Sydney, March 1, 2, 4, 5, 6 [1929]. This match had a most exciting finish, South Australia – set 446 to get – losing by only 60 runs. ... Bradman was seen at his best when New South Wales went in for the second time. ... Davidson and Walker both 'kept' admirably. Davidson caught six and stumped three and Walker [making his first-class debut] caught three and stumped five, so that between them they had a hand in taking seventeen wickets.

New South Wales

A. Fairfax lbw b Grimmett	17	–	st Walker b Grimmett	41
A. Jackson c Walker b Scott	6	–	st Walker b Grimmett	38
D. G. Bradman c Walker b Grimmett	35	–	c Walker b Carlton	175
*T. J. E. Andrews c Carlton b Whitfield	0	–	b Wall	23
S. McCabe c Grimmett b Wall	5	–	c Scott b Alexander	27
A. Marks run out	92	–	lbw b Grimmett	26
†H. Davidson run out	16	–	b Grimmett	13
F. Jordon st Walker b Grimmett	65	–	not out	19
H. Hooker st Walker b Grimmett	62	–	st Walker b Grimmett	6
W. Lampe c Richardson b Whitfield	3	–	run out	17
N. Morris not out	8			
B 7, l-b 7, w 1, n-b 2	17		B 5, l-b 3, w 1, n-b 5	14
	326		(nine wkts dec)	399

South Australia bowling: *First innings*—Wall 17–1–64–1; Scott 10–1–62–1; Whitfield 16–3–47–2; Grimmett 27–1–112–4; Carlton 6–0–24–0. *Second innings*—Wall 17–0–59–1; Scott 11–2–61–0; Whitfield 13–2–69–0; Grimmett 26.4–1–116–5; Carlton 18–2–47–1; Hack 4–0–23–0; Alexander 1–0–10–1.

South Australia

*V.Y. Richardson, G.W. Harris, A. Hack, H.E.P. Whitfield, †C.W. Walker, W.C. Alexander, P.M. Hutton, C.V. Grimmett, T.W. Wall, J.D. Scott and T.A. Carlton.
    First innings: 280 (Harris 107, Grimmett 43; Hooker three for 73, Andrews four for 34). *Second innings:* 385 (Harris 94, Hack 79, Richardson 56, Whitfield 91; Fairfax four for 55, Bradman one for 26).

Umpires: A.C. Jones and A.H. Farrow

ENGLAND v AUSTRALIA   18 (33, 34)
(FIFTH TEST MATCH)   4 (7, 8)

Played at Melbourne, Friday, Saturday, Monday, Tuesday, Wednesday, Thursday, Friday, Saturday, March 8, 9, 11, 12, 13, 14, 15, 16 [1929]. Lasting eight days – the greatest duration of any Test Match [at that time] – the concluding representative engagement saw Australia successful by five wickets. ... Judged from the English standpoint, the cricket all through proved dreadfully slow, but such keenness characterised the spectators – every ball being closely followed – that the rate of scoring was not noticed. ...

    Australia did well to reply [to England's first innings of 519] with a total of 491. Their batting was very sound throughout, the honours being carried off by Woodfull and Bradman. ... Fourth out at 203, Woodfull, with three 4's as his chief strokes, batted nearly five hours and a half. Then followed the stand which put Australia almost on terms, Bradman and Fairfax scoring 183 together for the fifth wicket in three hours and a half. Bradman put together a delightful innings of three hours and a half's duration, his strokeplay being remarkable, and his driving very powerful, well kept down and nicely placed. He hit eight 4's. ... Geary, bowling 81 overs – [at the time] a record for a Test Match – had a fine record, and on the fifth day actually obtained his five wickets for 51 runs. When the Australian innings ceased, play had lasted eighteen hours and twenty-seven minutes for 1,010 runs. ...

[On the second Saturday of the match, Australia having set out late on Thursday to attain a target of 286] two incidences occurred which probably affected the result. In the first case, Bradman, when five, gave a chance of stumping while Ryder, at 27, had his wicket thrown down by Leyland, who had run behind the bowler from mid-off. It was the general opinion that Ryder was at least a yard out, but to the obvious surprise and chagrin of the Englishmen, Jones, the umpire, gave the batsman in. The score at lunch was 248 and, in about twenty minutes afterwards, the remaining runs were hit off without further loss. Both Bradman and Ryder batted very well.

England

J.B. Hobbs, Mr D.R. Jardine, W.R. Hammond, E. Tyldesley, †G. Duckworth, E. Hendren, M. Leyland, H. Larwood, G. Geary, M.W. Tate and *Mr J.C. White.

First innings: 519 (Hobbs 142, Hammond 38, Tyldesley 31, Hendren 95, Leyland 137; Wall three for 123, Hornibrook three for 142). *Second innings:* 257 (Hobbs 65, Leyland 53 not out, Tate 54; Wall five for 66).

Australia

W. M. Woodfull c Geary b Larwood	102	–	b Hammond	35
A. Jackson run out	30	–	b Geary	46
A. F. Kippax c Duckworth b White	38	–	run out	28
J. Ryder c Tate b Hammond	30	–	not out	57
D. G. Bradman c Tate b Geary	123	–	not out	37
A. Fairfax lbw b Geary	65			
R. K. Oxenham c Duckworth b Geary	7			
W. A. Oldfield c and b Geary	6	–	b Hammond	48
C. V. Grimmett not out	38			
T. W. Wall c Duckworth b Geary	9			
P. M. Hornibrook lbw b White	26	–	b Hammond	18
B 6, l-b 9, w 2	17		B 12, l-b 6	18
	491		(five wkts)	**287**

England bowling: *First innings*—Larwood 34–7–83–1; Tate 62–26–108–0; Geary 81–36–105–5; White 75.3–22–136–2; Hammond 16–3–31–1; Leyland 3–0–11–0. *Second innings*—Larwood 32.1–5–85–0; Tate 38–13–72–0; Geary 20–5–31–1; White 18–8–28–0; Hammond 26–8–53–3.

Umpires: G. A. Hele and A. C. Jones

1929-30

To Don with best wishes from A.S.

Bradman with Bowral Town captain Alf Stephens on a return to his home town in 1930.
The young Don had been one of many Bowral cricketers who practised on the concrete
strip that Stephens put down in his backyard.

1929-30

A lack of good bowlers to support A. Fairfax largely accounted for the inability of New South Wales to retain the Shield, but a wealth of batting talent was available and, in D.G. Bradman, the outstanding batsman of Australia. For all first-class matches, Bradman had an aggregate of 1,586 runs and an average of 113.28. He made cricket history with a wonderful score of 452 not out – [then] the highest individual innings ever played – against Queensland at Sydney. …

Partly as a result of wet weather the receipts from the Sheffield Shield games generally showed a decided falling-off, but the New South Wales v Queensland match at Sydney brought in £1,088 as compared with £141 in 1928-29.

From 'Cricket in Australia: The Inter-State Matches'

QUEENSLAND v NEW SOUTH WALES   19 (35, 36)

Played at [Exhibition Ground] Brisbane, November 8, 9, 11, 12 [1929]. Despite fine all-round play by Oxenham, who in the course of the match scored 166 and took six wickets for 113, New South Wales won the first of the Sheffield Shield games by 23 runs. … New South Wales in their second innings did not repeat their previous batting success. Indeed, against skilful bowling by Hornibrook and Brew, half the side were out for 73. Bradman and Marks alone played with real skill. …

New South Wales

A. Fairfax lbw b Oxenham	49	–	lbw b Oxenham	21
A. Jackson c O'Connor b Oxenham	80	–	c Amos b Hornibrook	7
D. G. Bradman run out	48	–	c O'Connor b Brew	66
C. Andrews lbw b Amos	40	–	lbw b Amos	12
S. McCabe c Brew b Oxenham	77	–	b Hornibrook	3
Dr R. H. Bettington c O'Connor b Oxenham	9	–	c Nothling b Hornibrook	8
A. Marks c Brew b Amos	46	–	c O'Connor b Hornibrook	51
*†W. A. Oldfield run out	3	–	lbw b Brew	7
H. Hooker c O'Connor b Amos	2	–	not out	6
A. A. Mailey not out	4	–	c and b Brew	0
F. H. Dupain c Levy b Oxenham	10	–	b Brew	6
B 2, l-b 3	5		B 4, l-b 7	11
	373			**198**

Queensland bowling: *First innings*—Hornibrook 17–4–51–0; Amos 20–2–98–3; Brew 13–0–88–0; Oxenham 25–3–72–5; Bensted 5–0–17–0; Nothling 16–4–42–0. *Second innings*—Hornibrook 19–6–43–4; Amos 11–1–45–1; Brew 14–2–31–4; Oxenham 28–12–41–1; Nothling 9–1–27–0.

Queensland

R.M. Levy, †L.P. O'Connor, R.J. Higgins, R.K. Oxenham, V. Goodwin, *Dr O.E. Nothling, F.J. Gough, F.M. Brew, E.C. Bensted, G. Amos and P.M. Hornibrook.

First innings: 273 (O'Connor 35, Oxenham 49, Gough 69; Fairfax three for 47, Hooker three for 38, Mailey three for 103). *Second innings:* 275 (Oxenham 117; Fairfax three for 47, McCabe three for 41).

Umpires: J.P. Orr and J.A. Scott

MCC TEAM v NEW SOUTH WALES   20 (37)

Played at Sydney, November 22, 23, 25, 26 [1929]. To such an extent did the bat beat the ball in this match that 1,607 runs were scored for the loss of twenty-two wickets. Kippax twice declared but did not allow sufficient time for his bowlers to have much chance of winning the game and, with a draw inevitable, the last part of the cricket was not taken seriously. ... Handicapped [by illness and injury] the MCC attack underwent heavy punishment for seven hours. Jackson and Bradman added 117, Bradman and Kippax put on 149, and on the second day Allsopp and McCabe raised a partnership to 185. Bradman made 157 out of 266 obtained during his stay of less than three hours. Allsopp started his first-class career with almost equal freedom in scoring the third century of the innings. ...

New South Wales

A. Fairfax lbw b Allom	14	–	lbw b Worthington	19
A. Jackson c Benson b Allom	49	–	not out	168
D. G. Bradman b Worthington	157			
*A. F. Kippax c Dawson b Bowley	108			
A. Marks c and b Bowley	38	–	lbw b Woolley	26
A. Allsopp c Turnbull b Allom	117	–	not out	63
S. McCabe b Worthington	90			
C. Andrews not out	11	–	c and b Woolley	17
†W. A. Oldfield c Duleepsinhji b Worthington	3			
J. E. H. Hooker not out	6			
Byes, etc.	36		Byes, etc.	12
(eight wkts dec)	**629**		(three wkts dec)	**305**

F. H. Dupain did not bat.

MCC Team bowling: *First innings*—Barratt 30–1–130–0; Allom 27–1–127–3; Worthington 24–1–151–3; Bowley 13.3–0–80–2; Woolley 16–0–77–0; Duleepsinhji 4–0–28–0. *Second innings*—Allom 19–0–92–0; Worthington 13–1–63–1; Woolley 12–0–84–2; Duleepsinhji 4–0–24–0; Dawson 3–0–30–0.

MCC Team

Mr E.W. Dawson, *Mr A.H.H. Gilligan, K.S. Duleepsinhji, F.E. Woolley, Mr M.J. Turnbull, S. Worthington, Mr G.B. Legge, †Mr E.T. Benson, F. Barratt, Mr M.J.C. Allom and E.H. Bowley.

First innings: 469 (Gilligan 45, Duleepsinhji 34, Woolley 219, Turnbull 100, Legge 42; Fairfax four for 102, Bradman one for 83). *Second innings:* Two for 204 (Dawson 83 not out, Duleepsinhji 47, Legge 47 not out; Bradman none for 34).

Umpires: W.H. Bayfield and M. Carney

TEST TRIAL MATCH   21 (38, 39)

Played at Sydney, December 6, 7, 9, 10, 11 [1929]. The performance of Bradman in scoring two centuries in a match – the second time he had achieved the distinction – constituted the chief feature of some remarkable cricket in the trial arranged by the Australian Selectors with a view to choosing the team to tour England in 1930. Ryder's XI had so much the best of the game to begin with that the follow-on was enforced with Woodfull's side 354 in arrear. That policy, however, nearly brought about the defeat of Ryder's XI, who, left to get 188 to win, experienced such difficulty in playing Hornibrook and Blackie on a rain-damaged pitch that ultimately they only struggled home by one wicket. Jackson and Ponsford with a partnership of 278 laid the foundation of a huge score by Ryder's team. ... Bradman, however, overshadowed these successes by scoring 349 in his two innings. [He scored 275 of these on the third day, having opened the batting when Woodfull's XI followed on.] Rigg in the first innings and Kippax, who in the second made a splendid three-figure score, shared with Bradman in important stands and the three players between them were responsible for 592 of the 850 runs scored for Woodfull's XI. ... Eleven of the players taking part in the match afterwards made the trip to England.

J. Ryder's XI

A. Jackson, W.H. Ponsford, A. Marks, *J. Ryder, S. McCabe, W. Horrocks, H.E.P. Whitfield, R.K. Oxenham, †C.W. Walker, C.V. Grimmett and H.H. Alexander.

First innings: 663 (Jackson 182, Ponsford 131, Marks 83, McCabe 35, Whitfield 68, Oxenham 84 not out; Hornibrook three for 102, Blackie three for 163, Bradman one for 56). *Second innings:* Nine for 191 (McCabe 46; Hornibrook four for 67, Blackie three for 65).

W.M. Woodfull's XI

A. Fairfax c and b Alexander	27	–	st Walker b Grimmett	26
*W. M. Woodfull st Walker b Oxenham	36	–	c and b Grimmett	43
A. F. Kippax st Walker b Grimmett	17	–	c Walker b Oxenham	170
D. G. Bradman c Jackson b Oxenham	124	–	lbw b Grimmett	225
A. Allsopp b Oxenham	4	–	c McCabe b Grimmett	5
K. Rigg b Whitfield	73	–	c Ponsford b McCabe	9
A. O. Burrows b Oxenham	7	–	c and b Grimmett	0
†J. L. Ellis lbw b Oxenham	4	–	b Oxenham	24
D. D. Blackie c McCabe b Grimmett	0	–	b Grimmett	11
P. M. Hornibrook st Walker b Grimmett	2	–	c Alexander b Grimmett	1
T. W. Wall not out	0	–	not out	2
B 2, l-b 9, w 3, n-b 1	15		B 14, l-b 7, w 3, n-b 1	25
	309			**541**

J. Ryder's XI bowling: *First innings*—Alexander 11–1–73–1; Whitfield 12–2–46–1; Oxenham 14.6–3–42–5; Grimmett 15–2–68–3; McCabe 3–0–26–0; Marks 5–0–39–0. *Second innings*—Alexander 11–0–73–0; Whitfield 14–0–71–0; Oxenham 30.5–7–97–2; Grimmett 33–3–173–7; McCabe 7–1–42–1; Marks 6–0–45–0; Ryder 5–0–15–0.

Umpires: A.C. Jones and M. Carney

SOUTH AUSTRALIA v NEW SOUTH WALES   22 (40, 41)

Played at Adelaide, December 19, 20, 21, 23, 24 [1929]. New South Wales, after the failure of some of their leading run-getters, effected a good recovery but South Australia established a big lead on the first innings and won by five wickets. ... [In their second innings] thanks to Jackson and Bradman, New South Wales reduced their arrears of 194 to 22 before losing a wicket, and Allsopp and McCabe repeated their batting success of the opening day, but South Australia, set 241 to make, experienced no difficulty in completing their task.

[Following this match, Jackson, who had been diagnosed as suffering from TB, was admitted to hospital in Adelaide.]

New South Wales

A. Fairfax c Wall b Whitfield	39	–	c Hone b Grimmett		46
A. Jackson c Walker b Grimmett	19	–	c Pritchard b Grimmett		82
D. G. Bradman run out	2	–	lbw b Grimmett		84
*A. F. Kippax c Palmer b Wall	26	–	b Palmer		6
A. Marks c and b Wall	1	–	c Pritchard b Whitfield		23
S. McCabe b Wall	69	–	lbw b Grimmett		70
A. Allsopp c Walker b Grimmett	77	–	c and b Grimmett		73
S. C. Everett lbw b Whitfield	1	–	b Whitfield		10
H. Hooker not out	13	–	c Pritchard b Grimmett		9
†H. L. Davidson c Richardson b Grimmett	52	–	c and b Grimmett		7
J. N. Campbell c Pritchard b Whitfield	7	–	not out		4
L-b 3, n-b 5	8		B 13, l-b 5, n-b 2		20
	314				**434**

South Australia bowling: *First innings*—Wall 17–1–74–3; Whitfield 15.1–1–67–3; Grimmett 31–9–91–3; Palmer 13–2–74–0. *Second innings*—Wall 5–0–25–0; Whitfield 25–2–104–2; Grimmett 44.1–5–136–7; Palmer 26–3–121–1; Richardson 7–0–28–0.

South Australia

G. W. Harris, B. W. Hone, D. E. Pritchard, *V. Y. Richardson, H. C. Nitschke, A. R. Lonergan, C. V. Grimmett, H. E. P. Whitfield, †C. W. Walker, T. W. Wall and G. S. Palmer.

First innings: 508 (Harris 46, Hone 126, Pritchard 148, Richardson 64, Grimmett 35, Whitfield 45; Fairfax three for 80, Bradman two for 93). *Second innings:* Five for 244 (Hone 61, Pritchard 75, Richardson 44; Bradman none for 8).

Umpires: G. A. Hele and T. W. Cook

VICTORIA v NEW SOUTH WALES   23 (42, 43)

Played at Melbourne, December 26, 27, 28, 30, 31 [1929]. Victoria appeared a well-beaten side when, going in a second time, they lost five wickets and still required 47 to avert an innings reverse. By a wonderful recovery, as the outcome of which another 215 runs were added, however, they saved the game. Still, at the close New South Wales, with eight wickets to fall, needed only 26 to win.... New South Wales, after having two men out for 24, batted very consistently. Bradman, Kippax and McCabe were especially sound and attractive in their methods and the visitors, gaining the lead with six wickets in hand, finished the innings 173 ahead. Hendry hitting up a hundred and a'Beckett and Scaife showing much skill at a critical time, Victoria just managed to destroy New South Wales' hopes of winning.

Victoria

*J. Ryder, W. H. Ponsford, R. N. Ellis, H. L. Hendry, K. Rigg, E. L. a'Beckett, †J. L. Ellis, J. A. Scaife, D. D. Blackie, H. H. Alexander and H. Ironmonger.

First innings: 229 (Ponsford 65, Hendry 43, Rigg 44; Everett five for 57, Hooker three for 48). *Second innings:* 343 (Hendry 103, a'Beckett 50, J. L. Ellis 40, Scaife 60 not out, Blackie 37; Fairfax five for 104).

New South Wales

N. E. Phillips c Blackie b Alexander	10	–	st J. Ellis b Ryder	45
A. Fairfax c Blackie b a'Beckett	2	–	c and b Blackie	15
D. G. Bradman b Alexander	89	–	not out	26
*A. F. Kippax lbw b Blackie	80			
A. Marks b Alexander	68			
S. McCabe c J. Ellis b Ironmonger	70	–	not out	50
A. Allsopp c Ironmonger b a'Beckett	26			
†H. L. Davidson c J. Ellis b Blackie	24			
S. C. Everett lbw b Blackie	17			
H. Hooker c Ponsford b Ironmonger	3			
H. Chilvers not out	0			
B 6, l-b 6, n-b 1	13		B 8, n-b 1	9
	402		(two wkts)	**145**

Victoria bowling: *First innings*—Alexander 16–1–115–3; Blackie 20–4–71–3; Ironmonger 28.7–3–89–2; a'Beckett 19–2–48–2; R. Ellis 4–0–33–0; Hendry 4–0–27–0; Ryder 1–0–6–0. *Second innings*—Alexander 4–1–8–0; Blackie 6–0–31–1; Ironmonger 8–0–33–0; a'Beckett 7–2–12–0;R. Ellis 4–0–27–0; Hendry 1–0–2–0; Ryder 4–0–23–0.

Umpires: J. Richards and W. J. Moore

NEW SOUTH WALES v QUEENSLAND   24 (44, 45)

Played at Sydney, January 3, 4, 6, 7 [1930]. Everything else in this game paled before the phenomenal performance of Bradman who, in scoring 452 not out – a feat that occupied him 415 minutes – played the highest individual innings recorded in first-class cricket. That splendid exhibition led the way to a victory for New South Wales by 685 runs [the largest victory on record by a runs margin]. Displaying a wider range of strokes than usual, Bradman batted without a trace of error during his long stay and hit no fewer than forty-nine 4's. His prolific scoring followed upon comparatively low totals in the first innings of each side. ... New South Wales, going in again eight runs ahead, gained a complete mastery over the bowling. Bradman, batting with such brilliancy, made matters easy for his colleagues. ... Faced with the appalling task of getting 770 runs, Queensland offered scarcely any resistance. Half the wickets actually fell for 23, and on the last morning Everett finished off the innings. In the two spells of bowling he disposed of six batsmen at a cost of less than four runs each.

New South Wales

C. Andrews st Leeson b Hurwood	56	–	c Levy b Hurwood	16
D. G. Bradman c Leeson b Hurwood	3	–	not out	452
A. Marks c Hurwood b Thurlow	40	–	c Bensted b Hurwood	5
*A. F. Kippax lbw b Thurlow	15	–	lbw b Rowe	115
S. McCabe c Leeson b Thurlow	15	–	c Leeson b Hurwood	60
A. Allsopp c and b Hurwood	9	–	b Hurwood	66
A. Fairfax b Brew	20	–	st Leeson b Hurwood	10
S. C. Everett c Bensted b Brew	41	–	c Goodwin b Hurwood	4
†H. L. Davidson lbw b Hurwood	14	–	c and b Goodwin	22
S. Burt b Thurlow	10			
H. Chilvers not out	6			
B 3, l-b 3	6		B 6, l-b 1, w 2, n-b 2	11
	235		(eight wkts dec)	**761**

Queensland bowling: *First innings*—Thurlow 18.1–0–83–4; Hurwood 22–6–57–4; Bensted 6–0–39–0; Brew 8–0–50–2. *Second innings*—Thurlow 25–0–147–0; Hurwood 34–1–179–6; Bensted 12–0–70–0; Brew 6–0–61–0; Rowe 19–0–143–1; Thompson 15–0–90–0; Gough 4–0–40–0; Levy 2–0–20–0; Goodwin 0.1–0–0–1.

Queensland

R.M. Levy, *L.P. O'Connor, F.C. Thompson, W. Rowe, F.J. Gough, E.C. Bensted, V. Goodwin, A. Hurwood, F.M. Brew, †H. Leeson and H.M. Thurlow.

First innings: 227 (Bensted 51, Goodwin 67; Fairfax three for 53, McCabe five for 36). *Second innings:* 84 (Everett six for 23).

Umpires: G. Borwick and E.J. Shaw

NEW SOUTH WALES v SOUTH AUSTRALIA   25 (46)

Played at Sydney, January 9, 10, 11, 13 [1930]. Displaying all-round superiority, New South Wales won after three days' actual play by an innings and 220 runs. South Australia had very much the worst of the wicket which, following the completion of their opponents' innings of 535, was much damaged by rain. Still their batting, making every allowance for the conditions, was unusually weak. ... In the course of his innings on the opening day, Bradman [before scoring] received a blow on the head from the ball [thrown in from cover by Grimmett, forcing him to retire hurt until the fall of the fifth wicket] and did not afterwards field.

New South Wales

C. Andrews b Wall	9	A. Allsopp c Richardson b Grimmett	136
†H. S. Love st Walker b Whitfield	38	S. C. Everett b Whitfield	62
D. G. Bradman c Richardson b Whitfield	47	H. Hooker not out	39
*A. F. Kippax b Whitfield	14	H. Chilvers c Harris b Grimmett	52
A. Marks lbw b Grimmett	11	B 6, l-b 6, n-b 5	17
S. McCabe c Nitschke b Grimmett	81		**535**
A. Fairfax lbw b Whitfield	29		

South Australia bowling: Wall 26–2–145–1; Whitfield 26–2–106–5; Grimmett 33.7–3–163–4; Carlton 18–2–99–0; Richardson 2–1–5–0.

South Australia

G. W. Harris, B. W. Hone, D. E. Pritchard, *V. Y. Richardson, H. C. Nitschke, H. E. P. Whitfield, A. Hack, †C. W. Walker, C. V. Grimmett, T. A. Carlton and T. W. Wall.

First innings: 215 (Hone 42, Grimmett 42, Wall 33 not out; Fairfax three for 43, Chilvers four for 57). *Second innings:* 100 (Fairfax four for 19, Chilvers four for 38).

Umpires: A.C. Jones and G. Borwick

NEW SOUTH WALES v VICTORIA 26 (47)

Played at Sydney, January 24, 25, 27, 28, 29 [1930]. The return encounter between New South Wales and Victoria, one of the most important fixtures of the series, was almost completely spoiled by rain which prevented play on any of the first three days and so compelled a draw. Originally additional interest attached to the contest from the fact that during the struggle the team to tour England was to be announced, but in the adverse circumstances the Selectors naturally gained little or no assistance from such play as took place. Sent in to bat on a drying pitch New South Wales had five wickets down for 149, but some cautious, skilful work by Bradman, and successful efforts on the part of Allsopp and Fairfax, resulted in the addition of 181 more runs before the innings ended. ...

New South Wales

A. Jackson b a'Beckett	5	H. Chilvers c J. Ellis b Ironmonger	0
C. Andrews b Alexander	12	†H. L. Davidson b Hendry	22
D. G. Bradman c R. Ellis b Ironmonger	77	H. Hooker c Hendry b Ryder	30
*A. F. Kippax b Ironmonger	9	H. Theak not out	2
S. McCabe c Blackie b a'Beckett	29	B 6, l-b 7, n-b 2	15
A. Allsopp lbw b Blackie	65		**330**
A. Fairfax c J. Ellis b Hendry	64		

Victoria bowling: Alexander 14–0–79–1; a'Beckett 21–2–57–2; Ironmonger 20–0–100–3; Blackie 11–0–69–1; Hendry 2.1–0–4–2; Ryder 1–0–6–1.

Victoria

W. H. Ponsford, R. N. Ellis, H. L. Hendry, *J. Ryder, E. L. a'Beckett, K. Rigg, J. A. Scaife, †J. L. Ellis, H. Ironmonger, D. D. Blackie and H. H. Alexander.

First innings: Three for 222 (Hendry 95, Ryder 100 not out).

Umpires: A. C. Jones and G. Borwick

AN AUSTRALIAN XI MATCHES

At the end of the season, an Australian XI comprising the players selected to tour England in 1930 played two matches against Tasmania and one against Western Australia. These matches do not appear in *Wisden*.

[TASMANIA v AN AUSTRALIAN XI] 27 (48)

Played at Launceston, March 8, 10, 11 [1930]. The Australian XI won by ten wickets.
Tasmania: *J. A. Atkinson, D. C. Green, N. W. Davis, G. W. Martin, L. J. Nash, A. C. Newton, C. L. Badcock, G. T. H. James, V. L. Hooper, R. C. Townley and †E. A. Pickett.

First innings: 157 (Atkinson 50, Nash 31; Fairfax four for 36, Hornibrook three for 38). *Second innings:* 158 (Nash 49; Fairfax four for 43, Hornibrook three for 51).
An Australian XI: W. H. Ponsford, S. J. McCabe, A. F. Kippax, V. Y. Richardson, D. G. Bradman, A. G. Fairfax, *W. M. Woodfull, †W. A. Oldfield, A. Hurwood, P. M. Hornibrook and T. W. Wall.

First innings: 311 (Ponsford 36, McCabe 103, Richardson 33, Bradman lbw b Nash 20, Woodfull 50 not out; James five for 97). *Second innings:* None for 6.

Umpires: P. T. Henty and G. S. Pennfather

[TASMANIA v AN AUSTRALIAN XI]   28 (49)

Played at Hobart, March 13, 14, 15 [1930]. After the first day had been lost to the weather, the match ended as a draw.

Tasmania: *J. A. Atkinson, A. W. Rushforth, L. J. Nash, D. C. Green, A. O. Burrows, G. W. Martin, A. C. Newton, C. L. Badcock, †D. M. Vautin, G. T. H. James and R. C. Townley.

First innings: 131 (Green 47; Hornibrook three for 42, Grimmett five for 30). *Second innings:* Five for 174 (Nash 93; Bradman none for 21).

An Australian XI: W. H. Ponsford, S. J. McCabe, D. G. Bradman, A. F. Kippax, A. G. Fairfax, V. Y. Richardson, *W. M. Woodfull, C. V. Grimmett, †C. W. Walker, A. Hurwood and P. M. Hornibrook.

First innings: Four for 419 dec (Ponsford 166, Bradman c Rushforth b Atkinson 139, Kippax 53 not out, Fairfax 33).

Umpires: M. Leonard and W. T. Lonergan

[WESTERN AUSTRALIA v AN AUSTRALIAN XI]   29 (50)

Played at Perth, March 21, 22, 24 [1930]. The Australian XI won by an innings and 25 runs.

Western Australia: F. J. Bryant, H. K. Lang, W. J. Horrocks, R. J. Wilberforce, E. H. Bromley, *R. J. Bryant, M. Inverarity, W. A. Evans, H. E. Fidock, †W. J. Truscott and R. A. Halcombe.

First innings: 167 (Fidock 35; Grimmett six for 75). *Second innings:* 132 (Inverarity 30; a'Beckett four for 26, Bradman none for 5).

An Australian XI: S. J. McCabe, A. Jackson, D. G. Bradman, A. F. Kippax, *V. Y. Richardson, A. G. Fairfax, E. L. a'Beckett, C. V. Grimmett, A. Hurwood, †C. W. Walker and P. M. Hornibrook.

First innings: 324 (Bradman c R. J. Bryant b Evans 27, Kippax 114, Richardson 45, Grimmett 40; Evans three for 71).

Umpires: W. L. Menkens and F. R. Buttsworth

1930

Bradman batting at Trent Bridge in 1930: he hit a defiant second-innings century in an attempt to prevent the England victory.

1930

Even after the Australians had been here some time and had shown, only too clearly, that they would always be a difficult lot to beat, I don't think many people regarded them as likely to win the rubber. Admittedly in Woodfull, Ponsford, Bradman and Kippax, the tourists commanded the services of four exceptionally able batsmen, and in Grimmett those of a bowler puzzling even to players of the highest class, but in other respects the team, for a body of representative cricketers, appeared to be nothing out of the ordinary. Unhappily for England, the crack batsmen, except on that drying pitch on the Saturday afternoon at Trent Bridge, nearly always accomplished great things in the Test Matches, and on the big occasions Grimmett's only failure as a bowler was at Old Trafford where, incidentally, he rendered invaluable service as a batsman. That extraordinary young cricketer, Bradman, meeting with truly phenomenal success, put together scores of 334, 254, 232 and 131 in the course of the five Tests and the Australians' totals, after the first innings at Nottingham, were 335, 729 for six wickets, 566, 345 and 695. Those figures speak only too eloquently for the run-getting powers of our visitors. Against such performances practically no side could have prevailed. ...

From 'Notes by the Editor' (C. Stewart Caine), *Wisden 1931*

Coming to England while the experience of four consecutive defeats in Test Matches in their own land was still fresh in their memories, the seventeenth Australian team to visit this country accomplished a very fine performance. They not only achieved the great object of the tour by winning the rubber and so regaining possession of the Ashes but, in the course of thirty-one engagements against first-class sides, they were beaten but once – in the opening Test Match at Nottingham.

It is true that in the general results of the tour their record was unimpressive, for of the thirty-one important games they won only eleven, lost one and drew eighteen, while the encounter with Gloucestershire towards the latter part of August ended in a tie. ... The large proportion of drawn games was due to the fact that in most of them bad weather interfered. Indeed, the weather placed the Australians at a considerable disadvantage. In a number of their early matches they had to contend against not only a lot of wet but [also] a decidedly low temperature, feeling the cold so much that heavy underclothing under flannel shirts, and a couple of sweaters in addition, failed to keep them reasonably warm in the field. As no fewer than eleven of the fifteen who made the trip had not visited England before, the handicap under which they laboured may be imagined. Still, they triumphed in a remarkable fashion over the discomforts of a wet and cheerless English summer, and a chosen few of the newcomers adapted themselves, in a manner of which few people thought them capable, to the varying paces of the different wickets on which they had to play. ...

This particular tour will always be remembered by reason of the amazing batting successes which attended the efforts of Bradman. It is not too much to say that he took both England and the whole cricket world by storm. Those who, like myself, had seen him play in Australia against the team captained by A. P. F. Chapman were fully prepared for something out of the common but little did we dream that his progress would be of such a triumphal nature. Nothing like his series of colossal innings in the Test Matches had ever before been witnessed. He put the coping-stone on a – so far – very brief career when, in the Third Test Match at Leeds, following innings of 131 at Nottingham and 254 at Lord's, he made 334 which eclipsed the previous highest score ever obtained in Test Matches between England and Australia – 287 by the late R. E. Foster at Sydney during the MCC tour of 1903-04. As if that were not sufficient, Bradman, although failing at Manchester, wound up with 232 in the final Test Match at Kennington Oval.

He lost no time in demonstrating to the English public that he was a most remarkable young cricketer, for, leading off with 236 in the opening fixture against Worcestershire, he hit up, in addition to his four hundreds in representative engagements, seven other three-figure innings – one of them in a minor match. For Test Matches alone, without a not out to help him, he had an average of rather more than 139 with an aggregate of 974 runs in seven innings. Easily top – far away ahead of everyone else in this table of figures – he was also first in batting in first-class matches [27] with an aggregate of 2,960 and an average of over 98, while in all games [29] he scored 3,170 runs and averaged over 99.

Bradman had established himself before he reached this country, but it has been given to no Australian on his first experience of English wickets to enhance an already big reputation in so striking a manner, the performance, moreover, being all the more remarkable in view of the wet nature of the summer. In the course of the tour he demonstrated that he could play two entirely different games and that while, as at Lord's and at periods in his other Test Match innings, he could be brilliant to a degree, he could also, as in the second innings at Nottingham and in the last Test Match at The Oval, bat with a patience and restraint second only to that of Woodfull himself. There were several features about his batting with which one could not fail to be struck. To an eye almost uncanny in its power to gauge the length of a ball was allied really beautiful footwork. Bradman seldom played forward as a means of defence; he nearly always stepped back to meet the ball with a vertical bat. And this is where he had his limitations, for the tour proved that when he met a bowler either left-hand or right who could make the ball just go away, he never seemed quite such a master as against off-break or straight fast bowling. A glorious driver, he hit the ball very hard, while his placing was almost invariably perfect. He scored most of his runs by driving but he could cut, hook, or turn the ball to leg with nearly the same certainty. And only on rare occasions did he lift it. Without any disparagement to a batsman of abilities so pronounced, it is only fair to say that on more than one occasion his task was rendered the easier by the skilful manner in which Woodfull and Ponsford, by batting of different description, had taken the sting out of the England bowling.

Over and above his batting, Bradman showed himself to be a brilliant and dashing field. In match after match his work at deep mid-off and in the long field was a joy to watch. The number of potential 4's he turned into singles in the Test Match at The Oval was extraordinary. Possessed of a fine turn of speed, he picked up most cleanly and with deadly accuracy had the ball back to the wicket-keeper in a flash. Nothing during the whole tour could have been more dazzling than the manner in which at Leeds he threw Hobbs out from deep mid-off.

From 'The Australians in England', by S. J. Southerton

WORCESTERSHIRE v AUSTRALIANS 30 (51)

Played at Worcester, Wednesday, Thursday, Friday, April 30, May 1, 2 [1930]. The Australians opened their tour in most successful fashion, outplaying Worcestershire so completely that they won early on the third day by an innings and 165 runs. To no particularly high standard did the fielding attain, and the bowling, apart from that of Grimmett, was not impressive, but rather chilly weather handicapped the tourists who, moreover, had enjoyed little practice. Still, on the opening day the visitors, after disposing of Worcestershire for 131, put on 199 for the loss of one wicket. This was essentially the work of Woodfull and Bradman. Altogether the second-wicket partnership lasted two hours and ten minutes and produced 208 runs. ... Bradman put together the first of the many big scores he obtained during the summer. Batting for just over four hours and a half, he drove, hit to leg and hooked with wonderful power and certainty and, apart from a hard return when 215, gave no chance. Altogether he made 236 out of 423, among his strokes being twenty-eight 4's. The Australians registered their 492 runs in five hours and forty minutes. ...

Worcestershire

*Mr M.F.S. Jewell, L. Wright, M. Nichol, H.H. Gibbons, W.V. Fox, Mr C.F. Walters, F. Root, G. Brook, †S.W. Styler, Mr H.A. Gilbert and P. Jackson.

First innings: 131 (Gibbons 31 not out; Grimmett four for 38, Fairfax four for 36). *Second innings:* 196 (Walters 44, Root 48; Grimmett five for 46, Hornibrook three for 30).

Australians

*W. M. Woodfull b Brook	133	E. L. a'Beckett c Gilbert b Root	24
A. Jackson c Walters b Brook	24	†W. A. Oldfield c Jackson b Root	4
D. G. Bradman c Walters b Brook	236	C. V. Grimmett not out	15
S. McCabe c Root b Brook	15	T. W. Wall not out	9
V. Y. Richardson run out	24	B 4, l-b 2, w 1, n-b 1	8
A. Fairfax c Root b Jackson	0	(eight wkts dec)	**492**

P.M. Hornibrook did not bat.

Worcestershire bowling: Root 43–0–112–2; Jackson 25–1–105–1; Gilbert 4–0–30–0; Brook 36–1–148–4; Wright 18–1–68–0; Gibbons 2–0–21–0.

Umpires: J. Hardstaff and T. Oates

LEICESTERSHIRE v AUSTRALIANS   31 (52)

Played at [Aylestone Road] Leicester, Saturday, Monday, Tuesday, May 3, 5, 6 [1930]. Leaving off on Monday with only five men out and possessed of a lead of 217, the Australians might well have gained another single innings victory, but to such a condition had rain reduced the pitch on Tuesday that at eleven o'clock the captains decided to abandon the game. Bradman followed up his triumph at Worcester with another masterly display. Against bowling appreciably more formidable than that of Worcestershire, he found run-getting so difficult to begin with that his first 50 occupied him more than two hours. Afterwards he was not often seriously troubled, and when the second day's play came to an end he had brought his score to 185 in five hours and a quarter. Except for a difficult return chance when 44 he made no mistake and he hit sixteen 4's. Quite as notable as the batting of Bradman was the bowling of Grimmett, who on Saturday in one spell sent down seventeen overs for 29 runs and seven wickets. ... The Australians on Monday had four men out for 80, but Richardson rendered Bradman such excellent assistance that a partnership of two hours and a half produced 179 runs. Richardson drove in powerful fashion and hit cleanly to leg.

Leicestershire

A. Shipman, L.G. Berry, N.F. Armstrong, J.C. Bradshaw, H. Riley, Mr A.T. Sharp, W.E. Astill, G. Geary, *Mr J.A. de Lisle, †T.E. Sidwell and H.C. Snary.

First innings: 148 (Shipman 63, Berry 50; Wall three for 37, Grimmett seven for 46).

Australians

W. H. Ponsford lbw b Geary	25	*V. Y. Richardson c Armstrong b Geary	100
A. Jackson b Geary	4	A. Fairfax not out	21
D. G. Bradman not out	185	B 2, l-b 4	6
A. F. Kippax c Sidwell b Snary	22	(five wkts)	**365**
S. McCabe b Geary	2		

C. V. Grimmett, †C. W. Walker, A. Hurwood and T. W. Wall did not bat.

Leicestershire bowling: Shipman 22–2–59–0; Snary 29–6–89–1; Geary 35–9–85–4; Astill 30–2–99–0; Armstrong 9–2–27–0.

Umpires: W. Bestwick and W. A. Buswell

YORKSHIRE v AUSTRALIANS   32 (53)

Played at Sheffield, Saturday, Monday, Tuesday, May 10, 12, 13 [1930]. A splendid bowling performance on the part of Grimmett, who took all ten Yorkshire wickets for 37 runs, was the outstanding feature of a match in which rain, after interfering considerably with play on the first two days, ruined the pitch so completely that on the Tuesday no cricket could be attempted. ... From the time he went on at 46, Grimmett bowled with wonderful accuracy and varied his break and flight with delightful ingenuity. He received excellent assistance from Walker, who caught one batsman and stumped three. On two previous occasions all ten wickets in an innings had been taken in England by an Australian, Howell performing the feat in 1899 and Mailey in 1921. When the tourists went in, rain and bad light prevented much progress being made but 69 runs were scored for one wicket. So much rain fell on Sunday that on Monday the game could not be resumed until after two o'clock. Woodfull and Bradman, who had come together at 35, then played so well on the soft pitch that they raised the total to 142, Bradman by brilliant cricket making 78 out of 107 in a hundred minutes. ...

Yorkshire

P. Holmes, H. Sutcliffe, E. Oldroyd, M. Leyland, *Mr A. T. Barber, A. Mitchell, E. Robinson, †A. Wood, G.G. Macaulay, W. Rhodes and W. E. Bowes.

   First innings: 155 (Holmes 31, Sutcliffe 69; Grimmett ten for 37).

Australians

*W. M. Woodfull c Barber b Macaulay	121	C. V. Grimmett not out	23
W. H. Ponsford lbw b Robinson	6	†C. W. Walker c Macaulay b Leyland	3
D. G. Bradman c and b Macaulay	78	T. W. Wall c Robinson b Leyland	1
A. F. Kippax lbw b Leyland	3	P. M. Hornibrook st Wood b Rhodes	6
S. McCabe c Oldroyd b Robinson	16	L-b	4
V. Y. Richardson c Wood b Rhodes	45		**320**
E. L. a'Beckett st Wood b Rhodes	14		

Yorkshire bowling: Robinson 28–8–60–2; Bowes 26–7–63–0; Macaulay 28–2–80–2; Rhodes 31.5–5–95–3; Leyland 8–3–18–3.

Umpires: T. Oates and G. Beet

LANCASHIRE v AUSTRALIANS 33 (54, 55)

Played at Liverpool, Wednesday, Thursday, Friday, May 14, 15, 16 [1930]. Although 61 runs in arrear on the first innings, the Australians had the best of the game when stumps were pulled up soon after four o'clock on Friday, wanting only 90 runs and having eight wickets to fall. ... [In their first innings] the Australians, on a drying pitch, lost half their wickets for 63 and the next day, when play was delayed until nearly two o'clock, the last four wickets – despite a fine effort by Kippax – fell for 10 runs, the last three going down in one over from Hopwood.

Lancashire

F. Watson, C. Hallows, E. Tyldesley, J. Iddon, C. Hopwood, E. Paynter, *Mr P. T. Eckersley, F. M. Sibbles, †G. Duckworth, R. Tyldesley and E. A. McDonald.

First innings: 176 (Watson 37, Eckersley 54; Grimmett six for 57, Hornibrook three for 45, Bradman none for 5). *Second innings:* 165 (Eckersley 38; Hornibrook five for 38).

Australians

*W. M. Woodfull b R. Tyldesley	21			
A. Jackson lbw b McDonald	19	–	lbw b Sibbles	40
D. G. Bradman b McDonald	9	–	not out	48
A. F. Kippax not out	40	–	not out	6
V. Y. Richardson c Hopwood b McDonald	0	–	lbw b R. Tyldesley	39
†C. W. Walker lbw b R. Tyldesley	4			
A. Fairfax st Duckworth b Hopwood	18			
E. L. a'Beckett lbw b R. Tyldesley	3			
C. V. Grimmett c R. Tyldesley b Hopwood	0			
A. Hurwood c R. Tyldesley b Hopwood	0			
P. M. Hornibrook b Hopwood	0			
L-b	1		B 1, l-b 1, w 2	4
	115		(two wkts)	**137**

Lancashire bowling: *First innings*—McDonald 20–3–51–3; Sibbles 14–4–33–0; R. Tyldesley 14–7–17–3; Hopwood 10–4–13–4. *Second innings*—McDonald 11–1–36–0; Sibbles 15–6–18–1; R. Tyldesley 12–3–19–1; Hopwood 13–1–29–0; Iddon 4–0–16–0; Watson 4–0–7–0; E. Tyldesley 1–0–8–0.

Umpires: W. A. Buswell and A. Dolphin

MCC TEAM v AUSTRALIANS 34 (56, 57)

Played at Lord's, Saturday, Monday, Tuesday, May 17, 19, 20 [1930]. To meet the Australians, Marylebone placed in the field a distinctly strong side. At no time, however, did a definite issue appear likely to be reached and the end came with the Club having an innings to play and wanting 241 runs for victory. The Australians occupied the wickets for the whole of Saturday, the best batting being that of Bradman and Woodfull, who stayed together for a hundred minutes and put on 119 runs. ... [In their second innings] the tourists lost Woodfull and Bradman for 23 runs, but any cause for anxiety disappeared when next morning, after rain had delayed the game for eighty minutes, Hornibrook stayed with Jackson for an hour and a quarter. Jackson at length showed some approach to his Australian form.

Australians

*W. M. Woodfull c Lee b Kennedy	52	–	b Allom	7
A. Jackson c Lyon b Allom	0	–	c Hendren b Stevens	64
D. G. Bradman b Allom	66	–	lbw b Stevens	4
A. F. Kippax b Peebles	18	–	c Lyon b Allen	24
W. H. Ponsford not out	82	–	c Duleepsinhji b Allen	15
V. Y. Richardson c Hendren b Kennedy	34	–	c Duleepsinjhi b Kennedy	5
A. Fairfax lbw b Allom	1	–	st Lyon b Stevens	26
C. V. Grimmett b Allom	4	–	b Allen	15
†C. W. Walker c Lyon b Allom	0	–	not out	10
T. W. Wall lbw b Kennedy	5	–	b Allen	2
P. M. Hornibrook lbw b Peebles	6	–	b Peebles	11
B 11, l-b 6	17		B 18, l-b 9, w 1, n-b 2	30
	285			**213**

MCC bowling: *First innings*—Allen 16–5–38–0; Allom 32–11–67–5; Peebles 25.3–1–87–2; Kennedy 34–13–60–3; Stevens 9–2–16–0. *Second innings*—Allen 14–6–28–4; Allom 12–3–27–1; Peebles 19–4–48–1; Kennedy 10–3–16–1; Stevens 24.3–5–64–3.

MCC Team

H. W. Lee, †Mr M. D. Lyon, K. S. Duleepsinhji, E. Hendren, Mr D. R. Jardine, *Mr A. P. F. Chapman, Mr G. T. S. Stevens, Mr G. O. Allen, A. Kennedy, Mr M. J. C. Allom and Mr I. A. R. Peebles.

First innings: 258 (Duleepsinhji 92, Hendren 31, Stevens 48; Fairfax six for 54).

Umpires: J. Hardstaff and H. Young

DERBYSHIRE v AUSTRALIANS   35 (58)

Played at Chesterfield, Wednesday, Thursday, Friday, May 21, 22, 23 [1930]. Hornibrook, bowling in great form, obtained twelve wickets for 143 runs and the Australians gained a ten-wickets victory. ... Ponsford put together his first hundred of the tour, raising the score to 127 in company with Jackson and afterwards sharing in a partnership of 106 with Bradman. ... After [Ponsford] left, the Derbyshire bowlers, on a pitch which, from being extremely easy, turned rather difficult, secured eight wickets for 115 runs.

Derbyshire

G. M. Lee, H. Storer, A. E. Alderman, A. G. Slater, Mr N. M. Ford, S. Worthington, L. Townsend, *Mr G. R. Jackson, J. M. Hutchinson, †H. Elliott and T. B. Mitchell.

First innings: 215 (Storer 65, Ford 33, Worthington 79; Wall three for 48, Hornibrook six for 61, Bradman one for 24). Second innings: 181 (Alderman 38, Ford 48, Townsend 38; Hornibrook six for 82).

Australians

W. H. Ponsford c Hutchinson b Worthington	131	–	not out	30
A. Jackson c Elliott b Worthington	63	–	not out	18
D. G. Bradman c Elliott b Worthington	44			
A. F. Kippax c Elliott b Mitchell	25			
*V. Y. Richardson b Townsend	10			
S. McCabe c Hutchinson b Townsend	5			
A. Fairfax b Mitchell	20			
†W. A. Oldfield c and b Worthington	14			
A. Hurwood b Mitchell	15			
P. M. Hornibrook not out	2			
T. W. Wall lbw b Mitchell	0			
B 6, l-b 5, w 2, n-b 6	19		L-b 3, n-b 1	4
	348		(no wkt)	**52**

Derbyshire bowling: *First innings*—Slater 21–9–34–0; Worthington 38–6–103–4; Townsend 37–13–68–2; Mitchell 34.5–10–78–4; Lee 4–0–22–0; Storer 7–1–24–0. *Second innings*—Worthington 5–2–9–0; Townsend 6–1–11–0; Mitchell 6–3–3–0; Ford 2–0–9–0; Jackson 1.1–0–16–0.

Umpires: L. C. Braund and J. Hardstaff

SURREY v AUSTRALIANS   36 (59)

Played at Kennington Oval, Saturday, Monday, Tuesday, May 24, 26, 27 [1930]. To a single day's cricket was the first of the Australians' two matches with Surrey restricted, the ground, owing to rain, being reduced to such a muddy condition that not a ball could be bowled on either Monday or Tuesday, but the one day's play produced some wonderful batting on the part of Bradman. The remarkable young Australian had previously put together huge scores at Worcester and at Leicester so this further success occasioned no great surprise. Still, the performance reached an exceptionally high standard of excellence. Going in first wicket down at 11, Bradman – at great pains to play himself in – took an hour and a half to reach 50, but doubled that score in less than an hour and then travelled so fast that he went from 100 to 200 in eighty minutes. Altogether, in five hours and thirty-five minutes, he made 252 out of 368 and was still unbeaten when rain caused stumps to be drawn five minutes before the usual hour. Scoring at first chiefly on the leg side, he afterwards employed the late cut to fine purpose and in the course of the day brought almost every stroke into play. Not until his figures stood at 207 did he make a real mistake – at that point he gave a chance to short-leg – and among his hits were twenty-one 4's, ten 3's and twenty-six 2's. Woodfull played sound cricket for two hours and a quarter, using the drive as his chief scoring stroke and helping Bradman to put on 116. In another good stand Richardson and Bradman added 113 in seventy minutes but, although at tea there were 234 runs on the board and only two wickets had fallen, half the side were out for 250. There Surrey's measure of success ended, Fairfax, who took fifty minutes to reach double figures, rendering Bradman such stubborn help that subsequently 129 more runs were obtained without further loss. ...

Australians

*W. M. Woodfull c Shepherd b Fender	50	S. McCabe c Fender b Allom		2
A. Jackson c Brooks b Allom	9	A. Fairfax not out		28
D. G. Bradman not out	252	B 3, l-b 1, w 1		5
V. Y. Richardson c Stroud b Allom	32	(five wkts)		**379**
W. H. Ponsford lbw b Fender	1			

†W. A. Oldfield, P. M. Hornibrook, T. W. Wall and C. V. Grimmett did not bat.

Surrey bowling: Allom 34–8–74–3; Lock 22–5–73–0; Stroud 16–1–66–0; Fender 21–1–75–2; Shepherd 20–5–46–0; Gregory 10.4–1–40–0.

Surrey
*Mr P.G.H. Fender, Mr M.J.C. Allom, Mr D.R. Jardine, Mr E.G. Stroud, J.B. Hobbs, A. Sandham, A. Ducat, T. Shepherd, R.J. Gregory, †E.W. Brooks and H. Lock.

Umpires: J.H. King and W.A. Buswell

OXFORD UNIVERSITY v AUSTRALIANS   37 (60)
Played at [the Christ Church ground] Oxford, Wednesday, Thursday, May 28, 29 [1930]. Such a sorry figure did the University team cut that the Australians hit up 406 runs for the loss of only two wickets and, having declared at that score, proceeded to gain the easiest of victories by an innings and 158 runs. … Bradman, after batting nearly an hour, was bowled in playing back to a well-pitched-up ball. … Oxford's batting on an easy-paced pitch was truly pitiful.

Australians

S. McCabe b Garland-Wells	91	A.F. Kippax not out		56
W.H. Ponsford not out	220	B 3, l-b 2, w 1, n-b 1		7
D.G. Bradman b Garland-Wells	32	(two wkts dec)		**406**

*W. M. Woodfull, V. Y. Richardson, A. Fairfax, C. V. Grimmett, †C. W. Walker, T. W. Wall and A. Hurwood did not bat.

Oxford University bowling: Hill-Wood 25–2–75–0; Nevinson 23–3–72–0; Peebles 22–3–71–0; Garland-Wells 25–4–99–2; Melville 6–1–45–0; Moore 3–0–12–0; Kingsley 5–1–25–0.

Oxford University
*Mr P.G.T. Kingsley, Mr D.N. Moore, Nawab of Pataudi, Mr A. Melville, Mr N.M. Ford, Mr I. Akers-Douglas, Mr H.M. Garland-Wells, Mr C.K. Hill-Wood, Mr I.A.R. Peebles, †Mr J.F.N. Mayhew and Mr J.H. Nevinson.
First innings: 124 (Moore 34; Grimmett five for 48). *Second innings:* 124 (Ford 31; Wall four for 29, Bradman two for 19).

Umpires: W. Reeves and J.W. Day

HAMPSHIRE v AUSTRALIANS   38 (61)
Played at Southampton, Saturday, Monday, May 31, June 2 [1930]. Thanks mainly to Grimmett, who secured fourteen wickets for seven runs apiece, the Australians defeated Hampshire by an innings and eight runs. Of more general interest than the particular issue of the contest was the achievement of Bradman in completing his 1,000 runs by the end of May. In so doing Bradman accomplished a feat which no Australian had to his credit. Incidentally the circumstances attending Bradman's triumph were quite dramatic. The batsman required 46 runs to reach four figures and those had to be registered on the opening day. Hampshire batting first, there existed no small likelihood that Bradman would lack the chance of making the necessary runs. As it was, Grimmett's bowling provided the opportunity, but Bradman had only brought his aggregate to 1,001 when rain set in and stopped play for the day. Last man out, Bradman played exceptionally brilliant cricket, making his runs in four hours and giving no real chance. He off-drove splendidly and all through placed the ball with wonderful skill. Among his hits were one 6 and twenty-six 4's. McCabe on Monday played delightful cricket, hitting twelve 4's and helping Bradman to put on 141 in sixty-five minutes. …

Hampshire

†G. Brown, Mr A.L. Hosie, Mr W.G. Lowndes, C.P. Mead, J. Newman, A. Kennedy, Capt. T.O. Jameson, *Lord Tennyson, W.L. Creese, G.S. Boyes and O.W. Herman.

First innings: 151 (Brown 56; Grimmett seven for 39). *Second innings:* 175 (Brown 47; Hornibrook three for 51, Grimmett seven for 56).

Australians

D.G. Bradman c Mead b Boyes	191	†W.A. Oldfield lbw b Kennedy	1
A. Jackson c Boyes b Herman	0	C.V. Grimmett c Brown b Boyes	1
W.H. Ponsford b Newman	29	T.W. Wall lbw b Boyes	0
A.F. Kippax c Kennedy b Boyes	20	P.M. Hornibrook not out	0
*W.M. Woodfull st Brown b Boyes	4	B 4, l-b 2, w 1, n-b 2	9
S. McCabe b Lowndes	65		**334**
A. Fairfax c Hosie b Boyes	14		

Hampshire bowling: Kennedy 30–5–89–1; Herman 9–1–47–1; Newman 18–3–80–1; Boyes 26–4–90–6; Creese 2–0–13–0; Lowndes 3–0–6–1.

Umpires: F. Chester and W.R. Parry

MIDDLESEX v AUSTRALIANS   39 (62, 63)

Played at Lord's, Wednesday, Thursday, Friday, June 4, 5, 6 [1930]. Middlesex could not regain the ground lost by a poor batting performance on Wednesday and suffered defeat by five wickets. So badly did the side collapse before Hornibrook that after lunch eight wickets fell for 46 runs. The Australians also began badly, but when four batsmen had been dismissed for 72, Kippax and McCabe added 65. ...

Middlesex

Mr G.T.S. Stevens, H.W. Lee, J.W. Hearne, E. Hendren, Mr G.O. Allen, *Mr N. Haig, Mr H.J. Enthoven, Mr G.C. Newman, E.G. Canning, T.J. Durston and †W.F. Price.

First innings: 103 (Hornibrook seven for 42, Grimmett three for 36). *Second innings:* 287 (Hendren 138, Enthoven 38; Hornibrook four for 60, Grimmett three for 81).

Australians

W.H. Ponsford lbw b Allen	5	–	b Haig	10
A. Jackson c Canning b Stevens	14	–	lbw b Hearne	26
D.G. Bradman b Hearne	35	–	b Stevens	18
A.F. Kippax lbw b Allen	102	–	not out	17
*V.Y. Richardson lbw b Hearne	1	–	c Newman b Stevens	11
S. McCabe c Lee b Allen	31	–	c Allen b Stevens	18
A. Fairfax b Lee	34	–	not out	13
C.V. Grimmett b Allen	21			
A. Hurwood b Allen	1			
†C.W. Walker not out	5			
P.M. Hornibrook lbw b Allen	4			
B 9, l-b 6, n-b 2	17		B 2, l-b 4, w 2	8
	270		(five wkts)	**121**

Middlesex bowling: *First innings*—Allen 37.1–8–77–6; Haig 13–3–24–0; Durston 15–3–27–0; Stevens 23–2–70–1; Hearne 25–10–34–2; Lee 3–2–1–1; Enthoven 7–3–20–0. *Second innings*—Allen 7.4–3–19–0; Haig 11–3–18–1; Stevens 17–1–47–3; Hearne 13–3–27–1; Newman 1–0–2–0.

Umpires: P. Toone and A. Nash

CAMBRIDGE UNIVERSITY v AUSTRALIANS   40 (64)

Played at Cambridge, Saturday, Monday, Tuesday, June 7, 9, 10 [1930]. Beating Cambridge by an innings and 134 runs, the Australians, immediately prior to the First Test Match, registered their fourth consecutive victory. Killick put together two good scores in skilful fashion and, with the issue a foregone conclusion, the last three University wickets produced 126 runs, but otherwise the Light Blues gave almost as poor an exhibition as that of Oxford ten days earlier. Indeed, seeing that the Cambridge batsmen allowed themselves to be mastered by McCabe and Bradman, it might be contended that their failure was the more pronounced. ...

Cambridge University

Mr G. D. Kemp-Welch, Mr A. T. Ratcliffe, Mr E. T. Killick, Mr G. C. Grant, *†Mr J. T. Morgan, Mr T. W. T. Baines, Mr H. R. W. Butterworth, Mr R. H. C. Human, Mr F. R. Brown, Mr W. H. Webster and Mr A. H. Fabian.

First innings: 145 (Killick 48; McCabe four for 25, Bradman three for 35). *Second innings:* 225 (Killick 44, Human 47, Brown 52; McCabe four for 60, Bradman three for 68).

Australians

*W. M. Woodfull c Fabian b Webster	216	†W. A. Oldfield c Human b Webster	28
W. H. Ponsford b Kemp-Welch	7	P. M. Hornibrook b Human	6
D. G. Bradman c Baines b Human	32	T. W. Wall not out	9
S. McCabe run out	96	A. Hurwood not out	8
V. Y. Richardson c Kemp-Welch b Human	34	B 24, l-b 8, w 7, n-b 4	43
A. Jackson run out	25	(eight wkts dec)	**504**

C. W. Walker did not bat.

Cambridge University bowling: Kemp-Welch 30–3–100–1; Human 35–3–106–3; Fabian 26–4–104–0; Brown 31–5–72–0; Webster 21–8–45–2; Grant 1–0–13–0; Butterworth 2–0–21–0.

Umpires: G. Watts and J. W. Day

ENGLAND v AUSTRALIA   41 (65, 66)
(FIRST TEST MATCH)   5 (9, 10)

Played at Nottingham, Friday, Saturday, Monday, Tuesday, June 13, 14, 16, 17 [1930]. England won the first of the series of Test Matches shortly after half-past five on the fourth day by 93 runs. This was a satisfactory start but in gaining the initial success the England team were helped to no inconsiderable extent by the weather, Australia, on the second afternoon, having to bat on a pitch made difficult by hot sunshine following heavy rain during the night and early morning. As an offset to this, however, the Englishmen were greatly handicapped in Australia's last innings by being without Larwood for the whole of the concluding day. The Notts fast bowler, owing to an attack of gastritis, had to keep to his bed. Australia, who were set to get 429 runs to win, had scored 60 runs for the loss of Woodfull's wicket overnight, and with the England attack thus weakened made, thanks to Bradman, a very fine fight of it. Indeed, when shortly before three o'clock they had 229 runs on the board and only three men out, they possessed, with the wicket probably in better condition than at any previous time during the game, a reasonable chance of winning.

Bradman was well set and McCabe playing a bold and successful innings, but at that point McCabe fell to a splendid catch very low down at mid-on by Copley, a member of the ground staff at Trent Bridge fielding as substitute for Larwood. Copley made a lot of ground, took the ball at full length and, although rolling over, retained possession.

This catch, as it happened, turned the game in England's favour, for although Fairfax stayed some time and Richardson made a few hits, nobody, after Bradman's dismissal at 267, offered any real resistance. ...

[In England's first innings] play ceased with the score at 241 for eight wickets and the turf was so wet next day that not a ball could be bowled until a quarter past two. There were many who held that Chapman should have declared but, thanks to some fine hitting by Robins, 29 useful runs were added in twenty-five minutes. ...

By the time the Australians went in, the sun had come out and in less than an hour they lost Ponsford, Woodfull and Bradman for only 16 runs. Woodfull was out to a brilliant catch in the gully and Bradman completely beaten by a break-back. ...

[After England had batted a second time] fifty minutes remained for play when Australia entered upon their task of getting 429 runs to win. Duleepsinhji fielded as substitute for Sutcliffe, who had split his thumb. With only 12 scored, Woodfull was again caught in the gully but Ponsford and Bradman played out time, carrying the score to 60. The next morning Ponsford, playing back to a half-volley, was bowled at 93, but England without Larwood had to work tremendously hard for the rest of the day. Bradman, who had been quite brilliant overnight, played such an entirely different game that not until quarter to three did he hit another 4. ... Bradman and McCabe soon played themselves in after lunch and it was quickly obvious that they might rob England of victory, but then at 229 came the catch by the substitute Copley to which reference has been made.

The partnership realised 77 runs in seventy minutes. Bradman's fine innings ended at 267, Robins bowling him with a googly which the batsman made no attempt to play. At the wickets four hours and twenty minutes, Bradman hit ten 4's in scoring his hundred in his first Test Match in England. Off the first ball he received he made a lucky snick over slip's head, and when 60 he again snicked a ball which went off Duckworth's glove to Hammond's left hand and then on to the ground, while at 75 he was nearly bowled by a leg-break. Thus his display, if in the circumstances very remarkable, was not free from fault. ...

England

J. B. Hobbs, H. Sutcliffe, W. R. Hammond, F. E. Woolley, E. Hendren, *Mr A. P. F. Chapman, H. Larwood, Mr R. W. V. Robins, M. W. Tate, R. Tyldesley and †G. Duckworth.

First innings: 270 (Hobbs 78, Chapman 52, Robins 50 not out; Grimmett five for 107). *Second innings:* 302 (Hobbs 74, Sutcliffe 58 retired hurt, Hendren 72; Wall three for 67, Grimmett five for 94).

Australia

*W. M. Woodfull c Chapman b Tate	2	–	c Chapman b Larwood	4
W. H. Ponsford b Tate	3	–	b Tate	39
A. Fairfax c Hobbs b Robins	14	–	c Robins b Tate	14
D. G. Bradman b Tate	8	–	b Robins	131
A. F. Kippax not out	64	–	c Hammond b Robins	23
S. McCabe c Hammond b Robins	4	–	c sub b Tate	49
V. Y. Richardson b Tyldesley	37	–	lbw b Tyldesley	29
†W. A. Oldfield c Duckworth b Robins	4	–	c Hammond b Tyldesley	11
C. V. Grimmett st Duckworth b Robins	0	–	c Hammond b Tyldesley	0
P. M. Hornibrook lbw b Larwood	0	–	c Duckworth b Robins	5
T. W. Wall b Tyldesley	0	–	not out	8
B 4, l-b 4	8		B 17, l-b 5	22
	144			**335**

England bowling: *First innings*—Larwood 15–8–12–1; Tate 19–8–20–3; Tyldesley 21–8–53–2; Robins 17–4–51–4. *Second innings*—Larwood 5–1–9–1; Tate 50–20–69–3; Tyldesley 35–10–77–3; Robins 17.2–1–81–3; Hammond 29–5–74–0; Woolley 3–1–3–0.

Umpires: W. R. Parry and J. Hardstaff

SURREY v AUSTRALIANS   42 (67)

Played at Kennington Oval, Wednesday, Thursday, Friday, June 18, 19, 20 [1930]. To such a pronounced extent did the Australians, up to a point, outplay Surrey that, having established a lead of 226, they were able to declare with five men out. Hobbs, however, came to the rescue, putting together what was at once the second hundred recorded against the tourists and the 173rd of his career, with the result that in the end Surrey were 23 ahead and had eight wickets to fall. [On the first day] Play had lasted less than three hours, Surrey meanwhile losing five batsmen for 140, when rain flooded the ground. ...

Surrey

J. B. Hobbs, A. Sandham, T. H. Barling, T. Shepherd, E. F. Wilson, R. J. Gregory, *Mr P. G. H. Fender, H. G. Baldwin, H. A. Peach, Mr M. J. C. Allom and †E. W. Brooks.
    First innings: 162 (Shepherd 56; Grimmett six for 24). *Second innings:* Two for 249 (Hobbs 146 not out, Shepherd 65 not out; Bradman none for 31).

Australians

*W. M. Woodfull c Wilson b Shepherd	141	A. Jackson not out	37
A. Fairfax lbw b Shepherd	36	E. L. a'Beckett not out	67
D. G. Bradman c Allom b Shepherd	5	B 18, l-b 6	24
A. F. Kippax c and b Peach	36	(five wkts dec)	**388**
S. McCabe b Shepherd	42		

†C. W. Walker, A. Hurwood, C. V. Grimmett and T. W. Wall did not bat.

Surrey bowling: Allom 27–2–66–0; Peach 32–16–66–1; Fender 29–6–93–0; Gregory 28–6–74–0; Shepherd 27–6–65–4.

Umpires: F. Chester and W. Phillips

LANCASHIRE v AUSTRALIANS   43 (68, 69)

Played at Manchester, Saturday, Monday, Tuesday, June 21, 23, 24 [1930]. Rain caused several interruptions and the play generally being marked by rather pronounced restraint, there never existed much likelihood of a definite issue being reached. On the opening day, although the county attack was greatly weakened through the inability of McDonald to turn out, the Australians occupied four hours and forty minutes in making 231 for five wickets ... and in the end, batting more than eight hours, [they] registered the largest total obtained against Lancashire during the season. ...

Australians

*W. M. Woodfull st Duckworth b Sibbles	27			
A. Jackson b Hodgson	52			
D. G. Bradman c Duckworth b Sibbles	38	–	not out	23
A. F. Kippax st Duckworth b Hopwood	120			
S. McCabe c Duckworth b Hodgson	34	–	not out	36
V. Y. Richardson c R. Tyldesley b Hodgson	13	–	c Eckersley b Hodgson	12
A. Fairfax st Duckworth b R. Tyldesley	63			
†W. A. Oldfield not out	34			
A. Hurwood c Taylor b Hopwood	9			
T. W. Wall lbw b R. Tyldesley	0			
P. M. Hornibrook b Sibbles	20			
B 4, l-b 13	17		B	8
	427		(one wkt)	**79**

Lancashire bowling: *First innings*—Hodgson 37–7–97–3; Sibbles 50–6–89–3; R. Tyldesley 38–8–87–2; Hopwood 43–11–92–2; Watson 4–1–10–0; Iddon 16–4–35–0. *Second innings*—Hodgson 3–1–6–1; Sibbles 2–0–13–0; Watson 1–0–3–0; Eckersley 2–0–12–0; Duckworth 2–0–13–0; Hallows 2–0–15–0; E. Tyldesley 1–0–9–0.

Lancashire

F. Watson, C. Hallows, E. Tyldesley, J. Iddon, C. Hopwood, M.L. Taylor, *Mr P.T. Eckersley, F.M. Sibbles, †G. Duckworth, R. Tyldesley and G. Hodgson.

First innings: 259 (Watson 74, Hallows 42, Tyldesley 48, Hopwood 40; Wall four for 92, Fairfax four for 29, Bradman none for 24).

Umpires: W. Bestwick and W. R. Parry

ENGLAND v AUSTRALIA
(SECOND TEST MATCH)

44 (70, 71)
6 (11, 12)

Played at Lord's, Friday, Saturday, Monday, Tuesday, June 27, 28, 30, July 1 [1930]. Beating England, after a memorable struggle, by seven wickets Australia took ample revenge for their overthrow a fortnight previously at Trent Bridge. The batting of the Australians and particularly that of Bradman will assuredly live long in the minds of those who saw it but, while giving the visitors the fullest praise for winning so handsomely after having to face a first innings total of 425, it is only proper to observe that to a large extent England played right into the hands of their opponents. Briefly, the Englishmen lost a match which, with a little discretion on the last day, they could probably have saved. ... It can with truth be said, however, that the England bowling in no other game [of the series] not only looked but actually was so entirely lacking in sting and effect.

Records went by the board. Australia, in putting together a total of 729 before declaring with only six wickets down, broke four – the highest score by Australia in England, 551 at Kennington Oval in 1884; the highest score in this country, 576 by England at The Oval in 1899; the highest score by Australia, 600 at Melbourne in 1924; and the highest score in the whole series of Test Matches, 636 by England at Sydney in December, 1928. Bradman himself, with a score of 254, played the second-highest individual innings in the whole series of Test Matches between England and Australia, while Duleepsinhji not only made a hundred on the occasion of his first appearance in a Test Match against Australia but scored the highest number of runs ever obtained by an England player in these matches at Lord's. There was one other notable point, A. P. F. Chapman, after leading England to victory six times, captaining the losing side. As some set-off against that, he enjoyed, for the first time in his career, the distinction of making a hundred in a Test Match. ...

[Commencing their reply on Saturday morning] Australia, by skilful and judicious batting, remained in for the rest of the day and scoring 404 for the loss of only two batsmen left off no more than 21 runs behind – a very great performance. ... The Australians batted to a set plan, Woodfull and Ponsford steadily wearing down the bowling for Bradman later on to flog it. Nearly three hours were occupied over the first 162 runs, but in another two hours and three-quarters no fewer than 242 came. While in the end Bradman made most runs, very great credit was due to Woodfull and Ponsford, who, when England's bowling was fresh, put on 162 for the first wicket. Curiously enough the partnership terminated almost directly after a break in play while the members of both teams were presented to the King in front of the pavilion, Ponsford, who had batted very soundly, being caught at slip. ... Just before the King arrived, Woodfull, with his score at 52 playing forward to Robins, dragged his foot over the crease. Duckworth gathered the ball and swept it back to the stumps but omitted to remove the bails. That little error cost England dear. Bradman, who went in when Ponsford was out and the bowling had been mastered, seized his opportunity in rare style and, hitting all round the wicket with power and accuracy, scored in two hours and forty minutes 155 runs and was not out at the close. ...

On the Monday, Australia kept England in the field for another four hours and a half and added 325 runs for the loss of four more batsmen before declaring their innings closed at the tea interval. The partnership between Bradman and Kippax, which did not end until ten minutes to three when Bradman was caught right-hand at extra mid-off, produced 192 runs in less than three hours. In obtaining his 254, the famous Australian gave nothing approaching a chance. He nearly played on at 111 and, at 191, in trying to turn the ball to leg, he edged it deep into the slips but, apart from those trifling errors, no real fault could be found with his display. Like Woodfull he scarcely ever lifted the ball and, while his defence generally was perfect, he hit very hard in front of the wicket. Altogether he batted five and a half hours, his chief strokes being twenty-five 4's, three 3's, and twenty-six 2's. ... For their huge total Australia batted ten hours and ten minutes.

England thus found themselves requiring 304 runs to escape an innings defeat. [Although they accomplished this, the Australians then] had to make only 72 to win, but in twenty minutes there was much excitement. Ponsford was bowled at 16, Bradman caught low down at backward-point at 17, and Kippax taken at the wicket at 22. Visions of a remarkable collapse arose but Woodfull, exercising sound generalship by taking most of Robins' bowling himself, tided over an anxious period and by five o'clock he and McCabe had obtained the remaining runs.

In the course of the four days, 110,000 people watched the cricket, the takings being roughly £14,500.

England

J. B. Hobbs, F. E. Woolley, W. R. Hammond, K. S. Duleepsinhji, E. Hendren, *Mr A. P. F. Chapman, Mr G. O. Allen, M. W. Tate, Mr R. W. V. Robins, Mr J. C. White and †G. Duckworth.

First innings: 425 (Woolley 41, Hammond 38, Duleepsinhji 173, Hendren 48, Tate 54; Wall three for 118, Fairfax four for 101). *Second innings:* 375 (Hammond 32, Duleepsinhji 48, Chapman 121, Allen 57, sundries 30; Grimmett six for 167, Bradman none for 1).

Australia

*W. M. Woodfull st Duckworth b Robins	155	–	not out	26
W. H. Ponsford c Hammond b White	81	–	b Robins	14
D. G. Bradman c Chapman b White	254	–	c Chapman b Tate	1
A. F. Kippax b White	83	–	c Duckworth b Robins	3
S. McCabe c Woolley b Hammond	44	–	not out	25
V. Y. Richardson c Hobbs b Tate	30			
†W. A. Oldfield not out	43			
A. Fairfax not out	20			
B 6, l-b 8, w 5	19		B 1, l-b 2	3
(six wkts dec)	**729**		(three wkts)	**72**

C. V. Grimmett, P. M. Hornibrook and T. W. Wall did not bat.

England bowling: *First innings*—Allen 34–7–115–0; Tate 64–16–148–1; White 51–7–158–3; Robins 42–1–172–1; Hammond 35–8–82–1; Woolley 6–0–35–0. *Second innings*—Tate 13–6–21–1; White 2–0–8–0; Robins 9–1–34–2; Hammond 4.2–1–6–0.

Umpires: F. Chester and T. Oates

YORKSHIRE v AUSTRALIANS   45 (72)

Played at Bradford, Wednesday, Thursday, Friday, July 2, 3, 4 [1930]. Lacking the services of Sutcliffe, Yorkshire batted so poorly that a little play on the third day saw them beaten by ten wickets. Once again the big factor in the Australians' success was the bowling of Grimmett, who took eleven wickets for just over 12 runs apiece. In the course of the match Grimmett secured his 100th wicket [of the tour]. ... Yorkshire, although Bradman let off W. Barber, had four men out for 42 and ... could not retrieve the early disasters. ...

Australians

*W. M. Woodfull c Wood b Dennis	3			
W. H. Ponsford c and b Hall	143			
D. G. Bradman lbw b Robinson	1			
S. McCabe c Macaulay b Hall	40			
A. Jackson lbw b Macaulay	46			
V. Y. Richardson c Dennis b Robinson	3			
E. L. a'Beckett not out	30	–	not out	6
C. V. Grimmett c and b Hall	1			
A. Hurwood c A. T. Barber b Rhodes	4			
P. M. Hornibrook c Mitchell b Rhodes	10			
†C. W. Walker st Wood b Rhodes	6	–	not out	1
B 4, l-b 7, w 1, n-b 3	15			
	302		(no wkt)	**7**

Yorkshire bowling: *First innings*—Robinson 21–5–69–2; Dennis 13–6–25–1; Macaulay 32–10–58–1; Hall 24–6–61–3; Rhodes 25.3–8–49–3; Leyland 10–1–25–0. *Second innings*—Robinson 0.1–0–2–0; Hall 1–0–5–0.

Yorkshire

P. Holmes, A. Mitchell, *Mr A. T. Barber, M. Leyland, W. Barber, E. Robinson, W. Rhodes, F. Dennis, †A. Wood, G.G. Macaulay and C. Hall.

    First innings: 146 (Rhodes 35; a'Beckett three for 42, Grimmett six for 75). *Second innings:* 161 (W. Barber 42; Hurwood four for 35, Grimmett five for 58).

Umpires: G. Beet and A. Nash

ENGLAND v AUSTRALIA   46 (73)
(THIRD TEST MATCH)   7 (13)

Played at Leeds, Friday, Saturday, Monday, Tuesday, July 11, 12, 14, 15 [1930]. The Third Test Match, while it afforded that remarkable young batsman, Bradman, the opportunity of leaving all individual batting records in representative matches far behind, was in many respects an unsatisfactory affair. England had the worst of it from start to finish but escaped with a draw, a heavy storm on Sunday night, followed by further rain on the Monday, restricting the third day's play to forty-five minutes while, on the Tuesday, further delay occurred owing to defective light.

The game will go down to history on account of the wonderful batting performance accomplished by Bradman, who, with an innings of 334, beat the previous highest – 287 by R. E. Foster for England at Sydney – which had stood since December, 1903. In the course of this, Bradman achieved fame in other directions. Like C.G. Macartney on the same ground four years previously, he reached three figures before lunch-time on the first day. Not out 309 at the close he had then exceeded a total of 1,000 runs in Test cricket and reached an aggregate of exactly 2,000 runs for the season. In playing two consecutive innings of over 200 in Test Matches he equalled the performance of Hammond during the previous tour in Australia. He also equalled Macartney's performance of 1926 in scoring three separate hundreds in successive Test Matches. Truly could it be called 'Bradman's Match'. Bigger though it was and characterised by splendid strokeplay, Bradman's innings did not quite approach his 254 at Lord's in freedom from fault, but as to its extraordinary merit there could be no two opinions. As usual, he rarely lifted the ball and when making two or more consecutive scoring strokes seldom sent it in the same direction. His footwork was admirable as was the manner in which he played his defensive strokes to balls just short of a length. …

This time, Woodfull won the toss and Australia led off so brilliantly that, when the first day's play ended, they had 458 runs on the board with only three wickets down. The pitch, like those at Nottingham and Lord's, was, on the first day at any rate, lacking in life and pace and all in favour of batsmen. Opening the innings with Woodfull [because Ponsford was suffering from gastritis], Jackson off the fifth ball of the second over was caught at forward short-leg, but England had to wait until five minutes past three before they took another wicket, Woodfull and Bradman, in the meantime, putting on 192 runs in two hours and thirty-five minutes. This was very largely the work of Bradman, who, quick to settle down, completed 102 out of the first 127 in ninety-five minutes. All the same, Woodfull, by another great display of defensive cricket, rendered his side invaluable assistance. After Woodfull left, bowled in trying to hook a shortish ball, Bradman found another admirable partner in Kippax, who, if overshadowed by his colleague, played uncommonly well in helping to add 229 in rather less than two and three-quarter hours. The next day McCabe, who had batted twenty minutes overnight, stayed until 63 runs had been put on but nothing of any consequence was accomplished by the rest, the last seven wickets falling in a hundred minutes for 108 runs. Bradman, sixth out at 508, obtained his 334 in six hours and a quarter, his score being made up of forty-six 4's, six 3's, twenty-six 2's, and eighty singles. When he had made 141 he put up a ball towards mid-wicket and at 202 he skied a ball over Tate's head at mid-on. Indeed, a man a little quicker on his feet than Tate might have made a catch of it. Actually, Bradman gave only one chance, being missed at the wicket off Geary at 273 when the total was 385. He hit very hard in front of the wicket, scored splendidly on the leg side and very often cut in dazzling fashion. Nobody could have had a better reception than that accorded to Bradman on his return to the pavilion. …

[Bowled out for 391 in their first innings] England followed on 179 behind and, as over three hours remained for cricket, there was always the possibility of them losing. Hobbs and Sutcliffe opened the innings in a very poor light. After a quarter of an hour, they appealed against it and the players went in. For some extraordinary reason the crowd took this in very bad part, booing the batsmen and cheering the Australians, while on the game being resumed there was a continuance of this unseemly behaviour. With 24 scored, Hobbs was brilliantly thrown out by Bradman from deep mid-off but Sutcliffe and Hammond stayed nearly an hour to add 50. After Duleepsinhji had been caught at point off a ball which he afterwards confessed he did not see, another appeal against the light was made at ten minutes to six and no further cricket took place.

Australia

*W. M. Woodfull b Hammond	50	†W. A. Oldfield c Hobbs b Tate	2
A. Jackson c Larwood b Tate	1	C. V. Grimmett c Duckworth b Tyldesley	24
D. G. Bradman c Duckworth b Tate	334	T. W. Wall b Tyldesley	3
A. F. Kippax c Chapman b Tate	77	P. M. Hornibrook not out	1
S. McCabe b Larwood	30	B 5, l-b 8, w 1	14
V. Y. Richardson c Larwood b Tate	1		**566**
E. L. a'Beckett c Chapman b Geary	29		

England bowling: Larwood 33–3–139–1; Tate 39–9–124–5; Geary 35–10–95–1; Tyldesley 33–5–104–2; Hammond 17–3–46–1; Leyland 11–0–44–0.

England

J. B. Hobbs, H. Sutcliffe, W. R. Hammond, K. S. Duleepsinhji, M. Leyland, G. Geary, †G. Duckworth, *Mr A. P. F. Chapman, M. W. Tate, H. Larwood and R. Tyldesley.

First innings: 391 (Sutcliffe 32, Hammond 113, Duleepsinhji 35, Leyland 44, Duckworth 33, Chapman 45; Grimmett five for 135). *Second innings:* Three for 95 (Hammond 35).

Umpires: W. Bestwick and T. Oates

SCOTLAND v AUSTRALIANS 47

Played at Edinburgh, Wednesday, Thursday, Friday, July 16, 17, 18 [1930]. While a three-day fixture had been arranged for the meeting of Scotland with the Australians, the weather proved so unkind that progress with the game was restricted to something less than three hours on Wednesday. Play proceeded without interruptions up to lunch-time and was resumed at the usual hour, but after half an hour's more cricket rain caused a considerable delay and a further endeavour to continue the contest was, within a few minutes, checked by a downpour of so pronounced a description that nothing further could be done that day. Unhappily the rain continued through the night and next morning with the consequence that on Thursday play was out of the question, while on Friday when, with the weather clearing somewhat, it had been agreed to make a start after two o'clock, there came more rain, which compelled the abandonment of the match. ...

Scotland

Mr J. Kerr, *Mr G. W. A. Alexander, †Mr A. K. McTavish, Mr B. R. Tod, Mr W. Nicholson, Mr W. Anderson, Mr A. D. Baxter, Mr J. F. Jones, Mr R. W. Sievwright, Mr A. R. Simpson and Mr T. Watson.

First innings: Three for 129 (Alexander 51, McTavish 35; Bradman none for 4).

Australians

*W. M. Woodfull, V. Y. Richardson, W. H. Ponsford, A. Jackson, D. G. Bradman, A. F. Kippax, E. L. a'Beckett, C. V. Grimmett, P. M. Hornibrook, A. Hurwood and †C. W. Walker.

Umpires: R. A. Haywood and G. Deyes

A SCOTTISH XI v AUSTRALIANS

Played at Glasgow, Saturday, Monday, July 19, 21 [1930]. If not so deplorable as on the occasion of the match at Edinburgh, the weather associated with a two-day contest at Glasgow still left much to be desired. Indeed, on Saturday, when the Scotsmen batted with a measure of caution which neither the conditions nor the quality of the Australians' bowling justified, rain held up the game for seventy minutes in the course of the afternoon and bad light afterwards brought play to a close. On Monday the Scottish captain at once declared and the Australians put on 337 runs for the loss of nine wickets. Bradman, seizing upon the occasion to register his eighth hundred, gave a brilliant display, making 140 out of 210 in two hours and a half. He offered no chance and among his hits were a drive for 6 and nineteen 4's. Woodfull, also batting freely, helped to add 198 for the second wicket.

A Scottish XI

Mr J. Kerr, Mr B. W. G. Atkinson, Mr A. K. McTavish, *Mr G. W. A. Alexander, Mr W. Nicholson, Mr B. R. Tod, Ackroyd, Mr A. D. Baxter, †Mr D. A. Bompas, H. J. Preston and Mr T. Watson.

First innings: Six for 140 dec (Tod 34; Hornibrook three for 40).

Australians

*W. M. Woodfull c Kerr b Preston	65	A. Hurwood lbw b Watson	3
W. H. Ponsford b Baxter	6	P. M. Hornibrook b Preston	8
D. G. Bradman b Baxter	140	†C. W. Walker c Kerr b Baxter	0
A. F. Kippax lbw b Watson	0	T. W. Wall not out	2
S. McCabe b Baxter	1	B 8, l-b 8, n-b 1	17
A. Jackson not out	52	(nine wkts)	**337**
E. L. a'Beckett st Bompas b Tod	43		

A Scottish XI bowling: Baxter 35–8–89–4; Preston 40–7–94–2; Ackroyd 16–4–45–0; Watson 20–3–47–2; Tod 8–0–45–1.

Umpires: Guy and Joyce

[Although Bradman was not selected to play in the two-day match against Durham at Sunderland on July 23 and 24, readers may be interested to know that rain followed the Australians south from Scotland and prevented any play.]

ENGLAND v AUSTRALIA 48 (74)
(FOURTH TEST MATCH) 8 (14)

Played at Manchester, Friday, Saturday, Monday, Tuesday, July 25, 26, 28, 29 [1930]. Interfered with by rain to a much greater extent than was the case in the game at Leeds, the Fourth Test Match had also to be left drawn. Cricket went on without interruption on the first two days, but play lasted only forty-five minutes on the third afternoon – as at Leeds – and not a ball was bowled on the last day.

Under conditions which were expected to confer an advantage on the home team, England again had the worst of matters. For the fourth time the batting of the side proved inconsistent, a promising start being discounted by certain failures which were only partially retrieved, while the bowling, apart from that of Peebles, did not really inspire confidence or achieve the success anticipated when Australia, on winning the toss, batted on a soft wicket. ... So soft was the turf that the start had to be delayed for half an hour and the foothold proved so uncertain that Chapman, fielding at silly-mid-off, had to put down a lot of sawdust to prevent himself slipping.

Woodfull and Ponsford gave their side another fine start, staying in until a quarter to three and putting on 106 for the first wicket. Ponsford batted admirably ... Woodfull, until Peebles went on, also played extremely well, but for a long time before lunch he was definitely uncomfortable and uncertain in dealing with that bowler. The Middlesex amateur caused Ponsford little trouble; he constantly made Woodfull play false strokes. ...

Bradman had a most unhappy experience. He was nearly bowled first ball by Peebles and, when 10, gave a chance low down in the slips. He hit one 4 off a full-toss and then, trying to cut a leg-spinner, was nicely caught at second slip at 138. Just about this time, Peebles was bowling extremely well. ...

[When England batted, Hobbs and Sutcliffe put on 108 in two hours for the first wicket.] Sutcliffe ... gave a brilliant display of driving, pulling and hooking. ... He was out to a remarkable catch at long-leg off a big hit, Bradman taking the ball high up and then falling among the spectators. ...

Australia

*W. M. Woodfull c Duckworth b Tate	54	†W. A. Oldfield b Nichols	2
W. H. Ponsford b Hammond	83	C. V. Grimmett c Sutcliffe b Peebles	50
D. G. Bradman c Duleepsinhji b Peebles	14	P. M. Hornibrook c Duleepsinhji	
A. F. Kippax c Chapman b Nichols	51	b Goddard	3
S. McCabe lbw b Peebles	4	T. W. Wall not out	1
V. Y. Richardson b Hammond	1	B 23, l-b 3, n-b 7	33
A. Fairfax lbw b Goddard	49		**345**

England bowling: Nichols 21–5–33–2; Tate 30–11–39–1; Goddard 32.1–14–49–2; Peebles 55–9–150–3; Leyland 8–2–17–0; Hammond 21–6–24–2.

England

J. B. Hobbs, H. Sutcliffe, W. R. Hammond, K. S. Duleepsinhji, M. Leyland, *Mr A. P. F. Chapman, M. W. Tate, M. S. Nichols, Mr I. A. R. Peebles, †G. Duckworth and T. W. Goddard.

First innings: Eight for 251 (Hobbs 31, Sutcliffe 74, Duleepsinhji 54, Leyland 35; Wall three for 70, McCabe four for 41).

Umpires: F. Chester and J. Hardstaff

SOMERSET v AUSTRALIANS   49 (75)

Played at Taunton, Wednesday, Thursday, July 30, 31 [1930]. So completely did the Australians outplay Somerset that in the course of two days' cricket they defeated the western county by an innings and 158 runs. Batting first on a pitch of varying pace, the home side lost half their wickets for 30 and from that wretched start there was, as it happened, no recovery. For a blunder early in the Australians' innings a tremendously heavy price had to be paid. Ponsford was bowled at 13 and one run later Jackson, with his score at six, was missed by Wellard in the slips. To such an extent did Jackson profit by this escape that he remained to add, in company with Bradman, 231 runs for the second wicket, the partnership lasting just over three hours and a half. ... Following upon a very cautious start, Bradman batted with his customary skill and confidence, and hit thirteen 4's. After Bradman's dismissal, the last eight wickets fell for 116 runs. ... The match proved so large an attraction that on the opening day the holding capacity of the ground was taxed to its limit.

Somerset

A. Young, Mr E. F. Longrigg, Mr R. A. Ingle, F. S. Lee, *Mr J. C. White, Mr C. C. Case, Mr L. Hawkins, A. W. Wellard, J. W. Lee, G. Hunt and †Mr A. G. Marshall.

First innings: 121 (White 38, Wellard 38; Grimmett three for 38). *Second innings:* 81 (Grimmett seven for 33).

Australians

W. H. Ponsford b Hunt	8	C. V. Grimmett c Young b White	16
A. Jackson c J. W. Lee b Young	118	A. Hurwood hit wkt b Young	10
D. G. Bradman c and b Young	117	P. M. Hornibrook not out	4
S. McCabe c and b Young	1	†C. W. Walker c Wellard b White	0
*V. Y. Richardson c Hulme b Young	27	B 1, l-b 4	5
W. M. Woodfull c and b White	30		**360**
E. L. a'Beckett c Young b White	24		

Somerset bowling: Wellard 22–3–66–0; Hunt 38–13–91–1; J. W. Lee 19–8–37–0; White 30.4–8–91–4; Young 34–12–70–5.

Umpires: A. Morton and A. Nash

GLAMORGAN v AUSTRALIANS   50 (76, 77)

Played at Swansea, Saturday, Monday, Tuesday, August 2, 4, 5 [1930]. Although much interfered with by rain, which on Saturday prevented a start being made until after four o'clock and on Tuesday delayed play until a quarter to one, the match yielded a most interesting finish. The tourists, declaring with one man out in their second innings, set Glamorgan 218 to get in two hours and three-quarters and in the end there were 21 runs wanted and three wickets to fall. On Saturday the visitors scored 149 for the loss of Ponsford and Jackson, and on Monday, Bradman and McCabe raised the total to 196, but the last seven wickets produced only 49 runs. The Australians could not make their opponents follow on but on Tuesday they declared at lunch-time. Playing at first merely to avert defeat, Glamorgan scored 59 for two wickets but then Bates and Turnbull hit out so finely that 93 runs were obtained in sixty-five minutes. The attempt by other batsmen to force the runs, however, did not meet with success.

Australians

W. H. Ponsford b D. Davies	53	–	not out	35
A. Jackson c Hills b Mercer	39	–	c Clay b D. Davies	11
D. G. Bradman b Ryan	58	–	not out	19
S. McCabe c D. Davies b Ryan	53			
*V. Y. Richardson st Every b Ryan	3			
A. Fairfax c D. Davies b Ryan	8			
E. L. a'Beckett not out	18			
C. V. Grimmett c D. Davies b Ryan	0			
T. W. Wall c Turnbull b Ryan	2			
A. Hurwood lbw b Mercer	0			
†C. W. Walker b Mercer	1			
B 1, l-b 6, n-b 3	10		B 4, l-b 2	6
	245		(one wkt dec)	**71**

Glamorgan bowling: *First innings*—Mercer 32.3–7–70–3; E. Davies 6–0–31–0; Clay 16–3–35–0; Ryan 34–3–76–6; D. Davies 11–3–23–1. *Second innings*—Mercer 3–0–15–0; Clay 10–2–28–0; Ryan 4–1–13–0; D. Davies 4–1–9–1.

Glamorgan

W. Bates, A. H. Dyson, *Mr M. J. Turnbull, D. Davies, J. T. Bell, J. Hills, E. Davies, Mr J. C. Clay, J. Mercer, †G. Every and F. Ryan.

First innings: 99 (Grimmett four for 34). *Second innings:* Seven for 197 (Bates 73, Turnbull 52; Grimmett four for 69).

Umpires: J. H. King and A. Morton

NORTHAMPTONSHIRE v AUSTRALIANS   51 (78, 79)

Played at Northampton, Saturday, Monday, Tuesday, August 9, 11, 12 [1930]. Northamptonshire enjoyed the distinction of dismissing the Australians for the smallest score registered by the tourists during the tour. Still, the visitors drew the game in handsome style, leaving off 249 ahead with two wickets to fall. The county team occupied the wickets for the whole of Saturday ... Following upon a lot of rain on Sunday, the weather turned very bright. Jupp and Thomas bowled in deadly form, the former disposing of six batsmen for 32 runs. Bradman helped Woodfull to take the score from 15 to 51 but the last eight wickets fell for 42 runs. Made to follow on, the Australians, thanks to Woodfull and Jackson, cleared off 91 of their arrears before they lost a wicket. ...

Northamptonshire

C.N. Woolley, A.H. Bakewell, Mr A.P.R. Hawtin, J.E. Timms, *Mr V.W.C. Jupp, A.G. Liddell, A.L. Cox, A.D. Matthews, †B. Bellamy, Mr E.F. Towell and A.E. Thomas.

First innings: 249 (Bakewell 84, Timms 78; Hornibrook four for 45, Bradman none for 31).

Australians

*W.M. Woodfull b Jupp	15	–	c Bellamy b Towell	116
A. Jackson c and b Thomas	9	–	c and b Cox	52
D.G. Bradman b Jupp	22	–	c Hawtin b Cox	35
A. Fairfax b Jupp	1	–	c Bellamy b Timms	1
A.F. Kippax b Thomas	10	–	c Cox b Jupp	20
V.Y. Richardson c Bellamy b Thomas	7	–	c Jupp b Towell	116
E.L. a'Beckett c Bakewell b Matthews	13	–	c and b Matthews	22
A. Hurwood st Bellamy b Jupp	2	–	b Jupp	12
P.M. Hornibrook b Jupp	2	–	not out	16
T.W. Wall lbw b Jupp	3			
†C.W. Walker not out	0			
B 7, l-b 2	9		B 10, l-b 2, w 1, n-b 2	15
	93		(eight wkts)	**405**

Northamptonshire bowling: *First innings*—Thomas 29–14–29–3; Matthews 10–3–18–1; Jupp 23.4–10–32–6; Towell 3–0–5–0. *Second innings*—Thomas 25–12–32–0; Matthews 35.5–5–83–1; Jupp 21–5–47–2; Towell 24–4–84–2; Cox 28–2–87–2; Liddell 12–3–36–0; Timms 5–1–21–1.

Umpires: F. Chester and W.R. Parry.

ENGLAND v AUSTRALIA   52 (80)
(FIFTH TEST MATCH)   9 (15)

Played at Kennington Oval, Saturday, Monday, Tuesday, Wednesday, Thursday, Friday, August 16, 18, 19, 20, 21, 22 [1930]. Beating England in an innings with 39 runs to spare, Australia won the rubber and so regained possession of the Ashes they had lost four years previously on the same ground. Each side having proved successful once and the other two games being drawn, the concluding Test Match had to be played to a finish irrespective of the number of days involved. Including the Thursday when, owing to rain, not a ball could be bowled, the encounter was spread over six days – a longer time than had ever before been occupied by a Test Match in England.

Australia won the match fairly and squarely ... but just as rain had assisted England in the First Test Match at Nottingham, so it operated against them at The Oval. England had to play their second innings on a pitch so entirely suited to bowlers that in the circumstances they actually accomplished a good performance in scoring as many runs as they did on the last day. ... Admitting the weather bore hardly upon the losers, it is but proper to observe that England contributed to their undoing by faulty work in the field. To stress the mistakes of any particular individual is never a congenial task, but as a matter of history it must be set down that Duckworth, who, usually so dependable a wicket-keeper, had gone through the previous Australian tour in brilliant fashion, failed badly. At the very outset of the Australian innings he missed Woodfull, let off Ponsford twice before that batsman had made 50 and, on the Tuesday, failed to catch Bradman at the wicket. Between them these three Australian cricketers made 396 runs …

Once more Australia owed a great deal to Bradman, who followed up his previous batting successes at Nottingham, Lord's and Leeds with an innings of 232. As usual he scored well in front of the wicket but he obtained a large number of runs on the leg side, while from start to finish his defence was altogether remarkable. All the same he did not play in anything like the attractive style he had shown at Lord's; indeed, there were periods when he became monotonous. Scoring so heavily as he did, Bradman again overshadowed everyone else, but his task was made the easier by the good work accomplished, before he went in, by Ponsford and Woodfull, who once more wore the bowling down by their workmanlike and steady cricket. …

… Before Bradman reached the wicket there was a delay through defective light and a little while afterwards came a further break from the same cause. With the score up to 190, Woodfull was out … [and when] play ceased, Australia, with two men out for 215, were only 190 runs behind. In all, Bradman and Kippax added 73 for the third wicket. Then came the big stand of the innings, Bradman and Jackson not being separated until Wednesday at one o'clock, by which time they had put on 243 runs in four and a half hours. Jackson was nearly run out before he had scored and almost bowled when five, while Bradman, at 82, gave a chance at the wicket. Rain came on during lunch-time on the Tuesday, the score then standing at 371 for three wickets, and, play being resumed soon after three o'clock, a further break through rain and bad light just about four o'clock occurred with the score at 402. It looked as though there would be no more cricket that day but the players went out at twenty-five minutes past six and in the five minutes one more run was obtained. On the Wednesday morning the ball flew about a good deal, both batsmen frequently being hit on the body. The partnership might have ended at 458 had Leyland returned the ball to the right end, and on more than one occasion each player cocked the ball up dangerously but always, as it happened, just wide of the fieldsmen. Caught at length, at extra cover-point, Jackson played nothing like as well as those who saw him in Australia knew he could. For the most part he was very restrained and, except that it helped in a record Australia stand for the fourth wicket, his innings was hardly worthy of his reputation. Bradman all this time had gone steadily on but when joined by McCabe was overshadowed, the latter driving brilliantly. Another 64 runs were added and then Bradman, at 570, was caught by Duckworth standing back. In seven hours he made 232 out of 411 with sixteen 4's, ten 3's and twenty-eight 2's as his chief hits. …

England, 290 behind, went in again at a quarter to six. When Hobbs and Sutcliffe reached the wickets, the Australians gathered round Hobbs and gave three cheers as a tribute to the great batsman playing presumably his last innings for England. …

No play took place on the Thursday owing to rain. On Friday the sun shone and everyone realised that only a miracle could save England. … With [Leyland's] dismissal England's hope of saving the innings defeat disappeared. Hammond went on hitting but received no support. With the last man in Hammond was missed at long-off by Bradman, but three runs later he fell to a catch in the slips and at ten minutes to four the match was all over. …

Except towards the end of the first day, the Australian fielding in both innings was uncommonly good. Nobody did better than Bradman, who, whether at fine-leg or long-off, covered so much ground, picked up and returned so swiftly that many a possible four was turned into a single. …

In the course of the match, more than 110,000 people witnessed the cricket, the sum taken at the gates amounting to over £13,000. Very appropriately, the day on which Australia regained the Ashes with this victory coincided with the birthday of Woodfull, their captain, who was then 33.

England

J. B. Hobbs, H. Sutcliffe, W. Whysall, K. S. Duleepsinhji, W. R. Hammond, M. Leyland, *Mr R. E. S. Wyatt, M. W. Tate, H. Larwood, †G. Duckworth and Mr I. A. R. Peebles.

First innings: 405 (Hobbs 47, Sutcliffe 161, Duleepsinhji 50, Wyatt 64; Fairfax three for 52, Grimmett four for 135). *Second innings:* 251 (Sutcliffe 54, Duleepsinhji 46, Hammond 60; Hornibrook seven for 92).

Australia

*W. M. Woodfull c Duckworth b Peebles	54	†W. A. Oldfield c Larwood b Peebles	34
W. H. Ponsford b Peebles	110	C. V. Grimmett lbw b Peebles	6
D. G. Bradman c Duckworth b Larwood	232	T. W. Wall lbw b Peebles	0
A. F. Kippax c Wyatt b Peebles	28	P. M. Hornibrook c Duckworth b Tate	7
A. Jackson c Sutcliffe b Wyatt	73	B 22, l-b 18, n-b 4	44
S. McCabe c Duckworth b Hammond	54		**695**
A. Fairfax not out	53		

England bowling: Larwood 48–6–132–1; Tate 65.1–12–153–1; Peebles 71–8–204–6; Wyatt 14–1–58–1; Hammond 42–12–70–1; Leyland 16–7–34–0.

Umpires: J. Hardstaff and W. R. Parry

GLOUCESTERSHIRE v AUSTRALIANS 53 (81, 82)

Played at Bristol, Saturday, Monday, Tuesday, August 23, 25, 26 [1930]. There was a memorable finish to this match, the Australians, who had been set 118 to make to win, being all dismissed for 117 and the contest thus ending in a tie. Never before in England had a first-class match, in which an Australian team figured, terminated in this way. For a long time after the Australians entered upon their second innings the contest held out no promise of excitement. Indeed, of the 118 runs needed for victory no fewer than 59 – exactly half the number – were put on by Jackson and McCabe for the opening partnership. The pitch was obviously in a condition to assist the bowlers but to begin with Parker proved so erratic that the score reached 50 in forty minutes. Gradually, however, Parker not only found his length but a worn spot and thenceforward he was deadly in the extreme. ... [T]here were three men out for 67 at the luncheon interval.

... On play being resumed the game took a most dramatic turn. Six runs were added and then, with the total at 73, not only did Parker get Kippax leg before but Sinfield, picking up smartly and getting in a splendid return, threw out Ponsford from mid-on. Bradman still remained but neither he nor a'Beckett, against skilful bowling and most brilliant fielding, could get the ball away. Roused to tremendous excitement, the spectators cheered everything and their enthusiasm knew no bounds when at 81 Parker bowled Bradman. They had still further occasion for joy five runs later when a catch in the slips disposed of a'Beckett. [This left Australia needing 32 runs with three wickets in hand.] ...

Unhappily for the home side, there came just afterwards a blemish on what up to that point had been a superb display of fielding, Lyon, when Grimmett had made seven, getting his hand to a ball put up by that batsman but failing to effect the catch. ... Grimmett and Hurwood offered such a determined resistance to Parker and Goddard that they added 22 for the eighth wicket before Hurwood was leg before. Thus only 10 runs were wanted when Hornibrook joined Grimmett. The newcomer surviving two appeals for lbw, the score had been advanced to 115 – three to win – when Parker dismissed Grimmett, who had withstood the attack for an hour. Walker followed in and two singles brought the total to 117. With the scores level, there came three maidens in succession and then on a further appeal against Hornibrook being answered in the bowler's favour, the Australians were all out and the match ended in a tie. ...

On Monday [when Australia batted for the first time] the pitch, while still on the soft side, was, in the absence of sunshine, too slow to be really difficult. [Saturday's play had not begun until four o'clock because the ground was saturated.] Ponsford, second out at 78, batted in attractive fashion for an hour and a half but Bradman, although staying for an hour and three-quarters, never mastered the attack. Subsequent to lunch, seven wickets fell for 64 runs. ...

Gloucestershire

R. A. Sinfield, A. E. Dipper, W. R. Hammond, *Mr B. H. Lyon, †H. Smith, C. C. Dacre, Mr F. J. Seabrook, W. L. Neale, C. J. Barnett, C. Parker and T. W. Goddard.

First innings: 72 (Hurwood three for 13, Grimmett three for 28, Hornibrook four for 20). *Second innings:* 202 (Hammond 89; Hornibrook five for 49).

Australians

W. H. Ponsford b Sinfield	51	–	run out	0
A. Jackson b Goddard	8	–	lbw b Goddard	25
D. G. Bradman c Sinfield b Parker	42	–	b Parker	14
A. F. Kippax lbw b Sinfield	3	–	lbw b Parker	0
S. McCabe c Smith b Parker	5	–	b Parker	34
*V. Y. Richardson lbw b Goddard	12	–	st Smith b Parker	3
E. L. a'Beckett c Sinfield b Goddard	1	–	c Lyon b Parker	2
A. Hurwood b Goddard	0	–	lbw b Parker	14
C. V. Grimmett not out	7	–	c Seabrook b Parker	12
P. M. Hornibrook b Goddard	9	–	lbw b Goddard	4
†C. W. Walker c Seabrook b Parker	7	–	not out	0
B 5, l-b 7	12		B 2, l-b 7	9
	157			**117**

Gloucestershire bowling: *First innings*—Sinfield 14–5–18–2; Barnett 4–3–3–0; Goddard 26–7–52–5; Parker 30.5–9–72–3. *Second innings*—Goddard 34.1–10–54–2; Parker 35–14–54–7.

Umpires: W. A. Buswell and W. Huddleston

KENT v AUSTRALIANS   54 (83, 84)

Played at Canterbury, Wednesday, Thursday, Friday, August 27, 28, 29 [1930]. Yet another great display of batting on the part of Bradman was the outstanding feature of this drawn match, the famous young Australian in the second innings withstanding the Kent bowling for four hours and three-quarters and being still unbeaten with 205 runs to his credit when Woodfull made a belated declaration. In putting together his fifth score of more than 200 [sixth including his triple-century in the Third Test] Bradman did not give a single chance. ... [In Kent's first innings] Todd carried restraint to extreme limits, being at the wickets seventy-five minutes before he registered his second run and in all batting nearly three hours and a half for 42.

Australians

*W. M. Woodfull run out	16	–	lbw b Freeman	45
W. H. Ponsford c Ashdown b Freeman	21	–	b Ashdown	11
D. G. Bradman lbw b Freeman	18	–	not out	205
A. Jackson lbw b Freeman	11	–	not out	50
V. Y. Richardson c Ames b Ashdown	45			
A. Fairfax b Freeman	4			
E. L. a'Beckett run out	4			
C. V. Grimmett c Chapman b Ashdown	0			
A. Hurwood c Ames b Hardinge	45	–	run out	
T. W. Wall not out	12			
†C. W. Walker lbw b Freeman	1			
B 1, l-b 1, n-b 2	4		B 7, l-b 2	9
	181		(three wkts dec)	**320**

Kent bowling: *First innings*—Wright 7–2–18–0; Ashdown 18–4–38–2; Freeman 39.2–8–78–5; Hardinge 21–10–43–1. *Second innings*—Wright 16–4–40–0; Ashdown 21–4–68–1; Freeman 33–12–68–1; Hardinge 31–6–86–0; Woolley 16–7–21–0; Knott 2–0–28–0.

Kent

H. T. W. Hardinge, Mr J. L. Bryan, F. E. Woolley, †L. Ames, L. Todd, W. Ashdown, Mr A. P. F. Chapman, Mr C. H. Knott, *Mr G. B. Legge, C. Wright and A. P. Freeman.

First innings: 227 (Hardinge 39, Bryan 31, Todd 42 not out, Ashdown 48; Wall five for 60, Grimmett four for 80). *Second innings:* Two for 83 (Woolley 60 not out).

Umpires: J. Hardstaff and H. Young

AN ENGLAND XI v AUSTRALIANS 55 (85)

Played at Folkestone, Wednesday, Thursday, Friday, September 3, 4, 5 [1930]. Batting in strangely restrained fashion under conditions quite favourable for run-getting, the English team, although Grimmett owing to an injury could bowl very little, scored only 249 for five on the opening day and thenceforward a draw was always practically certain. ... Woodfull and Ponsford gave the Australians a capital start, staying together for an hour and three-quarters and raising the score to 117. ... Bradman and Jackson put on 103 in seventy minutes. ...

An England XI

Mr R. E. S. Wyatt, J. W. Hearne, W. R. Hammond, Jas. Langridge, †L. Ames, *Mr A. P. F. Chapman, Mr R. C. Robertson-Glasgow, M. W. Tate, Hon. F. S. G. Calthorpe, Mr M. J. C. Allom and A. P. Freeman.

First innings: Eight for 403 dec (Wyatt 51, Hearne 33, Hammond 54, Ames 121, Chapman 40, Tate 50; Wall three for 104, a'Beckett three for 81, Bradman none for 7). *Second innings:* One for 46.

Australians

*W. M. Woodfull run out	34	†W. A. Oldfield lbw b Freeman	10
W. H. Ponsford c Calthorpe b Allom	76	C. V. Grimmett c Langridge b Freeman	1
D. G. Bradman lbw b Allom	63	P. M. Hornibrook c Hearne b Freeman	43
A. F. Kippax lbw b Allom	0	T. W. Wall not out	40
A. Jackson b Langridge	78	B 9, l-b 11	20
S. McCabe b Allom	14		**432**
E. L. a'Beckett c Hammond b Freeman	53		

An England XI bowling: Tate 14–5–31–0; Allom 32–5–94–4; Freeman 41.5–3–131–4; Robertson-Glasgow 11–2–12–0; Langridge 16–1–54–1; Hammond 5–1–10–0; Wyatt 5–0–32–0; Calthorpe 5–2–12–0; Chapman 1–0–5–0; Hearne 8–2–31–0.

Umpires: F. Chester and A. E. Street

CLUB CRICKET CONFERENCE v AUSTRALIANS

Played at Lord's, Saturday, Monday, September 6, 8 [1930]. The two days set apart for the decision of this match proved sufficient for that purpose, the Australians winning by an innings and 41 runs. ... For the first and only time during the tour the wider and higher wicket was used [see page 182]. Bradman, despite some capital fast bowling by Smith and Brindley, batted so brilliantly that he scored 70 in seventy-five minutes and incidentally completed his 3,000 runs. ...

Australians

W. H. Ponsford c Summers b Brindley	0	†W. A. Oldfield b Smith	0
A. Fairfax b Brindley	25	A. Hurwood b Smith	0
D. G. Bradman c Whitehead b Nazeer Ali	70	P. M. Hornibrook lbw b Brindley	1
A. F. Kippax b Smith	63	C. W. Walker not out	7
S. McCabe b Brindley	0	B 18, l-b 11	29
E. L. a'Beckett b Smith	14		**278**
*W. M. Woodfull c Summers b Brindley	69		

Club Cricket Conference bowling: Smith 23–3–70–4; Brindley 30.1–4–71–5; Nazeer Ali 25–5–52–1; Taylor 14–1–45–0; Jarvis 4–0–11–0.

Club Cricket Conference

Mr T. G. Grinter, Mr L. W. Newman, Mr T. N. Pearce, Mr G. F. Summers, Mr W. T. Brindley, Mr S. Nazeer Ali, Mr H. Taylor, *Mr F. E. Whitehead, Mr V. E. Jarvis, Mr H. T. O. Smith and †Mr H. E. L. Piercy.

First innings: 133 (Summers 53, Brindley 34; Fairfax four for 41, Hurwood five for 14). *Second innings:* 104 (Pearce 30; a'Beckett three for 1, Hornibrook four for 37).

Umpires: Marshall and Dray

MR H. D. G. LEVESON GOWER'S XI v AUSTRALIANS   56 (86)

Played at Scarborough, Wednesday, Thursday, Friday, September 10, 11, 12 [1930]. In the concluding fixture of the tour rain caused a considerable loss of play and consequently there existed no chance of bringing the game to a definite issue. Richardson winning the toss sent the Englishmen in to bat ... Next day, when cricket proved impossible until a quarter to three, the Australians lost two wickets for 53 but Bradman and Kippax added 110 before bad light brought play to a close. Bradman should have been caught at mid-off first ball and just after reaching 60 was twice missed, all three chances being off Rhodes. Next day he ought, when 74, to have been easily run out. In the end he was bowled off his pads. The cricket when the Englishmen entered upon their second innings was taken in a very light-hearted spirit. ... Despite the weather the match attracted a large crowd each day.

Mr H. D. G. Leveson Gower's XI

J. B. Hobbs, H. Sutcliffe, K. S. Duleepsinhji, A. Sandham, M. Leyland, *Mr R. E. S. Wyatt, M. W. Tate, H. Larwood, W. Rhodes, †G. Duckworth and C. Parker.

First innings: Nine for 218 dec (Sutcliffe 45, Sandham 59; Hornibrook five for 69). *Second innings:* 247 (Hobbs 59, Duleepsinhji 41, Leyland 50; Hornibrook three for 100, Bradman three for 52).

Australians

A. Jackson b Rhodes	24	C. V. Grimmett c Wyatt b Rhodes	3
A. Fairfax st Duckworth b Rhodes	8	P. M. Hornibrook lbw b Parker	0
D. G. Bradman b Parker	96	T. W. Wall c Wyatt b Rhodes	6
A. F. Kippax b Larwood	59	†W. A. Oldfield absent hurt	0
S. McCabe c Larwood b Parker	24	B 6, l-b 3	9
*V. Y. Richardson not out	8		**238**
A. Hurwood b Rhodes	1		

Mr Leveson Gower's XI bowling: Larwood 14–4–34–1; Tate 10–3–14–0; Parker 31–7–81–3; Rhodes 30.5–5–95–5; Wyatt 2–0–5–0.

Umpires: D. Denton and A. Morton

THE DON

Bradman has attracted two new biographies, neither of which tells us much that is new, though both are thorough and thoughtful. *The Don*, by Roland Perry, draws on recent interviews with Bradman himself, but these are unrevealing; Perry has coaxed no revision or indiscretion from The Don in old age, though he himself goes over the old ground with enthusiasm. He is good on Bradman's unquenchable sense of competition and quotes from the diary in which Bradman recorded his tennis victories on the ship to England in 1930 ('beat Kippax 6–0 in the semi-final'). In 1939, when Bradman was working as a stockbroker, he played a bit of squash to keep fit, and reached the final of the South Australian championship, where he met a Davis Cup tennis player. He lost the first two games and was 1–5 down in the third, but he was beginning to get the hang of it. He ground his opponent down to win 10–8 in the fifth. The glory of Perry's biography is in the photographs. The picture of Bradman leaving the SCG in twilight, bat raised, after his last innings there in 1949 (courtesy of the Sydney *Sun*) and the one of him going out to bat at Leeds in 1938, walking modestly down a gangway of rapt, adoring faces (this one, alas, uncredited), are heart-stopping.

From 'Cricket Books, 1996', by Sebastian Faulks

1930-31

Don and Jessie Bradman at Kiama, NSW, April 1932. The couple were driving to Melbourne at the commencement of their honeymoon.

1930-31

The larger wicket* was used in all Sheffield Shield games during the 1930-31 season, which proved of particular interest by reason of the close rivalry between Victoria (holders) and New South Wales. In the end Victoria, for the thirteenth time, won the trophy, but New South Wales finished up no more than one point behind. ... Bradman, playing six innings for New South Wales [in the Sheffield Shield], scored 695 runs and returned an average of 115. In the game with South Australia at Adelaide, he and Jackson, by putting on 334 for the second wicket, set up a new record for Shield cricket. ...

Attendances at the games during the season were greatly affected by the bad weather often experienced. ... Sheffield Shield matches in 1930-31, however, were limited to four days, with no option of continuing play on the fifth day, and this arrangement, of course, caused some decline in aggregate attendances at some matches. ...

From 'Cricket in Australia: The Inter-State Matches'

*In the first change to the size of the wicket for 108 years, the height (i.e., stumps and bails) was increased by 1½ inches (3.81 cm) to 28½ inches (72.39 cm) and the width by 1 inch (2.54 cm) to 9 inches (22.86 cm). These have remained the dimensions of the wicket.

NEW SOUTH WALES v SOUTH AUSTRALIA   57 (87, 88)

Played at Sydney, November 7, 8, 10, 11 [1930]. The absence of Grimmett and Wall greatly weakened the bowling of South Australia, and although on the last day Nitschke ... played a strong defensive innings, New South Wales, with plenty of time to spare, won by 213 runs. Bradman, Fairfax and Hooker between them scored all but 51 of the New South Wales first innings total and Hooker, when South Australia went in, bowled with much skill, taking five wickets for 28. Left with a lead of 104, New South Wales, thanks to a hundred apiece from Bradman and Kippax, placed themselves in a very strong position, finishing up on the second day 421 ahead with half their wickets left. South Australia ultimately were set the tremendous task of scoring 501 to win. ...

New South Wales

C. Andrews b Deverson	6	–	c Parry b Carlton	0
O. W. Bill c Parry b Carlton	2	–	run out	5
D. G. Bradman c Pritchard b Deverson	61	–	c Waite b Deverson	121
*A. F. Kippax lbw b Tobin	19	–	b Deverson	104
A. Allsopp b Tobin	9	–	b Carlton	93
A. G. Fairfax b Carlton	62	–	b Deverson	6
†H. L. Davidson c Walsh b Deverson	2	–	c Tobin b Deverson	19
H. Hooker b Deverson	54	–	absent hurt	0
H. C. Chilvers b Carlton	3	–	c Lonergan b Lee	29
W. A. Hunt st Parry b Carlton	2	–	not out	7
G. L. Stewart not out	4	–	run out	2
W 1, n-b 3	4		B 4, l-b 1, w 1, n-b 4	10
	228			**396**

South Australia bowling: *First innings*—Deverson 15–1–60–4; Carlton 9.1–1–28–4; Lee 5–0–21–0; Tobin 9–0–75–2; Waite 9–0–40–0. *Second innings*—Deverson 19–1–86–4; Carlton 15.3–1–61–2; Lee 15–0–107–1; Tobin 3–0–25–0; Waite 16–1–107–0.

South Australia

G.W. Harris, H.C. Nitschke, *D.E. Pritchard, A.R. Lonergan, B.J. Tobin, L.S. Walsh, P.K. Lee, M.G. Waite, †C.N. Parry, T.A. Carlton and C.S. Deverson.

First innings: 124 (Nitschke 31, Lee 40; Stewart three for 25, Hooker five for 28). *Second innings:* 287 (Nitschke 141, Pritchard 30, Lee 36; Fairfax four for 54, Hunt three for 37, Bradman none for 41).

Umpires: W.H. Bayfield and M. Carney

AUSTRALIA v REST OF AUSTRALIA 58 (89, 90)

Played at Melbourne, November 14, 15, 17, 18 [1930]. A game arranged as a Testimonial to J. Ryder, Australia's former captain, also served to welcome the return of the victorious seventeenth Australian team in England. Unfortunately it was much interfered with by bad weather, the third day being entirely blank. On the Saturday, however, over 44,000 people attended and altogether Ryder received about £3,000. ... Bradman, Kippax and Woodfull batted skilfully, if with some lack of freedom, for Australia ... Set to get 118 in an hour and a half, Australia made a determined effort to win against the clock but lost half their wickets and failed by 22 runs.

Rest of Australia

G.W. Harris, H.L. Hendry, K.E. Rigg, *J. Ryder, A. Allsopp, T.J.E. Andrews, †J.L. Ellis, D.D. Blackie, H. Alexander, A.A. Mailey and H. Ironmonger.

First innings: 293 (Harris 108, Hendry 45, Ryder 38; Grimmett five for 89). *Second innings:* Three for 191 dec (Rigg 74, Ryder 65 not out; Bradman none for 27).

Australia

W. H. Ponsford lbw b Alexander	14	–	lbw b Ironmonger		0
A. A. Jackson c Ellis b Alexander	4	–	b Alexander		5
D. G. Bradman b Mailey	73	–	c and b Mailey		29
A. F. Kippax lbw b Blackie	70	–	b Blackie		17
S. J. McCabe c Alexander b Ironmonger	27	–	b Blackie		20
*W. M. Woodfull b Ironmonger	53	–	not out		13
A. G. Fairfax c Alexander b Ironmonger	39				
E. L. a'Beckett c Andrews b Mailey	30				
†W. A. Oldfield run out	18				
C. V. Grimmett b Mailey	28				
T. W. Wall not out	2				
B 4, l-b 5	9		B 8, l-b 2, w 1, n-b 1		12
	367		(five wkts)		**96**

Rest of Australia bowling: *First innings*—Alexander 15–1–64–2; Hendry 7–0–27–0; Blackie 17–2–45–1; Ironmonger 28–3–76–3; Mailey 23.3–2–126–3; Ryder 2–0–11–0; Andrews 2–0–9–0. *Second innings*—Alexander 5–1–24–1; Blackie 5.5–0–15–2; Ironmonger 6–0–17–1; Mailey 4–0–28–1.

Umpires: A. N. Barlow and D. Elder

WEST INDIES v NEW SOUTH WALES   59 (91, 92)

Played at Sydney, November 21, 22, 24, 25 [1930]. Defeat by four wickets from a powerful New South Wales XI was by no means an unsatisfactory start for the West Indies [in their first-ever first-class match in Australia. When in their second innings New South Wales were chasing 224 to win] the total reached 97 before a wicket fell, but Headley caught Bradman brilliantly in the long field and half the side were out for 131. ... On the second day nearly 20,000 people watched the cricket, and for the first two days the gate receipts amounted to £2,900.

West Indies

F. R. Martin, C. A. Roach, E. L. Bartlett, G. Headley, L. S. Birkett, *G. C. Grant, L. N. Constantine, G. N. Francis, †I. Barrow, E. St Hill and O. C. Scott.

First innings: 188 (Roach 43, Birkett 31, Grant 30; Chilvers four for 84, Fairfax three for 42, McCabe three for 23). *Second innings:* 241 (Headley 82, Grant 44, Constantine 59; Chilvers five for 73).

New South Wales

A. G. Fairfax b Constantine	9	–	not out		32
O. W. Bill c Constantine b St Hill	13	–	lbw b Martin		34
D. G. Bradman c Barrow b Francis	73	–	c Headley b Martin		22
*A. F. Kippax b Constantine	6				
S. J. McCabe b Constantine	18	–	not out		37
A. A. Jackson lbw b Constantine	13	–	b Martin		62
A. Allsopp run out	32	–	b Constantine		3
†W. A. Oldfield st Barrow b Scott	21	–	lbw b Constantine		0
W. A. Hunt b Francis	5				
H. C. Chilvers b Francis	8				
G. L. Stewart not out	1	–	c Roach b St Hill		20
L-b 1, n-b 6	7		B 3, l-b 4, n-b 7		14
	206		(six wkts)		**224**

West Indies bowling: *First innings*—Constantine 11–1–43–4; Francis 11–2–38–3; St Hill 10–2–46–1; Martin 3–0–22–0; Scott 8–0–50–1. *Second innings*—Constantine 11.1–2–53–2; Francis 8–0–37–0; St Hill 14–1–57–1; Martin 8–0–35–3; Scott 4–0–28–0.

Umpires: G. Borwick and W.G. French

AUSTRALIA v WEST INDIES   60 (93)
(FIRST TEST MATCH)   10 (16)

Played at Adelaide, December 12, 13, 15, 16 [1930]. Australia, with Hurwood for Hornibrook the only change from the eleven that beat England at The Oval during the previous [northern] summer, gained a decisive victory by ten wickets. Up to the point that Australia had lost their first three batsmen for 64, West Indies made a capital fight, but Kippax and McCabe added 182 by admirable cricket. Scott on the third morning took the last four wickets without conceding a run but West Indies were outplayed for the rest of the match. …

West Indies

C.A. Roach, L.S. Birkett, G. Headley, F.R. Martin, L.N. Constantine, *G.C. Grant, E.L. Bartlett, †I. Barrow, G.N. Francis, O.C. Scott and H.C. Griffith.

First innings: 296 (Roach 56, Martin 39, Grant 53 not out, Bartlett 84; Grimmett seven for 87, Hurwood three for 55, Bradman none for 7). *Second innings:* 249 (Birkett 64, Grant 71 not out; Grimmett four for 96, Hurwood four for 86, Bradman one for 8).

Australia

W. H. Ponsford c Birkett b Francis	24	–	not out	92
A. A. Jackson c Barrow b Francis	31	–	not out	70
D. G. Bradman c Grant b Griffith	4			
A. F. Kippax c Barrow b Griffith	146			
S. J. McCabe c and b Constantine	90			
*W. M. Woodfull run out	6			
A. G. Fairfax not out	41			
†W. A. Oldfield c Francis b Scott	15			
C. V. Grimmett c Barrow b Scott	0			
A. Hurwood c Martin b Scott	0			
T. W. Wall lbw b Scott	0			
B 2, l-b 10, n-b 7	19		B 8, w 1, n-b 1	10
	376		(no wkt)	**172**

West Indies bowling: *First innings*—Francis 18–7–43–2; Constantine 22–0–89–1; Griffith 28–4–69–2; Martin 29–3–73–0; Scott 20.5–2–83–4. *Second innings*—Francis 10–1–30–0; Constantine 9.3–3–27–0; Griffith 10–1–20–0; Martin 11–0–28–0; Scott 13–0–55–0; Birkett 2–0–2–0.

Umpires: G. A. Hele and A.G. Jenkins

SOUTH AUSTRALIA v NEW SOUTH WALES   61 (94)

Played at Adelaide, December 18, 19, 20, 22 [1930]. Brilliant batting by Bradman and Jackson largely determined the result of this return fixture, New South Wales winning by an innings and 134 runs. The South Australian bowlers, including Grimmett, went through a heart-breaking experience on the first day when Bradman hit up 258 in four hours and three-quarters and with Jackson, who played his usual stylish game, shared in a second-wicket stand which, extending over three hours and three-quarters, produced 334 runs. This was a record for the competition. At first uncomfortable against Grimmett, Bradman afterwards was completely master of the situation and hit so freely that 148 of his runs came in 4's. Next day the play went overwhelmingly in favour of bowlers. ...

New South Wales

J. H. Fingleton st Walker b Grimmett	6	†H. S. Love lbw b Grimmett	4
A. A. Jackson c Richardson b Waite	166	H. Hooker b Carlton	45
D. G. Bradman b Richardson	258	W. A. Hunt not out	15
*A. F. Kippax b Grimmett	42	H. C. Chilvers run out	23
S. J. McCabe lbw b Carlton	7	B 4, l-b 2	6
A. G. Fairfax b Grimmett	38		**610**
O. W. Bill lbw b Grimmett	0		

South Australia bowling: Wall 23–0–89–0; Carlton 20.2–0–99–2; Lee 38–4–144–0; Grimmett 48–5–180–5; Waite 7–0–54–1; Richardson 8–0–38–1.

South Australia

G. W. Harris, H. C. Nitschke, D. E. Pritchard, *V. Y. Richardson, A. Hack, P. K. Lee, M. G. Waite, T. A. Carlton, C. V. Grimmett, T. W. Wall and †C. W. Walker.

First innings: 166 (Nitschke 69; Hunt five for 36, Chilvers five for 68). *Second innings:* 310 (Nitschke 102, Wall 45 not out; Hunt four for 105, Bradman three for 54).

Umpires: G. A. Hele and A. G. Jenkins

VICTORIA v NEW SOUTH WALES   62 (95)

Played at Melbourne, December 24, 26, 27, 29 [1930]. Scoring 30 for the loss of three wickets on the opening day, Victoria, owing to rain, were unable to continue their batting until the last morning and not even a first innings decision could be reached. ...

Victoria

*W. M. Woodfull, W. H. Ponsford, H. L. Hendry, J. Ryder, K. E. Rigg, E. L. a'Beckett, L. Darling, †B. A. Barnett, D. D. Blackie, H. Alexander and H. Ironmonger.

First innings: 185 (Ponsford 109 not out; Fairfax four for 41).

New South Wales

J. H. Fingleton run out	9	A. G. Fairfax st Barnett b Ironmonger	3
A. A. Jackson not out	52	†W. A. Oldfield c Rigg b Ironmonger	8
D. G. Bradman c Hendry b a'Beckett	2	H. Hooker not out	2
S. J. McCabe b Blackie	10	L-b 3, n-b 4	7
*A. F. Kippax hit wkt b Blackie	4	(six wkts)	**97**

H. C. Chilvers, W. A. Hunt and G. L. Stewart did not bat.

Victoria bowling: Alexander 6–1–21–0; a'Beckett 10–2–26–1; Ironmonger 15–5–26–2; Blackie 7–2–16–2; Darling 1–0–1–0.

Umpires: A. N. Barlow and J. Richards

AUSTRALIA v WEST INDIES   63 (96)
(SECOND TEST MATCH)   11 (17)

Played at Sydney, January 1, 2, 3, 5 [1931]. Unfortunately for West Indies, rain that prevented any play on the second day completely altered the conditions which had obtained at the start and Australia won very easily by an innings and 172 runs. To add to their bad luck, West Indies had to bat a man short, Bartlett in catching Kippax from a powerful hit at mid-on having a finger crushed against his boot and being unable to take any further part in the match. Ponsford playing in his most resolute and skilful style, Australia scored 323 for four wickets on a perfect Sydney pitch, but after the rain the character of the cricket changed so completely that on the third day twenty wickets fell for 220 runs. ...

Australia

W. H. Ponsford b Scott	183	†W. A. Oldfield run out		0
A. A. Jackson c Francis b Griffith	8	C. V. Grimmett b Scott		12
D. G. Bradman c Barrow b Francis	25	A. Hurwood c Martin b Scott		5
A. F. Kippax c Bartlett b Griffith	10	H. Ironmonger not out		3
S. J. McCabe lbw b Scott	31	B 6, l-b 5, w 5, n-b 3		19
*W. M. Woodfull c Barrow b Constantine	58			**369**
A. G. Fairfax c Constantine b Francis	15			

West Indies bowling: Griffith 28–4–57–2; Constantine 18–2–56–1; Francis 27–3–70–2; Scott 15.4–0–66–4; Martin 18–1–60–0; Birkett 10–1–41–0.

West Indies

C. A. Roach, L. S. Birkett, G. Headley, F. R. Martin, L. N. Constantine, *G. C. Grant, G. N. Francis, †I. Barrow, H. C. Griffith, O. C. Scott and E. L. Bartlett.
    First innings: 107 (Fairfax three for 19, Grimmett four for 54). *Second innings:* 90 (Hurwood four for 22, Ironmonger three for 13).

Umpires: G. Borwick and W. G. French

AUSTRALIA v WEST INDIES   64 (97)
(THIRD TEST MATCH)   12 (18)

Played at [Exhibition Ground] Brisbane, January 16, 17, 19, 20 [1931]. Early on the fourth morning, Australia were successful by an innings and 217 runs, so winning the rubber with three consecutive victories. ... West Indies had an early encouragement in the fall of Jackson without scoring, but stands of 229 and 193 followed and, naturally, Australia never lost their hold on the game. Apart from a chance just before getting out, Ponsford batted faultlessly but Kippax was unsteady and Bradman, when four, was missed in the slips. Apart from this chance Bradman, in putting together the highest innings played for Australia in any Test Match in that country, showed that exceptional combination of skill and judgment that has produced for him so many triumphs. Next morning, on a pitch drying under the influence of strong sunshine, Bradman did not add to his overnight score. Batting for five hours, he hit twenty-four 4's. ...

Australia

W. H. Ponsford c Birkett b Francis	109	R. K. Oxenham lbw b Griffith		48
A. A. Jackson lbw b Francis	0	C. V. Grimmett c Constantine b Francis		4
D. G. Bradman c Grant b Constantine	223	H. Ironmonger c Roach b Griffith		2
A. F. Kippax b Birkett	84	†W. A. Oldfield not out		38
S. J. McCabe c Constantine b Griffith	17	B 2, l-b 7, n-b 7		16
*W. M. Woodfull c Barrow b Griffith	8			**558**
A. G. Fairfax c Sealy b Scott	9			

West Indies bowling: Francis 26–4–76–3; Griffith 33–4–133–4; Scott 24–0–125–1; Constantine 26–2–74–1; Martin 27–3–85–0; Sealy 3–0–32–0; Birkett 7–0–16–1; Grant 1–0–1–0.

West Indies

C.A. Roach, F.R. Martin, G. Headley, J.E.D. Sealy, *G.C. Grant, L.N. Constantine, L.S. Birkett, †I. Barrow, O.C. Scott, G.N. Francis and H.G. Griffith.

First innings: 193 (Headley 102 not out; Oxenham four for 39, Grimmett four for 95). *Second innings:* 148 (Grimmett five for 49).

Umpires: J.P. Orr and A.E. Wyeth

NEW SOUTH WALES v VICTORIA   65 (98, 99)

Played at Sydney, January 24, 26, 27, 28 [1931]. Victoria took first innings points from a drawn game marked by several good individual performances. Fairfax, batting doggedly for two hours, alone met Victoria's attack with resolution on the first day. ... Bradman, however, came out in brilliant form when New South Wales batted again. He played his third innings of over 200 during the season and with Bill added 234 in two hours and a quarter for the fifth wicket. Declaring, New South Wales left Victoria ten minutes under five hours in which to score 296 to win. Defensive batting was general. Rigg stayed over four hours for 98.

New South Wales

A.G. Fairfax c a'Beckett b Blackie	46	–	c O'Brien b Blackie	12
J.H. Fingleton b Alexander	6	–	st Barnett b Blackie	4
D.G. Bradman c Barnett b Alexander	33	–	c Rigg b Ironmonger	220
*A.F. Kippax b Alexander	6	–	c and b Blackie	26
S.J. McCabe c Barnett b Ironmonger	29	–	b Alexander	20
A.E. Marks b Blackie	9	–	b Ironmonger	9
O.W. Bill c a'Beckett b Blackie	39	–	b Blackie	100
†W.A. Oldfield c Barnett b a'Beckett	9	–	c Darling b Ironmonger	1
H. Hooker c Barnett b a'Beckett	0	–	not out	0
W.A. Hunt st Barnett b Blackie	15	–	c Rigg b Blackie	16
H.C. Chilvers not out	1			
B 1, l-b 1, w 1	3		B 3, l-b 4, w 2	9
	196		(nine wkts dec)	**417**

Victoria bowling: *First innings*—Alexander 13–0–43–3; a'Beckett 14–2–41–2; Ironmonger 16–5–56–1; Hendry 2–0–8–0; Blackie 12.3–0–45–4. *Second innings*—Alexander 15–1–89–1; a'Beckett 13–0–58–0; Ironmonger 22.4–0–91–3; Hendry 3–0–20–0; Blackie 23–2–101–5; Ryder 4–0–39–0; Darling 2–0–10–0.

Victoria

H.L. Hendry, L.P. O'Brien, K.E. Rigg, *J. Ryder, H.H. Oakley, L. Darling, E.L. a'Beckett, D.D. Blackie, †B.A. Barnett, H. Alexander and H. Ironmonger.

First innings: 318 (Hendry 39, O'Brien 119, Ryder 31; McCabe four for 46, Bradman none for 31). *Second innings:* Six for 202 (Rigg 98, Ryder 36; Hunt three for 38, Bradman none for 16).

Umpires: H. Armstrong and W.G. French

AUSTRALIA v WEST INDIES
(FOURTH TEST MATCH)
66 (100)
13 (19)

Played at Melbourne, February 13, 14 [1931]. Beaten in two days by an innings and 122 runs in the Fourth Test Match, West Indies gave their most disappointing batting display of the whole tour. On a pitch that seemed in perfectly good order they made a fair start, but Ironmonger brought about an astonishing collapse and in the second innings also bowled with considerable success. Altogether Ironmonger took eleven wickets for 79 and fairly shared with Bradman the chief honours of Australia's easy victory. Thanks to Woodfull and Bradman, Australia led by 98 at the end of the first day for the loss of Ponsford – dismissed at 50. Following upon rain in the night, Australia continued batting until three o'clock, when the closure was applied with eight wickets down for 328. Woodfull lost his wicket over an ill-judged run when the second partnership had realised 212, but Bradman – 92 overnight – went on batting brilliantly. Altogether at the wickets for four hours and three-quarters, Bradman hit fifteen 4's. West Indies ... never looked like taking the match into the third day.

West Indies

C. A. Roach, F. R. Martin, L. S. Birkett, G. Headley, E. L. Bartlett, *G. C. Grant, †I. Barrow, L. N. Constantine, O. C. Scott, H. C. Griffith and G. N. Francis.

First innings: 99 (Headley 33; Ironmonger seven for 23). *Second innings:* 107 (Fairfax four for 31, Ironmonger four for 56).

Australia

*W. M. Woodfull run out	83	A. G. Fairfax c Birkett b Martin	16
W. H. Ponsford st Barrow b Constantine	24	R. K. Oxenham c Constantine b Griffith	0
D. G. Bradman c Roach b Martin	152	†W. A. Oldfield not out	1
A. A. Jackson c Birkett b Constantine	15	B 7, l-b 3, n-b 1	11
S. J. McCabe run out	2	(eight wkts dec)	**328**
A. F. Kippax b Martin	24		

H. Ironmonger and C. V. Grimmett did not bat.

West Indies bowling: Francis 13–0–51–0; Griffith 8–1–33–1; Scott 11–0–47–0; Constantine 25–4–83–2; Martin 30.2–3–91–3; Birkett 3–0–12–0.

Umpires: A. N. Barlow and J. Richards

WEST INDIES v NEW SOUTH WALES
67 (101, 102)

Played at Sydney, February 21, 23, 24, 25 [1931]. Although New South Wales were much below full strength, West Indies in winning by 86 runs accomplished an admirable performance. Consistent batting followed by very good work in the field earned a first innings lead of 149 ... Further rapid scoring enabled Grant to declare with nine men out and there remained scarcely time for New South Wales to get 553 runs required for victory. Still, Kippax and McCabe batted so well that at tea-time the home team had made 373 with only four men out, but a collapse ensued. ...

West Indies

F. R. Martin, C. A. Roach, G. Headley, *G. C. Grant, J. E. D. Sealy, L. N. Constantine, O. S. Wight, †I. Barrow, O. C. Scott, G. N. Francis and H. C. Griffith.

First innings: 339 (Roach 55, Headley 70, Grant 36, Sealy 58, Constantine 41; Chilvers three for 56). *Second innings:* Nine for 403 dec (Martin 56, Sealy 92, Constantine 93, Barrow 45, Scott 67 not out; Chilvers three for 53).

New South Wales

†H. L. Davidson b Constantine	16	–	b Francis	32
O. W. Bill run out	41	–	lbw b Francis	11
D. G. Bradman b Constantine	10	–	lbw b Griffith	73
*A. F. Kippax lbw b Griffith	32	–	c Sealy b Griffith	141
S. J. McCabe b Constantine	26	–	c Barrow b Martin	100
A. Bennett b Griffith	0	–	c Barrow b Scott	16
W. A. Hunt b Constantine	2	–	c Sealy b Scott	6
H. Theak b Constantine	0	–	b Francis	2
J. H. Fingleton not out	32	–	lbw b Constantine	26
H. C. Chilvers c Headley b Scott	6	–	not out	43
L. McGuirk b Constantine	15	–	b Francis	2
B 6, l-b 3, n-b 1	10		B 9, l-b 5	14
	190			**466**

West Indies bowling: *First innings*—Constantine 10.3–0–45–6; Francis 8–0–25–0; Griffith 9–2–36–2; Scott 19–0–74–1. *Second innings*—Constantine 8–0–39–1; Francis 20.6–4–76–4; Griffith 19–0–115–2; Scott 19–0–107–2; Martin 19–2–68–1; Sealy 11–0–47–0.

Umpires: A. C. Jones and E. J. Shaw

AUSTRALIA v WEST INDIES 68 (103, 104)
(FIFTH TEST MATCH) 14 (20, 21)

Played at Sydney, February 27, 28, March 2, 3, 4 [1931]. Favoured by the conditions – rain over the weekend and subsequently [the] state of the pitch – West Indies gained a notable triumph by 30 runs. Apart from the result, the match was memorable for the fact that Grant twice applied the closure. Each time the wet wicket, becoming difficult under a hot sun, influenced the West Indies captain to adopt this course and on both occasions his judgment proved correct. Headley followed his success at Brisbane by scoring his second Test Match century. Martin, enjoying that distinction for the first time, carried out his bat when Grant declared on the second day. ... With the pitch again affected by sunshine after continuous rain, which prevented any cricket on Tuesday, Grant took the risk of leaving Australia to get 247 runs in unlimited time, it having been arranged to play the match to a finish. Half the wickets falling for 74 runs before lunch, the match seemed as good as over, but McCabe hit finely while Fairfax showed admirable defence until a catch by Grant broke up the partnership. ...

[Bradman's duck in the second innings was his first in Test cricket.]

West Indies

F. R. Martin, C. A. Roach, G. Headley, *G. C. Grant, J. E. D. Sealy, L. N. Constantine, E. L. Bartlett, †I. Barrow, O. C. Scott, G. N. Francis and H. C. Griffith.

First innings: Six for 350 dec (Martin 123 not out, Roach 31, Headley 105, Grant 62; Grimmett three for 100). *Second innings:* Five for 124 dec (Roach 34, Headley 30).

Australia

*W. M. Woodfull c Constantine b Martin	22	–	c Constantine b Griffith	18
W. H. Ponsford c Bartlett b Francis	7	–	c Constantine b Martin	28
D. G. Bradman c Francis b Martin	43	–	b Griffith	0
A. F. Kippax c Sealy b Constantine	3	–	c Roach b Constantine	10
K. E. Rigg c Barrow b Francis	14	–	c Barrow b Constantine	16
A. G. Fairfax st Barrow b Scott	54	–	not out	60
S. J. McCabe c Headley b Francis	21	–	c Grant b Martin	44
R. K. Oxenham c Barrow b Francis	0	–	lbw b Scott	14
†W. A. Oldfield run out	36	–	lbw b Griffith	0
H. Ironmonger b Griffith	1	–	run out	4
C. V. Grimmett not out	15	–	c Constantine b Griffith	12
B 1, l-b 7	8		B 3, l-b 7, w 2, n-b 2	14
	224			**220**

West Indies bowling: *First innings*—Francis 19–6–48–4; Griffith 13.2–3–31–1; Martin 27–3–67–2; Constantine 10–2–28–1; Scott 10–1–42–1. *Second innings*—Francis 16–2–32–0; Griffith 13.3–3–50–4; Martin 18–4–44–2; Constantine 17–2–50–2; Scott 11–0–30–1.

Umpires: H. Armstrong and W.G. French

1931-32

After a cricket match in Bowral, 1931.

1931-32

If the visit of the South Africans tended to lessen interest in Sheffield Shield cricket during 1931-32 and to deprive the States of the services of leading players when the Test Matches were in progress, the struggle for the Shield again proved remarkably close. South Australia, last on the list the previous year, developed much greater bowling strength and, by beating New South Wales at Sydney in the final game of the series, finished level on points with that State. New South Wales, however, had the better percentage on average and so carried off the trophy – their nineteenth success since the institution of the competition.

For the first time since a time limit was placed on Sheffield Shield fixtures, every one of the matches was played to a finish. To what extent this was due to the larger wicket – tried originally the preceding season – can only be conjectured. ...

S. J. McCabe (New South Wales) had a phenomenal batting record [his average from his three Shield innings was 438] ... D.G. Bradman also assisted New South Wales in three matches and hit up 167 against Victoria, but his average for five innings came out at no more than 42 as against 115 the previous year when he batted in six innings. Against South Africa, however, he showed brilliant form, and accomplished a feat unparalleled in Australian cricket by making seven centuries in successive matches.

From 'Cricket in Australia: The Inter-State Matches'

These particular ... matches served to emphasise the wonderful ability of Bradman as a batsman, for this marvellous young cricketer scored a hundred in every Test Match except the last, when he was injured. His name appeared in the list of those playing but he took no part in the game. Leading off with 226 in the First Test Match at Brisbane, he followed with 112 in the next at Sydney, 167 in the Third at Melbourne, and 299 not out at Adelaide in the Fourth. In addition to these huge scores he also made 219 and 135 for New South Wales. As the outcome of all this he headed the batting figures against the tourists with the extraordinary average of 201.50.

From 'The South African Team in Australia and New Zealand',
by S. J. Southerton

[With an aggregate of 1,190 runs against the South Africans, Bradman was the first, and until I. M. Chappell (1,062) v the West Indians in 1968-69 the only, batsman to score 1,000 runs against a touring team in Australia.]

QUEENSLAND v NEW SOUTH WALES 69 (105)

Played at Brisbane, November 6, 7, 9, 10 [1931]. Queensland, after being dismissed for 109, secured the wickets of Bill and Bradman [in Gilbert's first over] before their opponents scored a run, but afterwards their bowling was mastered and New South Wales won by an innings and 238 runs. Amos, with five wickets for 22, figured prominently in the early rout of Queensland, and a magnificent innings by McCabe went far towards deciding the issue. ...

Queensland

R. Higgins, *F. J. Gough, F. W. Sides, R. K. Oxenham, D. Hansen, K. Mossop, A. Hurwood, †L. Waterman, V. B. Suche, H. M. Thurlow and E. Gilbert.

First innings: 109 (Mossop 44 not out; Amos five for 22). Second innings: 85 (Hunt four for 25, Campbell three for 13).

New South Wales

O. W. Bill c Waterman b Gilbert	0	†W. A. Oldfield b Hurwood	46
J. H. Fingleton b Oxenham	93	J. N. Campbell c Oxenham b Hurwood	4
D. G. Bradman c Waterman b Gilbert	0	G. S. Amos lbw b Gilbert	2
*A. F. Kippax retired hurt	16	W. A. Hunt run out	3
A. Fairfax b Gilbert	5	B 17, l-b 9, n-b 5	31
S. J. McCabe not out	229		**432**
S. F. Hird lbw b Oxenham	3		

Queensland bowling: Thurlow 22–4–69–0; Gilbert 20.7–2–74–4; Hurwood 25–5–95–2; Oxenham 27–7–79–2; Suche 14–1–50–0; Gough 5–0–34–0.

Umpires: J. Bartlett and J. A. Scott

NEW SOUTH WALES v SOUTH AFRICANS 70 (106, 107)

Played at Sydney, November 13, 14, 16, 17 [1931]. A lot of runs were made in the first match in which the South Africans met New South Wales and in the end the game had to be left drawn. ... On the third day ... when rain stopped play at five o'clock the South Africans, with three men out for 190 [in their second innings], were 447 runs ahead. The innings was declared closed next morning, but so far from losing the match New South Wales went very close to winning it. Fingleton, who made a hundred, and McCabe played fine cricket but they were both overshadowed by Bradman, who hit up 135 in his most brilliant style. When at length stumps were pulled up and the match left drawn, New South Wales, with seven wickets to fall, were within 18 of victory. This was a great day's cricket on the part of the New South Wales team.

South Africans

J. A. J. Christy, S. H. Curnow, B. Mitchell, *†H. B. Cameron, H. W. Taylor, E. L. Dalton, D. P. B. Morkel, X. Balaskas, Q. McMillan, C. L. Vincent and A. J. Bell.

First innings: 425 (Curnow 39, Cameron 74, Taylor 124, Dalton 87, Morkel 30; McCabe three for 89, Hunt four for 84, Bradman none for 35). Second innings: Three for 190 dec (Curnow 79 not out, Mitchell 42, Cameron 49; Hunt three for 62).

New South Wales

J. H. Fingleton b Bell	30	–	c McMillan b Morkel	117
O. W. Bill b Bell	0	–	b Morkel	47
D. G. Bradman c and b McMillan	30	–	c Bell b Morkel	135
S. J. McCabe st Cameron b McMillan	37	–	not out	79
A. A. Marks b Vincent	16	–	not out	36
A. G. Fairfax c Dalton b Vincent	3			
S. F. Hird c Mitchell b McMillan	18			
*†W. A. Oldfield c Vincent b McMillan	10			
R. H. Bettington b Bell	7			
W. A. Hunt st Cameron b Bell	3			
G. S. Amos not out	3			
Byes, etc.	11		Byes, etc.	16
	168		(three wkts)	**430**

South Africans bowling: *First innings*—Bell 14.6–2–36–4; Morkel 5–0–23–0; Vincent 20–7–46–2; McMillan 13–1–52–4. *Second innings*—Bell 27–2–100–0; Morkel 18–1–80–3; Vincent 27–4–125–0; McMillan 8–0–72–0; Balaskas 4–1–27–0.

Umpires: G. Borwick and W.G. French

AUSTRALIA v SOUTH AFRICA 71 (108)
(FIRST TEST MATCH) 15 (22)

Played at Brisbane, November 27, 28, 30, December 1, 2, 3 [1931]. Entering upon the first of their five Test Matches against Australia with a very moderate record behind them, South Africa cut a poor figure and … they suffered a heavy defeat, Australia winning in an innings with 163 runs to spare. Still, South Africa were served a very bad turn by the weather. They had to field out while Australia were putting together their total on a firm, true pitch, and in reply had made 126 for three wickets on the Saturday. Then rain came to prevent any cricket at all on the Monday and Tuesday, and for the rest of the match the conditions were all against the visitors. The outstanding feature of the game was the splendid innings of 226 put together by Bradman. He and Woodfull added 163 for the second wicket, and later on Oldfield played well, but nobody else on the side accomplished anything of note. Bradman enjoyed a good deal of luck, being missed off Quinn when 11 and again at 15. After those escapes he completely mastered the bowling and, before being leg-before in trying to force Vincent to the on, he hit twenty-two 4's. …

Australia

*W. M. Woodfull lbw b Vincent	76	†W. A. Oldfield not out	56
W. H. Ponsford c Mitchell b Bell	19	C. V. Grimmett b Bell	14
D. G. Bradman lbw b Vincent	226	T. W. Wall lbw b Quinn	14
A. F. Kippax c Cameron b Vincent	1	H. Ironmonger b Quinn	2
S. J. McCabe c Vincent b Morkel	27	B 5, l-b 1, w 1, n-b 1	8
H. C. Nitschke c Cameron b Bell	6		**450**
R. K. Oxenham b Bell	1		

South Africa bowling: Bell 42–5–120–4; Morkel 13–1–57–1; Quinn 38.3–6–113–2; Vincent 34–0–100–3; McMillan 10–0–52–0.

South Africa

J. A. J. Christy, S. H. Curnow, B. Mitchell, *†H. B. Cameron, H. W. Taylor, E. L. Dalton, Q. McMillan, D. P. B. Morkel, C. L. Vincent, N. A. Quinn and A. J. Bell.

First innings: 170 (Mitchell 58, Taylor 41; Ironmonger five for 42). *Second innings:* 117 (Taylor 47; Wall five for 14, Ironmonger four for 44).

Umpires: G. A. Hele and G. Borwick

NEW SOUTH WALES v SOUTH AFRICANS 72 (109)

Played at Sydney, December 5, 7, 8, 9 [1931]. Restricted to two days owing to rain on the first and last afternoons, the return match of the South Africans with New South Wales was left drawn. However, it afforded Bradman the opportunity of making another big innings against the tourists. New South Wales lost their first two wickets for 12 runs but Bradman, playing in brilliant fashion, hit up 219 in rather less than four hours. He was caught at mid-off, this being the first chance he had offered. Among his hits were fifteen 4's. ...

New South Wales

J. H. Fingleton lbw b Morkel	2	W. A. Hunt c Curnow b McMillan	45
O. W. Bill c Morkel b Bell	10	S. Hird c Cameron b McMillan	101
D. G. Bradman c Curnow b McMillan	219	G. S. Amos st Cameron b McMillan	24
S. J. McCabe c Christy b Bell	28	H. Theak not out	10
A. A. Marks c Cameron b Bell	6	Byes, etc.	15
C. Solomon st Cameron b McMillan	11		**500**
*†W. A. Oldfield c Mitchell b McMillan	29		

South Africans bowling: Bell 26–2–107–3; Morkel 8–0–33–1; Vincent 11–0–51–0; Quinn 20–1–105–0; McMillan 23.4–0–189–6.

South Africans

J. A. J. Christy, S. H. Curnow, D. P. B. Morkel, B. Mitchell, *†H. B. Cameron, K. F. Viljoen, X. Balaskas, Q. McMillan, C. L. Vincent, A. J. Bell and N. A. Quinn.

First innings: One for 185 (Curnow 81 not out, Morkel 70 not out).

Umpires: G. Borwick and W.G. French

AUSTRALIA v SOUTH AFRICA 73 (110)
(SECOND TEST MATCH) 16 (23)

Played at Sydney, December 18, 19, 21 [1931]. Although the conditions did not operate against them as they had at Brisbane, South Africa fared no better in the Second Test Match and suffered defeat at the end of three days' cricket, Australia winning in an innings with 155 runs to spare. On the opening day the visitors could do little with the bowling of Grimmett. Indeed, before lunch that player kept batsmen in such subjection that of the sixty-six balls he delivered only four were scored off. ...

South Africa were all out for 153, after which Australia made 78 for one wicket, and on the next afternoon the home side ran their score to 444 for seven wickets. ... Rigg ... enjoyed the distinction of making a hundred in his first Test Match. He and Bradman added 111 runs before Rigg was out, and then Bradman and McCabe put on 93, Bradman being out to a glorious catch in the long field. Fourth to leave at 347, Bradman, although suffering from a slightly strained leg, batted in brilliant fashion for about two hours and three-quarters, being very severe on the South African slow bowlers. ...

South Africa

J. A. J. Christy, B. Mitchell, D. P. B. Morkel, *†H. B. Cameron, H. W. Taylor, K. F. Viljoen, E. L. Dalton, C. L. Vincent, L. S. Brown, N. A. Quinn and A. J. Bell.

First innings: 153 (Viljoen 37, Vincent 31 not out; McCabe four for 13, Grimmett four for 28). *Second innings:* 161 (Christy 41, Vincent 35; Grimmett four for 44, Ironmonger three for 22).

Australia

*W. M. Woodfull c Mitchell b Vincent	58	†W. A. Oldfield c Cameron b Bell		8
W. H. Ponsford b Quinn	5	C. V. Grimmett not out		9
K. E. Rigg b Bell	127	T. W. Wall c Morkel b Bell		6
D. G. Bradman c Viljoen b Morkel	112	H. Ironmonger c Cameron b Bell		0
S. J. McCabe c Christy b Vincent	79	B 5, l-b 12, w 1		18
H. C. Nitschke b Bell	47			**469**
P. K. Lee c Cameron b Brown	0			

South Africa bowling: Bell 46.5–6–140–5; Quinn 42–10–95–1; Brown 29–3–100–1; Vincent 24–5–75–2; Morkel 12–2–33–1; Mitchell 1–0–8–0.

Umpires: G. A. Hele and G. Borwick

AUSTRALIA v SOUTH AFRICA (THIRD TEST MATCH)

74 (111, 112)
17 (24, 25)

Played at Melbourne, December 31 [1931], January 1, 2, 4, 5, 6 [1932]. South Africa made a much better fight of it with their opponents in the Third Test Match, but in the end had to admit defeat by 169 runs. This result gave Australia the rubber. Australia did not start in a manner which suggested their ultimate victory for, losing Ponsford, Woodfull and Bradman for 25 runs, they were all out for a total of 198 ... and altogether the innings lasted just over three hours and a half. ...

[The South Africans scored 358 and] Australia thus had to go in a second time 160 runs behind, but any anxiety they may have had was soon dispelled, Ponsford and Woodfull putting on 54 for the first wicket and Woodfull and Bradman then carrying the score to 206 without being separated. Thus the situation had been retrieved and on the Monday the Australian score stood, at the close of play, at 554 for nine wickets. Woodfull and Bradman were not separated until the total reached 328, their partnership for the second wicket having realised 274 runs. This beat the previous highest for the second wicket in Test Matches of 235 made by Macartney and Woodfull against England at Leeds in 1926. The South Africans bowled and fielded well, but Bradman scored with much freedom during the three hours he was at the wicket. In his 167 he hit eighteen 4's, his batting generally being of high order. The only bowler to trouble him was Vincent. ...

Australia

*W. M. Woodfull c Cameron b Bell	7	–	c Mitchell b McMillan	161
W. H. Ponsford b Bell	7	–	c Mitchell b Bell	34
D. G. Bradman c Cameron b Quinn	2	–	lbw b Vincent	167
A. F. Kippax c Bell b Quinn	52	–	c Curnow b McMillan	67
S. J. McCabe c Morkel b Bell	22	–	c Mitchell b McMillan	71
E. L. a'Beckett c Mitchell b Quinn	6	–	b Vincent	4
†W. A. Oldfield c Vincent b Quinn	0	–	lbw b McMillan	0
K. E. Rigg c Mitchell b Bell	68	–	c Mitchell b Vincent	1
C. V. Grimmett c Morkel b Bell	9	–	not out	16
T. W. Wall not out	6	–	b Vincent	12
H. Ironmonger run out	12	–	b Quinn	0
B 1, l-b 4, w 1, n-b 1	7		B 17, l-b 3, n-b 1	21
	198			**554**

South Africa bowling: *First innings*—Bell 26.1–9–69–5; Quinn 31–13–42–4; Morkel 3–0–12–0; Vincent 12–1–32–0; McMillan 2–0–22–0; Christy 3–0–14–0. *Second innings*—Bell 36–0–101–1; Quinn 36.4–6–113–1; Morkel 4–0–15–0; Vincent 55–16–154–4; McMillan 33–3–150–4.

South Africa

S. H. Curnow, B. Mitchell, J. A. J. Christy, H. W. Taylor, D. P. B. Morkel, *†H. B. Cameron, C. L. Vincent, K. F. Viljoen, Q. McMillan, N. A. Quinn and A. J. Bell.

First innings: 358 (Curnow 47, Morkel 33, Cameron 39, Viljoen 111; Wall three for 98, Ironmonger three for 72). *Second innings:* 225 (Mitchell 46, Christy 63, Taylor 38, Vincent 34; Ironmonger four for 54, Grimmett six for 92, Bradman none for 2).

Umpires: G. A. Hele and G. Borwick

NEW SOUTH WALES v VICTORIA   75 (113, 114)

Played at Sydney, January 22, 23, 25, 26 [1932]. Two brilliant hundreds by McCabe, a big second innings by Bradman, and a plucky effort for Victoria by Oakley were the features of this match, which New South Wales won by 239 runs. McCabe proved the mainstay of New South Wales in their first innings, and on the third day he and Bradman placed their State in such a strong position that a declaration was made possible with only four wickets down. Bradman completed his 1,000 runs in first-class cricket for the season for the fourth successive year. ...

New South Wales

O. W. Bill c Barnett b McCormick	27	–	lbw b McCormick	15
J. H. Fingleton c a'Beckett b Nagel	40	–	lbw b Smith	40
D. G. Bradman c Smith b Ironmonger	23	–	b Nagel	167
S. J. McCabe c Barnett b Ironmonger	106	–	not out	103
R. N. Nutt c Darling b a'Beckett	15	–	not out	8
S. F. Hird c Barnett b McCormick	23			
*A. F. Kippax c and b Darling	36	–	c Barnett b McCormick	44
†W. A. Oldfield c Oakley b Darling	2			
W. A. Hunt c Darling b Ironmonger	0			
W. J. O'Reilly not out	26			
H. J. Theak run out	17			
B 16, l-b 11, w 5, n-b 1	33		B 3, l-b 3, w 4, n-b 2	12
	348		(four wkts dec)	**389**

Victoria bowling: *First innings*—McCormick 15.4–4–42–2; a'Beckett 15–3–44–1; Ironmonger 20–2–94–3; Nagel 14–1–63–1; Smith 5–0–33–0; Darling 8–0–39–2. *Second innings*—McCormick 13–0–54–2; a'Beckett 13.3–0–68–0; Ironmonger 17–4–52–0; Nagel 12–1–57–1; Smith 14–1–100–1; Darling 3–0–34–0; Ryder 4–0–12–0.

Victoria

J. Thomas, L. P. O'Brien, L. Darling, *J. Ryder, E. L. a'Beckett, †B. A. Barnett, H. H. Oakley, L. E. Nagel, E. L. McCormick, S. A. Smith and H. Ironmonger.

First innings: 204 (O'Brien 38, Oakley 48, Nagel 30; McCabe three for 57, O'Reilly three for 52, Bradman none for 6). *Second innings:* 294 (Thomas 70, O'Brien 34, Oakley 93 not out; Bradman one for 4).

Umpires: H. Armstrong and W.G. French

AUSTRALIA v SOUTH AFRICA
(FOURTH TEST MATCH)

76 (115)
18 (26)

Played at Adelaide, January 29, 30, February 1, 2 [1932]. Up to a point South Africa rendered a fairly good account of themselves but, as in previous matches, the combination of Bradman and Grimmett as batsman and bowler proved too much for them and Australia won the Fourth Test Match by ten wickets. Bradman played a great innings of 299 not out, while Grimmett took fourteen wickets – seven in each innings – for 199 runs. Rarely in a Test Match can two men have contributed so materially to the defeat of the opposing side. ...

... In reply to [South Africa's first innings of 308] Australia made 302 for four wickets [by stumps on the second day]. This was almost entirely the work of Woodfull and Bradman, who added 176 for the second wicket. Rigg, later, gave Bradman useful assistance, the latter at the close being 170 not out.

On Monday the Australian total amounted to 513, Bradman remaining undefeated until the end. In his attempt to reach his 300th run, however, he ran Thurlow out [on his Test debut]. Bradman's score of 299 was the highest ever made by one man in a Test Match in Australia, but it fell short by 35 of his record made against England at Leeds in 1930. He dominated the proceedings on this day after he and Rigg had increased their overnight partnership to 114. There were times, however, when he was not at all comfortable. During one particular hour he scored only 25 runs and survived several appeals for leg-before and catches at the wicket. Oldfield and Grimmett gave valuable help, and with O'Reilly [another playing in his first Test] 78 runs were added. The innings closed just before tea, South Africa being left to get 205 to save the innings defeat. ...

South Africa

S.H. Curnow, B. Mitchell, J.A.J. Christy, H.W. Taylor, *†H.B. Cameron, D.P.B. Morkel, K.F. Viljoen, C.L. Vincent, Q. McMillan, N.A. Quinn and A.J. Bell.

First innings: 308 (Mitchell 75, Taylor 78, Cameron 52, Vincent 48; Grimmett seven for 116). *Second innings:* 274 (Mitchell 95, Christy 51, Taylor 84; Grimmett seven for 83).

Australia

*W. M. Woodfull c Morkel b Bell	82	–	not out	37
W. H. Ponsford b Quinn	5	–	not out	27
D. G. Bradman not out	299			
A. F. Kippax run out	0			
S. J. McCabe c Vincent b Bell	2			
K. E. Rigg c Taylor b Bell	35			
†W. A. Oldfield lbw b Vincent	23			
C. V. Grimmett b Bell	21			
W. A. Hunt c Vincent b Quinn	0			
W. J. O'Reilly b Bell	23			
H. M. Thurlow run out	0			
B 18, l-b 3, w 1, n-b 1	23		B 4, l-b 5	9
	513		(no wkt)	**73**

South Africa bowling: *First innings*—Bell 40–2–142–5; Quinn 37–5–114–2; Vincent 34–5–110–1; McMillan 9–0–53–0; Morkel 18–1–71–0. *Second innings*—Quinn 3–0–5–0; Vincent 7–0–31–0; McMillan 7.2–0–23–0; Morkel 2–0–5–0.

Umpires: G. A. Hele and G. Borwick

AUSTRALIA v SOUTH AFRICA
(FIFTH TEST MATCH)

77
19

Played at Melbourne, February 12, 13, 15 [1932]. Before proceeding to New Zealand, South Africa engaged in their concluding Test Match with Australia and for the fifth time were defeated, Australia, although scoring only 153, winning in an innings with 72 runs to spare. For this game Australia brought in L. Nash, a Tasmanian fast bowler ... Short, but of powerful build, Nash made the ball rise in very awkward fashion, several of them getting head high. He and Ironmonger proved so effective on a pitch slightly on the soft side that in a little more than ninety minutes South Africa were dismissed for the sorry total of 36. This was not their lowest total in Test cricket for they had twice been got rid of previously by England for 30 – at Port Elizabeth in 1895-96 and at Birmingham in 1924. Their lowest score before this in Test Matches against Australia was 80 at Melbourne in 1910-11. Cameron alone reached double figures [11] ...

Before the day was over there were further surprises, Australia being got rid of for 153. ... Woodfull was out first ball ... [and] Australia's total was their smallest against South Africa, the previous lowest being 175 at Johannesburg in 1902-03. [Bradman took no part in the first day's play, having twisted his ankle when his sprigs caught in the dressing-room matting as he was going out to field.] South Africa, 117 behind, lost one wicket for five runs before play ceased for the day, and on the Saturday no cricket took place, heavy rain during the night and a further downpour soon after two o'clock preventing any chance of a resumption. On the Monday, however, there came more sensational play.

The game was not proceeded with until quarter-past two, and then in less than an hour and a half the last nine South African wickets went down for another 40 runs. Thus South Africa were twice dismissed for an aggregate of 81, the lowest total for two innings ever recorded in the history of Test Match cricket [as indeed is the match aggregate]. The wicket was very difficult and Ironmonger once more proved practically unplayable. ... Five batsmen failed to score and only Curnow [16] reached double figures ...

South Africa

B. Mitchell, S. H. Curnow, J. A. J. Christy, H. W. Taylor, K. F. Viljoen, *†H. B. Cameron, D. P. B. Morkel, C. L. Vincent, Q. McMillan, N. A. Quinn and A. J. Bell.

First innings: 36 (Nash four for 18, Ironmonger five for 6). *Second innings:* 45 (Ironmonger six for 18, O'Reilly three for 19).

Australia

*W. M. Woodfull b Bell	0	C. V. Grimmett c Cameron b Quinn	9
J. H. Fingleton c Vincent b Bell	40	W. J. O'Reilly c Curnow b McMillan	13
K. E. Rigg c Vincent b Quinn	22	H. Ironmonger not out	0
A. F. Kippax c Curnow b McMillan	42	D. G. Bradman absent hurt	0
S. J. McCabe c Cameron b Bell	0	L-b 3	3
L. J. Nash b Quinn	13		**153**
†W. A. Oldfield c Curnow b McMillan	11		

South Africa bowling: Bell 16–0–52–3; Quinn 19.3–4–29–3; Vincent 11–2–40–0; McMillan 8–0–29–3.

Umpires: G. A. Hele and G. Borwick

NEW SOUTH WALES v SOUTH AUSTRALIA

78 (116, 117)

Played at Sydney, March 19, 21, 22 [1932]. Winning a thoroughly interesting struggle by 132 runs, South Australia finished level with New South Wales in the matter of points, but the latter State won the Shield by virtue of their better averages. ... [In the New South Wales second innings] with McCabe still unfit to bat, Bradman dismissed without scoring and Grimmett's skilful bowling too much for all their batsmen except Fingleton and Bill, New South Wales were easily overcome.

South Australia

*V.Y. Richardson, H.C. Nitschke, A.R. Lonergan, W.E. Catchlove, H.E.P. Whitfield, M.G. Waite, P.K. Lee, C.V. Grimmett, †C.W. Walker, T.W. Wall and T.A. Carlton.

First innings: 272 (Nitschke 45, Lonergan 68, Whitfield 51; Theak three for 68, O'Reilly five for 68).
Second innings: 225 (Nitschke 119; O'Reilly five for 59).

New South Wales

J. H. Fingleton b Wall	0	– b Grimmett	24
W. A. Hunt b Wall	0	– c Richardson b Lee	1
R. N. Nutt b Lee	33	– b Whitfield	6
S. J. Hird lbw b Carlton	2	– lbw b Grimmett	5
D. G. Bradman b Carlton	23	– b Wall	0
J. Donnelly c Walker b Wall	57	– c Carlton b Grimmett	18
O. W. Bill not out	76	– st Walker b Grimmett	46
*†W. A. Oldfield lbw b Grimmett	31	– c Richardson b Lee	6
W. J. O'Reilly c Richardson b Lee	5	– run out	0
H. J. Theak st Walker b Lee	1	– not out	4
S. J. McCabe absent hurt	0	– absent hurt	0
B 8, l-b 7, w 1, n-b 3	19	B 3, l-b 5	8
	247		**118**

South Australia bowling: *First innings*—Wall 16–1–63–3; Whitfield 8–0–31–0; Carlton 8–1–30–2; Grimmett 16–1–75–1; Lee 7.1–2–29–3. *Second innings*—Wall 5–0–24–1; Whitfield 4–1–8–1; Carlton 4–1–12–0; Grimmett 19–9–32–4; Lee 14.2–1–34–2.

Umpires: G. Borwick and W.G. French

1932

AUSTRALIAN TOUR IN AMERICA

During the summer months of 1932 a strong team of Australian cricketers under the captaincy of V.Y. Richardson visited Canada and the United States. They played no fewer than fifty-one matches – the majority of minor interest, though Canada and British Columbia were met – and of these forty-four were won, six drawn, and one lost – to Vancouver.

D.G. Bradman secured remarkable batting figures, scoring 3,782 runs in fifty-one innings (fourteen times not out), giving an average of 102.21 with a highest of 260 against Western Ontario on July 4, which constitutes a Canadian record. He followed this with 200 (not out) against Montreal and in all played eighteen three-figure innings. ... Against a Victoria XV, [he] captured six wickets in an eight-ball over ...

1932-33

Bradman shaking hands with New York Yankees baseball star Babe Ruth, 1932. US newspapers captioned Bradman 'the Babe Ruth of Australian cricket'.

1932-33

Owing to the presence in Australia of the English cricketers, several of the Sheffield Shield matches were contested with teams which did not include leading players, and consequently interest in the competition temporarily diminished. ... New South Wales won the Shield fairly easily. ... Outstanding performances in the competition were the splendid batting of Bradman and the bowling of O'Reilly and Grimmett. Bradman, again the predominating Australian batsman, played in only three Shield matches, but scored 600 runs with a highest innings of 238 and an average of 150. In addition to his double-century against Victoria, he scored 157 against the same State in the return match. ...

From 'Cricket in Australia: The Inter-State Matches'

At the moment of writing these notes the Third Test Match has just ended in a handsome victory for England, but while followers of cricket in this country rejoice exceedingly over that success the public in Australia appear to be getting very excited about the fast bowling of some of the Englishmen and what is variously known as the 'leg theory', 'shock tactics' and 'Bodyline methods'. Leg theory, as we have understood that kind of bowling, ... consisted in the delivery ... of a slow ball, with an off-break, pitched on the leg stump or well outside it, with three or four men fielding close in at leg and to the on. ...

The ball to which such strong exception is being taken in Australia is not slow or slow-medium but fast. It is dropped short and is alleged in certain quarters to be aimed at the batsman rather than at the wicket. It may at once be said that, if the intention is to hit the batsman and so demoralise him, the practice is altogether wrong – calculated, as it must be, to introduce an element of pronounced danger and altogether against the spirit of the game of cricket. Upon this point practically everybody will agree. No one wants such an element introduced. That English bowlers, to dispose of their opponents, would of themselves pursue such methods or that Jardine would acquiesce in such a course is inconceivable. ...

... In suggesting, as has the Australian Board of Control, that bowling such as that of the Englishmen has become a menace to the best interests of the game, is causing intensely bitter feelings between players and, unless stopped at once, is likely to upset the friendly relations between England and Australia, the Commonwealth cricket authorities seem to have lost their sense of proportion. ...

From 'Notes by the Editor' (C. Stewart Caine), *Wisden 1933*

... I have purposely omitted to use the expression 'Bodyline bowling'. It may have conveyed to those to whom it was presented at the outset the meaning the inventor of it wished to infer, but to my mind it was an objectionable term, utterly foreign to cricket, and calculated to stir up strife when the obvious aim of everybody should have been directed towards the prevention of any breach. ...

Happily the controversy is now at an end, and little reason exists, therefore, to flog what we can regard as a 'dead horse'. But, obviously from the historical point of view, something on the subject must be said. I hope and believe that the ventilation of their grievances by the Australians, and the placatory replies of the MCC, will have done much towards imparting a better spirit to Test Matches which of recent years have become battles rather than pleasurable struggles. A false atmosphere has pervaded them. During the last few tours of MCC teams in Australia, and the visits of the Australians to this country, one could not fail to detect a subtle change taking place in the conduct of Test Matches – reflected unfortunately in the style of the cricketers themselves. The result of the contests was given a prominence out of keeping with the importance of Test Matches, and the true sense of perspective stood in danger of disappearing altogether. ...

And now, what of this fast leg-theory method of bowling to which not only the Australian players themselves, but a vast majority of the people of Australia took such grave exception? With the dictum of the MCC that any form of bowling which constitutes a direct attack by the bowler on the batsman is contrary to the spirit of the game, everyone must unquestionably concur. D. R. Jardine, on his return to England, stated definitely in his book that the bowling against which the Australians demurred was not of this description, and Larwood, the chief exponent of it, said with equal directness that he had never intentionally bowled at a man. On the other hand, there are numerous statements by responsible Australians to the effect that the type of bowling adopted was calculated to intimidate batsmen, pitched as the ball was so short as to cause it to fly shoulder and head high and make batsmen, with the leg side studded with fieldsmen, use the bat as a protection for their bodies or their heads rather than in defence of the wicket or to make a scoring stroke. Victor Richardson, the South Australian batsman, has said that when he took his ordinary stance at the wicket he found the ball coming on to his body; when he took guard slightly more to the leg side he still had the ball coming at him; and with a still wider guard the ball continued to follow him. I hold no brief either for Jardine or Larwood or for Richardson, Woodfull or Bradman; but while some of the Australians may have exaggerated the supposed danger of this form of bowling, I cling to the opinion that they cannot all be wrong. When the first mutterings of the storm were heard, many people in this country were inclined to the belief that the Australians, seeing themselves in danger of losing the rubber, were not taking defeat in the proper spirit always expected from honourable opponents. I will confess that I thought they did not relish what seemed to me at that stage to be a continuous good-length bombardment by our fast bowlers on to their leg stump. This idea I afterwards found was not quite correct. ...

From 'The Bowling Controversy', by the Editor (S. J. Southerton),

Wisden 1934

MCC TEAM v A COMBINED AUSTRALIAN XI   79 (118, 119)

Played at Perth, October 27, 28, 29 [1932]. Despite deadly bowling by Verity, MCC, though they carried off all the honours, could not win. Sutcliffe and the Nawab of Pataudi [shared] in a second-wicket stand of 283 – a record for the ground ... The Australians replied with 59 without loss on the second day but, the pitch becoming sticky, Verity sent back the first six batsmen up to tea-time for 23 runs and altogether took seven wickets for just over five runs apiece. ...

MCC Team

H. Sutcliffe, M. Leyland, Nawab of Pataudi, W. R. Hammond, L. E.G. Ames, *Mr D. R. Jardine, Mr G. O. Allen, E. Paynter, H. Verity, T. B. Mitchell and †G. Duckworth.

First innings: Seven for 583 dec (Sutcliffe 169, Pataudi 129, Hammond 77, Jardine 98, Paynter 32 not out; Bradman two for 106).

A Combined Australian XI

J. H. Fingleton c Duckworth b Verity	29	–	not out	53
V. Y. Richardson c Sutcliffe b Verity	27	–	b Allen	0
D. G. Bradman c Hammond b Verity	3	–	c Pataudi b Allen	10
A. R. Lonergan c Duckworth b Verity	10	–	b Paynter	23
S. J. McCabe b Paynter	43			
W. Hill-Smith c Jardine b Verity	17	–	c Duckworth b Ames	32
*R. Bryant c Mitchell b Verity	0	–	not out	12
†O. Lovelock c Hammond b Mitchell	11			
A. Evans c Allen b Verity	0			
E. Martin st Duckworth b Mitchell	1			
R. Halcombe not out	1			
B 11, l-b 5, n-b 1	17		L-b 7, w 1, n-b 1	9
	159		(four wkts)	139

MCC Team bowling: *First innings*—Allen 4–0–24–0; Hammond 9–1–29–0; Mitchell 13–2–37–2; Verity 18–7–37–7; Leyland 2–0–15–0; Paynter 0.2–0–0–1. *Second innings*—Allen 7–2–16–2; Hammond 3–1–7–0; Verity 1–0–2–0; Leyland 8–1–23–0; Paynter 12–1–31–1; Ames 6–0–25–1; Sutcliffe 3–0–18–0; Jardine 2–1–8–0.

Umpires: F. Buttsworth and J. Hart

NEW SOUTH WALES v VICTORIA   80 (120, 121)

Played at Sydney, November 4, 5, 7, 8 [1932]. Great individual performances marked this game, which New South Wales won by nine wickets. Ponsford, who could not bat a second time as he twisted an ankle while fielding, and Woodfull scored 138 for Victoria's first wicket, Ponsford playing a fine innings which lasted four and a half hours. Bradman's display for New South Wales was, however, one of the most brilliant exhibitions ever seen on the Sydney ground. During a stay of three and a quarter hours [in which he hit the fastest double-hundred in a Shield match] he hit thirty-two 4's. ...

Victoria

*W. M. Woodfull, W. H. Ponsford, L. P. O'Brien, K. E. Rigg, L. S. Darling, J. Thomas, †B. A. Barnett, D. D. Blackie, L. O'B. Fleetwood-Smith, H. H. Alexander and H. Ironmonger.

First innings: 404 (Woodfull 74, Ponsford 200, Barnett 36, Fleetwood-Smith 38; O'Reilly five for 81, Hird three for 115, Bradman one for 8). *Second innings:* 150 (Woodfull 83; Hird six for 56).

New South Wales

J. H. Fingleton lbw b Alexander	6	–	not out	20
O. W. Bill b Fleetwood-Smith	19	–	b Alexander	8
D. G. Bradman c O'Brien b Fleetwood-Smith	238	–	not out	52
*A. F. Kippax c Barnett b Alexander	52			
S. J. McCabe c Fleetwood-Smith b Alexander	56			
S. F. Hird c Barnett b Alexander	6			
F. S. Cummins b Alexander	13			
W. J. O'Reilly c Barnett b Alexander	0			
†W. A. Oldfield not out	22			
C. Hill b Ironmonger	10			
H. J. Theak b Alexander	39			
B 8, l-b 6	14		B 1, l-b 1	2
	475		(one wkt)	82

Victoria bowling: *First innings*—Alexander 22–1–95–7; Darling 7–0–40–0; Fleetwood-Smith 19–0–145–2; Ironmonger 26.1–3–96–1; Blackie 19–1–85–0. *Second innings*—Alexander 3–0–23–1; Darling 1–0–7–0; Fleetwood-Smith 5–0–27–0; Ironmonger 5–2–17–0; Blackie 1.2–0–6–0.

Umpires: G. Borwick and W.G. French

MCC TEAM v AN AUSTRALIAN XI   81 (122, 123)

Played at Melbourne, November 18, 19, 21, 22 [1932]. Rain interfering when play had become very exciting – the Australian XI wanted 106 to win with eight wickets in hand – this match was left drawn. The Englishmen, with the exception of Sutcliffe, Allen and Leyland, gave a most disappointing batting display on an easy pitch. … The Australians, too, fared only moderately. During one period after tea on the second day six wickets went down for 58 runs … On the last day Larwood brought some consolation [to MCC] by sending back Bradman and Woodfull at small cost before the rain came on.

[The total attendance of 109,501 was a record for a first-class match in Australia, other than a Test Match, as was the attendance of 53,916 on the second day, which saw the introduction of Bodyline tactics in the Australian XI's first innings.]

MCC Team

*Mr R. E. S. Wyatt, H. Sutcliffe, Nawab of Pataudi, M. Leyland, Mr G. O. Allen, E. Paynter, H. Larwood, Mr F. R. Brown, W. Voce, †G. Duckworth and W. E. Bowes.

First innings: 282 (Sutcliffe 87, Leyland 38, Allen 48; Nash three for 39, Oxenham five for 53). *Second innings:* 60 (Nagel eight for 32).

An Australian XI

*W. M. Woodfull lbw b Bowes	18	–	c Duckworth b Larwood	0
L. P. O'Brien b Larwood	46	–	not out	5
D. G. Bradman lbw b Larwood	36	–	b Larwood	13
K. E. Rigg c Brown b Bowes	13	–	not out	0
L. S. Darling b Bowes	4			
R. K. Oxenham c Larwood b Voce	12			
L. J. Nash b Larwood	0			
P. K. Lee c Paynter b Brown	28			
†B. Barnett b Voce	20			
L. E. Nagel lbw b Larwood	15			
H. Ironmonger not out	5			
B 11, l-b 2, n-b 8	21		B	1
	218		(two wkts)	**19**

MCC Team bowling: *First innings*—Larwood 14–0–54–4; Bowes 15–2–63–3; Voce 15.5–2–55–2; Brown 7–0–25–1. *Second innings*—Larwood 3.7–1–5–2; Allen 3–1–13–0.

Umpires: A. N. Barlow and J. Richards

MCC TEAM v NEW SOUTH WALES   82 (124, 125)

Played at Sydney, November 25, 26, 28, 29 [1932]. Bradman [who was unwell] failing twice, New South Wales proved no real match for the tourists, who won deservedly by an innings and 44 runs. … Jardine allowed [H.S.] Love, not even twelfth man, to act as wicket-keeper in the absence of Oldfield, ill. [In addition to catching Jardine, Love also effected the first stumpings by a substitute in Australian first-class cricket.]

New South Wales

O. W. Bill c Jardine b Tate	22	–	b Voce	1
J. H. Fingleton not out	119	–	b Brown	18
D. G. Bradman lbw b Tate	18	–	b Voce	23
*A. F. Kippax c Voce b Tate	3	–	c Sutcliffe b Voce	24
S. J. McCabe c Allen b Tate	67	–	c Brown b Voce	29
S. J. Hird c Ames b Allen	9	–	c Tate b Voce	15
F. S. Cummins lbw b Voce	0	–	c Jardine b Brown	71
†W. A. Oldfield c Sutcliffe b Allen	5	–	absent ill	0
W. J. O'Reilly b Allen	0	–	b Allen	11
H. J. Theak b Allen	9	–	b Allen	4
W. Howell b Allen	7	–	not out	0
L-b 8, n-b 6	14		B 2, l-b 6, w 1, n-b 8	17
	273			**213**

MCC Team bowling: *First innings*—Allen 16.2–2–69–5; Voce 19–3–53–1; Tate 17–2–53–4; Brown 5–0–28–0; Hammond 5–0–26–0; Verity 6–1–30–0. *Second innings*—Allen 10–1–52–2; Voce 15–1–85–5; Tate 6–1–21–0; Brown 5.5–0–19–2; Hammond 4–0–12–0; Verity 4–1–7–0.

MCC Team

Mr R.E.S. Wyatt, H. Sutcliffe, W.R. Hammond, Nawab of Pataudi, Mr F.R. Brown, †L.E.G. Ames, *Mr D.R. Jardine, Mr G.O. Allen, W. Voce, H. Verity and M.W. Tate.

First innings: 530 (Wyatt 72, Sutcliffe 182, Pataudi 61, Ames 90, Voce 46, sundries 30; O'Reilly four for 86, Hird six for 135, Bradman none for 24).

Umpires: G. Borwick and W.G. French

ENGLAND v AUSTRALIA
(FIRST TEST MATCH)

Played at Sydney, December 2, 3, 5, 6, 7 [1932]. Leading off in fine style in the series of Test Matches, England won this, the first, early on the fifth day by ten wickets. ...

Reference to the fact that Bradman, owing to illness, was unable to play in the match must not be omitted, although in view of subsequent events it is, to say the least, questionable if his presence would have staved off disaster.

VICTORIA v NEW SOUTH WALES   83 (126)

Played at Melbourne, December 23, 24, 26, 27 [1932]. This game could not be started until the third of the four days set apart for it, but when play commenced the sun shone and the good crowd [21,187] was provided with some bright cricket. New South Wales, put in by Woodfull, were given a useful start with an opening partnership of 145 by Fingleton and Brown, who retired injured but returned, and Bradman played a fine innings. After completing his hundred in two and three-quarter hours, he took his score to 157 in another thirty minutes [becoming with his 130th run the youngest player (24 years and 121 days) to score 10,000 runs in first-class cricket] ...

New South Wales

J. H. Fingleton lbw b Nagel	85			
W. Brown not out	35			
D. G. Bradman c Bromley b Ironmonger	157			
S. J. McCabe lbw b Alexander	48			
*A. F. Kippax c King b Ironmonger	17			
S. F. Hird c Barnett b Ironmonger	3			
F. S. Cummins c Bromley b Ironmonger	15			
†H. S. Love lbw b Alexander	1			
W. J. O'Reilly c and b Alexander	2	–	not out	7
W. Howell b Alexander	5			
G. L. Stewart c Darling b Ironmonger	7	–	not out	1
B 6, l-b 7	13			
	388		(no wkt)	**8**

Victoria bowling: *First innings*—Alexander 26–3–107–4; L. E. Nagel 24–1–90–1; Ironmonger 30.2–6–87–5; Fleetwood-Smith 14–0–73–0; Darling 4–0–18–0. *Second innings*—Bromley 1–0–8–0.

Victoria

*W. M. Woodfull, W. H. Ponsford, L. P. O'Brien, L. S. Darling, S. P. King, E. H. Bromley, †B. A. Barnett, L. E. Nagel, L. O'B. Fleetwood-Smith, H. H. Alexander and H. Ironmonger.

First innings: 258 (O'Brien 53, King 30, Bromley 84, Barnett 39; Howell four for 69, O'Reilly four for 52, Bradman none for 8).

Umpires: A. N. Barlow and W. J. Moore

ENGLAND v AUSTRALIA   84 (127, 128)
(SECOND TEST MATCH)   20 (27, 28)

Played at Melbourne, December 30, 31 [1932], January 2, 3 [1933]. ... Jardine again lost the toss, but England started even better than they had done at Sydney and, at the end of the first day, Australia had seven men out for 194. This splendid work was not followed up at all well when it came England's turn to bat and the match – over in four days – resulted in a victory for Australia by 111 runs. ... Having recovered from his indisposition, Bradman was able to play for Australia ... [and] dismissed for nought on the opening day [he] afterwards scored a brilliant 103 not out ...

For a Test Match in Australia, this was a game of small scores ... and it can be said at once that the pitch proved quite different from any experienced in former tours by England cricketers. For some reason or other it lacked the usual firmness of bounce associated with wickets at the Victorian capital and Jardine, playing all his pace bowlers by including Bowes for Verity, was completely misled in his assumption that fast bowling would be likely to win the match. ... Australia had their worst shock when Bradman was out first ball to Bowes. He tried to hook it, but edged it down on to the stumps. Previously Woodfull had also been dismissed cheaply. At times the ball bounced a good deal, Woodfull on one occasion being struck over the heart. ...

On the third day there was a record crowd of nearly 70,000 people [68,238] present. The England innings was finished off for 169, which gave Australia a lead of 59 runs. At their second attempt Australia, thanks almost entirely to Bradman, made 191, and towards the end of the day England, left to get 251 in the last innings, had forty-five minutes' batting. ... The day's cricket really was dominated by Bradman, who, after a succession of failures, simply took his courage in both hands and played a wonderful innings. In a way his batting was masterly. He went in when two wickets had fallen for 27 runs; resisted a lot of good bowling for over three hours and a half to complete his hundred when Ironmonger, the last man, was in with him. While Wall and O'Reilly were his partners he sacrificed many runs in order to keep the bowling.

To few other Australian batsmen could such an innings as Bradman played have been possible. The England bowling was very good all the time, Hammond doing excellent work.

So, on the last day, England, with all their wickets in hand, required 208 runs, but O'Reilly and Ironmonger proved too much for them on a pitch which by this time took the spin of the ball to a pronounced degree and England were all out for 139. ... The fact that in fine weather forty wickets went down in four days for an aggregate of 727 runs clearly suggested that at no time was the pitch all that it should have been.

Australia

J. H. Fingleton b Allen	83	–	c Ames b Allen	1
*W. M. Woodfull b Allen	10	–	c Allen b Larwood	26
L. P. O'Brien run out	10	–	b Larwood	11
D. G. Bradman b Bowes	0	–	not out	103
S. J. McCabe c Jardine b Voce	32	–	b Allen	0
V. Y. Richardson c Hammond b Voce	34	–	lbw b Hammond	32
†W. A. Oldfield not out	27	–	b Voce	6
C. V. Grimmett c Sutcliffe b Voce	2	–	b Voce	0
T. W. Wall run out	1	–	lbw b Hammond	3
W. J. O'Reilly b Larwood	15	–	c Ames b Hammond	0
H. Ironmonger b Larwood	4	–	run out	0
B 5, l-b 1, w 2, n-b 2	10		B 3, l-b 1, w 4, n-b 1	9
	228			**191**

England bowling: *First innings*—Larwood 20.3–2–52–2; Voce 20–3–54–3; Allen 17–3–41–2; Hammond 10–3–21–0; Bowes 19–2–50–1. *Second innings*—Larwood 15–2–50–2; Voce 15–2–47–2; Allen 12–1–44–2; Hammond 10.5–2–21–3; Bowes 4–0–20–0.

England

H. Sutcliffe, Mr R. E. S. Wyatt, W. R. Hammond, Nawab of Pataudi, M. Leyland, *Mr D. R. Jardine, †L. E. G. Ames, Mr G. O. Allen, H. Larwood, W. Voce and W. E. Bowes.

First innings: 169 (Sutcliffe 52, Allen 30; Wall four for 52, O'Reilly five for 63). *Second innings*: 139 (Sutcliffe 33; O'Reilly five for 66, Ironmonger four for 26).

Umpires: G. A. Hele and G. Borwick

ENGLAND v AUSTRALIA (THIRD TEST MATCH)

85 (129, 130)
21 (29, 30)

Played at Adelaide, January 13, 14, 16, 17, 18, 19 [1933]. The Third Test Match of the tour, in which England – well on top when an innings had been completed on each side – were victorious by no fewer than 338 runs, will go down to history as probably the most unpleasant ever played. So hostile was the feeling of the Australian public against Jardine that, on the days before the game started, people were excluded from the ground when the Englishmen were practising. As Jardine won the toss and England batted first, nothing out of the common occurred to begin with, but later on, when Australia went in and Woodfull was hit over the heart again while Oldfield had to retire owing to a blow he received on the head, the majority of the spectators completely lost all hold on their feelings. Insulting remarks were hurled at Jardine, and when Larwood started to bowl his leg theory he came in for his share of the storm of abuse. Not to put too fine a point on it, pandemonium reigned. A passage of words between P. F. Warner [the MCC team's co-manager] and Woodfull in the dressing-room increased the bitter feeling prevalent in the crowd, and the dispatch of the cablegram protesting against 'Bodyline' bowling served no purpose in whatever endeavours were made to appease tempers already badly frayed by the various happenings.

[In their second innings Australia's target was 532 to win, on a wicket showing 'definite signs of wear'.] Before the fifth day's play ended, [they] lost four of their best batsmen for 120 runs and to all intents and purposes the game was as good as over. ... Fingleton and Ponsford [were] out with only 12 runs on the board, but then came an excellent stand by Woodfull and Bradman, 88 being put on in an hour and a quarter. Bradman was in first-rate form, hitting a 6 and ten 4's, but just when he was becoming dangerous Verity caught him from a hard return. ... The greatest praise is due to Woodfull, who for the second time in his career in a Test Match carried his bat through the innings. He was in for nearly four hours, making most of his runs from strokes on the leg side. ...

England

H. Sutcliffe, *Mr D.R. Jardine, W.R. Hammond, †L.E.G. Ames, M. Leyland, Mr R.E.S. Wyatt, E. Paynter, Mr G.O. Allen, H. Verity, W. Voce and H. Larwood.

First innings: 341 (Leyland 83, Wyatt 78, Paynter 77, Verity 45; Wall five for 72). *Second innings:* 412 (Jardine 56, Hammond 85, Ames 69, Leyland 42, Wyatt 49, Verity 40, sundries 32; O'Reilly four for 79, Ironmonger three for 87, Bradman one for 23).

Australia

J. H. Fingleton c Ames b Allen	0	–	b Larwood	0
*W. M. Woodfull b Allen	22	–	not out	73
D. G. Bradman c Allen b Larwood	8	–	c and b Verity	66
S. J. McCabe c Jardine b Larwood	8	–	c Leyland b Allen	7
W. H. Ponsford b Voce	85	–	c Jardine b Larwood	3
V. Y. Richardson b Allen	28	–	c Allen b Larwood	21
†W. A. Oldfield retired hurt	21	–	absent hurt	0
C. V. Grimmett c Voce b Allen	10	–	b Allen	6
T. W. Wall b Hammond	6	–	b Allen	0
W. J. O'Reilly b Larwood	0	–	b Larwood	5
H. Ironmonger not out	0	–	b Allen	0
B 2, l-b 11, n-b 1	14		B 4, l-b 2, w 1, n-b 5	12
	222			193

England bowling: *First innings*—Larwood 25–6–55–3; Allen 23–4–71–4; Hammond 17.4–4–30–1; Voce 14–5–21–1; Verity 16–7–31–0. *Second innings*—Larwood 19–3–71–4; Allen 17.2–5–50–4; Hammond 9–3–27–0; Voce 4–1–7–0; Verity 20–12–26–1.

Umpires: G. A. Hele and G. Borwick

MCC TEAM v NEW SOUTH WALES   86 (131, 132)

Played at Sydney, January 26, 27, 28 [1933]. MCC won a game of low scoring by four wickets. New South Wales on the first day lost four batsmen for 68, but Brown and Rowe brought about an improvement in a stand of 101. A rain-damaged pitch next day gave bowlers everything their own way, sixteen wickets going down for 246 runs. The last five New South Wales wickets fell for 11, and MCC had to fight hard for a lead of 19 runs. ... In [a second] innings marked by a curious mixture of good and bad strokes, Bradman on the last day saved New South Wales from collapse, but MCC needed only 110 to win. ...

New South Wales

J. H. Fingleton b Mitchell	19	–	lbw b Tate	7
W. Brown c Ames b Bowes	69	–	c Duckworth b Hammond	25
D. G. Bradman b Mitchell	1	–	c Ames b Hammond	71
*A. F. Kippax c Mitchell b Bowes	3	–	c Verity b Hammond	1
F. Cummins b Mitchell	0	–	c Verity b Hammond	3
R. Rowe c Mitchell b Verity	70	–	c Bowes b Hammond	11
†H. S. Love c Ames b Hammond	4	–	b Verity	2
C. Hill c Verity b Hammond	0	–	c Mitchell b Hammond	0
H. Chilvers lbw b Hammond	4	–	run out	0
W. Howell c Brown b Verity	0	–	b Verity	6
G. L. Stewart not out	0	–	not out	0
B 7, l-b 2, n-b 1	10		B 1, l-b 1	2
	180			**128**

MCC Team bowling: *First innings*—Bowes 15–2–48–2; Tate 10–1–42–0; Mitchell 10–1–32–3; Hammond 8.5–1–22–3; Verity 5–1–9–2; Brown 3–0–17–0. *Second innings*—Bowes 7–1–19–0; Tate 4–0–10–1; Mitchell 5–0–28–0; Hammond 13–1–43–6; Verity 9.1–3–26–2.

MCC Team

*Mr R. E. S. Wyatt, Nawab of Pataudi, W. R. Hammond, H. Verity, L. E. G. Ames, M. Leyland, Mr F. R. Brown, M. W. Tate, †G. Duckworth, W. E. Bowes and T. B. Mitchell.

First innings: 199 (Wyatt 63, Verity 33; Hill three for 39, Chilvers five for 73). *Second innings:* Six for 110 (Leyland 33; Chilvers three for 29).

Umpires: G. Borwick and W.G. French

NEW SOUTH WALES v SOUTH AUSTRALIA   87 (133, 134)

Played at Sydney, February 3, 4, 6 [1933]. Despite a great bowling feat by Wall, South Australia lost this return match by 98 runs. On the opening day New South Wales had 87 on the board for two wickets, but after lunch Wall's fast bowling was almost unplayable. Fingleton, McCabe, Rowe and Cummins were sent back in one over without a run being scored, and Wall took all ten wickets for 36 runs – nine for five runs after the interval and six clean-bowled. [This was the first instance of a bowler taking all ten wickets in the Sheffield Shield, and the second of a bowler doing so in a first-class match in Australia.] The pitch gave him little assistance, but a stiff breeze helped him swing the ball. ... When New South Wales went in again, Brown, Bradman and McCabe batted freely, and South Australia were set 356 for victory. ... [Bradman brought both South Australian innings to an end when he had Shepherd caught in the first and Wall stumped in the second.] The win of New South Wales enabled them to retain the Shield.

New South Wales

J. H. Fingleton b Wall	43	–	c Tobin b Wall	0
W. Brown c Whitington b Wall	0	–	c Walker b Wall	79
D. G. Bradman c Ryan b Wall	56	–	b Lee	97
S. J. McCabe c Walker b Wall	0	–	lbw b Grimmett	67
R. Rowe b Wall	0	–	c Tobin b Lee	19
F. S. Cummins c Walker b Wall	0	–	b Grimmett	36
*†H. S. Love b Wall	1	–	lbw b Ryan	31
C. Hill b Wall	0	–	not out	9
W. Howell b Wall	0	–	b Ryan	8
W. J. O'Reilly b Wall	4	–	c Walker b Lee	5
G. L. Stewart not out	2	–	b Lee	0
L-b 1, w 1, n-b 5	7		B 1, l-b 2, n-b 2	5
	113			356

South Australia bowling: *First innings*—Wall 12.4–2–36–10; Tobin 5–0–23–0; Grimmett 11–0–47–0. *Second innings*—Wall 22–1–91–2; Tobin 12–0–69–0; Grimmett 20–2–84–2; Ryan 17–3–38–2; Lee 16.5–2–69–4.

South Australia

*V.Y. Richardson, H.C. Nitschke, A.R. Lonergan, A.J. Ryan, R.S. Whitington, B.J. Tobin, A.G. Shepherd, P.K. Lee, C.V. Grimmett, T.W. Wall and †C.W. Walker.

First innings: 114 (Shepherd 32; Howell five for 31, Bradman one for 4). *Second innings:* 257 (Richardson 35, Nitschke 105, Ryan 33; O'Reilly five for 56, Hill four for 61, Bradman one for 36).

Umpires: G. Borwick and W.G. French

ENGLAND v AUSTRALIA (FOURTH TEST MATCH)

88 (135, 136)
22 (31, 32)

Played at Brisbane, February 10, 11, 13, 14, 15, 16 [1933]. England won the Fourth Test Match by six wickets, so being successful in the rubber and regaining the Ashes. ... Their cricket in this game proved from first to last better than that of the Australians. Once more Jardine captained his side with remarkable skill, his management of his bowlers and his placing of the field being worthy of great praise. In this respect he certainly outshone Woodfull, who had under his command three new men ... Bromley and Darling were brought into the Australian XI as left-handers likely to counteract the effect of Larwood's leg-theory bowling, and Love kept wicket as Oldfield was not well enough to take his usual place behind the stumps [the blow to his head by a ball from Larwood in the Third Test had fractured his skull].

The Australians at times seemed to have more than a reasonable chance, but they failed to drive home a temporary advantage, and generally speaking they did not appear to be a well-balanced side, while there is no doubt that nearly all of them were overawed by Larwood. The match will always be memorable for the great part played in the victory of England by Paynter. Suffering from an affection of the throat, he left a sick-bed to bat, and put together a splendid innings of 83, while he enjoyed the additional satisfaction later on of making the winning hit with a 6.

Woodfull again won the toss, and this time took in with him to open the Australian innings Victor Richardson. This move proved highly successful ... and thanks to their opening partnership of 133 Australia on the first day stayed in all afternoon to make 251 for the loss of three wickets ... Richardson after lunch made some splendid hits and Bradman carried on the good work, being 71 not out when stumps were pulled up. ... In getting rid of Australia for less than 400 runs, the Englishmen could congratulate themselves. Larwood did great work in taking four wickets, bowling Bradman at 264 and Ponsford at 267. The quick dismissal of these two renowned batsmen meant a great deal to the visiting team. Bradman did not play at all well in the closing stages of his innings, drawing away more than once from Larwood's bowling. After that there was little of note in the batting. ... The third day did not go quite so well for England, for at the close England had eight men out for 271 and thus were still 69 runs behind. ... [The] negative kind of batting following the opening partnership of 114 runs was disappointing. ... Paynter, ill and weak, obviously could not force matters, but he was 24 not out at the close of the day, and on the next morning he gave a superb exhibition. ... He was in for nearly four hours ... As near as possible England were batting ten hours for their total of 356, which on the face of it seemed absurd.

In the last two and a half hours of the day, however, they atoned for this by some splendid bowling and fielding so that Australia lost four wickets in their second innings for 108 and wound up only 92 runs in front. Richardson led off in rare style, and Bradman batted brightly before falling once more to Larwood at 79. ... Once more, the Australians showed what a long tail they had to their team, the last five men scoring between them only 16 runs.

England were thus left with only 160 runs to get ... and play ceased [for the day] with the score at 107 for two wickets. On the last day the flags all round the ground were at half-mast owing to the death that morning of Archie Jackson [at the age of twenty-three]. ... Soon after the match was won rain came on and poured steadily for twelve hours. ...

Australia

*W. M. Woodfull b Mitchell	67	–	c Hammond b Mitchell	19
V. Y. Richardson st Ames b Hammond	83	–	c Jardine b Verity	32
D. G. Bradman b Larwood	76	–	c Mitchell b Larwood	24
S. J. McCabe c Jardine b Allen	20	–	b Verity	22
W. H. Ponsford b Larwood	19	–	c Larwood b Allen	0
L. Darling c Ames b Allen	17	–	run out	39
E. H. Bromley c Verity b Larwood	26	–	c Hammond b Allen	7
†H. S. Love lbw b Mitchell	5	–	lbw b Larwood	3
T. Wall not out	6	–	c Jardine b Allen	2
W. J. O'Reilly c Hammond b Larwood	6	–	b Larwood	4
H. Ironmonger st Ames b Hammond	8	–	not out	0
B 5, l-b 1, n-b 1	7		B 13, l-b 9, n-b 1	23
	340			**175**

England bowling: *First innings:* Larwood 31–7–101–4; Allen 24–4–83–2; Hammond 23–5–61–2; Mitchell 16–5–49–2; Verity 27–12–39–0. *Second innings*—Larwood 17.3–3–49–3; Allen 17–3–44–3; Hammond 10–4–18–0; Mitchell 5–0–11–1; Verity 19–6–30–2.

England

*Mr D. R. Jardine, H. Sutcliffe, W. R. Hammond, Mr R. E. S. Wyatt, M. Leyland, †L. E. G. Ames, Mr G. O. Allen, E. Paynter, H. Larwood, H. Verity and T. B. Mitchell.

First innings: 356 (Jardine 46, Sutcliffe 86, Paynter 83; O'Reilly four for 120, Ironmonger three for 69, Bradman none for 17). *Second innings:* Four for 162 (Leyland 86).

Umpires: G. A. Hele and G. Borwick

ENGLAND v AUSTRALIA
(FIFTH TEST MATCH)

89 (137, 138)
23 (33, 34)

Played at Sydney, February 23, 24, 25, 27, 28 [1933]. The rubber having been won by England, the batting of both sides in their first innings in the last Test Match was generally much brighter than that which previously had been seen. The strain was lifted from both sides, but Australia gave a poor display in the second innings and England demonstrated their superiority over their opponents in no uncertain fashion in winning by eight wickets. Unfortunately the match was marred by bad catching, each side being at fault [in Australia's first innings 'it was ... estimated that England missed no fewer than fourteen catches'], and to Victor Richardson in particular it must have proved a dismal memory, for going in first again with Woodfull he was dismissed without scoring in each innings. ... Larwood, although damaging his foot when bowling [in the second innings; he suffered a broken toe], came out as a batsman with a splendid innings of 98. What a pity he could not have capped his great bowling successes by obtaining a hundred in a Test Match! ... For the fourth time Jardine lost the toss, and in the first over Richardson was out. Woodfull and Bradman carried the score to 59, but then Woodfull played on and in the next over Bradman left at 64. Thenceforward, matters went well for Australia. ... On the Saturday, England batted all day and finished up only 17 runs behind with two wickets to fall. Continuing his innings, Hammond did not play in quite the same brilliant style, and most of the applause was earned by Larwood [who had joined Hammond on Friday evening as night-watchman], who drove in glorious fashion and treated the spectators to a great display ... [until], trying to place the ball to the on for a two to reach three figures, [he] did not time his stroke properly and was caught by Ironmonger, a notoriously bad fieldsman. Larwood treated the bowling as no other of the Englishmen had previously done. He made his runs in two hours and a quarter, hitting a 6, a 5 and nine 4's, and ... was loudly cheered. ...

Monday was full of sensation. England increasing their score to 454 gained a lead of 19 runs ... When Australia went in again the first wicket once more fell before a run had been scored, but then Woodfull and Bradman put on 115. Bradman was in his most daring mood, often stepping back to the leg-theory bowling of Voce and Larwood and forcing the ball to the off. Verity, however, bowled Bradman when the batsman misjudged the flight of the ball, and with his dismissal a breakdown occurred. ... [Later] Verity dismissed O'Reilly and Alexander with consecutive balls, and as Ironmonger was next in the Yorkshireman had a good chance of doing the 'hat-trick'. This he did not accomplish. ...

[When England batted again, requiring 164 to win], Jardine, who took Wyatt in with him, complained about Alexander running down the pitch after his delivery [as the Englishmen had in the first innings], and the crowd booed and hooted. Alexander then bumped several balls down to Jardine, and when the England captain was struck on the thigh, sections of the crowd cheered. A disgraceful exhibition. ... [When Jardine and Leyland were out] Hammond surprised everyone by on-driving O'Reilly for 6 – one of the biggest hits ever seen on the Sydney ground. Hammond, after that, played in brilliant fashion and finished the match in dramatic style with another big 6 [off the bowling of Lee].

Australia

V. Y. Richardson c Jardine b Larwood	0	–	c Allen b Larwood	0
*W. M. Woodfull b Larwood	14	–	b Allen	67
D. G. Bradman b Larwood	48	–	b Verity	71
L. P. O'Brien c Larwood b Voce	61	–	c Verity b Voce	5
S. J. McCabe c Hammond b Verity	73	–	c Jardine b Voce	4
L. S. Darling b Verity	85	–	c Wyatt b Verity	7
†W. A. Oldfield run out	52	–	c Wyatt b Verity	5
P. K. Lee c Jardine b Verity	42	–	b Allen	15
W. J. O'Reilly b Allen	19	–	b Verity	1
H. H. Alexander not out	17	–	lbw b Verity	0
H. Ironmonger b Larwood	1	–	not out	0
B 13, l-b 9, w 1	23		B 4, n-b 3	7
	435			**182**

England bowling: *First innings*—Larwood 32.2–10–98–4; Voce 24–3–80–1; Allen 25–1–128–1; Hammond 8–0–32–0; Verity 17–3–62–3; Wyatt 2–0–12–0. *Second innings*—Larwood 11–0–44–1; Voce 10–0–34–2; Allen 11.4–2–54–2; Hammond 3–0–10–0; Verity 19–9–33–5.

England
H. Sutcliffe, *Mr D.R. Jardine, W.R. Hammond, H. Larwood, M. Leyland, Mr R.E.S. Wyatt, †L.E.G. Ames, E. Paynter, Mr G.O. Allen, H. Verity and W. Voce.
  First innings: 454 (Sutcliffe 56, Hammond 101, Larwood 98, Leyland 42, Wyatt 51, Allen 48; O'Reilly three for 100, Lee four for 111). *Second innings:* Two for 168 (Wyatt 61 not out, Hammond 75 not out).

Umpires: G.A. Hele and G. Borwick

BRADMAN: AN AUSTRALIAN HERO

Charles Williams in *Bradman: An Australian Hero* ventures on to more technical ground [than Roland Perry in *The Don*, see page 180] by trying to analyse why Bradman was so pre-eminent; he looks at stance, grip, stillness of head, follow-through and so on. This is a more successful project than Perry's attempt to show by 'biochemical' graphs (the so-called Bell curve) that Bradman was better at cricket than anyone else has ever been at any sport. Charles Williams also goes more deeply into the question of Australian identity and what sort of national need was satisfied by Bradman's pre-eminence in the sporting world; the fact that Bradman sprang from such a decent, modest, archetypically Australian background was ideal for a hero-hungry public in the depressed 1930s, though it made him unpopular with a certain Irish element in the Australian team. Both authors agree, as have their predecessors, on Bradman's shy, private personality, on his honour, determination and self-discipline; both are tactful to the point of reticence on the extent to which his illnesses in the war years were of physical or partly psychological origin; but Williams, formerly the biographer of de Gaulle, is the subtler. His book is also well illustrated (it includes the farewell to the SCG picture) and it is shorter – not a bad thing in a well-known story. Neither of these new biographies, however, replaces the gripping *Don Bradman's Book* (1930) on the stump-and-tennis-ball years (Williams has it in his bibliography; Perry does not), or Irving Rosenwater's *Sir Donald Bradman* (1978) for the mature years.

From 'Cricket Books, 1996', by Sebastian Faulks

1933-34

Batting against England in the Fifth Test at Sydney, Februrary 1933.

1933-34

For the third time in five seasons Victoria carried off the Sheffield Shield. The result of the competition was not decided until the final match – that between New South Wales and Victoria at Sydney. New South Wales had to win outright to retain the trophy, but as they could only lead on the first innings their opponents finished one point in front. ...

Bradman again proved the outstanding batsman for New South Wales ... and of the season. Scoring 922 runs in Shield matches he had the remarkable figures of 184.40 per innings, and put together two double-centuries, both against Queensland, and two hundreds against Victoria. He and Kippax created a new Sheffield Shield third-wicket record, the pair putting on 363 against Queensland at Sydney. [This remained the highest third-wicket partnership in Australia until 1981-82.] In all first-class games, Bradman exceeded a thousand runs for the sixth successive season, a performance unequalled by any player in Australia. ...

Before the commencement of the 1933-34 season the Inter-State conference decided to adopt the Australian Board of Control's 'anti-Bodyline' law for the Sheffield Shield competition. The law reads: 'Any ball delivered which, in the opinion of the umpire at the bowler's end, is bowled at the batsman with intent to intimidate or injure him, shall be considered unfair and "no-ball" shall be called and the bowler notified of the reason. If the offence be repeated by the same bowler in the same innings, he shall be immediately instructed by the umpire to cease bowling and the over shall be regarded as completed. Such bowler shall not again be permitted to bowl during the course of the innings then in progress.'

From 'Cricket in Australia: Inter-State Matches 1933-34'

QUEENSLAND v NEW SOUTH WALES   90 (139)

Played at Brisbane, November 3, 4, 6, 7 [1933]. Splendid bowling by O'Reilly ... followed by brilliant batting from Bradman were outstanding features of a one-sided match that New South Wales won by an innings and 171 runs. ... When New South Wales went in, Bradman scored 200 runs, including twenty-six 4's, in 184 minutes. He and Brown put on 294 in less than three hours and made a record second-wicket stand for their State against Queensland. Heavy rain caused a blank Monday, but, Queensland's batsmen again failing before O'Reilly on a bowler's wicket, New South Wales won easily.

Queensland

*R.M. Levy, T. Allen, C.W. Andrews, F.C. Thompson, E.C. Bensted, R.K. Oxenham, R.C. Raymond, †H. Leeson, H.S. Gamble, F. Yeates and E.R.H. Wyeth.

First innings: 183 (Andrews 59, Bensted 70; O'Reilly six for 58). *Second innings:* 140 (Levy 37, Andrews 31; O'Reilly seven for 53, Mair three for 30).

New South Wales

J. H. Fingleton c Leeson b Yeates	53	S. J. McCabe c Thompson b Oxenham	20
W. A. Brown st Leeson b Yeates	154	R. Rowe not out	13
D. G. Bradman c Andrews b Levy	200	B 2, l-b 1, n-b 5	8
*A. F. Kippax not out	46	(four wkts dec)	**494**

†W. A. Oldfield, F. Mair, C. J. Hill, W. J. O'Reilly and W. Howell did not bat.

Queensland bowling: Gamble 24–6–89–0; Bensted 8–3–33–0; Oxenham 30–8–81–1; Raymond 12–0–57–0; Wyeth 10–3–54–0; Yeates 22–1–155–2; Thompson 1–0–11–0; Levy 1–0–6–1.

Umpires: J. A. Scott and J. Bartlett

W. M. WOODFULL'S XI v V. Y. RICHARDSON'S XI   91 (140, 141)

Played at Melbourne, November 17, 18, 20, 21, 22 [1933]. This [Test Trial] match ... primarily intended as a Benefit to Blackie and Ironmonger, was left drawn. Rain prevented a start on Friday, and after lunch on Saturday the weather stopped further proceedings until Monday. ... Unfortunately for Woodfull, Ironmonger, owing to an injured knee, could do little bowling [nor was he able to bat]. ... [After the teams had batted once] Bradman dominated the remaining cricket. Of the 169 runs scored in Richardson's XI's second innings before the game was given up, he obtained 101 by hard and well-timed strokes all round the wicket.

V. Y. Richardson's XI

*V. Y. Richardson run out	28			
J. H. Fingleton lbw b McCabe	105	–	b Wall	0
D. G. Bradman c Woodfull b Wall	55	–	c Darling b Blackie	101
K. E. Rigg b Blackie	94	–	b McCabe	2
L. P. O'Brien c Ponsford b Fleetwood-Smith	90	–	run out	42
P. K. Lee lbw b Fleetwood-Smith	17			
†B. A. Barnett st Oldfield b Blackie	60			
H. I. Ebeling c Wall b Blackie	4			
C. V. Grimmett not out	16			
L. E. Nagel not out	8			
W. J. O'Reilly (did not bat)		–	not out	20
B 6, l-b 7, n-b 1	14		L-b 3, n-b 1	4
(eight wkts dec)	**491**		(four wkts)	**169**

W.M. Woodfull's XI bowling: *First innings*—Wall 25–2–104–1; McCabe 14–1–51–1; Fleetwood-Smith 36–3–140–2; Ironmonger 20–5–88–0; Darling 5–0–25–0; Blackie 25–5–69–3. *Second innings*—Wall 10–5–20–1; McCabe 11–3–25–1; Fleetwood-Smith 9–0–49–0; Darling 2–0–16–0; Blackie 11.7–2–36–1; Kippax 2–0–19–0.

W.M. Woodfull's XI

*W.M. Woodfull, W.H. Ponsford, H.C. Nitschke, S.J. McCabe, A.F. Kippax, L.S. Darling, †W.A. Oldfield, D.D. Blackie, T.W. Wall, L. O'B. Fleetwood-Smith and H. Ironmonger.

First innings: 350 (Woodfull 118, Ponsford 42, McCabe 82, Kippax 34, Darling 30; Ebeling five for 72, Bradman none for 18).

Umpires: G.A. Hele and A.N. Barlow

NEW SOUTH WALES v REST OF AUSTRALIA 92 (142, 143)

Played at Sydney, November 24, 25, 27, 28 [1933]. The second Benefit Trial Match – played as a Testimonial for Collins, Andrews and Kelleway – which the Rest won by two wickets, yielded several good performances. ... [When] New South Wales batted again Fingleton, Bradman, Kippax and Rowe all made good scores. ... Declaring with a lead of 408, New South Wales found their opponents in great batting form. Woodfull's soundness, and dashing innings by Darling and Nitschke, saw the Rest secure a rather unexpected but well-deserved victory in the last over of the day.

New South Wales

J.H. Fingleton b Ebeling	33	–	c Walker b Ebeling	78
W.A. Brown b Nash	8	–	b Chilvers	29
D.G. Bradman c Walker b Chilvers	22	–	b Ebeling	92
*A.F. Kippax c Walker b Chilvers	15	–	not out	111
S.J. McCabe c Walker b Darling	110	–	st Walker b Chilvers	8
R. Rowe c Walker b Ebeling	66	–	not out	66
F. Mair b Ebeling	2			
†W.A. Oldfield c Bromley b Ebeling	4			
C.J. Hill c Walker b Darling	2			
W.J. O'Reilly c Darling b Ebeling	4			
W. Howell not out	1			
B 3, l-b 2, w 1	6		B 5, l-b 1	6
	273		(four wkts dec)	**390**

Rest of Australia bowling: *First innings*—Nash 10–0–48–1; Ebeling 22.1–3–66–5; Lee 14–2–39–0; Chilvers 19–2–69–2; Bromley 7–1–31–0; Darling 6–1–14–2. *Second innings*—Nash 11–0–57–0; Ebeling 28–4–87–2; Lee 23–2–67–0; Chilvers 26–2–95–2; Bromley 7–0–33–0; Darling 8–0–45–0.

Rest of Australia

*W.M. Woodfull, W.H. Ponsford, L.P. O'Brien, L.S. Darling, H.C. Nitschke, E.H. Bromley, P.K. Lee, L.J. Nash, H.I. Ebeling, H.C. Chilvers and †C.W. Walker.

First innings: 255 (Ponsford 70, Lee 69; O'Reilly three for 59, Mair three for 81). *Second innings:* Eight for 409 (Woodfull 129, O'Brien 44, Darling 77, Nitschke 76, Bromley 42; Bradman one for 30, Kippax three for 10).

Umpires: G. Borwick and W.G. French

SOUTH AUSTRALIA v NEW SOUTH WALES   93 (144, 145)

Played at Adelaide, December 15, 16, 18 [1933]. South Australia, in the Ernest Jones Benefit game, accomplished an excellent performance in beating the [Shield] holders by ten wickets. ... [In their first innings] New South Wales generally [showed] to very poor advantage. ... In [their] second innings, Bradman and Kippax got runs readily without ever appearing quite comfortable against Grimmett, who took advantage of a worn patch, and Lee. ...

New South Wales

J. H. Fingleton c Walker b Tobin	27	–	c Walker b Grimmett	30
W. A. Brown c Ryan b Wall	4	–	c Walker b Collins	38
D. G. Bradman b Collins	1	–	c Wall b Grimmett	76
*A. F. Kippax b Tobin	9	–	st Walker b Grimmett	90
R. Rowe c Wall b Tobin	1	–	b Wall	6
†W. A. Oldfield run out	0	–	c Richardson b Grimmett	20
H. C. Chilvers not out	16	–	b Grimmett	0
F. Mair b Grimmett	14	–	lbw b Lee	2
W. J. O'Reilly c Richardson b Grimmett	6	–	not out	2
C. J. Hill run out	24	–	b Lee	1
W. Howell b Lee	1	–	b Lee	0
B 1, l-b 1, n-b 3	5		L-b	6
	108			**271**

South Australia bowling: *First innings*—Wall 10–3–24–1; Collins 9–1–30–1; Tobin 8–1–20–3; Lee 4.1–0–12–1; Grimmett 6–2–17–2. *Second innings*—Wall 18–1–66–1; Collins 13–0–43–1; Tobin 10–0–49–0; Lee 5–2–4–3; Grimmett 33–3–103–5.

South Australia

*V. Y. Richardson, H. C. Nitschke, A. R. Lonergan, A. J. Ryan, A. G. Shepherd, B. J. Tobin, F. H. Collins, P. K. Lee, †C. W. Walker, C. V. Grimmett and T. W. Wall.

First innings: 316 (Nitschke 82, Lonergan 50, Ryan 94 not out, Shepherd 43; Chilvers three for 48, Mair four for 69). *Second innings:* None for 65 (Nitschke 44 not out).

Umpires: J. D. Scott and E. H. Kitson

VICTORIA v NEW SOUTH WALES   94 (146, 147)

Played at Melbourne, December 22, 23, 26, 27 [1933]. Victoria gained innings points after much splendid cricket. ... Despite good defence by Fingleton and splendidly accurate batting on the part of Bradman, New South Wales lost six men for 259. Then Bradman scored all but 16 of the 96 runs realised by the remaining wickets, the visitors finishing 27 behind. O'Reilly, spinning and flighting the ball skilfully, followed by dismissing nine Victorian batsmen ... Only Ponsford and Darling dealt effectively with him. New South Wales, set 228 to get, finished in the better position, Bradman again carrying his bat.

Victoria

*W. M. Woodfull, W. H. Ponsford, L. P. O'Brien, K. E. Rigg, L. S. Darling, E. H. Bromley, †B. A. Barnett, L. E. Nagel, H. I. Ebeling, L. O'B. Fleetwood-Smith and H. Ironmonger.

First innings: 382 (Woodfull 60, Ponsford 30, O'Brien 86, Darling 91, Ebeling 32; Howell five for 97, O'Reilly three for 92). *Second innings:* 200 (Ponsford 40, Darling 53; O'Reilly nine for 50).

New South Wales

J. H. Fingleton lbw b Ebeling	76			
W. A. Brown lbw b Fleetwood-Smith	23			
D. G. Bradman not out	187	–	not out	77
*A. F. Kippax b Fleetwood-Smith	23	–	c Barnett b Ebeling	28
A. McGilvray b Fleetwood-Smith	11			
R. Rowe c Barnett b Fleetwood-Smith	5	–	not out	39
†W. A. Oldfield c Darling b Fleetwood-Smith	2			
H. C. Chilvers b Ironmonger	5			
W. J. O'Reilly lbw b Fleetwood-Smith	6			
F. Mair c Barnett b Ironmonger	3			
W. Howell b Fleetwood-Smith	2			
B 8, l-b 2, n-b 2	12			
	355		(one wkt)	**144**

Victoria bowling: *First innings*—Ebeling 29–7–53–1; Nagel 20–3–70–0; Ironmonger 30–10–51–2; Fleetwood-Smith 32–3–138–7; Bromley 7–0–31–0. *Second innings*—Ebeling 10–0–56–1; Nagel 3–0–28–0; Ironmonger 9–0–26–0; Bromley 3–0–26–0; Darling 2–0–8–0.

Umpires: A. N. Barlow and G. A. Hele

NEW SOUTH WALES v QUEENSLAND   95 (148)

Played at Sydney, December 30 [1933], January 1, 2, 3 [1934]. Another great double-century by Bradman against Queensland featured [in] the victory of New South Wales by an innings and 84 runs. ... Bradman surpassed everyone. Exploiting all the strokes, he dealt unmercifully with the bowling, actually scoring his 253 in less than three and a half hours. His execution of the cut, drive, pull and leg-glance was perfect. Kippax was by no means overshadowed. Batting with his usual grace he reached his hundred in two hours. His record third-wicket stand of 363 with Bradman occupied only two and a quarter hours. ...

Queensland

G.G. Cook, F.M. Brew, C.W. Andrews, F.C. Thompson, *R.M. Levy, E.C. Bensted, T. Allen, R.K. Oxenham, A. Tait, †H. Leeson and H.S. Gamble.

First innings: 372 (Andrews 38, Thompson 92, Levy 45, Allen 86, Oxenham 51; Hill three for 51, Bradman none for 2). *Second innings:* 158 (Tait 35; Chilvers six for 62).

New South Wales

J. H. Fingleton c Bensted b Brew	42	A. G. Chipperfield c Leeson b Andrews	84
W. A. Brown c Levy b Oxenham	50	A. McGilvray not out	34
D. G. Bradman b Brew	253	C. J. Hill not out	2
*A. F. Kippax c sub b Oxenham	125	B 8, l-b 2, w 5, n-b 2	17
R. Rowe c Leeson b Oxenham	7	(six wkts dec)	**614**

†A. Easton, H. C. Chilvers and W. Howell did not bat.

Queensland bowling: Gamble 6–0–17–0; Bensted 19–2–97–0; Brew 25–1–176–2; Oxenham 42–0–116–3; Tait 10–1–77–0; Cook 4–0–32–0; Andrews 3–0–19–1; Levy 5–0–63–0.

Umpires: G. Borwick and H. Armstrong

NEW SOUTH WALES v VICTORIA 96 (149)

Played at Sydney, January 26, 27, 29, 30 [1934]. A draw won Victoria the Sheffield Shield by a single point. For New South Wales, Bradman [in what was to be his last game for his home State] hit four 6's and seventeen 4's in an hour and a half; Brown combined caution with aggression in a sound 205, and Fingleton made 145 after being given out when 86 only to be recalled following a talk between Woodfull and Borwick, the umpire. [Having been dropped at slip, Fingleton left his ground to tap down the pitch and was adjudged run out by Borwick, standing at square-leg, when wicket-keeper Barnett removed the bails.] ...

New South Wales

J. H. Fingleton c Bromley b Ironmonger	145	H. C. Chilvers run out	42
W. A. Brown lbw b Fleetwood-Smith	205	†W. A. Oldfield run out	2
D. G. Bradman c Darling b Fleetwood-Smith	128	C. J. Hill not out	32
*A. F. Kippax c Barnett b McCormick	44	W. J. O'Reilly not out	11
R. Rowe run out	42	B 4, l-b 8	12
A. G. Chipperfield c Barnett b Ebeling	9	(eight wkts dec)	**672**

H. Theak did not bat.

Victoria bowling: McCormick 35–1–148–1; Ebeling 29–1–154–1; Fleetwood-Smith 31–0–178–2; Ironmonger 22–3–86–1; Bromley 6–0–42–0; Darling 9–0–52–0.

Victoria

*W. M. Woodfull, L. P. O'Brien, K. E. Rigg, J. Scaife, L. S. Darling, E. H. Bromley, †B. A. Barnett, H. I. Ebeling, E. L. McCormick, L. O'B. Fleetwood-Smith and H. Ironmonger.

First innings: 407 (Woodfull 83, Scaife 120, Bromley 92; Hill three for 40). *Second innings:* Five for 274 (Rigg 35, Scaife 80, Darling 93, Bromley 33 not out; Bradman none for 19).

Umpires: G. Borwick and H. Armstrong

1934

Bradman leaves the field after straining a thigh muscle on the third afternoon of the 1934 Headingley Test.

1934

The Australian team of 1934 arrived in [the United Kingdom] with the knowledge that during the previous series of Test Matches in Australia they had been beaten four times and successful only once, and to the majority of people at home the idea of England losing the rubber was as remote as it had been in 1930. Australia, however, won two Test Matches to England's one – the struggles at Manchester and Leeds being left drawn – and, by a remarkable coincidence, Woodfull, again as in 1930, led his side at The Oval to the victory which regained the Ashes, on the anniversary of his birthday – August 22....

There is no need here to go deeply into those occurrences which, marring the enjoyment of the tour of the MCC team in 1932, so nearly ended in a breach of the cricketing relations between this country and Australia. Yet it is necessary to refer to the upheaval which the so-called 'Bodyline' bowling, as practised during that tour, caused. Matters were smoothed over sufficiently to ensure the visit of the Australians ... but the echoes of the controversy continually arose and the Australian team themselves were just a trifle doubtful as to the kind of welcome they would receive. Happily for everyone concerned, any fears our visitors may have entertained on this point were quickly removed by the enthusiasm expressed about their cricket during the early matches and the genuine feeling of goodwill shown towards them at public receptions and at most places they went to play....

The advent of fine, sunny weather, after very miserable conditions prior to their opening match, enabled them to jump almost at once into form, and with the exception of the debacle in the Test Match at Lord's they remained at their very best until the end. Still, they had their troubles in the way of illness and accident. Quite early ... they had to contend with an epidemic of influenza.... After the First Test Bradman hurt his leg, catching it in a rope when running off the field, at Nottingham ... illness kept Ponsford out of the Second Test, at Lord's ... another epidemic, this time described as 'Wimbledon throat', swept through the team during the Manchester Test Match so that Chipperfield and Kippax were detained in an isolation hospital ... and then at Leeds Bradman had to leave the field with a strained thigh. ... Finally Bromley, on the eve of the last Test Match, developed appendicitis and underwent an operation while, when the tour had been completed, Bradman was also operated on for appendicitis and prevented from leaving England with the rest of his colleagues. Few, if any, teams visiting this country, therefore, can have experienced such an anxious time ... as did the Australians last summer. ...

The batting of the team was tremendously strong. In all first-class matches six men scored over 1,000 runs each, Bradman heading the list with an average of over 84 and an aggregate of 2,020. [The other five were McCabe (2,078), Ponsford (1,784), Brown (1,308), Woodfull (1,268) and Darling (1,022).] ... For purposes of comparison Bradman obtained 940 fewer runs than in 1930 ... In Test Matches ... despite innings of 304 at Leeds and 244 at The Oval, [he] totalled, in eight appearances as against five, 216 fewer runs, his average dropping from 139 to 94. ...

Bradman [who was vice-captain of the touring team] had a curious season. He reached three figures seven times ... As in 1930 he led off in the opening match with an innings of over 200 against Worcestershire but then for a time he was, for Bradman, less than normal. Indeed, after his 206 at Worcester his only three-figure innings until the middle of July at Sheffield was 160 against Middlesex at Lord's. Yet that 160 was, in all probability, the most dazzling exhibition he gave throughout the tour. On the first afternoon he reached his hundred off the last ball of the day, having obtained these runs out of 135 in seventy-five minutes. Although going at such a tremendous pace his timing and placing were so certain and his execution so powerful that he did not make a single mistake. Old habitués of Lord's were almost unanimous afterwards in saying that they had never before seen such a brilliant and perfect display. Bradman finished the season in great style, his 140 against Yorkshire being the prelude to a succession of big scores, of which 304 in the Leeds Test was most noteworthy. He was out of the team for five first-class matches after this; then came his 244 at The Oval and he ended with 149 not out at Folkestone and 132 at Scarborough. It was noticeable that in many innings Bradman lifted the ball to a far greater extent than when he came here first, and there were many occasions on which he was out to wild strokes. Indeed at one period he created the impression that, to some extent, he had lost control of himself and went in to bat with an almost complete disregard for anything in the shape of a defensive stroke. To those, however, who watched him closely in his big innings, it was obvious that in the course of four years he had improved his technique almost out of knowledge. He was much more interesting to look at because of the wider range of his scoring strokes. At his best he was probably harder to get out than ever, and at times so marvellous was his footwork and power of execution that all bowlers were at a complete loss as to where they should pitch the ball. An amazingly brilliant batsman, he retained that faculty, given to most really great players, of delaying his stroke until the last possible moment. ...

... [A]s in 1930, the team went through their programme of matches with only one defeat – in the Second Test Match at Lord's. Including minor engagements they won fifteen of the thirty-four fixtures arranged and drew eighteen. Actually, apart from the match they lost, they never really looked to be in danger.

From 'The Australians in England', by S. J. Southerton

WORCESTERSHIRE v AUSTRALIANS   97 (150)

Played at Worcester, Wednesday, Thursday, May 2, 3 [1934]. A great innings by Bradman and the skilful bowling of Grimmett had most to do with the overwhelming victory by an innings and 297 runs gained by the Australians in the opening engagement of the tour. ... Bradman immediately settled down to his finest form, driving, pulling and hooking with perfect timing and strength. He and Woodfull added 114 for the second wicket, and McCabe and Bromley joined with Bradman in partnerships that yielded 70 and 111 respectively. Sixth out at 359, Bradman, except for one chance of stumping, made no mistake during nearly three and a half hours at the crease. He punished fully any deliveries of imperfect length, twice scoring 14 runs in an over, and he hit twenty-seven 4's. ...

Worcestershire

*Mr C.F. Walters, H.H. Gibbons, Nawab of Pataudi, M. Nichol, S.H. Martin, C.H. Bull, †Mr B.W. Quaife, R. Howorth, G.W. Brook, P.F. Jackson and R.T.D. Perks.

First innings: 112 (Walters 32; Grimmett five for 53). Second innings: 95 (Grimmett five for 27, O'Reilly four for 25).

Australians

*W. M. Woodfull c Perks b Martin	48	C. V. Grimmett c Brook b Howorth	7
W. H. Ponsford c Nichol b Jackson	13	H. I. Ebeling b Perks	13
D. G. Bradman b Howorth	206	T. W. Wall lbw b Brook	24
A. F. Kippax b Jackson	0	W. J. O'Reilly not out	25
S. J. McCabe c Brook b Perks	20	B 26, l-b 5, n-b 5	36
E. H. Bromley c Brook b Howorth	45		**504**
†W. A. Oldfield c Martin b Howorth	67		

Worcestershire bowling: Perks 26–2–83–2; Jackson 30–4–95–2; Martin 14–4–41–1; Brook 22–2–114–1; Howorth 23–0–135–4.

Umpires: T. Oates and A. Dolphin

LEICESTERSHIRE v AUSTRALIANS 98 (151)

Played at [Aylestone Road] Leicester, Saturday, Monday, Tuesday, May 5, 7, 8 [1934]. Though leading by 216 on the first innings, the Australians could not force a win. Their bowlers laboured under the handicap of a wet ball on the last day ... The pitch on Saturday helped O'Reilly to take seven wickets ... but the turf rolled out well on Monday when, aided by fielding errors, the Australians played themselves into an impregnable position. Brown and Bradman made 65 together. ... Bradman declaring with five men out, Leicestershire faced a heavy task, but Dawson and Berry, in a third-wicket stand of 116, pulled the game round. [After a collapse] Astill and Geary came to the rescue.

Leicestershire

Mr E.W. Dawson, A. Shipman, N.F. Armstrong, L.G. Berry, *Mr A.G. Hazlerigg, Mr A.G. Weston, A. Riddington, G. Geary, W.E. Astill, H.A. Smith and †P. Corrall.

First innings: 152 (Shipman 30; O'Reilly seven for 39). *Second innings:* Nine for 263 (Dawson 91, Berry 48, Astill 50 not out; O'Reilly four for 40, Fleetwood-Smith four for 83).

Australians

W. H. Ponsford lbw b Geary	9	S. J. McCabe not out	108
W. A. Brown b Smith	28	†B. A. Barnett not out	30
*D. G. Bradman b Geary	65	B 1, l-b 2, n-b 1	4
A. F. Kippax c Armstrong b Shipman	89	(five wkts dec)	**368**
L. S. Darling c Corrall b Shipman	35		

W. J. O'Reilly, L. O'B. Fleetwood-Smith, E. H. Bromley and H. I. Ebeling did not bat.

Leicestershire bowling: Shipman 25–1–88–2; Smith 34–7–81–1; Geary 31–8–48–2; Riddington 14–1–37–0; Astill 24–4–69–0; Armstrong 7–0–17–0; Hazlerigg 5–0–24–0.

Umpires: F. Chester and J. Stone

CAMBRIDGE UNIVERSITY v AUSTRALIANS 99 (152)

Played at Cambridge, Wednesday, Thursday, Friday, May 9, 10, 11 [1934]. The Australian bowling meeting with little resistance, the tourists won easily by an innings and 163 runs. On Wednesday the Australians lost three wickets for 71 – Bradman failed to score for the first time in England – but subsequently the University attack, lacking a bowler of real pace, was mastered. Batting throughout an innings lasting six and a quarter hours, Ponsford put together, up to then, his highest score in England. ... Brown, in a stylish innings, registered his first century of the tour in the course of a partnership of 262 – a record fifth stand for an Australian team in England. ...

Australians

*W. M. Woodfull c Cox b Davies	21	W. A. Brown c Barlett b Grimshaw	105
W. H. Ponsford not out	229	†B. A. Barnett not out	1
D. G. Bradman b Davies	0	B 5, l-b 5, w 1, n-b 1	12
S. J. McCabe c Human b Grimshaw	15	(five wkts dec)	**481**
L. S. Darling c Human b Cox	98		

T. W. Wall, L. O'B. Fleetwood-Smith, H, I. Ebeling and C. V. Grimmett did not bat.

Cambridge University bowling: Jahangir Khan 41–5–127–0; Cox 42–8–115–1; Davies 39–11–89–2; Grimshaw 43–5–102–2; Human 6–0–36–0.

Cambridge University

Mr A.W. Allen, Mr A.F. Skinner, Mr R.de W.K. Winlaw, Mr H.P. Dinwiddy, Mr H.T. Bartlett, *Mr J.H. Human, Mr J.G.W. Davies, M. Jahangir Khan, Mr H.R. Cox, †Mr A.G. Powell and Mr J.W. T. Grimshaw.

First innings: 158 (Jahangir Khan 33; Grimmett nine for 74). *Second innings:* 160 (Cox 51 not out; Fleetwood-Smith three for 31).

Umpires: A. Morton and L.C. Braund

MCC TEAM v AUSTRALIANS   100 (153)

Played at Lord's, Saturday, Monday, Tuesday, May 12, 14, 15 [1934]. To two members of the MCC team, Wyatt and Hendren, belonged chief credit for a draw. Between them, this pair scored 326 of the runs obtained by their side, and each completed a hundred. ... The Australian innings was practically a one-partnership affair, Ponsford and McCabe, against an attack containing no pace bowler, establishing a third-wicket record by adding 389 in four and a half hours. Ponsford made his highest score in England ...

MCC Team

Mr R.E.S. Wyatt, Rev. E.T. Killick, Mr M.J. Turnbull, E. Hendren, Mr B.H. Valentine, *Mr A.P.F. Chapman, Mr F.R. Brown, Mr J.C. White, Mr I.A.R. Peebles, †Mr P.C. Oldfield and Mr C.S. Marriott.

First innings: 362 (Wyatt 72, Turnbull 33, Hendren 135, Valentine 40, Chapman 46 not out; Wall six for 74). *Second innings:* Eight for 182 (Wyatt 102 not out; O'Reilly three for 29, Grimmett four for 90).

Australians

*W. M. Woodfull c White b Brown	20	W. A. Brown c Oldfield b Brown	2
W. H. Ponsford not out	281	†W. A. Oldfield b Brown	7
D. G. Bradman c and b Brown	5	C. V. Grimmett not out	26
S. J. McCabe b Peebles	192	B 9, l-b 6	15
L. S. Darling c Hendren b White	11	(six wkts dec)	**559**

T. W. Wall, W. J. O'Reilly and L. O'B. Fleetwood-Smith did not bat.

MCC bowling: Wyatt 9–1–38–0; Valentine 6–0–28–0; Peebles 40–5–141–1; Marriott 41–9–126–0; Brown 37–2–134–4; White 28–4–77–1.

Umpires: A. Morton and J. Hardstaff

OXFORD UNIVERSITY v AUSTRALIANS   101 (154)

Played at [the Christ Church ground] Oxford, Saturday, Monday, May 19, 21 [1934]. On a pitch that generally proved helpful to bowlers, the Australians overwhelmed the University by an innings and 33 runs. Darling and Ponsford, for the tourists, and de Saram, for Oxford, were the only batsmen really to overcome the conditions. ... Bradman played a subdued innings. ...

Australians

W. H. Ponsford c Singleton b Dyson	75	†W. A. Oldfield b Tindall		8
W. A. Brown lbw b Townsend	20	C. V. Grimmett b Tindall		0
*D. G. Bradman lbw b Dyson	37	H. I. Ebeling c Walker b Tindall		0
L. S. Darling lbw b Tindall	100	L. O'B. Fleetwood-Smith not out		2
S. J. McCabe b Tindall	15	B 13, l-b 4, n-b 2		19
E. H. Bromley b Barlow	3			**319**
A. G. Chipperfield c Stainton b Barlow	40			

Oxford University bowling: Tindall 24–3–94–5; Barlow 32.4–2–102–2; Townsend 9–3–18–1; Singleton 7–0–38–0; Dyson 17–4–48–2.

Oxford University

Mr D. F. Walker, Mr D. C. H. Townsend, Mr F. C. de Saram, Mr N. S. Mitchell-Innes, *Mr F.G. H. Chalk, Mr R.G. Stainton, Mr R.G. Tindall, Mr E. A. Barlow, †Mr M. H. Matthews, Mr A. P. Singleton and Mr J. H. Dyson.

    First innings: 70 (Ebeling four for 34, Fleetwood-Smith five for 30). *Second innings:* 216 (de Saram 128; Grimmett seven for 109).

Umpires: A. Stoner and J. H. King

HAMPSHIRE v AUSTRALIANS   102 (155)

Played at Southampton, Wednesday, Thursday, Friday, May 23, 24, 25 [1934]. Bad light caused a match full of variety and changing fortune to end tamely in a draw, though a definite result appeared unlikely some time before the finish. Arnold saved Hampshire from a second innings collapse that might have meant defeat, despite the highest total to date from the Australian bowling and the best partnership against the tourists by Mead and Lowndes [who] put on 247 in less than three hours for the fourth wicket ...

Hampshire

J. Arnold, Mr R. H. Moore, A. E. Pothecary, C. P. Mead, *Mr W.G. Lowndes, Lord Tennyson, W. L. Creese, A. Kennedy, G. S. Boyes, †N. McCorkell and Mr A. E.G. Baring.

    First innings: 420 (Mead 139, Lowndes 140, Tennyson 56; McCabe four for 79, O'Reilly three for 123). *Second innings:* Seven for 169 dec (Arnold 109 not out; Fleetwood-Smith three for 86, O'Reilly four for 34).

Australians

*W. M. Woodfull c and b Baring	2			
W. A. Brown c McCorkell b Baring	0			
D. G. Bradman c Mead b Baring	0			
S. J. McCabe c McCorkell b Baring	79	–	not out	0
L. S. Darling lbw b Kennedy	96	–	c McCorkell b Lowndes	1
A. F. Kippax c Tennyson b Boyes	38			
E. H. Bromley lbw b Boyes	37			
A. G. Chipperfield not out	116	–	not out	5
†W. A. Oldfield b Lowndes	22			
W. J. O'Reilly lbw b Baring	23			
L. O'B. Fleetwood-Smith c sub b Kennedy	4			
B 9, l-b 7	16		B	4
	433		(one wkt)	**10**

Hampshire bowling: *First innings*—Baring 26–1–121–5; Kennedy 23.5–3–81–2; Creese 7–0–34–0; Lowndes 21–3–95–1; Boyes 23–6–86–2. *Second innings*—Kennedy 1–1–0–0; Creese 2–0–6–0; Lowndes 1.1–1–0–1.

Umpires: W. Reeves and D. Hendren

MIDDLESEX v AUSTRALIANS 103 (156)

Played at Lord's, Saturday, Monday, May 26, 28 [1934]. Until the second day, Middlesex fought hard, but then they broke down badly and the Australians won easily by ten wickets. ... An amazing innings by Bradman overshadowed everything else in the Australian reply. After the quick fall of two wickets, he hit the bowling all over the field. He and Darling put on 132 and he and Kippax 84, while altogether Bradman obtained 160 out of 225 in just over two hours. For all his freedom, Bradman gave no chance. Enthoven accomplished the 'hat-trick' after lunch on Monday, but the Australians led by 87 and, Middlesex losing eight wickets in clearing the arrears, the result was soon beyond doubt. ...

Middlesex

†W. F. Price, G. E. Hart, J. Hulme, E. Hendren, Mr R. W. V. Robins, Mr G. C. Newman, Mr G. O. Allen, *Mr H. J. Enthoven, J. Smith, Mr P. F. Judge and Mr I. A. R. Peebles.

  First innings: 258 (Hendren 115, Robins 65; Wall three for 41, Grimmett three for 80). *Second innings:* 114 (Hendren 35; O'Reilly three for 34, Grimmett five for 27).

Australians

*W. M. Woodfull lbw b Smith	0			
W. H. Ponsford lbw b Smith	0			
D. G. Bradman c Hulme b Peebles	160			
L. S. Darling c Price b Smith	37	–	not out	9
A. F. Kippax lbw b Robins	56			
A. G. Chipperfield c and b Enthoven	35			
†B. A. Barnett b Smith	40	–	not out	14
C. V. Grimmett c Price b Enthoven	8			
H. I. Ebeling st Price b Enthoven	0			
T. W. Wall b Enthoven	0			
W. J. O'Reilly not out	7			
B 1, l-b 1	2		B 4, l-b 1, w 1	6
	345		(no wkt)	**29**

Middlesex bowling: *First innings*—Smith 20.2–2–99–4; Judge 6–0–41–0; Enthoven 16–2–59–4; Robins 12–1–61–1; Peebles 16–0–83–1. *Second innings*—Hulme 2–0–8–0; Allen 1.4–0–15–0.

Umpires: A. Skelding and W. A. Buswell

SURREY v AUSTRALIANS 104 (157)

Played at Kennington Oval, Wednesday, Thursday, Friday, May 30, 31, June 1 [1934]. As many as 1,266 runs being scored for the loss of nineteen wickets, the game never looked like providing a definite result. ... . [The] Australians gained the lead without much difficulty. McCabe, let off time and again, shared with Ponsford in the first opening stand of three figures during the tour ... Bradman helped add 130 for the second wicket, and the tourists finished 154 ahead ...

Surrey

J. B. Hobbs, A. Sandham, R. J. Gregory, H. S. Squires, †E. W. Brooks, T. H. Barling, *Mr E. R. T. Holmes, Mr H. M. Garland-Wells, Mr F. R. Brown, Mr P. G. H. Fender and A. R. Gover.

First innings: Seven for 475 dec (Sandham 219, Gregory 116, Barling 44). *Second innings:* Two for 162 (Gregory 59 not out, Brown 54 not out).

Australians

W. H. Ponsford c Brooks b Holmes	125	†W. A. Oldfield not out	33
S. J. McCabe c Fender b Garland-Wells	240	C. V. Grimmett b Gover	25
D. G. Bradman c Squires b Gover	77	W. J. O'Reilley c Brooks b Gover	8
A. F. Kippax b Gover	5	T. W. Wall c Fender b Holmes	10
A. G. Chipperfield b Gover	34	B 3, l-b 3, w 1, n-b 8	15
*W. M. Woodfull c Fender b Holmes	1		**629**
E. H. Bromley c Gregory b Fender	56		

Surrey bowling: Gover 34–4–147–5; Holmes 25.2–5–136–3; Fender 24–2–114–1; Brown 20–0–108–0; Garland-Wells 19–1–76–1; Gregory 4–0–15–0; Squires 2–0–18–0.

Umpires: F. Chester and F. Walden

ENGLAND v AUSTRALIA (FIRST TEST MATCH)

105 (158, 159)
24 (35, 36)

Played at Nottingham, Friday, Saturday, Monday, Tuesday, June 8, 9, 11, 12 [1934]. Australia began the series of Test Matches with a splendid victory by 238 runs. On the first three days, at any rate, the fortunes of the game changed sufficiently to keep interest at its highest pitch, while on the last afternoon everyone was on the tip-toe of excitement in watching England's desperate but unavailing effort to stave off defeat. Thus it came about that the decision of the contest was not determined until only ten more minutes remained for play. ...

As a matter of fact, England up to a point fared quite satisfactorily, for, after Woodfull and Ponsford had made 77 together in ninety-five minutes, two wickets fell before lunch, and shortly before quarter to four Australia had five men out for 153. Ponsford made his runs by varied strokes and hit eight 4's; Woodfull was very solid for nearly two hours; Bradman hit six 4's in half an hour; and Brown stayed for eighty minutes, but the fact remained that Australia, up to then, had scarcely made sufficient use of their opportunity of batting first on a nice easy wicket. ... On Saturday McCabe was out at 234, but unexpected assistance was given to Chipperfield by Oldfield and Grimmett ... Chipperfield, in his first Test Match, just missed the distinction of making a hundred. He was 99 at lunch-time, and out third ball afterwards. ...

... England fared well for a time ... [but] were all out by three o'clock [on Monday], and they found themselves 106 runs behind. Still, Australia at their second attempt lost their first three wickets for 69 before the game turned once more with a partnership between McCabe and Brown ... All the other batsmen on the Tuesday morning went out for runs in order to give Woodfull the chance of declaring at the earliest possible moment. He did not do this until half-past twelve ... [by which time] the wicket was showing signs of wear ... O'Reilly bowled superbly. Clever variation in flight and pace combined with spin off the worn turf made him very difficult, and he deserved all the congratulations showered upon him at the close by his delighted colleagues.

Australia

*W. M. Woodfull c Verity b Farnes	26	–	b Farnes	2
W. H. Ponsford c Ames b Farnes	53	–	b Hammond	5
W. A. Brown lbw b Geary	22	–	c Ames b Verity	73
D. G. Bradman c Hammond b Geary	29	–	c Ames b Farnes	25
S. J. McCabe c Leyland b Farnes	65	–	c Hammond b Farnes	88
L. S. Darling b Verity	4	–	c Hammond b Farnes	14
A. G. Chipperfield c Ames b Farnes	99	–	c Hammond b Farnes	4
†W. A. Oldfield c Hammond b Mitchell	20	–	not out	10
C. V. Grimmett b Geary	39	–	not out	3
W. J. O'Reilly b Farnes	7	–	c Verity b Geary	18
T. W. Wall not out	0			
B 4, l-b 5, n-b 1	10		B 22, l-b 9	31
	374		(eight wkts dec)	**273**

England bowling: *First innings*—Farnes 40.2–10–102–5; Geary 43–8–101–3; Hammond 13–4–29–0; Verity 34–9–65–1; Mitchell 21–4–62–1; Leyland 1–0–5–0. *Second innings*—Farnes 25–3–77–5; Geary 23–5–46–1; Hammond 12–5–25–1; Verity 17–8–48–1; Mitchell 13–2–46–0.

England

*Mr C.F. Walters, H. Sutcliffe, W.R. Hammond, Nawab of Pataudi, M. Leyland, E. Hendren, †L.E.G. Ames, G. Geary, H. Verity, Mr K. Farnes and T.B. Mitchell.

First innings: 268 (Sutcliffe 62, Hendren 79, Geary 53; Grimmett five for 81, O'Reilly four for 75).
Second innings: 141 (Walters 46; Grimmett three for 39, O'Reilly seven for 54).

Umpires: A. Dolphin and F. Chester

NORTHAMPTONSHIRE v AUSTRALIANS   106 (160, 161)

Played at Northampton, Wednesday, Thursday, Friday, June 13, 14, 15 [1934]. After dismissing the Australians for the two lowest totals of the tour to date, Northamptonshire, needing 332 to win, collapsed badly on Friday and narrowly avoided defeat. The finish was most exciting, nine minutes remaining when the last county batsman went in. Although Ponsford and Brown scored 93 for the opening wicket, half the Australian side were out for 116 on Wednesday, and only a stand of 127 by Chipperfield and Bradman saved the tourists. ... [In Northamptonshire's first innings] Snowden, putting together his first hundred in big cricket, went in first and was last out. ... Brown, opening the innings and being last to leave, averted a second innings breakdown by the tourists.

Australians

W. H. Ponsford lbw b Pitt	56	–	c Bellamy b Matthews	11
W. A. Brown b Partridge	30	–	c Bellamy b Matthews	113
L. S. Darling b Bakewell	3	–	c Bellamy b Pitt	17
A. F. Kippax lbw b Matthews	12	–	c and b Partridge	9
E. H. Bromley c Bakewell b Partridge	5	–	c and b Partridge	3
*D. G. Bradman c Bakewell b Matthews	65	–	b Matthews	25
A. G. Chipperfield c Pitt b Partridge	71	–	run out	0
†B. A. Barnett c Partridge b Matthews	7	–	b Matthews	44
W. J. O'Reilly not out	13	–	c Timms b Matthews	4
H. I. Ebeling b Matthews	14	–	c Matthews b Pitt	1
L. O'B. Fleetwood-Smith run out	0	–	not out	1
B 1, l-b 7	8		B 3, l-b 3	6
	284			**234**

Northamptonshire bowling: *First innings*—Matthews 23–0–71–4; Pitt 12–1–53–1; Partridge 24.1–2–67–3; Towell 11–1–27–0; Bakewell 11–1–38–1; Cox 7–1–20–0. *Second innings*—Matthews 26.5–3–87–5; Pitt 14–2–42–2; Partridge 27–8–57–2; Towell 8–0–20–0; Bakewell 3–0–22–0.

Northamptonshire

Mr A. W. Snowden, A. H. Bakewell, N. Grimshaw, J. E. Timms, †B. Bellamy, A. L. Cox, Mr E. F. Towell, A. D. Matthews, *Mr W. C. Brown, R. J. Partridge and Mr T. A. Pitt.

First innings: 187 (Snowden 105; Fleetwood-Smith five for 63, O'Reilly three for 46). *Second innings:* Nine for 133 (Bakewell 53, Timms 50; Ebeling three for 26, Fleetwood-Smith five for 29).

Umpires: J. Stone and W. Reeves

ENGLAND v AUSTRALIA   107 (162, 163)
(SECOND TEST MATCH)   25 (37, 38)

Played at Lord's, Friday, Saturday, Monday, June 22, 23, 25 [1934]. For their defeat at Trent Bridge, England took an ample revenge at Lord's, winning the match in three days in an innings with 38 runs to spare. This was England's first success in a Test Match against Australia at Lord's since 1896 when Lohmann and Tom Richardson, in a memorable struggle, swept the Australians off their feet. While everyone in England naturally was jubilant over the triumph of the Englishmen, it could not be denied that they were helped in a pronounced degree by the weather.

Winning the toss, England stayed in until nearly three o'clock on the Saturday ... but before the end of the day Australia had 192 runs on the board with only two men out. In view of this splendid start by the visitors there existed no sound reason why they should not have closely approached if not even passed the England total, but they suffered the cruellest luck, rain falling during the weekend and rendering their chances almost hopeless. Fortunately England had in the team a bowler capable of taking full advantage of the conditions that prevailed, and Verity, obtaining seven wickets in the first innings for 61 runs, followed this up with eight in the second for 43, to be the chief factor in giving England such a pronounced success. ... Verity had taken one of the Australian wickets which fell on Saturday [that of Bradman], and on the Monday he dismissed fourteen men for 80 runs, six of them after tea at a cost of 15. ... Verity's length was impeccable and he made the ball come back and lift so abruptly that most of the Australians were helpless. The majority of them had had no experience in England of such a pitch ['it could scarcely be described as genuinely "sticky" except for one period after lunch'], and they showed no ability or skill in dealing with bowling like that of Verity under these conditions. Those who tried to play forward did not get far enough, and their efforts at playing back were, to say the least, immature. ...

[In Australia's first innings] Bradman, with seven 4's, hit up 36 [of 73 runs scored while he was at the wicket] but actually he never looked like staying very long, making many of his strokes without restraint. ... [In their second innings, following on,] Verity, coming on at 17, quickly got to work again, dismissing McCabe and Bradman at 43 and 57, while after tea Woodfull, who had defended stubbornly for two hours, was fourth to leave at 94. The rest of the innings was a mere procession ...

England

Mr C. F. Walters, H. Sutcliffe, W. R. Hammond, E. Hendren, *Mr R. E. S. Wyatt, M. Leyland, †L. E. G. Ames, G. Geary, H. Verity, Mr K. Farnes and W. E. Bowes.

First innings: 440 (Walters 82, Wyatt 33, Leyland 109, Ames 120; Wall four for 108, Chipperfield three for 91).

Australia

*W. M. Woodfull b Bowes	22	–	c Hammond b Verity	43
W. A. Brown c Ames b Bowes	105	–	c Walters b Bowes	2
D. G. Bradman c and b Verity	36	–	c Ames b Verity	13
S. J. McCabe c Hammond b Verity	34	–	c Hendren b Verity	19
L. S. Darling c Sutcliffe b Verity	0	–	b Hammond	10
A. G. Chipperfield not out	37	–	c Geary b Verity	14
E. H. Bromley c Geary b Verity	4	–	c and b Verity	1
†W. A. Oldfield c Sutcliffe b Verity	23	–	lbw b Verity	0
C. V. Grimmett b Bowes	9	–	c Hammond b Verity	0
W. J. O'Reilly b Verity	4	–	not out	8
T. W. Wall lbw b Verity	0	–	c Hendren b Verity	1
B 1, l-b 9	10		B 6, n-b 1	7
	284			**118**

England bowling: *First innings*—Farnes 12–3–43–0; Bowes 31–5–98–3; Geary 22–4–56–0; Verity 36–15–61–7; Hammond 4–1–6–0; Leyland 4–1–10–0. *Second innings*—Farnes 4–2–6–0; Bowes 14–4–24–1; Verity 22.3–8–43–8; Hammond 13–0–38–1.

Umpires: F. Chester and J. Hardstaff

SOMERSET v AUSTRALIANS   108 (164)

Played at Taunton, Wednesday, Thursday, June 27, 28 [1934]. Somerset proved no match for the Australians, who won in an innings with 77 runs to spare. The county were unfortunate in getting the worst of the wicket on the opening day, for Ingle, who won the toss, could not be blamed for taking first innings. Heavy rain preceded the match and the wicket, though covered, gave bowlers considerable assistance. O'Reilly seized his opportunity … Keeping a perfect length and concentrating on the leg stump, he caused trouble to everybody, nine wickets falling to him after lunch for 75 runs. Frank Lee, who carried his bat through the innings, alone offered much resistance. By the time the tourists went in, the turf had recovered … Going in again 193 behind, Somerset soon experienced trouble with Fleetwood-Smith, losing three men for 14 runs. …

Somerset

J. W. Lee, F. S. Lee, Mr G. M. Bennett, Mr J. C. White, Mr C. C. Case, *Mr R. A. Ingle, Mr H. D. Burrough, A. W. Wellard, Mr J. H. Cameron, Mr P. J. Davey and †W. T. Luckes.

    First innings: 116 (F. S. Lee 59 not out; O'Reilly nine for 38). *Second innings:* 116 (Ebeling three for 24, Fleetwood-Smith six for 56).

Australians

*W. M. Woodfull run out	84		†B. A. Barnett b Wellard	51
W. H. Ponsford st Luckes b White	17		H. I. Ebeling c sub b Wellard	21
D. G. Bradman c Luckes b White	17		W. J. O'Reilly not out	22
L. S. Darling c Davey b Wellard	79		L. O'B. Fleetwood-Smith b Wellard	0
A. F. Kippax c Luckes b Wellard	1		L-b	4
A. G. Chipperfield hit wkt b Wellard	12			**309**
E. H. Bromley lbw b J. W. Lee	1			

Somerset bowling: Wellard 36.4–6–111–6; J. W. Lee 30–9–70–1; White 27–4–92–2; Cameron 3–0–18–0; Davey 8–1–14–0.

Umpires: W. Reeves and E. J. Smith

SURREY v AUSTRALIANS 109 (165, 166)

Played at Kennington Oval, Saturday, Monday, Tuesday, June 30, July 2, 3 [1934]. Surrey did so well in their first game with the Australians that they were expected to put up a good fight in their second meeting. Although their bowlers performed satisfactorily, however, the county batting failed and the tourists won by six wickets. ... Surrey gave a disappointing display in their first innings. The Australians, too, found run-getting no easy matter on an excellent pitch ... [but in their second innings, needing 109 to win,] Bradman, batting in his best form, destroyed any possibility of a surprise result, he and Darling, after three wickets fell cheaply, adding 73 together.

Surrey

A. Sandham, R. J. Gregory, H. S. Squires, T. H. Barling, *Mr E. R. T. Holmes, Mr F. R. Brown, E. A. Watts, Mr P. G. H. Fender, A. R. Gover, Mr M. J. C. Allom and †E. W. Brooks.
    First innings: 175 (Gregory 48, Brooks 32; McCabe four for 24, Grimmett four for 64). *Second innings:* 184 (Gregory 48, Brown 46; Grimmett five for 33, Fleetwood-Smith three for 48).

Australians

W. H. Ponsford c Holmes b Allom	85	–	c Allom b Gover	10
W. A. Brown lbw b Allom	34	–	c Fender b Gover	0
L. S. Darling c Watts b Fender	20	–	lbw b Holmes	31
*D. G. Bradman c Brooks b Holmes	27	–	not out	61
†B. A. Barnett c Holmes b Gover	1			
S. J. McCabe b Fender	0	–	not out	0
A. F. Kippax b Gover	50			
E. H. Bromley c Holmes b Allom	0	–	c Gover b Allom	3
C. V. Grimmett c Brooks b Watts	7			
H. I. Ebeling b Allom	12			
L. O'B. Fleetwood-Smith not out	2			
B 1, l-b 5, w 1, n-b 6	13		B 1, l-b 3, n-b 2	6
	251		(four wkts)	**111**

Surrey bowling: *First innings*—Gover 22–3–73–2; Allom 17.4–2–60–4; Brown 6–0–14–0; Fender 18–4–58–2; Watts 5–0–18–1; Holmes 5–1–15–1. *Second innings*—Gover 6–0–36–2; Allom 6–0–23–1; Fender 3.2–0–28–0; Watts 2–0–14–0; Holmes 2–1–4–1.

Umpires: D. Hendren and J. Hardstaff

ENGLAND v AUSTRALIA 110 (167)
(THIRD TEST MATCH) 26 (39)

Played at Manchester, Friday, Saturday, Monday, Tuesday, July 6, 7, 9, 10 [1934]. The Third Test Match had to be left drawn, the scoring being so heavy that in the course of the four days 1,307 runs were obtained and only twenty wickets fell. For more than one reason, however, the game will always be remembered by those who saw it. Changed at the request of Lancashire from its usual order in the rota of Tests – Old Trafford for some years had been the scene of the fourth encounter in the series of Test Matches in this country – the alteration from the point of view of weather was more than justified. Seldom, indeed, can an International engagement in this country have been played throughout the whole of four days under such wonderful conditions. From first to last the sun blazed down, the heat being at times almost unbearable.

    Another point of remembrance was the fact that the Australians played through the greater part of the game under a very serious handicap, an affection of the throat seizing Bradman, Chipperfield and Kippax in particular and others in a lesser degree, so that at one period it was feared that an attack of diphtheria had overtaken the visitors. ... In these circumstances, therefore, the Australians – kept in the field until nearly four o'clock on the Saturday while England were scoring, in nine and a half hours, a total of 627 for nine wickets – naturally played in rather a depressed spirit, but they did not allow this to affect their skill and, replying to the big total of their opponents with a score of 491, practically made certain, unless something phenomenal happened, of avoiding defeat.

[In England's first innings, O'Reilly dismissed Walters, Wyatt and Hammond in four balls, transforming their position from no wicket for 68 to three for 72. When Australia batted, McCabe 'went along at a fine pace' on Saturday evening and Monday. Later] Woodfull [who had been dropped first ball at second slip] and Bradman put on 58 in sixty-five minutes, but Bradman, when 26, gave Hammond a sharp return chance. ... Australia, [having avoided the follow-on in the first session on Tuesday,] found themselves 136 behind, but they had kept England in the field for over ten hours. The rest of the cricket on the last day was of no particular interest. ...

England

Mr C.F. Walters, H. Sutcliffe, *Mr R.E.S. Wyatt, W.R. Hammond, E. Hendren, M. Leyland, †L.E.G. Ames, J.L. Hopwood, Mr G.O. Allen, H. Verity and E.W. Clark.

First innings: Nine for 627 dec (Walters 52, Sutcliffe 63, Hendren 132, Leyland 153, Ames 72, Allen 61, Verity 60 not out; O'Reilly seven for 189). *Second innings:* None for 123 dec (Walters 50 not out, Sutcliffe 69 not out).

Australia

W. A. Brown c Walters b Clark	72	–	c Hammond b Allen	0
W. H. Ponsford c Hendren b Hammond	12	–	not out	30
S. J. McCabe c Verity b Hammond	137	–	not out	33
*W. M. Woodfull run out	73			
L. S. Darling b Verity	37			
D. G. Bradman c Ames b Hammond	30			
†W. A. Oldfield c Wyatt b Verity	13			
A. G. Chipperfield c Walters b Verity	26			
C. V. Grimmett b Verity	0			
W. J. O'Reilly not out	30			
T. W. Wall run out	18			
B 20, l-b 13, w 4, n-b 6	43		B 1, l-b 2	3
	491		(one wkt)	**66**

England bowling: *First innings*—Clark 40–9–100–1; Allen 31–3–113–0; Hammond 28.3–6–111–3; Verity 53–24–78–4; Hopwood 38–20–46–0. *Second innings*—Clark 4–1–16–0; Allen 6–0–23–1; Hammond 2–1–2–0; Verity 5–4–2–0; Hopwood 9–5–16–0; Hendren 1–0–4–0.

Umpires: J. Hardstaff and F. Walden

DERBYSHIRE v AUSTRALIANS   111 (168, 169)

Played at Chesterfield, Wednesday, Thursday, Friday, July 11, 12, 13 [1934]. Collapsing in deplorable fashion on the last day, Derbyshire fell easy victims by nine wickets. Of the county's first innings total of 145, three men between them scored 101. ... The Australians got to within 23 of the Derbyshire score for the loss of four wickets, but, thanks to fine bowling by Mitchell, with flight, break and variation of pace, they led by only 110. Bradman made top score, but scarcely appeared at his best. Derbyshire began the last day 36 behind with eight wickets in hand ... In one spell, Fleetwood-Smith dismissed five batsmen for 18 runs.

Derbyshire

H. Storer, A. E. Alderman, L. F. Townsend, D. Smith, *Mr A. F. Skinner, Mr G. R. Jackson, Mr N. M. Ford, T. S. Worthington, †H. Elliott, T. B. Mitchell and W. Copson.

First innings: 145 (Storer 40, Ford 37; Ebeling five for 28). Second innings: 139 (Storer 47, Smith 32; Fleetwood-Smith five for 38).

Australians

E. H. Bromley b Mitchell	31	–	not out	16
W. A. Brown st Elliott b Mitchell	17	–	b Jackson	10
D. G. Bradman c Elliott b Townsend	71	–	not out	6
S. J. McCabe c Elliott b Mitchell	3			
L. S. Darling b Mitchell	14			
*W. M. Woodfull run out	44			
W. H. Ponsford lbw b Townsend	11			
†B. A. Barnett b Mitchell	48			
H. I. Ebeling b Mitchell	1			
T. W. Wall not out	2			
L. O'B. Fleetwood-Smith b Mitchell	0			
B 8, l-b 5	13			
	255		(one wkt)	32

Derbyshire bowling: First innings—Worthington 12–2–25–0; Copson 16–5–45–0; Mitchell 34.5–6–105–7; Townsend 25–3–67–2. Second innings—Jackson 2.5–0–21–1; Ford 2–0–11–0.

Umpires: A. Skelding and W. A. Buswell

YORKSHIRE v AUSTRALIANS   112 (170)

Played at Sheffield, Saturday, Monday, Tuesday, July 14, 16, 17 [1934]. Thanks largely to a capital three-figure innings by Sellers – his first for the county – Yorkshire effected a creditable draw. The performance was the more praiseworthy as Sutcliffe retired from the game after pulling a muscle early on Saturday. ... Bradman once again took the batting honours for the Australians, scoring 140 out of 189 added with Woodfull, but, Bowes bowling admirably, the tourists led by only eight runs. Sent in to open Yorkshire's second innings, Wood saved his side from collapse. ... Sellers helped him put on 58, and the Australians were set an impossible task.

Yorkshire

H. Sutcliffe, A. Mitchell, W. Barber, M. Leyland, C. Turner, *Mr A. B. Sellers, H. Verity, T. F. Smailes, †A. Wood, G. G. Macaulay and W. E. Bowes.

First innings: 340 (Mitchell 36, Barber 37, Leyland 43, Sellers 104, Smailes 30, Macaulay 40 not out; Grimmett four for 113). Second innings: 157 (Wood 59; Wall three for 36, Fleetwood-Smith three for 39.)

Australians

*W. M. Woodfull c Sellers b Smailes	54			
W. A. Brown c Macaulay b Bowes	14	–	lbw b Macaulay	12
D. G. Bradman b Leyland	140			
S. J. McCabe b Bowes	21	–	not out	14
L. S. Darling c sub b Bowes	45			
E. H. Bromley lbw b Macaulay	16			
†B. A. Barnett b Bowes	7			
C. V. Grimmett b Bowes	8			
H. I. Ebeling b Bowes	27			
T. W. Wall b Bowes	1			
L. O'B. Fleetwood-Smith not out	1			
B 10, l-b 3, n-b 1	14		W	2
	348		(one wkt)	28

Yorkshire bowling: *First innings*—Bowes 29.2–4–100–7; Smailes 21–2–68–1; Macaulay 19–5–41–1; Turner 9–0–53–0; Verity 6–0–33–0; Leyland 4–0–39–1. *Second innings*—Bowes 3–1–6–0; Smailes 2–1–5–0; Macaulay 5–1–13–1; Turner 4–3–2–0.

Umpires: L. C. Braund and C. N. Woolley

ENGLAND v AUSTRALIA   113 (171)
(FOURTH TEST MATCH)   27 (40)

Played at Leeds, Friday, Saturday, Monday, Tuesday, July 20, 21, 23, 24 [1934]. Just as at Lord's rain came to damage the wicket and ruin Australia's chance of making an even fight of it, so in the Fourth Test Match on the Headingley ground at Leeds did one of the shortest but heaviest rainstorms seen at a cricket match for years arrive just in time to rob Australia of victory and enable England to draw a game in which they were completely outplayed. Escaping defeat in the luckiest manner possible, the England team accomplished nothing in the match on which they could congratulate themselves. ...

His good fortune in the matter of winning the toss again attended Wyatt and for the third consecutive game England enjoyed the advantage of batting first. Wyatt himself described the wicket as being 'like a feather-bed', whatever that may have meant. The assumption at the time was that it would be slow and easy. There was nothing in the way it played during the first day to suggest that it was otherwise, yet England, giving one of the worst displays of batting probably ever seen under similar conditions, were all dismissed between twenty-five minutes to twelve and twenty-five minutes past five for a paltry total of 200. It can be said that O'Reilly, Grimmett and Chipperfield bowled very well, but nothing they accomplished with the ball was quite sufficient to account for the shocking exhibition of weak and hesitant batting given by the Englishmen. ...

Before cricket ended, however, further surprises were in store for the crowd. Bowes and Hammond started the bowling for England and both Ponsford and Brown played them so easily that there seemed no reason to expect any pronounced success for the England attack up to half-past six. Bowes, however, changed ends and, coming on again at 37 from the Pavilion wicket, bowled Brown at 37 and two runs later sent back Oldfield and Woodfull in one over. Stumps were then pulled up, Bowes having sent down ten balls from the Pavilion end and dismissed three batsmen without conceding a run. ... Those, however, were the last crumbs of comfort England were destined to enjoy in this disastrous match. Bradman joined Ponsford the next morning and not until ten minutes to six on Saturday evening did another wicket fall. Giving a great display of batting, the two famous Australian run-getters beat all previous partnership records in Test Matches. They carried the score in five and a half hours to 427 before Ponsford, hooking a short ball from Verity, trod on his wicket ... Altogether their stand realised no fewer than 388 runs. They always scored at a good rate but, as usual with Australians, unless the bowling is exceptionally steady, pushed along very quickly after tea when, in an hour, 98 runs were put on. Up to lunch-time they scored 129 in two hours and twenty-five minutes and between lunch and tea 161 in two hours and five minutes.

Ponsford's innings was very good indeed. In the course of the partnership each batsman gave a chance, for Ponsford when 70 should have been caught by Mitchell at cover-point while Bradman at 71 was let off by Hopwood. ... For the greater part of the day Bradman, who unlike Ponsford obtained most of his runs in front of the stumps, batted with the utmost certainty, but during the last thirty-five minutes when he and McCabe were raising the score to 494 he played in a more light-hearted spirit. Twice he lifted the ball over the ring for 6, and hit Hopwood for 15 runs in one over.

Australia, therefore, began the third day in a most comfortable position, being 294 runs on with six wickets to fall, and altogether Bradman and McCabe added 90 in an hour before McCabe was out. Thanks to some most effective bowling by Bowes, Australia's innings was finished off in a hundred minutes, the last six wickets falling on Monday morning for 90 runs. Bradman, sixth out at 550, made his 304 in six hours and fifty-five minutes. Going in third wicket down, he took the leading part in adding 511 runs while as many more wickets fell. Not out on Saturday with 271 he was perhaps lucky in reaching 300 because when 280 he was missed at third slip by Verity. He did not play so well during the fifty minutes he was in on Monday morning as he had done previously, but all the same his innings was a masterly affair. He hit the ball very hard and placed his strokes beautifully, while until joined by McCabe on Saturday evening he rarely sent the ball into the air. He hit two 6's, forty-three 4's, one 3, fifteen 2's and eighty-seven singles. ... England went in again at one o'clock 384 runs behind, so that the most they could hope for was a draw. ... [Three wickets fell for 87] but by dint of very hard work and much watchful batting Hendren and Wyatt added 65 in rather less than two hours. During this stand Bradman, trying to stop the ball in the long field with his foot, strained his leg and had to retire. ... Heavy rain fell in the night and the wicket was very wet, while a further shower caused a delay soon after cricket had been resumed. Then Hendren was out at 190 and when Ames left at 213 the end seemed very near. Just before one o'clock a thunderstorm broke over the ground and, although it lasted only ten minutes, the downpour was so severe that no further cricket was possible. Not until six o'clock, however, was the decision to abandon the match arrived at. Not only the pitch but parts of the outfield and especially that in front of the pavilion were, even then, far too wet for cricket to be proceeded with.

England

Mr C.F. Walters, W.W. Keeton, W.R. Hammond, E. Hendren, *Mr R.E.S. Wyatt, M. Leyland, †L.E.G. Ames, J.L. Hopwood, H. Verity, T.B. Mitchell and W.E. Bowes.

First innings: 200 (Walters 44, Hammond 37; Grimmett four for 57, O'Reilly three for 46). *Second innings:* Six for 229 (Walters 45, Hendren 42, Wyatt 44, Leyland 49 not out; Grimmett three for 72).

Australia

W. A. Brown b Bowes	15	A. G. Chipperfield c Wyatt b Verity	1
W. H. Ponsford hit wkt b Verity	181	C. V. Grimmett run out	15
†W. A. Oldfield c Ames b Bowes	0	W. J. O'Reilly not out	11
*W. M. Woodfull b Bowes	0	T. W. Wall lbw b Verity	1
D. G. Bradman b Bowes	304	B 8, l-b 9	17
S. J. McCabe b Bowes	27		**584**
L. S. Darling b Bowes	12		

England bowling: Bowes 50–13–142–6; Hammond 29–5–82–0; Mitchell 23–1–117–0; Verity 46.5–15–113–3; Hopwood 30–7–93–0; Leyland 5–0–20–0.

Umpires: J. Hardstaff and A. Dolphin

THE ARMY v AUSTRALIANS

Played at Aldershot, Wednesday, August 15 [1934]. Main interest in this match, which gave the Australians an easy victory, centred in the first appearance of Bradman since he injured himself in the Fourth Test at Leeds. Bradman made top score in the game, scoring his 79 at almost one a minute. None of the Army batsmen ever looked comfortable.

The Army

*Lieut. R. E. H. Hudson, Lieut. C. P. Hamilton, Lieut. P. M. Nelson, Capt. G. J. Bryan, Lieut. R. J. Packe, Lieut. J. W. A. Stephenson, Maj. M. A. Green, Lieut. J. H. N. Foster, Lieut. R.G. W. Melsome, Lieut. P. M. Hughes and †Lieut. T. F. Winnington.

First innings: 110 (O'Reilly three for 17, Bromley three for 21).

Australians

W. H. Ponsford c Hudson b Hamilton	48	†B. A. Barnett b Nelson	7
L. S. Darling c Packe b Stephenson	6	W. A. Oldfield not out	3
E. H. Bromley c Packe b Melsome	7	W. A. Brown not out	10
*D. G. Bradman c Melsome b Stephenson	79	B	5
W. J. O'Reilly b Stephenson	6	(seven wkts)	**194**
H. I. Ebeling c Hamilton b Nelson	23		

A. F. Kippax and L. O'B. Fleetwood-Smith did not bat.

The Army bowling: Stephenson 20–5–47–3; Melsome 18–0–70–1; Hughes 5–1–18–0; Hamilton 9–1–42–1; Nelson 4–0–12–2.

Umpires: G. Moore and Regt. Sgt-Major Marrison

ENGLAND v AUSTRALIA 114 (172, 173)
(FIFTH TEST MATCH) 28 (41, 42)

Played at Kennington Oval, Saturday, Monday, Tuesday, Wednesday, August 18, 20, 21, 22 [1934]. Each side having won once with two games left drawn, the Fifth and concluding Test Match was entered upon without any restrictions as to the time involved in reaching a definite result. As it happened four days proved sufficient for Australia to win by 562 runs. Thus they regained the Ashes. Being successful in the rubber by two victories to one, they brought their number of wins in the whole series of encounters between the two countries to 52 as against 51 by England. Under conditions which, apart from the winning of the toss, favoured neither side unduly, the result was a fitting tribute to the superior all-round skill of Australia. ...

The law of averages suggested that it was Woodfull's turn to win the toss. This he did and when Clark, coming on at 20, bowled Brown at 21 with the best ball sent down all day long, it seemed as though the England attack on a hard wicket was about to come into its own. Never were hopeful anticipations more rudely dispelled. Between them Ponsford and Bradman gave another glorious display of batting, staying together until nearly half-past six and engaging in a partnership which left that of Leeds far behind and produced 451 runs in five hours and a quarter. This time Bradman was the first to leave, hitting over his head at a bouncing ball and being caught behind the wicket at 472. ... It would be hard to speak in too high terms of praise of the magnificent displays of batting given by Ponsford and Bradman. Before Bradman joined him, Ponsford had shown an inclination to draw away from the bowling of Bowes but he received inspiration from the example of his partner, who from the very moment he reached the centre and took up his stance was coolness and mastery personified. The pitch did not help bowlers at all. ... Clark and the others tried all sorts of theories ['Clark tried leg-theory with a packed leg-side field but ... his bowling ... scarcely came under the category of what is known as "Bodyline"] but they had no effect on Bradman, who, as the afternoon wore on, invested his batting with increasing daring. He drove and cut with the utmost certainty and power, and when the ball did bounce he just stepped back and hooked it. Included in his hits were a 6 and thirty-two 4's and, having regard to the rate at which he as well as Ponsford scored, a better display has rarely been seen. Ponsford was not quite so sure as Bradman and he frequently turned his back to the ball to receive blows on the thigh. ... As during the day about 80 runs an hour were obtained it can be realised that too many long-hops and half-volleys were sent down. This great partnership meant that in consecutive representative encounters Bradman and Ponsford in two stands scored 839 runs in ten hours and three-quarters. Ponsford offered three very difficult chances and one when 115 comparatively easy; Bradman's batting, as far as was seen, was flawless.

On Monday, England had further trouble before the innings, which lasted nearly ten hours, closed at twenty minutes to five for 701 runs – the second highest in the history of Test Matches between England and Australia. ... Tuesday was a black day for England and except for a superbly aggressive display by Maurice Leyland the batting proved deplorable. ... Australia, 380 ahead, scored 186 for two wickets before the end of the day, Brown leaving at 13 and Ponsford at 42. ... Bradman and McCabe scored at a fine pace, making 144 together in ninety minutes. Light rain fell during the night but the wicket the next morning was not greatly affected. ... [Bowes] soon dismissed Bradman, who, with McCabe, had added 150 in ninety-five minutes and then for the first time England's bowling got really on top so that Australia were all out by half-past two ... England were thus left with no fewer than 708 to get to win – only 34 short of the number England had set Australia in the First Test Match at Brisbane during the 1928-29 tour. [They] made a shocking start ... and shortly before six o'clock, with Allen stumped, the innings was all over for 145 ... Grimmett bowled superbly.

Australia

W. A. Brown b Clark	10	–	c Allen b Clark	1
W. H. Ponsford hit wkt b Allen	266	–	c Hammond b Clark	22
D. G. Bradman c Ames b Bowes	244	–	b Bowes	77
S. J. McCabe b Allen	10	–	c Walters b Clark	70
*W. M. Woodfull b Bowes	49	–	b Bowes	13
A. F. Kippax lbw b Bowes	28	–	c Walters b Clark	8
A. G. Chipperfield b Bowes	3	–	c Woolley b Clark	16
†W. A. Oldfield not out	42	–	c Hammond b Bowes	0
C. V. Grimmett c Ames b Allen	7	–	c Hammond b Bowes	14
H. I. Ebeling b Allen	2	–	c Allen b Bowes	41
W. J. O'Reilly b Clark	7	–	not out	15
B 4, l-b 14, w 2, n-b 13	55		B 37, l-b 8, w 1, n-b 4	50
	701			**327**

England bowling: *First innings*—Bowes 38–2–164–4; Allen 34–5–170–4; Clark 37.2–4–110–2; Hammond 12–0–53–0; Verity 43–7–123–0; Wyatt 4–0–28–0; Leyland 3–0–20–0. *Second innings*—Bowes 11.3–3–55–5; Allen 16–2–63–0; Clark 20–1–98–5; Hammond 7–1–18–0; Verity 14–3–43–0.

England

Mr C. F. Walters, H. Sutcliffe, F. E. Woolley, W. R. Hammond, *Mr R. E. S. Wyatt, M. Leyland, †L. E. G. Ames, Mr G. O. Allen, H. Verity, E. W. Clark and W. E. Bowes.

First innings: 321 (Walters 64, Sutcliffe 38, Leyland 110, Ames 33 retired hurt; Ebeling three for 74, Grimmett three for 103). *Second innings:* 145 (Hammond 43; Grimmett five for 64).

Umpires: F. Chester and F. Walden

SUSSEX v AUSTRALIANS 115 (174)

Played at Hove, Saturday, Monday, Tuesday, August 25, 27, 28 [1934]. The form of Sussex in county engagements had suggested the likelihood of a close fight, but the Australians won readily by an innings and 35 runs. ...

Sussex

John Langridge, J. H. Parks, *Mr A. Melville, T. Cook, Jas. Langridge, H. W. Parks, E. H. Bowley, G. Pearce, †J. Eaton, M. W. Tate and J. Cornford.

First innings: Eight for 304 dec (J. H. Parks 60, Cook 60, Jas. Langridge 57, Tate 40 not out; Fleetwood-Smith five for 114). *Second innings:* 221 (John Langridge 53, Bowley 63, J. H. Parks 32, Melville 40; Fleetwood-Smith five for 87, O'Reilly four for 49).

Australians

W. H. Ponsford b Cornford	6	†B. A. Barnett not out	27
W. A. Brown hit wkt b Jas. Langridge	66	H. I. Ebeling b Bowley	10
A. G. Chipperfield c Eaton b Cornford	0	W. J. O'Reilly c Pearce b Bowley	4
A. F. Kippax c H. Parks b Pearce	250	L. O'B. Fleetwood-Smith c Cornford	
S. J. McCabe lbw b Cornford	46	b Bowley	0
L. S. Darling b Tate	117	B 10, l-b 2, w 2, n-b 1	15
*D. G. Bradman b Pearce	19		**560**

Sussex bowling: Tate 31–4–101–1; Cornford 26–2–129–3; J. Parks 20–0–91–0; Pearce 17–0–90–2; Jas. Langridge 12–0–63–1; Bowley 13.2–0–71–3.

Umpires: F. Chester and C. N. Woolley

KENT v AUSTRALIANS 116

Played at Canterbury, Wednesday, Thursday, Friday, August 29, 30, 31 [1934]. Only thirty-five minutes' cricket being possible on the first day and rain putting play on the second entirely out of the question, a drawn game became inevitable. ... Set to get 176 to avoid defeat in a single innings, Kent fared disastrously, but, so little time remaining, they were never in much danger.

Kent

W. H. Ashdown, F. E. Woolley, L. J. Todd, Mr B. H. Valentine, Mr C. H. Knott, Mr F. G. H. Chalk, Mr J. G. W. Davies, *Mr A. P. F. Chapman, †Mr W. H. V. Levett, A. E. Watt and A. P. Freeman.

First innings: Two for 21 dec. *Second innings:* Seven for 74 (Fleetwood-Smith four for 30).

Australians

W. H. Ponsford not out	82
S. J. McCabe lbw b Woolley	108
B 2, l-b 4, n-b 1	7
(one wkt dec)	**197**

*D. G. Bradman, A. G. Chipperfield, C. V. Grimmett, A. F. Kippax, L. S. Darling, †B. A. Barnett, H. I. Ebeling, W. J. O'Reilly and L. O'B. Fleetwood-Smith did not bat.

Kent bowling: Ashdown 14–2–36–0; Watt 13–2–30–0; Davies 10–1–27–0; Todd 9–0–42–0; Freeman 10–0–49–0; Woolley 3.5–0–6–1.

Umpires: J. Stone and J. Newman

AN ENGLAND XI v AUSTRALIANS   117 (175)

Played at Folkestone, Saturday, Monday, Tuesday, September 1, 3, 4 [1934]. Cricket on the first two days being limited by rain to two hours forty minutes, a draw was inevitable, but the game will always be remembered for a brilliant and spectacular display of hard, clean hitting by Bradman, who made 149 not out in an hour and three-quarters. When play began at three o'clock on Monday, Woolley, Walters and Hobbs compensated the crowd for their disappointment ... and the sight of Woolley and Hobbs together at the crease brought back vivid memories of their wonderful feats for England in the past. ... Bradman's display provided a glorious finish to the match. Taking full advantage of an escape when one, Bradman reached three figures out of 166 in ninety minutes, trounced Freeman for three 6's and three 4's in one over, and in one period of seven minutes he scored 31! In addition to four 6's, Bradman obtained seventeen 4's. Brown, Ponsford and Woodfull also showed capital form.

An England XI

Mr C.F. Walters, J.B. Hobbs, F.E. Woolley, W.R. Hammond, †L.E.G. Ames, Mr B.H. Valentine, Lord Tennyson, M. Jahangir Khan, Mr M.J.C. Allom, *Mr A.P.F. Chapman and A.P. Freeman.

First innings: 279 (Hobbs 38, Woolley 66, Hammond 54, Allom 47 not out; O'Reilly four for 55, Fleetwood-Smith five for 137).

Australians

W. H. Ponsford b Freeman	45	D. G. Bradman not out	149
W. A. Brown c Ames b Woolley	73	*W. M. Woodfull not out	62
S. J. McCabe lbw b Freeman	10	B 2, l-b 1, w 2	5
A. F. Kippax c Ames b Hammond	21	(four wkts)	**365**

†W. A. Oldfield, C. V. Grimmett, T. W. Wall, W. J. O'Reilly and L. O'B. Fleetwood-Smith did not bat.

An England XI bowling: Jahangir Khan 16–1–52–0; Allom 20–1–81–0; Hammond 15–0–71–1; Woolley 8–0–28–1; Freeman 31–5–128–2.

Umpires: F. Chester and A. E. Street

MR H.D.G. LEVESON GOWER'S XI v AUSTRALIANS   118 (176)

Played at Scarborough, Saturday, Monday, Tuesday, September 8, 10, 11 [1934]. Centuries by Bradman and McCabe and splendid bowling by Fleetwood-Smith were the chief features of the Australians' fine win by an innings and 48 runs. With runs coming at the rate of over 90 an hour, the crowd of 10,000 experienced a thoroughly enjoyable day's cricket on Saturday. Bradman, in his most joyous mood, hit up 132 before lunch-time and became the first Australian to reach 2,000 runs during the tour. Bradman took only ninety minutes over his runs and, giving a masterly display of all the strokes, he hit a 6 and twenty-four 4's. In five minutes he scored 31! ...

Australians

W. H. Ponsford c and b Nichols	92	†W. A.. Oldfield c Duckworth b Nichols	16
W. A. Brown b Farnes	3	H. I. Ebeling c Nichols b Farnes	18
D. G. Bradman st Duckworth b Verity	132	W. J. O'Reilly c Duckworth b Farnes	9
S. J. McCabe c Duckworth b Farnes	124	L. O'B. Fleetwood-Smith not out	1
*W. M. Woodfull lbw b Verity	9	B 2, l-b 9, w 1, n-b 1	13
L. S. Darling b Bowes	19		**489**
A. G. Chipperfield b Farnes	53		

Mr H. D. G. Leveson Gower's XI bowling: Farnes 31.3–4–132–5; Bowes 23–2–111–1; Nichols 28–5–126–2; Townsend 3–0–23–0; Verity 21–3–84–2.

Mr H. D. G. Leveson Gower's XI

*Mr R. E. S. Wyatt, H. Sutcliffe, M. Leyland, E. Hendren, Mr J. H. Human, M. S. Nichols, L. F. Townsend, H. Verity, †G. Duckworth, Mr K. Farnes and W. E. Bowes.

First innings: 223 (Human 31, Nichols 75, Townsend 37; Fleetwood-Smith four for 111, O'Reilly three for 35). *Second innings:* 218 (Sutcliffe 36, Leyland 42, Hendren 42, Townsend 39 not out; Fleetwood-Smith six for 90).

Umpires: J. Newman and A. Dolphin

NORTH OF SCOTLAND v AUSTRALIANS

Played at Forres, Friday, September 14 [1934]. The Australians wound up their tour with a splendid victory by an innings and 20 runs over North of Scotland in one day. On a pitch which may have been too liberally watered, batsmen experienced such an unhappy time that thirty wickets went down for an aggregate of 312 runs. Neither Wall nor Ebeling bowled at his usual pace but ... the Scotsmen put up a poor fight and were all out in seventy minutes for the lowest total made against the tourists [all] summer. ... Bradman altered his batting order and the main ambition of the Australians seemed to be to register as many 6's as possible. All of them hit out recklessly, the innings finishing in under ninety minutes ... O'Reilly, going in first, hit four 6's in making his highest score of the tour. Peebles bowled unchanged, and Kemp had the distinction of dismissing Bradman and McCabe [both of whom had scored 2,000 first-class runs on tour] with successive deliveries. North of Scotland fared little better at their second attempt and were put out in an hour and a half. To compensate the spectators, play went on next day as an exhibition.

North of Scotland

Mr A. C. Bremner, Mr J. F. Gray, Mr J. F. Grant, Mr P. D. C. R. Clark, Mr J. C. Richardson, †Lieut. J. A. Grant-Peterkin, Mr I. A. R. Peebles, Mr J. R. Braid, Major K. S. Clarke, Mr J. I. Kemp and Mr N. Wigram.

First innings: 48 (O'Reilly three for 11, Fleetwood-Smith three for 4). *Second innings:* 98 (Wall three for 13, O'Reilly three for 5).

Australians

T. W. Wall lbw b Peebles	0	S. J. McCabe lbw b Kemp	16
W. J. O'Reilly c and b Peebles	47	*D. G. Bradman c Richardson b Kemp	7
L. O'B. Fleetwood-Smith st Grant-Peterkin		A. F. Kippax st Grant-Peterkin b Peebles	15
b Peebles	8	L. S. Darling b Peebles	14
W. A. Brown b Grant	21	H. I. Ebeling not out	0
†B. A. Barnett c Clark b Braid	16	B 15, l-b 3, n-b 1	19
A. G. Chipperfield lbw b Braid	3		**166**

North of Scotland bowling: Peebles 13–2–84–5; Braid 7–1–29–2; Kemp 5–0–34–2; Grant 0.2–0–0–1.

Umpires: G. R. Coutts and R. Corbett

1934–36

Bradman illustrates his driving technique, 1935.

1934-35

In a particularly interesting season, Victoria retained the Sheffield Shield with 25 points out of a possible 30 ... Even without Bradman, who joined South Australia but did not play for that State owing to illness, New South Wales ... were strong enough to finish second. ...

From 'Cricket in Australia: Inter-State Matches, 1934-35'

1935-36

Going through the season undefeated, South Australia carried off the Sheffield Shield for the first time since 1926-27, and for the fifth time in all.

The competition lost something in interest because of the absence of well-known players with the Australian team in South Africa and with the Maharaj of Patiala's side in India. South Australia missed Richardson and Grimmett, and Queensland were without Oxenham, but their disadvantages in this respect were trifling compared with those of the two other States. New South Wales lacked the services of Fingleton, McCabe, Brown, Chipperfield, O'Reilly and Oldfield, and Victoria were nearly as hard hit through the absence of Darling, O'Brien, Barnett, Fleetwood-Smith, McCormick and Sievers.

Despite the weakened opposition, South Australia, who had by far the biggest proportion of experienced players, did well to take the honours by the decisive margin of twelve points. Bradman, of course, was the dominant factor in their success. Leading the team for the first time in State matches, he totalled 739 runs with an average of 123.16, and in his first three innings scored 117, 233 and 357. His form during the series demonstrated his complete recovery to good health and proved a big incentive to his colleagues. In the full Australian season, he scored 1,173 runs (average 130.33). ...

From 'Cricket in Australia: Inter-State Matches, 1935-36'

MCC TEAM v SOUTH AUSTRALIA   119 (177, 178)

Played at Adelaide, Friday, Saturday, Monday, Tuesday, November 8, 9, 11, 12 [1935]. MCC [who played six matches in Australia on their way to New Zealand] won by 36 runs. Although Bradman, appearing for the first time since his operation in England in 1934, captained South Australia, MCC proved slightly the better team. On the first day bright batting ... enabled the touring side to score 314 for the loss of half their wickets, but, Waite performing the 'hat-trick', the innings closed for the addition of 57 runs. South Australia would have failed but for a seventh-wicket stand of 65 between Walker and Waite, and when

MCC went in again 49 in front, bowlers gained the upper hand. ... South Australia were left with plenty of time to score 224 for victory, but Bradman, who drove splendidly, alone caused much trouble.

MCC Team

D. Smith, J. H. Parks, J. Hardstaff, Mr N. S. Mitchell-Innes, Mr J. H. Human, James Langridge, J. Sims, *Hon. C. J. Lyttelton, †Mr A. G. Powell, Mr A. D. Baxter and Mr H. D. Read.

First innings: 371 (Smith 52, Parks 67, Hardstaff 90, Human 87; Ward four for 127, Waite five for 42).
Second innings: 174 (Langridge 34, Lyttelton 31; Ward four for 62, Ryan four for 13).

South Australia

R. Parker c and b Sims	30	–	lbw b Sims	18
C. L. Badcock c Powell b Read	45	–	c Parks b Baxter	14
*D. G. Bradman lbw b Sims	15	–	lbw b Parks	50
E. J. R. Moyle c and b Langridge	39	–	b Baxter	2
A. J. Ryan c Hardstaff b Langridge	13	–	b Parks	27
M. G. Waite c Mitchell-Innes b Read	58	–	b Read	30
R. Williams c Powell b Read	24	–	b Sims	9
†C. W. Walker not out	65	–	c Powell b Sims	5
F. H. Collins b Sims	6	–	b Read	0
F. Ward lbw b Langridge	7	–	not out	10
H. Thompson b Sims	7	–	run out	12
B 5, l-b 1, n-b 7	13		B 5, l-b 1, n-b 4	10
	322			**187**

MCC Team bowling: *First innings*—Baxter 17–3–53–0; Read 20–2–81–3; Sims 34.7–3–134–4; Parks 3–0–16–0; Langridge 17–4–25–3. *Second innings*—Baxter 9–0–35–2; Read 5–0–14–2; Sims 20–0–76–3; Parks 12–1–32–2; Langridge 6.5–0–20–0.

Umpires: R. A. Nelson and J. D. Scott

SOUTH AUSTRALIA v NEW SOUTH WALES   120 (179)

Played at Adelaide, December 18, 19, 20, 21 [1935]. South Australia won by an innings and five runs. Bradman made a highly successful appearance for South Australia. Parker helped Badcock score 139 for the first wicket and then Bradman assisted the hard-hitting Tasmanian to add 202 in two and a half hours. Ward turned the ball sufficiently to trouble nearly all the New South Wales batsmen, and ... they had to follow on 224 behind. ...

South Australia

R. Parker c White b Cooper	74	†C. W. Walker run out	28
C. L. Badcock c Lonergan b Robinson	150	F. H. Collins c and b Mudge	0
*D. G. Bradman c and b Robinson	117	F. Ward b Howell	32
E. J. Moyle c Easton b Mudge	98	T. W. Wall not out	10
M. G. Waite c Little b Cooper	22	B 6, l-b 4, w 1, n-b 4	15
A. J. Ryan b Howell	5		**575**
T. O'Connell b Cooper	24		

New South Wales bowling: Cooper 27–3–103–3; McGilvray 14–2–36–0; White 37–7–97–0; Mudge 28–3–113–2; Howell 25.4–5–98–2; Little 4–0–24–0; Robinson 9–0–53–2; Marks 17–3–36–0.

New South Wales

L. Fallowfield, H. Mudge, R. Little, A.E. Marks, A.R. Lonergan, R. Robinson, E.S. White, †F. Easton, *A. McGilvray, W. Howell and A. Cooper.

First innings: 351 (Fallowfield 54, Little 76, Robinson 102; Ward six for 127). *Second innings:* 219 (Fallowfield 38, Marks 31, Lonergan 39, Robinson 39, Easton 42; Wall three for 15, Ryan four for 27).

Umpires: J.D. Scott and R.A. Nelson

SOUTH AUSTRALIA v QUEENSLAND   121 (180)

Played at Adelaide, December 24, 26, 27, 28 [1935]. South Australia won by an innings and 226 runs. Bradman demoralised the Queensland attack, his glorious strokeplay bringing him runs almost at will, and he occupied little more than three hours over his 233. [It was Bradman's third consecutive double-hundred against Queensland.] Badcock and his captain added 183 and Walker, Waite and Ryan hit in fine style. Four Queensland bowlers had a hundred runs hit off them. ...

South Australia

C.L. Badcock c Tallon b Gilbert	91	A.J. Ryan b Christy	72
R. Parker c Levy b Fisher	10	T. O'Connell c Honour b Gilbert	41
*D.G. Bradman c Tallon b Levy	233	F.H. Collins not out	0
†C.W. Walker c Andrews b Fisher	71	B 7, l-b 3, w 1, n-b 1	12
E.J. Moyle b Levy	13	(eight wkts dec)	**642**
M.G. Waite lbw b Cook	99		

F. Ward and T.W. Wall did not bat.

Queensland bowling: Gilbert 27.5–1–121–2; Cook 29–3–108–1; Fisher 20–2–103–2; Wyeth 20–2–98–0; Allen 7–0–52–0; Levy 19–0–116–2; Christy 11–2–24–1; Andrews 1–0–8–0.

Queensland

T. Allen, G.G. Cook, C.W. Andrews, V. Honour, D. Hansen, †D. Tallon, *R.M. Levy, J.A. Christy, A. Fisher, E. Gilbert and E.R. Wyeth.

First innings: 127 (Allen 54; Wall three for 13, Waite three for 29). *Second innings:* 289 (Allen 30, Cook 34, Hansen 80, Tallon 88; Collins four for 41, Ward three for 95).

Umpires: R.A. Nelson and J.D. Scott

VICTORIA v SOUTH AUSTRALIA   122 (181)

Played at Melbourne, January 1, 2, 3, 4 [1936]. South Australia won on the first innings. Big crowds enjoyed a feast of interesting cricket between two unbeaten sides. Bradman overshadowed everyone else. His 357, which followed innings of 233 and 117 in the two previous Shield matches, was his fifth score of 300 and his twenty-third of 200. [It was also the highest score against Victoria.] Bradman, when 18, passed his 5,000 runs in Shield cricket. Picking out the loose ball with unhurried but masterly decision, Bradman made 229 before the close of the first day and, next morning, he gave a scintillating display, hitting up 128 in less than two hours. In all he batted just over seven hours, gave no chance and hit forty 4's; he scored his runs out of 502 and used every stroke with equal facility ... [When Victoria followed on] a fine fighting innings by Rigg was primarily responsible for his side saving the game.

South Australia

A. J. Ryan run out	7	†C. W. Walker lbw b Welch	8
R. Parker c Rigg b Welch	63	F. H. Collins not out	37
*D. G. Bradman c Quin b Bromley	357	F. Ward st Quin b Welch	29
E. J. Moyle c Quin b Welch	9	T. W. Wall lbw b Smith	0
M. G. Waite b Gregory	24	L-b 4, n-b 2	6
A. F. Richter c Smith b Welch	7		**569**
T. O'Connell c Quin b Plant	22		

Victoria bowling: Ebeling 4–1–9–0; Nagel 25–5–85–0; Plant 27–2–86–1; Smith 14.1–2–56–1; Welch 25–1–155–5; Gregory 19–1–101–1; Bromley 14–2–71–1.

Victoria

K. E. Rigg, †S. Quin, I. S. Lee, J. W. Scaife, V. Nagel, E. H. Bromley, R. Gregory, H. J. Plant, S. Smith, *H. I. Ebeling and C. Welch.

First innings: 313 (Quin 52, Lee 50, Scaife 48, Gregory 80, Plant 42; Wall four for 77). *Second innings:* Five for 250 (Rigg 124, Quin 47; O'Connell three for 42, Bradman none for 0).

Umpires: A. N. Barlow and C. Dwyer

QUEENSLAND v SOUTH AUSTRALIA   123 (182)

Played at Brisbane, January 10, 11, 13, 14 [1936]. South Australia won by ten wickets. Bradman's policy of sending in Queensland to bat was completely justified but he disappointed a big crowd who came expecting to see him continue his run of centuries. [The attendance on the second day was 15,716, compared with 3,892 on the first day.] Queensland showed moderate batting form on a wicket affected by rain, and South Australia, apart from a timely hundred by Ryan, were little more impressive. Gilbert bowled exceptionally well and at his top pace. Bradman was never comfortable against him and, not properly getting over a rising ball, he gave backward-point a simple catch. ...

Queensland

T. Allen, R. Rogers, C. W. Andrews, *J. A. Christy, D. Hansen, V. Honour, H. Thomsett, †G. Gunthorpe, E. R. Wyeth, A. Muhl and E. Gilbert.

First innings: 205 (Rogers 39, Andrews 30, Honour 32; Waite three for 45, Ward four for 52). *Second innings:* 163 (Hansen 35, Gunthorpe 46; Waite three for 44, Ward three for 36).

South Australia

R. Parker c Allen b Gilbert	1	–	not out	12
C. L. Badcock b Thomsett	16	–	not out	16
*D. G. Bradman c Wyeth b Gilbert	31			
A. J. Ryan lbw b Wyeth	144			
E. J. Moyle c Hansen b Gilbert	21			
M. G. Waite c Rogers b Muhl	41			
T. O'Connell c Gunthorpe b Gilbert	36			
†C. W. Walker b Wyeth	0			
R. G. Williams c Wyeth b Gilbert	23			
F. Ward lbw b Wyeth	12			
T. W. Wall not out	7			
B 5, l-b 2, n-b 1	8		L-b	1
	340		(no wkt)	**29**

Queensland bowling: *First innings*—Gilbert 29–6–87–5; Andrews 5–0–25–0; Wyeth 31.2–9–101–3; Thomsett 7–0–26–1; Christy 6–0–9–0; Muhl 15–3–48–1; Allen 10–0–36–0. *Second innings*—Gilbert 3–1–11–0; Andrews 3–0–9–0; Muhl 2–0–6–0; Allen 1–0–2–0.

Umpires: J. A. Scott and J. Bartlett

NEW SOUTH WALES v SOUTH AUSTRALIA   124 (183)

Played at Sydney, January 17, 18, 20 [1936]. Abandoned. Rain prevented play on the first day, and owing to the death of King George V there was no cricket on the last day [January 21]. When the game started after lunch on Saturday, McGilvray sent South Australia in, and White (eight for 31) nonplussed the batsmen on an awkward wicket. However, he did not have the satisfaction of disposing of Bradman, who was out without scoring through Little showing smart anticipation in moving to fine short-leg and holding a glide off Hynes. South Australia took nearly three hours over their 94. ...

South Australia

C. L. Badcock c McGilvray b White	24	†C. W. Walker c Robinson b White	7
R. Parker c McGilvray b White	14	R. G. Williams run out	10
*D. G. Bradman c Little b Hynes	0	F. Ward c Mudge b White	12
A. J. Ryan c Little b White	2	T. W. Wall run out	0
M. G. Waite c Marks b White	0	B 2, l-b 2, w 1, n-b 2	7
E. J. Moyle b White	5		**94**
T. O'Connell c Marks b White	13		

New South Wales bowling: Cooper 9–3–11–0; McGilvray 4–0–11–0; Hynes 11.3–2–25–1; White 19–8–31–8; Chilvers 3–0–9–0.

New South Wales

L. Fallowfield, H. Mudge, R. Little, A. E. Marks, R. Robinson, L. R. Hynes, †F. Easton, E. S. White, *A. McGilvray, H. C. Chilvers and A. Cooper.
    First innings: Six for 286 (Fallowfield 53, Little 30, Robinson 94 not out, Hynes 41; Ward three for 57).

Umpires: G. Borwick and H. Armstrong

SOUTH AUSTRALIA v VICTORIA   125 (184)

Played at Adelaide, February 21, 22, 24, 25 [1936]. South Australia won by an innings and 190 runs. Despite the failure of Bradman – caught at second slip off an out-swinger – Victoria were outplayed in every department. Ward's slow bowling was always too clever for their batsmen, none of whom, with the exception of Hassett in the first innings, managed to pass 50, and Badcock overwhelmed the Victoria bowling. The young Tasmanian [21], in making the highest score of his career, gave a great exhibition. Solid rather than brilliant, he did not force the pace but produced the right stroke for nearly every ball he received during his long stay of nine and a quarter hours. His hands were blistered in the latter stages of his innings but his drives, cuts, hooks and hits to leg lost little power in consequence. He hit thirty-four 4's. Badcock took part in three century stands [including a South Australian record of 210 for the first wicket] ...

Victoria

K. E. Rigg, †S. Quin, I. S. Lee, J. W. Scaife, R. Gregory, J. Ledward, A. Hassett, H. J. Plant, W. Y. Wilson, *H. I. Ebeling and R. B. Scott.

First innings: 201 (Quin 30, Hassett 73; Wall three for 21, Ward five for 74). *Second innings:* 174 (Scaife 33, Ledward 47; Ward four for 72, Waite four for 29).

South Australia

R. Parker c Scott b Wilson	88	M. G. Waite c Rigg b Wilson	8
C. L. Badcock c Rigg b Gregory	325	†C. W. Walker not out	33
*D. G. Bradman c Ledward b Ebeling	1	B 6, l-b 12, w 1, n-b 9	28
E. J. Moyle b Ebeling	5	(six wkts dec)	**565**
A. J. Ryan b Wilson	77		

F. H. Collins, F. Ward, T. W. Wall and R. G. Williams did not bat.

Victoria bowling: Scott 30–3–110–0; Ebeling 41–6–97–2; Wilson 30–4–122–3; Gregory 22.6–1–99–1; Plant 36–11–109–0.

Umpires: J. D. Scott and R. A. Nelson

SOUTH AUSTRALIA v TASMANIA 126 (185)

At Adelaide, February 29, March 2, 3 [1936]. South Australia won by an innings and 349 runs. In addition to the Sheffield Shield matches and the games played by the MCC, [in other matches played in Australia in 1935-36] Tasmania met Victoria three times and South Australia once. In the last-mentioned game Bradman made 369, his second score of over 350 during the season; he had scored 357 against Victoria at Melbourne earlier in the year. [Containing four 6's and forty-six 4's, Bradman's sixth triple-hundred was the highest score by a South Australian batsman, while South Australia's 688 was the State's highest innings total.]

Tasmania: M. J. Combes, R. V. Thomas, E. H. Smith, C. L. Jeffery, A. L. Pearsall, *A. W. Rushforth, J. M. Walsh, G. T. H. James, †J. Gardiner, G. A. Combes and R. C. Townley.

First innings: 158 (Smith 62, Thomas 42; Ward three for 35). *Second innings:* 181 (Rushforth 73, Thomas 44; Waite three for 28, Ward six for 47).

South Australia: C. L. Badcock, †C. W. Walker, *D. G. Bradman, R. A. Hamence, B. H. Leak, R. M. Stanford, M. G. Waite, T. O'Connell, F. Ward, H. J. Cotton and H. R. Shepherdson.

First innings: 688 (Bradman c and b Townley 369, Hamence 121, O'Connell 53, Waite 43; Townley three for 169).

1936-37

Bradman is bowled Verity for 82 on the last day of the Second Test against England at the SCG in December 1936.

1936-37

Recording their third success in four seasons and their ninth since the war, Victoria regained the Sheffield Shield championship they last held in 1934-35. The destination of the trophy was not decided until the last match of the series. Victoria, with 19 points, and South Australia, with 17 points, were the contesting teams and South Australia, who needed an outright win to retain the Shield, lost by nine wickets.

The visit of the MCC team overshadowed the Shield competition, but the absence of leading players on Test Match duty provided chances for the aspiring youngsters ...

South Australia, champions in the previous season, when Bradman and Badcock showed phenomenal batting form, fell below expectations. Playing the same number of innings as in 1935-36, Bradman scored 323 fewer runs; Badcock's aggregate declined by 373 and his average dropped from 124.40 to 49.80. ...

From 'Cricket in Australia: Inter-State Matches, 1936-37'

Although the MCC team which toured Australia in 1936-37 under the captaincy of G. O. Allen failed in their quest to regain the mythical Ashes, it is probable that they would have achieved their object had not some wonderful batting feats by Bradman for Australia turned the scale. After winning two Tests, England were beaten in the remaining three, and so for the first time a side which lost the first two games of a series came out on top. Australia must be heartily congratulated on the success. It is a point worth recording that in each of the five games the captain who won the toss led the winning eleven. ...

The fluctuating nature of the Test struggles gripped the interest of the Australian public and financially the tour broke all records. The total number of people who watched the five games was over 900,000 and the receipts amounted to £90,909. ... On examination of individual performances, Bradman emerges as the star player of the Tests. After a disappointing start, he had an aggregate of 810 runs, in which were included scores of 82, 270, 212 and 169, and an average of 90. Though McCabe was next with an aggregate of 491 runs, Hammond had rather the better average – 58 as against 54. ...

From 'MCC Team in Australia'

V. Y. RICHARDSON'S TEAM v D.G. BRADMAN'S TEAM
(TESTIMONIAL MATCH)   127 (186, 187)

At Sydney, October 9, 10, 12, 13 [1936]. D.G. Bradman's team won by six wickets. The Testimonial match for W. Bardsley and J. M. Gregory brought a double-hundred from Bradman, but the deciding factor was the slow bowling of Ward. Brown, McCabe and Oldfield were the only batsmen to play him confidently. O'Brien cut and drove stylishly for Bradman's team, but the captain overshadowed everyone. He used all the strokes with equal brilliance and scored almost at will. [This was the first time Bradman had played against O'Reilly in a first-class match, though he had faced him in country matches before either played for New South Wales. On one of those occasions, at the age of seventeen, he had also notched up a double-hundred.]

V. Y. Richardson's Team

W. A. Brown, J. H. Fingleton, S. J. McCabe, L. S. Darling, *V. Y. Richardson, A. G. Chipperfield, M. W. Sievers, †W. A. Oldfield, C. V. Grimmett, W. J. O'Reilly and E. L. McCormick.

First innings: 363 (Brown 111, McCabe 76, Oldfield 78, McCormick 30 not out; Ward seven for 127). *Second innings:* 180 (Darling 35, Sievers 43 not out; Ward five for 100).

D.G. Bradman's Team

L. P. O'Brien lbw b McCormick	85	–	lbw b O'Reilly	18
C. L. Badcock c Fingleton b O'Reilly	18	–	c Darling b Grimmett	43
R. H. Robinson b O'Reilly	2	–	c Fingleton b Grimmett	57
R. O. Morrisby b O'Reilly	4	–	not out	19
†D. Tallon b Sievers	3	–	not out	0
*D. G. Bradman c O'Reilly b Grimmett	212	–	c Fingleton b Grimmett	13
A. D. McGilvray st Oldfield b Grimmett	42			
E. S. White b O'Reilly	2			
F. Ward not out	5			
H. I. Ebeling lbw b Grimmett	1			
T. Leather st Oldfield b Grimmett	0			
B 4, l-b 2, n-b 5	11		B 7, l-b 4	11
	385		(four wkts)	**161**

V. Y. Richardson's Team bowling: *First innings*—McCormick 13–0–50–1; Sievers 13–1–49–1; O'Reilly 22–0–96–4; Grimmett 20.7–2–146–4; McCabe 4–1–21–0; Chipperfield 1–0–12–0. *Second innings*—McCormick 6–0–30–0; Sievers 3–0–11–0; O'Reilly 13.6–4–27–1; Grimmett 16–2–82–3.

Umpires: G. Borwick and A. Christie

MCC TEAM v SOUTH AUSTRALIA

At Adelaide, October 30, 31, November 2, 3 [1936]. MCC Team won by 105 runs. ... Bradman, the South Australia captain, stood down because of the death of his baby son.

VICTORIA v SOUTH AUSTRALIA   128 (188)

At Melbourne, November 13, 14, 16, 17 [1936]. Drawn. So far from profiting after putting Victoria in first, South Australia had their bowling trounced. ... A superb innings by Bradman was chiefly responsible for South Australia making a fight of the first innings issue. Although he had a strained leg, Bradman batted brilliantly and at one period scored nearly 100 runs in an hour. Altogether, during a stay of three hours, he hit thirty-three 4's. ...

Victoria

L. P. O'Brien, K. E. Rigg, L. S. Darling, I. S. Lee, R. G. Gregory, M. W. Sievers, †B. A. Barnett, H. J. Plant, J. Frederick, *H. I. Ebeling and E. L. McCormick.

First innings: 401 (O'Brien 30, Rigg 97, Darling 39, Lee 38, Gregory 85, Sievers 54; Ward six for 107). *Second innings:* Seven for 403 (Rigg 105, Darling 102, Lee 93, Barnett 55; Waite four for 65).

South Australia

C. L. Badcock lbw b McCormick	2	M. G. Waite c and b Ebeling	11
R. A. Parker st Barnett b Sievers	33	C. V. Grimmett c Barnett b Ebeling	8
A. J. Ryan lbw b McCormick	9	F. A. Ward not out	3
*D. G. Bradman c O'Brien b Gregory	192	H. J. Cotton lbw b Ebeling	0
V. Y. Richardson lbw b Sievers	38	B 12, l-b 1, w 2, n-b 4	19
R. A. Hamence b Frederick	37		**386**
†C. W. Walker b Ebeling	34		

Victoria bowling: McCormick 15–1–85–2; Ebeling 26.2–5–74–4; Sievers 13–3–36–2; Frederick 15–2–90–1; Plant 15–6–50–0; Gregory 10–3–27–1; Darling 2–0–5–0.

Umpires: A. N. Barlow and C. Dwyer

MCC TEAM v AN AUSTRALIAN XI   129 (189)

At Sydney, November 20, 21, 23, 24 [1936]. Drawn. When time expired, the MCC team, with eight men out and Duckworth suffering from a broken finger, required 11 runs to avoid defeat in a single innings. … Fingleton and Brown gave the Australian side a fine start with a careful partnership of 103, and Bradman scored readily, but chief honours in the innings fell to Badcock … Facing a deficit of 256, MCC lost three men for 50 and … dropped catches alone enabled the visitors to escape.

MCC Team

A. Fagg, T. S. Worthington, L. E. G. Ames, M. Leyland, J. Hardstaff, L. B. Fishlock, *Mr R. W. V. Robins, H. Verity, W. Voce, †G. Duckworth and Mr K. Farnes.

First innings: 288 (Fagg 49, Ames 76, Leyland 80, Robins 53; Chipperfield eight for 66). *Second innings:* Eight for 245 (Ames 37, Leyland 118 not out, Robins 33).

An Australian XI

J. H. Fingleton lbw b Verity	56	A. G. Chipperfield c Duckworth b Voce	39
W. A. Brown lbw b Farnes	71	†D. Tallon c Hardstaff b Robins	31
*D. G. Bradman b Worthington	63	A. J. Ryan not out	40
C. L. Badcock c Farnes b Verity	182	M. G. Waite not out	11
R. H. Robinson c Worthington b Farnes	0	B 14, l-b 15, n-b 8	37
R. G. Gregory c Worthington b Verity	14	(eight wkts dec)	**544**

H. Ebeling did not bat.

MCC Team bowling: Farnes 24–4–112–2; Voce 27–4–89–1; Robins 13–0–72–1; Verity 48–5–130–3; Worthington 25–5–81–1; Leyland 4–0–23–0.

Umpires: G. Borwick and H. Armstrong

ENGLAND v AUSTRALIA   130 (190, 191)
(FIRST TEST MATCH)   29 (43, 44)

At Sydney, December 4, 5, 7, 8, 9 [1936]. England won by 322 runs. England gained a totally unexpected but wholly meritorious victory before lunch on the fifth day. Prior to this match, the record of the team had been so poor that on form it was impossible to concede them more than an outside chance of making a good show. Batsmen who had gone to Australia lauded as leaders in the recovery of English cricket – Fishlock, Hardstaff and Fagg – had played lamentably, being made sport of by every slow leg-break bowler they met, some bowlers barely good enough to gain a regular place in an English county side. ... That England became transformed in a single night into a great and victorious side was entirely due to the example and enthusiasm of G. O. Allen, the captain; and this match will go down to history as 'Allen's Test'. Aided by Robins, Wyatt, Hammond and Leyland, who formed the advisory selection committee, Allen sprang surprises in his make-up of the eleven, and his choices succeeded. He followed this up by winning the toss.

Don Bradman will have reason to remember his first essay as captain of Australia, for he lost the toss, was in some Australian quarters criticised for his captaincy, and he failed with the bat.

A thunderstorm threatened when play opened, but actually no rain fell until the night between the fourth and fifth days. The Brisbane wicket is always lively for an hour and a half or so on the first day of a match and ... McCormick was able to make the ball lift during that spell before lunch. His height aided the natural conditions, and he had three of England in the pavilion with only 20 on the board. Worthington was caught at the wicket off the first ball of the match [and the] loss of Hammond, also out first ball, was a severe blow to English hopes. ... [England recovered to reach six for 263 at stumps and ended with a total of 358.]

Bradman had been seriously handicapped on the Saturday by the inability to bowl of McCormick, who was attacked by lumbago and made only fitful appearances for the remainder of the game. At the end of the second day England's worst fears [an Australian first innings score of 500] looked like being justified, for Australia's score was 151 for two wickets, Fingleton being 61 and McCabe 37. It is true that Bradman had been dismissed, caught in the gully off Voce, but the third-wicket pair looked formidable and seemed capable of a huge partnership on such a good wicket.

But on Monday, the third day, the game swung round completely, England showed fight before lunch and Voce ran through the Australian team afterwards. ... England's batting ... once more disappointed in the second innings. ... On the fourth day there came a further improvement, led by the captain ... The way Allen played O'Reilly was a revelation of concentration and masterly batting ... Australia opened their last innings [with half an hour remaining on the fourth day] wanting 381 to win. In a poor light, against which five appeals were made, Fingleton [who in the first innings had become the first batsman to make four hundreds in successive Test innings] was bowled first ball by Voce. A storm threatened, but even had not rain fallen during the night, it was felt that Australia's task of getting 378 still needed, with Fingleton out and McCormick a cripple, would be beyond their compass.

The last shower before the fifth ... day's play occurred about 6 a.m., and the wicket, already worn, assumed the properties of a 'sticky dog'. In former days, fast bowlers would not have been able to get a foothold, but with the runs-up to the wicket protected, Voce and Allen were able to bowl from first to last and Verity was not called upon. The Australian batting was deplorable. Badcock went out to Allen's second ball of the day, and the England captain dismissed Sievers and Bradman with the fourth and sixth balls of his second over. With Bradman's departure, Australia's last hope disappeared. Half the side were dismissed with only 16 on the board, and Australia were all out, McCormick not batting, for the paltry total of 58. ...

Fingleton's century stood out for Australia. The placing of the field in England's second innings was remarkably good, and little fault could be found with Bradman's tactics. ... Oldfield, when he stumped Hardstaff in England's second innings, set up a new record for Test cricket, surpassing Lilley's figures of eighty-four successes when keeping wicket for England.

England

T.S. Worthington, C.J. Barnett, A. Fagg, W.R. Hammond, M. Leyland, †L.E.G. Ames, J. Hardstaff, Mr R.W.V. Robins, *Mr G.O. Allen, H. Verity and W. Voce.

First innings: 358 (Barnett 69, Leyland 126, Hardstaff 43, Robins 38, Allen 35; McCormick three for 26, O'Reilly five for 102). *Second innings:* 256 (Leyland 33, Allen 68; Sievers three for 29, Ward six for 102).

Australia

J.H. Fingleton b Verity	100	–	b Voce	0
C.L. Badcock b Allen	8	–	c Fagg b Allen	0
*D.G. Bradman c Worthington b Voce	38	–	c Fagg b Allen	0
S.J. McCabe c Barnett b Voce	51	–	c Leyland b Allen	7
R.H. Robinson c Hammond b Voce	2	–	c Hammond b Voce	3
A.G. Chipperfield c Ames b Voce	7	–	not out	26
M.W. Sievers b Allen	8	–	c Voce b Allen	5
†W.A. Oldfield c Ames b Voce	6	–	b Voce	10
W.J. O'Reilly c Leyland b Voce	3	–	b Allen	0
F. Ward c Hardstaff b Allen	0	–	b Voce	1
E.L. McCormick not out	1	–	absent ill	0
B 4, l-b 1, n-b 5	10		N-b	6
	234			**58**

England bowling: *First innings*—Allen 16–2–71–3; Voce 20.6–5–41–6; Hammond 4–0–12–0; Verity 28–11–52–1; Robins 17–0–48–0. *Second innings*—Allen 6–0–36–5; Voce 6.3–0–16–4.

Umpires: G. Borwick and J.D. Scott

ENGLAND v AUSTRALIA   131 (192, 193)
(SECOND TEST MATCH)   30 (45, 46)

At Sydney, December 18, 19, 21, 22 [1936]. England won by an innings and 22 runs. Possibly even more than in the First Test, the winning of the toss was of paramount importance. Owing to the long drought, the groundsman feared the wicket would not last as well as is usual in Test Matches at Sydney. The prospect of unsettled weather contributed to uncertainty about the way the wicket would play after the first day or two. ...

A much-discussed feature of play before lunch, when 100 runs were scored for one wicket, concerned five overs sent down by McCormick, who was not only erratic but pitched short, so that the ball flew all over the place. It should be made clear, however, that suggestions of 'Bodyline' bowling were uncalled for. McCormick merely used the recognised methods of the fast bowler and did not set an exaggerated leg field. Batsmen experienced little trouble in playing him during the later stages of the match; he had not fully recovered from his attack of lumbago and never again attained any real speed. ...

Barnett lost his wicket immediately after lunch ... Then Leyland came on the scene to dash the hopes of the Australians. This was not one of the Yorkshire left-hander's most attractive displays [and he was] criticised even more than Hammond for his slow play by Australian experts who neglected to give their own bowlers and captain full credit for limiting the batsmen's scoring scope by the nature of their attack and the setting of the field. ...

... There was a curious incident [on the second day] when Hardstaff had scored 11. Robinson, the twelfth man, was fielding behind the square-leg umpire and Hardstaff hit a ball from O'Reilly hard into his hands. A shower had rendered the ball as slippery as wet soap and the catch was missed. Apparently both umpires were watching the fieldsman, for when Bradman called attention to the fact that the Nottinghamshire man had stepped on to his wicket sufficiently to dislodge a bail when making the stroke, Hardstaff was given the benefit of the doubt.

Heavy rain in the night created a problem for Allen next morning, and as events proved he was right in declaring straightaway. Australia, as at Brisbane, were caught on a wet wicket and figured in an inglorious collapse – all out for 80.

Nothing more sensational can be imagined than their first dreadful quarter of an hour, when O'Brien, Bradman and McCabe were all sent back without scoring. Voce dismissed them with his seventh, eighth and tenth balls ... Seven wickets were down for 31, but with lunch-time approaching O'Reilly played a desperate innings and hit three 6's, one off Verity and two off Sims. ... During lunch Allen decided to put Australia in again. Already the wicket had shown signs of recovery, and it rolled out a perfect batting wicket, so that he took a risk which might have cost him the match.

The general opinion was that Australia's batsmen had exaggerated the dangers of the wicket, which was damp, not sticky. They did much better on going in again, and at the close of the third day Fingleton (67) and Bradman (57) were together with the score 145 for one wicket.

The English victory was said by Australian critics to have been registered at five minutes to one on the fourth day, when Bradman, having surpassed Clem Hill's aggregate of 2,660 runs in Test Matches for Australia v England, was bowled by Verity for 82. McCabe alone refused to be unnerved. He proceeded after lunch to give the brightest batting exhibition of the whole match ...

Tea-time came with the score 309 for five wickets and odds on England having to bat again. The interval gave England's bowlers fresh heart; Voce once more found top form, and he and Hammond, bringing about another sensational Australian collapse, won the match. Though it was Hammond's steadiness as a bowler that clinched England's superiority, which he himself had established with his great innings of 231 not out, Voce again came out with fine figures ... England enjoyed all the luck that was going ... while Australia were hard hit by Badcock being ill; he could not bat in the first innings, and although he left a sick bed to bat in the second, he made only two. ...

England

A. Fagg, C. J. Barnett, W. R. Hammond, M. Leyland, †L. E. G. Ames, *Mr G. O. Allen, J. Hardstaff, H. Verity, Mr R. W. V. Robins, W. Voce and J. Sims.

First innings: Six for 426 dec (Barnett 57, Hammond 231 not out, Leyland 42).

Australia

J. H. Fingleton c Verity b Voce	12	–	b Sims	73
L. P. O'Brien c Sims b Voce	0	–	c Allen b Hammond	17
*D. G. Bradman c Allen b Voce	0	–	b Verity	82
S. J. McCabe c Sims b Voce	0	–	lbw b Voce	93
A. G. Chipperfield c Sims b Allen	13	–	b Voce	21
M. W. Sievers c Voce b Verity	4	–	run out	24
†W. A. Oldfield b Verity	1	–	c Ames b Voce	1
W. J. O'Reilly not out	37	–	b Hammond	3
E. L. McCormick b Allen	10	–	lbw b Hammond	0
F. Ward b Allen	0	–	not out	1
C. L. Badcock absent ill	0	–	lbw b Allen	2
B 1, l-b 1, n-b 1	3		L-b 3, n-b 4	7
	80			**324**

England bowling: *First innings*—Voce 8–1–10–4; Allen 5.7–1–19–3; Verity 3–0–17–2; Hammond 4–0–6–0; Sims 2–0–20–0; Robins 1–0–5–0. *Second innings*—Voce 19–4–66–3; Allen 19–4–61–1; Verity 19–7–55–1; Hammond 15.7–3–29–3; Sims 17–0–80–1; Robins 7–0–26–0.

Umpires: G. Borwick and J. D. Scott

ENGLAND v AUSTRALIA
(THIRD TEST MATCH)

132 (194, 195)

31 (47, 48)

At Melbourne, January 1, 2, 4, 5, 6, 7 [1937]. Australia won by 365 runs. England were not disgraced even though the margin was a large one; outside influences had much to do with the result. The faith of the Australians that their [revamped] side ... would atone for the two previous disappointments was reflected in the attendances. All records for attendances and receipts at a cricket match were broken. On the third day alone there were 87,798 people present – the takings were £7,405 – and the aggregate attendance for the match was 350,534 and the full receipts £30,124.

As things turned out, Bradman won the match for Australia when he won the toss, and his tactics influenced the result. On the second day he took the unusual procedure in a played-to-a-finish Test Match of declaring his first innings closed [as Allen had England's in the previous Test] and sent England in to bat on a pitch from which the ball often reared up almost straight and at other times kept low. It is important to mention that on the first day, when Australia were batting, the wicket was lifeless and unhelpful to spin bowling, and yet England got down six wickets for 130 and would probably have done still better had not rain set in and led to the bowlers being handicapped by the wet ball. Next day rain held up a resumption of the match until after lunch. The difficulties of the wicket quickly became apparent, and batsmen experienced such an unhappy time that in about three hours thirteen wickets fell. England, after losing nine wickets for 76, also declared, so that for the first time in Test cricket each side closed its first innings.

It is possible England would have done better had Allen's declaration been made earlier but, as one authority put it, the England captain could not be expected to possess second sight. At the close of play on the second day, one Australian – O'Reilly [first ball] – had been dismissed for three runs [Bradman had sent in O'Reilly, Fleetwood-Smith and Ward first to protect his top-order batting] and a Sunday without rain enabled the wicket to recover so that when Australia took up their second innings again the conditions were more favourable for batting than at any previous time in the match. ...

Australia batted all the third day. It was inevitable that Bradman should find his form soon, and he chose the moment of his country's greatest need to do so. Rain fell in the afternoon, and between – and during – the showers the England bowlers were handicapped by a wet ball which they wiped with a towel between each delivery. Bradman took full advantage of this and, though not quite his old scintillating self, and eschewing the off-drive, he thrilled the crowd and subdued the bowlers. Scoring 270, he played his highest innings against England in Australia. Not until the evening was it revealed that Bradman was suffering from a severe chill. That explained his sedateness. In Rigg he found a splendid partner: a man who had been on the fringe of the Australian XI for a long time and looked good enough a cricketer to have gained a place earlier. [This was, in fact, Rigg's sixth Test but his first against England!] ... Hereabouts came the first glimpse during the tour of the Bradman known in England. It was after a stoppage for rain and he faced Voce. He took 13 off the over (of eight balls) and two and three off the first two balls of Allen's next over. Another shower cut short the burst of hitting.

The fact that, on the fourth day, Bradman and Fingleton put up a sixth-wicket record of 346 – actually the highest stand for any wicket in a Test Match [and first-class match] in Australia – was due to Bradman sending in his tail-end batsmen first. Usually those two players would have been associated for the second wicket. The pitch had become as perfect as any batsman could wish, and though the England bowlers remained steady they had little chance of beating Bradman or Fingleton. ...

Bradman, still suffering from mild influenza, was quickly dismissed on the morning of the fifth day, and immediately after lunch England opened their second innings wanting 689 runs to win. Such a task had never before been achieved in Test history, but the wicket was still very easy and a dour fight was anticipated. However, [only] Leyland alone of the earlier batsmen, and Robins, towards the end of the day, batted really well. ...

Australia

J. H. Fingleton c Sims b Robins	38	–	c Ames b Sims	136
W. A. Brown c Ames b Voce	1	–	c Barnett b Voce	20
*D. G. Bradman c Robins b Verity	13	–	c Allen b Voce	270
K. E. Rigg c Verity b Allen	16	–	lbw b Sims	47
S. J. McCabe c Worthington b Voce	63	–	lbw b Allen	22
L. S. Darling c Allen b Verity	20	–	b Allen	0
M. W. Sievers st Ames b Robins	1	–	not out	25
†W. A. Oldfield not out	27	–	lbw b Verity	7
W. J. O'Reilly c Sims b Hammond	4	–	c and b Voce	0
F. Ward st Ames b Hammond	7	–	c Hardstaff b Verity	18
L. O'B. Fleetwood-Smith (did not bat)	0	–	c Verity b Voce	0
B 2, l-b 6, n-b 2	10		B 6, l-b 2, w 1, n-b 10	19
(nine wkts dec)	**200**			**564**

England bowling: *First innings*—Voce 18–3–49–2; Allen 12–2–35–1; Sims 9–1–35–0; Verity 14–4–24–2; Robins 7–0–31–2; Hammond 5.3–0–16–2. *Second innings*—Voce 29–2–120–3; Allen 23–2–84–2; Sims 23–1–109–2; Verity 37.7–9–79–3; Robins 11–2–46–0; Hammond 22–3–89–0; Worthington 4–0–18–0.

England

T. S. Worthington, C. J. Barnett, W. R. Hammond, M. Leyland, J. Sims, †L. E. G. Ames, Mr R. W. V. Robins, J. Hardstaff, *Mr G. O. Allen, H. Verity and W. Voce.

First innings: Nine for 76 dec (Hammond 32; Sievers five for 21, O'Reilly three for 28). *Second innings:* 323 (Hammond 51, Leyland 111 not out, Robins 61; O'Reilly three for 65, Fleetwood-Smith five for 124).

Umpires: G. Borwick and J. D. Scott

MCC TEAM v SOUTH AUSTRALIA   133 (196)

At Adelaide, January 22, 23, 25, 26 [1937]. Drawn. Rain and the state of the pitch prevented cricket on the last two days. The MCC batsmen exercised great care. … Fishlock, who stayed two hours, received a blow on the hand in Cotton's opening over and, a bone being fractured, he was kept out of the team until early March. [Owing to a strained leg, Bradman batted with a runner during his innings.]

MCC Team

C. J. Barnett, L. B. Fishlock, W. R. Hammond, M. Leyland, Mr R. E. S. Wyatt, †L. E. G. Ames, Mr R. W. V. Robins, *Mr G. O. Allen, H. Verity, W. Voce and Mr K. Farnes.

First innings: 301 (Barnett 78, Fishlock 40, Wyatt 53, Ames 36, Allen 60; Cotton three for 76, Grimmett four for 77).

South Australia

A. J. Ryan c sub b Verity	71	R. S. Whitington not out	33
†C. W. Walker c Verity b Farnes	29	R. Hamence not out	3
C. L. Badcock c Ames b Voce	13	L-b 6, n-b 1	7
*D. G. Bradman c Ames b Barnett	38	(four wkts)	**194**

H. Cotton, C. V. Grimmett, V. Y. Richardson, F. Ward and M. G. Waite did not bat.

MCC Team bowling: Voce 8–0–32–1; Allen 9–1–44–0; Farnes 10–1–28–1; Hammond 2–0–11–0; Robins 7–0–36–0; Verity 12–2–33–1; Barnett 2–0–3–1.

Umpires: J. D. Scott and A. J. Richardson

ENGLAND v AUSTRALIA
(FOURTH TEST MATCH)

134 (197, 198)

32 (49, 50)

Played at Adelaide, January 29, 30, February 1, 2, 3, 4 [1937]. Australia won by 148 runs. Two factors lost England the match, which might have been won despite Bradman succeeding in the toss. One was England's batting collapse on the Monday, when the immense advantage gained by getting Australia out for the small total of 288 was frittered away by a deplorable display after Barnett and Leyland had put the side in a splendid position. The other was Bradman's second innings of 212....

The wicket was perfect throughout the match, and for the only time in the series no rain came to interfere with play. The batting failures, therefore, were inexplicable. Australia's win roused cricket enthusiasm in the country to a high pitch because it meant the final Test being the decider of the rubber.

The first day's play was witnessed by 39,000 people. Australia ... in the five hours allotted scored 267 for the loss of seven wickets; a good day's work by England. ... Bradman, who, unusually restrained, took 68 minutes to score 26 runs, was clean bowled by Allen when trying one of his favourite hook shots. Gregory, making his Test debut at the age of twenty, showed promise, and McCabe indulged in an exhilarating burst of scoring immediately after the tea interval ... At twenty minutes to one on the second day Australia were out for 288, and by the close of play England had hit 174 for two wickets, Barnett being 92 and Leyland 35. England appeared to be in a very strong position, and Barnett's first Test century was completed early on the morning of the third day ... Then the game swung Australia's way ... five England wickets were lost for 259 with Australia still 29 runs on – not as comfortable a position as had been promised.

... [Next day] England finished only 42 ahead. By close of play Australia were 21 on with nine wickets in hand, and Bradman in his most dangerous mood. The fourth day's play virtually settled the issue; a stubborn stand between Bradman and McCabe realised 109, and a big fifth-wicket partnership ensued between Bradman and Gregory. This, producing 135, was not broken until the fifth day when Bradman showed signs of tiredness. Bradman's innings was not one of his most brilliant efforts but he has never looked more sure of himself. He seemed to go in to bat with the fixed determination of winning the match, and though England bowled with any amount of skill and heart he hit 212 in 437 minutes. In that score there were only fourteen 4's – an indication of the dourness of his fight. Incidentally, it was Bradman's seventh double-century in Tests against England [and his seventeenth Test hundred in all, surpassing the record set by H. Sutcliffe]. On his dismissal the four remaining wickets went down for 11 runs ... At the close of the fifth day there was still a ray of hope for England because Hammond and Leyland were together with 148 of the 392 runs required already scored and seven wickets in hand. The wicket, considering the amount of play on it, was in wonderful order. Fleetwood-Smith, however, was in an inspired mood and utilised the pitch to his needs as no bowler on the English side could have done. ...

Australia

J. H. Fingleton run out	10	–	lbw b Hammond	12
W. A. Brown c Allen b Farnes	42	–	c Ames b Voce	32
K. E. Rigg c Ames b Farnes	20	–	c Hammond b Farnes	7
*D. G. Bradman b Allen	26	–	c and b Hammond	212
S. J. McCabe c Allen b Robins	88	–	c Wyatt b Robins	55
R. W. Gregory lbw b Hammond	23	–	run out	50
A. G. Chipperfield not out	57	–	c Ames b Hammond	31
†W. A. Oldfield run out	5	–	c Ames b Hammond	1
W. J. O'Reilly c Leyland b Allen	7	–	c Hammond b Farnes	1
E. L. McCormick c Ames b Hammond	4	–	b Hammond	1
L. O'B. Fleetwood-Smith b Farnes	1	–	not out	4
L-b 2, n-b 3	5		B 10, l-b 15, w 1, n-b 1	27
	288			**433**

England bowling: *First innings*—Voce 12–0–49–0; Allen 16–0–60–2; Farnes 20.6–1–71–3; Hammond 6–0–30–2; Verity 16–4–47–0; Robins 7–1–26–1. *Second innings*—Voce 20–2–86–1; Allen 14–1–61–0; Farnes 24–2–89–2; Hammond 15.2–1–57–5; Verity 37–17–54–0; Robins 6–0–38–1; Barnett 5–1–15–0; Leyland 2–0–6–0.

England

H. Verity, C.J. Barnett, W.R. Hammond, M. Leyland, Mr R.E.S. Wyatt, †L.E.G. Ames, J. Hardstaff, *Mr G.O. Allen, Mr R.W.V. Robins, W. Voce and Mr K. Farnes.

First innings: 330 (Barnett 129, Leyland 45, Ames 52; Fleetwood-Smith four for 129, O'Reilly four for 51). *Second innings:* 243 (Hardstaff 43, Hammond 39, Leyland 32, Wyatt 50; Fleetwood-Smith six for 110).

Umpires: G. Borwick and J.D. Scott

QUEENSLAND v SOUTH AUSTRALIA 135 (199)

At Brisbane, February 12, 13, 15 [1937]. South Australia won by ten wickets. Bowlers were so much on top that, apart from Bradman, only two players scored over 50. … In contrast to the hesitant methods of Queensland [in their first innings] was the certainty of Bradman, who drove, cut, hooked and pulled in masterly style. Badcock, too, batted well and helped his captain in a stand of 109. Queensland failed a second time … Ward finished matters in summary fashion by taking the last four wickets for three runs [three were stumpings by Walker].

Queensland

W.A. Brown, G.G. Cook, R. Rogers, T. Allen, †D. Tallon, G. Baker, J. Maddern, *R.K. Oxenham, G. Amos, E.R.H. Wyeth and P.L. Dixon.

First innings: 137 (Allen 68, Baker 39; Cotton three for 27, Grimmett four for 18). *Second innings:* 139 (Rogers 46, Tallon 48; Cotton three for 50, Ward four for 3).

South Australia

†C.W. Walker c Maddern b Cook	13			
A.J. Ryan b Wyeth	15			
V.Y. Richardson b Wyeth	8			
C.L. Badcock c Amos b Dixon	56			
*D.G. Bradman st Tallon b Wyeth	123			
R.A. Hamence b Wyeth	28			
M.G. Waite lbw b Dixon	0	–	not out	6
R.G. Williams lbw b Dixon	2	–	not out	13
F. Ward c Baker b Dixon	1			
C.V. Grimmett run out	2			
H.J. Cotton not out	0			
B 7, l-b 2	9		W	1
	257		(no wkt)	**20**

Queensland bowling: *First innings*—Dixon 19.7–4–70–4; Cook 12–1–56–1; Oxenham 10–2–16–0; Wyeth 23–4–52–4; Amos 8–0–54–0. *Second innings*—Dixon 3–0–7–0; Wyeth 2.7–1–9–0; Amos 1–0–3–0.

Umpires: J.A. Scott and J. Bartlett

NEW SOUTH WALES v SOUTH AUSTRALIA   136 (200, 201)

At Sydney, February 19, 20, 22, 23 [1937]. Drawn. Good innings were played by Badcock and White, and the former gained a place in the last Test largely through his display in this match. ... With Bradman unable to find his form, a big burden devolved on Badcock, and so well did he shoulder it that he defied the attack for three hours. ...

New South Wales

J.H. Fingleton, R. Beattie, R.H. Robinson, *S.J. McCabe, V. Jackson, S. Barnes, J.G. Lush, L.C. Hynes, †W.A. Oldfield, E.S. White and W.J. O'Reilly.

First innings: 355 (Robinson 47, McCabe 39, Barnes 31, Oldfield 63, White 108 not out; Grimmett four for 71). *Second innings:* 242 (McCabe 68, Jackson 32, Barnes 44, Lush 40; Grimmett three for 77, Ward four for 89).

South Australia

†C. W. Walker c Fingleton b O'Reilly	4	–	b O'Reilly	11
A. J. Ryan c Hynes b Lush	0	–	b O'Reilly	41
R. S. Whitington c Beattie b Lush	29			
*D. G. Bradman lbw b O'Reilly	24	–	not out	38
C. L. Badcock c White b Jackson	136	–	not out	27
R. A. Hamence c Oldfield b Robinson	27			
V. Y. Richardson st Oldfield b Robinson	9			
R. G. Williams lbw b O'Reilly	2			
F. A. Ward b O'Reilly	0	–	c Oldfield b White	8
C. V. Grimmett b Lush	12			
H. J. Cotton not out	12			
B 4, l-b 1, n-b 10	15		B 4, l-b 1, n-b 2	7
	270		(three wkts)	**132**

New South Wales bowling: *First innings*—Lush 16–2–77–3; Hynes 18–1–76–0; Jackson 5–2–9–1; O'Reilly 20–8–40–4; White 10–1–16–0; Robinson 9–0–37–2. *Second innings*—Lush 5–0–24–0; Hynes 8–0–38–0; Jackson 6–2–14–0; O'Reilly 10–3–12–2; White 12–2–36–1.

Umpires: G. Borwick and F. Lyons

ENGLAND v AUSTRALIA   137 (202)
(FIFTH TEST MATCH)   33 (51)

Played at Melbourne, February 26, 27, March 1, 2, 3 [1937]. Australia won by an innings and 200 runs and thereby retained the Ashes. The weather was glorious for the first two days but was less settled on the third, and a thunderstorm during the early hours of the fourth day denied England the chance of making a closer match of it, though by then their position was precarious, to say the least. Again Bradman showed the way, after winning the toss for the third successive time, and his brilliant display – one of the finest of his career – made it easy for his colleagues to help build up the mammoth total of 604 in the first innings. This was the highest total Australia have ever amassed against England in their own country [subsequently overtaken in 1946-47] ...

All the bright, attacking stroke-making batting came from Australia. On the first day, Bradman and McCabe broke another record by putting on 249 for the third wicket, and Bradman, reaching three figures, equalled Hobbs' record of twelve hundreds in England-Australia Tests. At close of play Australia were 342 for three, a total that should never have been achieved, as four important catches were dropped, all at short-leg behind the umpire. ...

This first day's play was a tragic one for England. Fingleton was dropped twice, when one and two, while McCabe was missed early in his innings and again when 86. The fillip the fast bowlers would have gained had all the catches been taken was incalculable. ... Right through his innings [however], Bradman did not once put the ball into the air; nor did he give the semblance of a chance. The heat had its effect and next morning he seemed unable to concentrate; he added only four more runs. Bradman batted over three and a half hours and hit fifteen 4's. ...

As the pitch was still perfect, giving no assistance to any bowler, England had a wonderful chance to make a telling reply but, after a dazzling start by Barnett and Worthington, there was a disastrous collapse. ... The fourth day clinched matters, for England [four for 184 overnight] had to bat on a wet wicket that O'Reilly was able to exploit. Faulty timing was the cause of Hardstaff's early dismissal and accounted for the failure of most of the other batsmen, but Wyatt met a ball from O'Reilly that turned and popped up suddenly. The last four wickets fell for three runs and at the lunch interval England were all out and had to follow on 365 behind. ... England that night had lost eight second innings wickets for 165, and two balls by Fleetwood-Smith on the following morning accounted for Voce and Farnes. ... A notable point about the match was that only one bye was conceded.

Australia

J. H. Fingleton c Voce b Farnes	17	L. J. Nash c Ames b Farnes	17
K. E. Rigg c Ames b Farnes	28	W. J. O'Reilly b Voce	1
*D. G. Bradman b Farnes	169	E. L. McCormick not out	17
S. J. McCabe c Farnes b Verity	112	L. O'B. Fleetwood-Smith b Farnes	13
C. L. Badcock c Worthington b Voce	118	B 1, l-b 5, w 1, n-b 4	11
R. G. Gregory c Verity b Farnes	80		**604**
†W. A. Oldfield c Ames b Voce	21		

England bowling: Allen 17–0–99–0; Farnes 28.5–5–96–6; Voce 29–3–123–3; Hammond 16–1–62–0; Verity 41–5–127–1; Worthington 6–0–60–0; Leyland 3–0–26–0.

England

C. J. Barnett, T. S. Worthington, J. Hardstaff, W. R. Hammond, M. Leyland, Mr R. E. S. Wyatt, †L. E. G. Ames, *Mr G. O. Allen, H. Verity, W. Voce and Mr K. Farnes.
First innings: 239 (Worthington 44, Hardstaff 83, Wyatt 38; Nash four for 70, O'Reilly five for 51).
Second innings: 165 (Barnett 41, Hammond 56; O'Reilly three for 58, Fleetwood-Smith three for 36).

Umpires: G. Borwick and J. D. Scott

SOUTH AUSTRALIA v VICTORIA   138 (203, 204)

At Adelaide, March 12, 13, 15 [1937]. Victoria won by nine wickets. Their bowling strength decided the match and the Shield. South Australia, who needed an outright win to carry off the honours, were puzzled in the first innings by Fleetwood-Smith, and in the second broke down completely against McCormick. McCormick, very fast, was rarely hit in front of the wicket and at one point he seemed likely to take all ten wickets. ...

South Australia

A. J. Ryan b McCormick	0	–	c Hassett b McCormick	19
†C. W. Walker lbw b Fleetwood-Smith	7	–	c Sievers b McCormick	0
R. S. Whitington c Pearson b Sievers	30	–	c Hassett b McCormick	13
*D. G. Bradman c Ebeling b Fleetwood-Smith	31	–	c Hassett b McCormick	8
C. L. Badcock c Hassett b McCormick	28	–	b McCormick	0
R. A. Hamence lbw b Fleetwood-Smith	35	–	c Lee b McCormick	4
M. G. Waite c Sievers b McCormick	0	–	hit wkt b McCormick	7
C. V. Grimmett b Fleetwood-Smith	7	–	b McCormick	0
R. G. Williams b Fleetwood-Smith	7	–	b Sievers	9
F. Ward c Barnett b Fleetwood-Smith	25	–	c Sievers b McCormick	11
H. J. Cotton not out	4	–	not out	0
B 1, l-b 4, n-b 2, w 1	8		B 1, l-b 3, w 1, n-b 3	8
	182			**79**

Victoria bowling: *First innings*—McCormick 14–1–56–3; Ebeling 6–1–16–0; Sievers 10–0–36–1; Fleetwood-Smith 20.4–3–66–6. *Second innings*—McCormick 11–1–40–9; Ebeling 8–0–21–0; Sievers 0.6–0–4–1; Fleetwood-Smith 2–1–6–0.

Victoria

K. E. Rigg, I. S. Lee, R. G. Gregory, A. L. Hassett, J. D. Ledward, W. E. Pearson, †B. A. Barnett, M. W. Sievers, *H. I. Ebeling, E. L. McCormick and L. O'B. Fleetwood-Smith.

First innings: 213 (Rigg 33, Lee 109 not out; Grimmett three for 52, Waite four for 35). *Second innings:* One for 49.

Umpires: J. D. Scott and A. J. Richardson

1937-38

In the nets, 1937.

1937-38

Sheffield Shield cricket in 1937-38 aroused exceptional interest because the Australian players to tour England were to be chosen towards the close of the season. After a lapse of five years, New South Wales regained the trophy with 21 points ... [runners-up] South Australia fell away slightly, but Victoria, winning only one match, dropped from first to third place. ...

In Bradman, South Australia again provided the outstanding batsman in Australian cricket. For the ninth time in ten playing seasons, he scored over 1,000 runs in first-class cricket, and so surpassed the [Sheffield Shield] record aggregate ... previously held with 6,274 by Clem Hill. Bradman scored 983 runs in Shield cricket for an average of 98.30, and, up to the end of 1937-38, Bradman, during his three seasons with South Australia, had made 2,138 runs in 24 innings at the remarkable average of 101.80. He hit four centuries in Shield games, and in scoring 113 and 107 against Queensland at Brisbane he became the first player, since the inception of the Shield competition, to twice perform the feat of getting two centuries in a match. Badcock, Whitington, Waite and Williams played many good innings, but Bradman overshadowed them all in his complete mastery of the bowlers. ...

From 'Cricket in Australia: Inter-State Matches, 1937-38'

SOUTH AUSTRALIA v NEW ZEALANDERS 139 (205)

At Adelaide, November 5, 6, 8 [1937]. South Australia won by ten wickets. Following their tour in England in 1937, the New Zealanders played three matches in Australia – against South Australia, Victoria and New South Wales – before returning home.

New Zealanders: H.G. Vivian, J.L. Kerr, W.M. Wallace, D.A.R. Moloney, M.P. Donnelly, G.L. Weir, *M.L. Page, A.W. Roberts, C.K. Parsloe, †E.W.T. Tindill and J. Cowie.

First innings: 151 (Weir 38; Grimmett three for 21, Ward four for 59). Second innings: 186 (Vivian 64, Wallace 37; Ward seven for 62).

South Australia: C.L. Badcock, †C.W. Walker, V.Y. Richardson, *D.G. Bradman, R.H. Robinson, R.A. Hamence, M.G. Waite, R.G. Williams, F.A. Ward, C.V. Grimmett and H.J. Cotton.

First innings: 331 (Badcock 114, Bradman c Tindill b Cowie 11, Hamence 56, Waite 45, Ward 41 not out; Cowie three for 72, Vivian three for 84). Second innings: None for 7.

Umpires: A.G. Jenkins and J.D. Scott

D.G. BRADMAN'S XI v V.Y. RICHARDSON'S XI   140 (206)
(TESTIMONIAL MATCH)

At Adelaide, November 26, 27, 29, 30 [1937]. Drawn. Play in this game was restricted through rain to the first two days, but the subscription lists proved so successful that Richardson and Grimmett each received £1,028. The ability of Sievers to make the ball lift awkwardly brought discomfiture to Bradman's men and Grimmett, with his cunning slow bowling, was also difficult to get away; he completely beat Bradman. ...

D.G. Bradman's XI

J. H. Fingleton c Oldfield b McCormick	32	J. G. Lush b Sievers	28
W. A. Brown b Sievers	42	F. A. Ward not out	7
*D. G. Bradman b Grimmett	17	†C. W. Walker b O'Reilly	29
A. L. Hassett c Oldfield b Grimmett	13	L. O'B. Fleetwood-Smith b Sievers	4
R. G. Gregory c Oldfield b Grimmett	1	B 3, n-b 2	5
V. Jackson b Sievers	0		**184**
L. C. Hynes b McCabe	6		

V. Y. Richardson's XI bowling: McCormick 9–0–34–1; Sievers 9.4–0–27–4; O'Reilly 14–6–21–1; Grimmett 18–3–39–3; Chipperfield 3–0–22–0; McCabe 5–2–10–1; Robinson 4–0–26–0.

V.Y. Richardson's XI

C.L. Badcock, K.E. Rigg, M.W. Sievers, A.G. Chipperfield, S.J. McCabe, *V.Y. Richardson, R.H. Robinson, C.V. Grimmett, †W.A. Oldfield, W.J. O'Reilly and E.L. McCormick.

First innings: Nine for 380 (Badcock 102, Sievers 32, Chipperfield 41, McCabe 72, Richardson 42, Robinson 37 not out; Ward four for 71).

Umpires: J.D. Scott and A.G. Jenkins

SOUTH AUSTRALIA v WESTERN AUSTRALIA   141 (207)

At Adelaide, December 3, 4, 6 [1937]. South Australia won by ten wickets. [A feature of Ridings' debut for South Australia was the appearance of his father as one of the umpires.]

Western Australia: F.J. Alexander, J.A. Jeffreys, J.A. Shea, *W.T. Rowlands, †O.I. Lovelock, W.F. Buttsworth, R.J. Wilberforce, G.C. Arthur, G.A. Gardiner, A.G. Zimbulis and G. Eyres.

First innings: 100. *Second innings:* 185 (Alexander 44; Oswald three for 89, Roberts four for 35).

South Australia: †C.W. Walker, M.E.C. Mueller, R.A. Hamence, B.H. Leak, M.G. Waite, *D.G. Bradman, C.L. Badcock, P.L. Ridings, W.M. Roberts, N.H. Oswald and J.A. Scott.

First innings: 264 (Walker 30, Mueller 56, Bradman c Wilberforce b Eyres 101; Eyres five for 58, Zimbulis three for 98). *Second innings:* None for 22.

Umpires: R.B. Ridings and J.D. Scott

SOUTH AUSTRALIA v NEW SOUTH WALES   142 (208, 209)

At Adelaide, December 17, 18, 20, 21 [1937]. New South Wales won by 33 runs. The craft of O'Reilly turned the fortune of an exciting game. The Test bowler narrowly missed taking all ten wickets in South Australia's first innings – at one point he sent back five men for one run – and when the home side batted a second time, needing 225 to win, his skilful control of length, flight and spin proved the winning factor. South Australia were 153 for four but O'Reilly dashed their hopes of success. ... Bradman, who shared with Whitington and Badcock in partnerships of 141 and 121, was South Australia's most effective batsman, and Grimmett bowled extremely well.

New South Wales

J.H. Fingleton, A.G. Cheetham, *S.J. McCabe, S.G. Barnes, A.G. Chipperfield, V. Jackson, L.C. Hynes, †W.A. Oldfield, E.S. White, W.J. O'Reilly and L.J. O'Brien.

First innings: 337 (Fingleton 81, McCabe 106, Barnes 79; Grimmett five for 103). *Second innings:* 104 (Cotton three for 22, Grimmett four for 51).

South Australia

C.L. Badcock lbw b O'Brien	2	–	b O'Brien	77
R.S. Whitington c Fingleton b O'Reilly	54	–	lbw b O'Brien	1
*D.G. Bradman c O'Brien b O'Reilly	91	–	c Chipperfield b O'Reilly	62
R.H. Robinson b O'Reilly	0	–	c O'Brien b O'Reilly	16
R.A. Hamence c Oldfield b O'Reilly	17	–	b O'Brien	4
M.G. Waite c Oldfield b O'Reilly	3	–	c Oldfield b McCabe	7
†C.W. Walker b O'Reilly	1	–	lbw b O'Reilly	9
F.A. Ward c Chipperfield b O'Reilly	23	–	run out	0
R.G. Williams c Chipperfield b O'Reilly	6	–	c and b O'Reilly	0
C.V. Grimmett lbw b O'Reilly	4	–	c Fingleton b O'Reilly	3
H.J. Cotton not out	10	–	not out	10
L-b 2, n-b 4	6		L-b 1, n-b 1	2
	217			**191**

New South Wales bowling: *First innings*—O'Brien 19–1–67–1; Hynes 11–1–34–0; O'Reilly 33.6–12–41–9; Jackson 8–3–14–0; Cheetham 6–1–20–0; White 11–3–35–0. *Second innings*—O'Brien 12–0–58–3; Hynes 6–0–24–0; O'Reilly 20–8–57–5; Jackson 5–2–7–0; Cheetham 2–0–17–0; White 7–0–17–0; McCabe 2.1–0–9–1.

Umpires: J.D. Scott and A.G. Jenkins

SOUTH AUSTRALIA v QUEENSLAND   143 (210, 211)

At Adelaide, December 25, 27, 28, 29 [1937]. South Australia won by eight wickets. Queensland recovered finely, but they lacked a bowler who could trouble Bradman. Williams, making the ball swing appreciably in the heavy atmosphere, was responsible for Queensland's poor show at the start, and when South Australia lost three men for 50 it seemed there might be a keen struggle. Bradman, however, soon dominated affairs, and with all the strokes at his command in a magnificent exhibition lasting six hours he hit twenty 4's. ... [Although Queensland rallied in their second innings] South Australia needed only 91 for victory, and in helping to knock off the runs Bradman brought his match aggregate to 285 for once out.

Queensland

*W.A. Brown, G.G. Cook, J. Coats, C.A. Loxton, R.E. Rogers, †D. Tallon, T. Allen, G. Baker, E.R. Wyeth, J. Govan and P.L. Dixon.

First innings: 93 (Williams six for 21). *Second innings:* 426 (Brown 132, Rogers 181; Ward four for 152).

South Australia

C. L. Badcock c Dixon b Cook	10	–	st Tallon b Govan	45
†C. W. Walker run out	11	–	c Loxton b Dixon	0
*D. G. Bradman c Baker b Dixon	246	–	not out	39
F. A. Ward c Tallon b Loxton	0			
R. G. Williams c Baker b Govan	34			
R. H. Robinson c Loxton b Dixon	49			
R. A. Hamence c Tallon b Dixon	5	–	not out	9
R. S. Whitington run out	3			
M. G. Waite not out	52			
C. V. Grimmett not out	5			
B 3, l-b 8, n-b 3	14			
(eight wkts dec)	**429**		(two wkts)	**93**

H. J. Cotton did not bat.

Queensland bowling: *First innings*—Dixon 24–0–130–3; Cook 23–1–87–1; Loxton 11–0–41–1; Govan 12–0–72–1; Wyeth 24–3–70–0; Baker 3–1–15–0. *Second innings*—Dixon 4–0–22–1; Cook 10–1–30–0; Loxton 4–1–11–0; Govan 1.2–0–9–1; Wyeth 3–0–12–0; Baker 1–0–9–0.

Umpires: J. D. Scott and A.G. Jenkins

VICTORIA v SOUTH AUSTRALIA   144 (212, 213)

At Melbourne, December 31 [1937], January 1, 3, 4 [1938]. Drawn. The match was important from the point of view of the Selectors, for in the sides there were at least a dozen probables for the England tour. Several of them enhanced their reputations. Fleetwood-Smith took chief honours in the early play, for with his tantalising slow bowling he dismissed nine South Australian batsmen. … Victoria looked set for a big lead, but Grimmett, bowling cleverly, restricted it to 60. Without doing anything extraordinary, South Australia showed consistent form in their second innings …

South Australia

C. L. Badcock c Pearson b Fleetwood-Smith	50	–	b McCormick	0
R. S. Whitington c Rigg b Fleetwood-Smith	81	–	lbw b Fleetwood-Smith	29
*D. G. Bradman c Sievers b Gregory	54	–	c Sievers b Gregory	35
R. H. Robinson c Rigg b Fleetwood-Smith	12	–	run out	62
R. A. Hamence st Barnett b Fleetwood-Smith	8	–	c Hassett b McCormick	64
M. G. Waite c Pearson b Fleetwood-Smith	30	–	c Barnett b Gregory	51
†C. W. Walker c Pearson b Fleetwood-Smith	13	–	run out	25
R. G. Williams b Fleetwood-Smith	15	–	st Barnett b Fleetwood-Smith	11
F. A. Ward not out	26	–	c Gregory b Fleetwood-Smith	9
C. V. Grimmett c Pearson b Fleetwood-Smith	4	–	c Barnett b Sievers	31
H. J. Cotton c Ledward b Fleetwood-Smith	8	–	not out	18
L-b 1, n-b 2	3		B 13, l-b 3, w 1, n-b 4	21
	304			**356**

Victoria bowling: *First innings*—McCormick 16–1–60–0; Sievers 17–5–39–0; Pearson 17–3–41–0; Fleetwood-Smith 31.3–1–135–9; Gregory 10–1–26–1. *Second innings*—McCormick 20–1–91–2; Sievers 18.2–4–45–1; Pearson 3–0–13–0; Fleetwood-Smith 37–3–137–3; Gregory 16–1–46–2; Ledward 1–0–3–0.

Victoria

*K. E. Rigg, I. S. Lee, R. G. Gregory, A. L. Hassett, J. D. Ledward, M. W. Sievers, F. W. Sides, W. E. Pearson, †B. A. Barnett, E. L. McCormick and L. O'B. Fleetwood-Smith.

First innings: 364 (Rigg 118, Lee 67, Gregory 61, Sides 47; Grimmett six for 95). *Second innings:* Four for 144 (Lee 34, Ledward 58 not out).

Umpires: A. N. Barlow and W. J. Moore

QUEENSLAND v SOUTH AUSTRALIA 145 (214, 215)

At Brisbane, January 8, 10, 11, 12 [1938]. Drawn. Bradman's unique feat of making two separate hundreds in a Sheffield Shield match for the second time was the outstanding event of the game. Scoring much as he pleased, Bradman, in his second brilliant display, exactly equalled Bardsley's record aggregate of 17,461 [for an Australian in first-class matches. Record books have subsequently and retrospectively credited Bardsley with only 17,025 runs in matches deemed first-class.] South Australia were helped to their useful first total by Williams and Grimmett, who added 100 for the ninth wicket. ... [In the second innings] Waite gave Bradman useful assistance in an entertaining fifth-wicket stand of 103, and a declaration left Queensland [whose captain, Brown, was unable to bat in either innings] the too heavy task of getting 494 to win. This would have proved far beyond them, but the weather saved them from defeat. ...

South Australia

C. L. Badcock c Tallon b Christ	37	–	b Dixon	1
R. S. Whitington c Loxton b Christ	28	–	b Cook	18
*D. G. Bradman c Tallon b Dixon	107	–	c Hackett b Allen	113
R. H. Robinson c Govan b Christ	43	–	st Tallon b Cook	0
R. A. Hamence c Rogers b Loxton	16	–	st Tallon b Christ	11
M. G. Waite c Rogers b Cook	16	–	c Webb b Cook	58
†C. W. Walker c Loxton b Cook	11	–	not out	25
R. G. Williams not out	75	–	c Rogers b Cook	37
F. A. Ward lbw b Cook	10	–	not out	15
C. V. Grimmett c Rogers b Dixon	46			
H. J. Cotton lbw b Cook	1	–	c Tallon b Dixon	1
L-b 6, n-b 2	8		B 2, l-b 3, n-b 3	8
	398		(eight wkts dec)	287

Queensland bowling: *First innings*—Dixon 17–1–85–2; Cook 20.6–2–69–4; Loxton 5–0–15–1; Govan 17–0–105–0; Christ 26–2–99–3; Baker 2–0–17–0. *Second innings*—Dixon 14–1–60–2; Cook 22–1–108–4; Govan 3–0–30–0; Christ 16.5–2–66–1; Allen 3–0–15–1.

Queensland

*W. A. Brown, G. G. Cook, C. Loxton, T. Allen, R. E. Rogers, †D. Tallon, G. Baker, J. Hackett, J. Govan, C. Christ and P. L. Dixon.

First innings: 192 (Tallon 48, Baker 70 not out; Cotton four for 37, Grimmett three for 42). *Second innings:* Eight for 155 (Allen 55; Ward five for 66).

Umpires: K. Fagg and J. Bartlett

NEW SOUTH WALES v SOUTH AUSTRALIA   146 (216, 217)

At Sydney, January 15, 17, 18, 19 [1938]. New South Wales won by four wickets. The moderately cheap dismissal of Bradman at the start influenced the course of the game ... [However, he] did quite well when he kept wicket in place of Walker, who injured a finger. Bradman at his second attempt put together a fine century, during which he reached 1,000 runs for the season. Badcock also drove hard in making a hundred, but New South Wales were not left a very serious task. They wanted 227 and, despite some first-rate wicket-keeping by Bradman, who caught three men, they won comfortably.

South Australia

C. L. Badcock c O'Reilly b O'Brien	6	–	run out	132
R. S. Whitington b McCabe	4	–	st Oldfield b O'Reilly	29
*D. G. Bradman c McCabe b O'Brien	44	–	not out	104
R. H. Robinson b Jackson	13	–	lbw b McCabe	21
R. A. Hamence c Oldfield b Mair	49	–	lbw b O'Reilly	13
M. G. Waite lbw b O'Reilly	21	–	lbw b O'Brien	7
†C. W. Walker run out	0	–	absent hurt	0
R. G. Williams b O'Reilly	12	–	c Oldfield b O'Brien	6
F. A. Ward not out	11	–	c Fingleton b O'Reilly	8
C. V. Grimmett run out	1	–	c Chipperfield b O'Brien	0
H. J. Cotton run out	18	–	c Chipperfield b O'Reilly	3
B 7, l-b 1	8		B 8, l-b 3	11
	187			**334**

New South Wales bowling: *First innings*—O'Brien 9–0–42–2; McCabe 5–0–12–1; Jackson 6–0–20–1; O'Reilly 16–3–36–2; Mair 11.6–0–59–1; White 2–0–10–0. *Second innings*—O'Brien 22–2–90–3; McCabe 12–1–39–1; Jackson 12–4–28–0; O'Reilly 25.6–7–65–4; Mair 7–1–26–0; White 11–0–38–0; Chipperfield 6–0–37–0.

New South Wales

*S. J. McCabe, J. H. Fingleton, B. V. McCauley, S.G. Barnes, A.G. Chipperfield, V. Jackson, E. S. White, †W. A. Oldfield, F. Mair, W. J. O'Reilly and L. J. O'Brien.

First innings: 295 (McCabe 83, Chipperfield 31, Jackson 63, Mair 39; Williams three for 93, Ward four for 51). *Second innings:* Six for 227 (McCabe 39, Fingleton 74, Chipperfield 30, White 36 not out; Waite three for 55).

Umpires: G. Borwick and F. Lyons

SOUTH AUSTRALIA v VICTORIA   147 (218, 219)

At Adelaide, February 4, 5, 7, 8 [1938]. South Australia won by 125 runs. ... Waite, an all-rounder chosen for the England tour, demonstrated his usefulness with the bat after Bradman was clean bowled for three, but South Australia were never at ease against Sievers, whom the Selectors passed over. Victoria did not fare much better, and with Bradman finding his form in the second innings, South Australia recovered their lost ground. Whitington shared with Bradman in a stand of 113, and when Victoria wanted 303 for victory, Waite damped their hopes by taking the first three wickets in nine overs for seven runs.

South Australia

R. S. Whitington c Rigg b Thorn	42	–	run out		86
M. E. Mueller lbw b Sievers	1	–	c Thorn b Rayson		37
*D. G. Bradman b McCormick	3	–	c Ledward b Thorn		85
R. H. Robinson lbw b Sievers	19	–	b Pearson		8
R. A. Hamence c Pearson b Sievers	0	–	run out		18
B. H. Leak b Sievers	9	–	b Pearson		31
M. G. Waite not out	45	–	c Pearson b Sievers		10
†J. A. J. Horsell c Barnett b McCormick	9	–	lbw b Pearson		1
R. G. Williams b Sievers	5	–	st Barnett b Rayson		29
F. A. Ward c Barnett b Rayson	1	–	c Rigg b Thorn		22
C. V. Grimmett c Pearson b Sievers	2	–	not out		1
B 17, l-b 1, n-b 3	21		B 5, l-b 3, n-b 4		12
	157				**340**

Victoria bowling: *First innings*—McCormick 9–1–27–2; Sievers 12.7–2–43–6; Pearson 8–1–22–0; Thorn 11–1–37–1; Rayson 2–1–7–1. *Second innings*—McCormick 16–1–54–0; Sievers 25–5–73–1; Pearson 17–1–70–3; Thorn 13–0–53–2; Rayson 11.7–0–78–2.

Victoria

*K. E. Rigg, I. S. Lee, A. L. Hassett, J. D. Ledward, P. Beames, W. E. Pearson, †B. A. Barnett, M. W. Sievers, M. Rayson, E. L. McCormick and F. Thorn.

First innings: 195 (Lee 44; Williams three for 60, Grimmett three for 56). *Second innings:* 177 (Pearson 36, Barnett 41; Williams five for 52, Waite three for 28).

Umpires: J. D. Scott and A. G. Jenkins

TASMANIA v AUSTRALIAN TOURING TEAM   148 (220)

At Launceston, February 26, 28, March 1 [1938]. Australian Touring Team won by 386 runs.
Australian Touring Team: J. H. Fingleton, †B. A. Barnett, A. L. Hassett, *D.G. Bradman, S. J. McCabe, C. L. Badcock, S.G. Barnes, M.G. Waite, E. S. White, F. A. Ward and L. O'B. Fleetwood-Smith.
First innings: 477 (Fingleton 66, Hassett 75, Bradman c Sankey b Thomas 79, McCabe 83, Badcock 36, Barnes 53 not out, Waite 38; Thollar five for 116). *Second innings:* Four for 172 dec (Badcock 42, Barnes 89).
Tasmania: *R. O.G. Morrisby, R. V. Thomas, E. H. Smith, M. J. Combes, C. J. Sankey, C. L. Jeffery, J. N. W. Nicolson, †J. Gardiner, G. T. H. James, J. I. Murfett and D. H. Thollar.
First innings: 112 (Thomas 30; Fleetwood-Smith four for 22, Ward three for 26). *Second innings:* 151 (Morrisby 38, Combes 37; Fleetwood-Smith four for 56, Ward three for 65).

Umpires: G. T. Godden and E. C. Knight

TASMANIA v AUSTRALIAN TOURING TEAM   149 (221)

At Hobart, March 3, 4, 5 [1938]. Australian Touring Team won by 485 runs.
Australian Touring Team: J. H. Fingleton, W. A. Brown, C. L. Badcock, *D.G. Bradman, S.G. Barnes, A.G. Chipperfield, M.G. Waite, †B. A. Barnett, E. S. White, W. J. O'Reilly and L. O'B. Fleetwood-Smith.
First innings: 520 (Fingleton 47, Brown 46, Badcock 159, Bradman b Jeffery 144, Chipperfield 42; James three for 86, Putman four for 155). *Second innings:* Three for 240 dec (Fingleton 109, Brown 108).

Tasmania: *R. O.G. Morrisby, R. V. Thomas, M. J. Combes, S. W. L. Putman, E. H. Smith, G. T. H. James, C. J. Sankey, C. L. Jeffery, †J. Gardiner, J. I. Murfett and C. J.G. Oakes.

First innings: 194 (Putman 40, Smith 37; O'Reilly five for 34, Fleetwood-Smith three for 70). *Second innings:* 81 (O'Reilly six for 16).

Umpires: D.G. Hickman and S. J. Alford

WESTERN AUSTRALIA v AUSTRALIAN TOURING TEAM
150 (222)

At Perth, March 18, 19, 21 [1938]. Australian Touring Team won by an innings and 126 runs.

Western Australia: J. A. Jeffreys, F. J. Alexander, J. A. Shea, *W. T. Rowlands, K. S. Jeffreys, †O. I. Lovelock, M. O. Bessen, A.G. Zimbulis, G. A. Gardiner, G. Eyres and R. A. Halcombe.

First innings: 192 (Bessen 39, Zimbulis 33, Eyres 41; O'Reilly four for 65). *Second innings:* 73 (O'Reilly five for 12, Fleetwood-Smith three for 5).

Australian Touring Team: W. A. Brown, C. L. Badcock, *D.G. Bradman, S. J. McCabe, A. L. Hassett, A.G. Chipperfield, †C. W. Walker, F. A. Ward, W. J. O'Reilly, E. L. McCormick and L. O'B. Fleetwood-Smith.

First innings: 391 (Badcock 34, Bradman st Lovelock b Zimbulis 102, McCabe 122, Chipperfield 42; Zimbulis three for 160, Halcombe three for 43).

Umpires: F. R. Buttsworth and E. T. Tonkinson

1938

Bradman is carried from the field by Ted White and 'Chuck' Fleetwood-Smith after injuring his ankle when bowling in the final Test of the 1938 Ashes series.

1938

A warning note is also sounded concerning the effect on the counties generally of any serious decline in the popularity of Test Match cricket. Consequently the news that, for the Test Matches of 1938 with Australia, agreement has been reached to restrict the games to four days apiece and to reduce the hours of play by one and a half hours in each match, came as a surprise. A reason advanced for the change is that neither Australian nor English cricketers relish a period of two and a half hours play before lunch-time after the first day. To my mind, it is a retrograde step. There is no gainsaying the assertion that the long pre-lunch spell imposes a severe test upon bowlers, but the policy is directly opposed to the movement in England to revive the interest of the public in the game of cricket. Are we to have another run of purposeless drawn games with the possibility of one 'play-to-a-finish' Test deciding the rubber? Not since 1905 has an England-Australia match at Old Trafford produced a definite result, and the last three encounters at Leeds were drawn. Who can argue with conviction that a reduction of the time in which a Test Match has to be decided is on all fours with the urgent need to enlist more support for the game generally by getting more definite results? It has been encouraging to note the growth of favourable opinion, both in England and in the Commonwealth, upon the idea of allocating more than four days to all Test Matches between England and Australia in this country, and events during the series of 1938 may bring further support for the suggestion.

... An intriguing and vital question at the time of writing is that of the [England] captaincy. On this point, much has been said and written regarding W.R. Hammond, who in future will play as an amateur. ... Without going into the question as to whether Hammond possesses the essential qualities for leadership, I am strongly against him being saddled with the task of leading England. Hammond once more should be free to concentrate upon batting and be spared anything prejudicial to his individual prowess. It is true that the batting abilities of Bradman did not decline after he assumed the captaincy of Australia. But Bradman had for some time led the South Australian team and he undertook his more responsible post after a good deal of experience in leading an eleven.

From 'Notes by the Editor' (Wilfrid H. Brookes), *Wisden 1938*

I am not in a position to make any comparison between the players of the past and those of the present time, but the attempt of certain writers to *The Times* to compare by statistics the doings of W.G. Grace and D.G. Bradman in matches between England and Australia is unfortunate. For this reason: 'W.G.' began playing for England against Australia in 1880 when thirty-two years of age and continued until he was fifty-one; Bradman began when twenty and is now thirty – two years younger than Grace when, in the first contest with Australia in England, he scored 152. As *Wisden* has been quoted in the published correspondence, it is interesting to recall that Sydney H. Pardon, then *The Times* cricket correspondent, wrote of 'W.G.' as follows: 'His early fame as a batsman culminated in the season of 1876 when in August he scored in successive innings 344, 177 and 318. Soon after that, he passed his examination as a surgeon, thinking to settle down as a general practitioner. That he changed his plans was mainly due to the appearance of the first Australian XI in England in 1878. The most brilliant part of his career ended before this invasion ...'

From 'Notes by the Editor' (Wilfrid H. Brookes), Wisden 1939

The visit of the Australian team coincided with a marked revival in English cricket, several young players of high merit coming to the front. Yet the Australians, although having the atrocious luck of losing the toss in each of the four Test Matches played, drew the rubber and thereby retained the Ashes. That this was a most creditable performance is not likely to be questioned even by the severest critics of the team.

It would be a delicate task to compare this Australian side with the previous combinations which have come over from the Commonwealth, and as very little would be gained by embarking on such an effort, it is not attempted here. The result of more than four months' cricket was that the Australians remained undefeated by any county XI and only once – after they had won the Fourth Test at Leeds – did they go down before England.

Like the team of 1921, the side also suffered a reverse in the Festival match at Scarborough [their final fixture in England], but against the two defeats they could set fifteen wins in first-class engagements, and outside the representative matches they rarely encountered formidable opposition. ...

The strength of the team lay in batting and fielding; the weakness in bowling. There were more individual failures than usually occur in an Australian touring side and had a serious accident happened to either Bradman or O'Reilly at an early stage of the season the record must have been much less imposing. The very appearance of Bradman in the field was sufficient to inspire confidence in his colleagues. Nothing that occurred seemed to disturb his equanimity and the influence he held over the other members of the team, combined with his own brilliant performances, was an extremely important factor in the results accomplished.

In every Test in which he batted, Bradman made a century. When on the third day of the Fifth Test he damaged his right ankle and was carried off The Oval ground, England were already in a position which made their success a foregone conclusion, but there is not a shadow of doubt that the moral effect of the loss of their captain, coupled with an injury to Fingleton, accounted, to a very large extent, for the complete rout of Australia that followed.

Bradman did not play again, and yet in twenty-six innings he scored 2,429 runs with an average of 115.66. Not only was this a far better record than he made on either of his two previous visits, except for his 1930 aggregate, but he was the first Australian to average 100 runs an innings in England. He also beat Victor Trumper's feat of hitting eleven centuries during a tour, for he played thirteen three-figure innings, three over 200. Leading off with an innings of 258 at Worcester, he completed 1,000 runs before the end of May, so repeating his achievement of 1930, and 2,000 runs before any other Australian or Englishman. Both in the first-class averages for the tour and those for the four Test Matches his name came out at the top.

One did not detect any waning of his powers. Judged by the standard he himself set, he was perhaps a shade better. The responsibility of leadership certainly did not interfere with his individual play, and his concentration, as shown when in the first two Test Matches the state of affairs demanded that he should bat cautiously, was astonishing. To say that he was a popular captain and a most astute one is not fulsome praise; under his charge the Australians revealed a wonderful team spirit which counted a great deal towards their many triumphs. A point that impressed itself upon the mind was his quickness to note the strength of an opposing batsman and to make a move directed towards countering effective strokeplay. ...

… Measured by what English followers of cricket have seen from other post-war Australian sides, the fielding was not found wanting. One could deduce from the live, intense and often brilliant out-cricket the influence of Bradman when the players were picked for the tour. To those whose duties brought them into close touch with Bradman and his colleagues, the happy spirit pervading the team was very evident. Wherever they went, they made friends. …

From 'The Australians in England', by Wilfrid H. Brookes

WORCESTERSHIRE v AUSTRALIANS   151 (223)

At Worcester, April 30, May 2, 3 [1938]. Australians won by an innings and 77 runs. Lyttelton caused astonishment when after winning the toss he sent in the touring team to bat on a true and easy wicket. By the end of the first day 474 runs had been scored for the loss of six wickets, and in the end the Australians made their highest total against Worcestershire. Batting in biting, wintry weather, Bradman, as on his two previous matches on the ground, began the tour with a double-hundred. Starting in a cautious way, he developed capital form and, during an innings lasting four hours fifty minutes, offered no semblance of a chance. Pulling, driving, cutting and placing the ball with skill, he hit thirty-three 4's. Badcock, on his first appearance in England, created a big impression and he helped Bradman to put on 277 for the fourth wicket. … Monday's play furnished a most remarkable happening. McCormick, the fast bowler, repeatedly went over the crease and during his first three overs was no-balled nineteen times by umpire Baldwin. His first over actually comprised fourteen balls and the second over fifteen. … In the match, McCormick was no-balled thirty-five times.

Australians

J. H. Fingleton c Crisp b Howorth	41	E. S. White b Crisp	26
W. A. Brown lbw b Crisp	2	W. J. O'Reilly b Perks	11
*D. G. Bradman c Martin b Howorth	258	E. L. McCormick b Crisp	5
S. J. McCabe b Perks	34	L. O'B. Fleetwood-Smith not out	6
C. L. Badcock c Singleton b Perks	67	B 13, l-b 15, w 2, n-b 2	32
A. L. Hassett c Howorth b Perks	43		**541**
†B. A. Barnett b Crisp	16		

Worcestershire bowling: Crisp 37.3–5–170–4; Perks 34–3–147–4; Martin 29–8–70–0; Howorth 21–1–85–2; Singleton 3–0–37–0.

Worcestershire

*Hon. C. J. Lyttelton, C. H. Bull, E. Cooper, H. H. Gibbons, S. H. Martin, Mr R. H. C. Human, R. Howorth, Mr A. P. Singleton, †S. Buller, R. T. D. Perks and Mr R. J. Crisp.

First innings: 268 (Lyttelton 50, Bull 37 not out, Cooper 61; Fleetwood-Smith eight for 98). *Second innings:* 196 (Lyttelton 35, Bull 69; O'Reilly three for 56, Fleetwood-Smith three for 38).

Umpires: J. Smart and H. G. Baldwin

OXFORD UNIVERSITY v AUSTRALIANS 152 (224)

Played at the Christ Church ground, Oxford, May 4, 5, 6 [1938]. Australians won by an innings and 487 runs. This match was played far too early in the term for the University to do themselves justice. They were little more than a scratch side and the Australians, winning the toss, batted until lunch-time on the second day, when Bradman declared. ... Fingleton and Brown led off with a stand of 140 and altogether there were five three-figure partnerships. ... On the last day, when Walker had a damaged finger, Fingleton ... stumped three men.

Australians

J. H. Fingleton c Whetherly b Evans	124	A. L. Hassett b Darwall-Smith	146
W. A. Brown c Evans b Macindoe	72	M. G. Waite c Kimpton b Evans	54
*D. G. Bradman lbw b Evans	58	†C. W. Walker not out	31
S. J. McCabe b Macindoe	110	B 21, l-b 9, w 1	31
A. G. Chipperfield c Whetherly b Darwall-Smith	53	(seven wkts dec)	**679**

F. Ward, E. L. McCormick and L. O'B. Fleetwood-Smith did not bat.

Oxford University bowling: Darwall-Smith 39.4–4–162–2; Macindoe 68–11–207–2; Evans 47–9–171–3; Kimpton 13–1–53–0; Murray-Wood 9–1–55–0.

Oxford University

Mr M. M. Walford, Mr E. J. H. Dixon, Mr J. D. Eggar, †Mr R. C. M. Kimpton, *Mr J. N. Grover, Mr E. D. R. Eagar, Mr W. Murray-Wood, Mr G. Evans, Mr D. H. Macindoe, Mr R. F. H. Darwall-Smith and Mr R. E. Whetherly.

    First innings: 117 (Eggar 51 not out; Fleetwood-Smith five for 28). *Second innings:* 75 (Ward three for 16, Fleetwood-Smith four for 31).

Umpires: D. Hendren and N. Harris

CAMBRIDGE UNIVERSITY v AUSTRALIANS 153 (225)

At Cambridge, May 11, 12, 13 [1938]. Australians won by an innings and 425 runs. This was their fourth single-innings victory in succession [having beaten Leicestershire by an innings and 163 runs on May 7, 9, 10]. ... [For Cambridge] Gibb carried his bat through the second innings; otherwise, the batting was poor and the bowling, except for that of Wild, inaccurate. The Australians, putting together their highest total of the tour and the biggest ever made at Fenner's, again demonstrated their great batting powers. Brown failed, but Fingleton and Bradman added 215. ... Bradman, who [like Fingleton] completed his second century of the tour, scored twenty boundaries. ... Cambridge, 588 behind, began their second innings without hope.

Cambridge University

†Mr P. A. Gibb, Mr J. V. Wild, Mr J. D. A. Langley, *Mr N. W. D. Yardley, Mr M. St J. Packe, Mr F.G. Mann, Mr P. M. Studd, Mr M. A. C. P. Kaye, Mr S. M. A. Banister, Mr H.G. Jameson and Mr W. R. Rees-Davies.

    First innings: 120 (Yardley 67; Waite five for 23, O'Reilly five for 55). *Second innings:* 163 (Gibb 80 not out; White three for 22, Ward six for 64).

Australians

J. H. Fingleton b Kaye	111	A. G. Chipperfield st Gibb b Banister	8
W. A. Brown lbw b Rees-Davies	0	M. G. Waite not out	30
*D. G. Bradman c Mann b Wild	137	B 10, l-b 5, w 1	16
C. L. Badcock c Mann b Rees-Davies	186	(five wkts dec)	**708**
A. L. Hassett not out	220		

†B. A. Barnett, W. J. O'Reilly, F. Ward and E. S. White did not bat.

Cambridge University bowling: Rees-Davies 43–2–214–2; Jameson 29–4–127–0; Kaye 17–0–100–1; Wild 45–12–143–1; Banister 22–2–91–1; Yardley 5–1–17–0.

Umpires: W. Wainwright and J. J. Hills

MCC TEAM v AUSTRALIANS 154 (226)

At Lord's, May 14, 16, 17 [1938]. Drawn. Rain prevented play on the last day when MCC, having followed on 288 behind, needed 201 to avoid an innings defeat with nine wickets in hand. A superb innings by Bradman overshadowed everything else in the game. Batting for six hours, he made no serious mistake till, attempting to square cut a bad ball, he was well taken at cover. Though he did not drive much and at first experienced difficulty with the bowling of Stephenson, he played masterly cricket and hit a 6 and thirty-five 4's. Fingleton helped him in a stand of 138 and Hassett, strong in driving, stayed while 162 were added. McCormick, taking a shorter run, showed increased accuracy when MCC batted, and he sent down only one no-ball. He dismissed Human and Maxwell with consecutive deliveries, but a collapse was prevented by Wyatt ... McCormick, having strained a tendon, retired during the MCC first innings ... So large was the crowd on the first day, when some 32,000 were present, that about three o'clock the gates were closed.

Australians

J. H. Fingleton b Smith	44	†B. A. Barnett lbw b Stephenson	1
W. A. Brown b Farnes	5	W. J. O'Reilly c Compton b Smith	17
*D. G. Bradman c Robins b Smith	278	E. L. McCormick c Maxwell b Smith	9
S. J. McCabe b Smith	33	L. O'B. Fleetwood-Smith not out	3
C. L. Badcock b Stephenson	14	B 2, l-b 11, n-b 1	15
A. L. Hassett c Maxwell b Compton	57		**502**
M. G. Waite lbw b Smith	26		

MCC bowling: Farnes 32–3–88–1; Smith 42.5–9–139–6; Stephenson 29–5–112–2; Robins 18–2–69–0; Wyatt 7–0–27–0; Compton 10–2–37–1; Edrich 2–0–15–0.

MCC Team

Mr D. R. Wilcox, W. J. Edrich, D. Compton, Mr R. E. S. Wyatt, Mr F. G. H. Chalk, Mr J. H. Human, †Mr C. R. Maxwell, *Mr R. W. V. Robins, Capt. J. W. A. Stephenson, J. Smith and Mr K. Farnes.
  First innings: 214 (Edrich 31, Wyatt 84 not out; O'Reilly three for 42, Fleetwood-Smith four for 69). *Second innings:* One for 87 (Edrich 53 not out).

Umpires: J. Hardstaff and J. Newman

NORTHAMPTONSHIRE v AUSTRALIANS 155 (227)

At Northampton, May 18, 19, 20 [1938]. Australians won by an innings and 77 runs. Northamptonshire gave early promise of repeating their performance in 1934, when they drew with the tourists, but the Australians had things all their own way on the last day. Against a weak attack the Australians scored 126 without loss during a restricted opening day's play ... [Next day] Partridge, bowling medium-fast and making the ball swing, sent back Badcock, Bradman and McCabe in eleven overs for 15 runs. ... Eighty minutes on the third morning saw the last seven Northamptonshire [first innings] wickets fall for 55 runs, Ward, on a pitch responsive to spin, carrying all before him. McCabe, taking four wickets for a single, did the damage in the follow-on ...

Australians

W. A. Brown not out	194	M. G. Waite lbw b Timms		43
C. L. Badcock c James b Partridge	72	†B. A. Barnett lbw b Timms		1
*D. G. Bradman c James b Partridge	2	C. W. Walker not out		29
S. J. McCabe c Merritt b Partridge	13	B 22, l-b 12		34
A. G. Chipperfield lbw b Timms	18	(six wkts dec)		**406**

E. S. White, F. Ward and L. O'B. Fleetwood-Smith did not bat.

Northamptonshire bowling: Partridge 36–7–82–3; Herbert 30–6–75–0; Timms 20–4–68–3; Nelson 14–1–56–0; Merritt 16–0–81–0; O'Brien 3–0–10–0.

Northamptonshire

Mr R. P. Nelson, H. W. Greenwood, Mr A. W. Snowden, J. E. Timms, D. Brookes, Mr G. B. Cuthbertson, F. P. O'Brien, †K. C. James, W. E. Merritt, R. J. Partridge and E. J. Herbert.
 First innings: 194 (Nelson 74, Brookes 37; Ward six for 75). *Second innings:* 135 (Greenwood 43; Waite three for 28, McCabe four for 28).

Umpires: F. Chester and A. Dolphin

SURREY v AUSTRALIANS   156 (228)

At [Kennington] Oval, May 21, 23, 24 [1938]. Drawn. The Australians made no effort to win for, although they led by 257 runs, Bradman, on the score that some of his players badly needed rest, did not enforce the follow-on. On a perfect wicket, the Australians batted until nearly lunch-time on the second day. Bradman played another big innings, driving to the off and pulling with special skill, and in a stay of three hours and twenty minutes he hit eleven 4's. His unhurried display contained no serious blemish. ... Brown helped his captain to put on 120. Bradman's decision to bat a second time caused a mild demonstration among the crowd, and as Surrey tried as many as eight bowlers, a first-wicket partnership of 206 by Badcock and Barnett lost much of its importance. ...

Australians

J. H. Fingleton b Brown	47			
W. A. Brown c Brooks b Watts	96			
*D. G. Bradman c Brooks b Watts	143			
C. L. Badcock c and b Brown	32	–	c Watts b Gregory	95
A. L. Hassett c Squires b Berry	98			
A. G. Chipperfield b Gover	20	–	c Brooks b Gregory	6
M. G. Waite c Brooks b Watts	35			
†B. A. Barnett not out	33	–	not out	120
E. S. White b Berry	7	–	not out	5
F. Ward b Brown	0			
W. J. O'Reilly c Brooks b Brown	0			
B 8, l-b 8, n-b 1	17		B 4, l-b 1, n-b 1	6
	528		(two wkts dec)	**232**

Surrey bowling: *First innings*—Gover 20–4–100–1; Watts 23–4–69–3; Berry 33–6–92–2; Brown 35–0–147–4; Squires 20–2–68–0; Gregory 9–3–23–0; Garland-Wells 3–0–12–0. *Second innings*—Gover 6–0–20–0; Watts 10–1–47–0; Berry 6–3–12–0; Brown 5–0–23–0; Squires 8–2–29–0; Gregory 7–4–10–2; Garland-Wells 15–1–62–0; Holmes 4–0–23–0.

Surrey

R. J. Gregory, L. B. Fishlock, H. S. Squires, T. H. Barling, *Mr E. R. T. Holmes, Mr H. M. Garland-Wells, Mr F. R. Brown, F. Berry, E. A. Watts, †E. W. Brooks and A. R. Gover.

First innings: 271 (Gregory 60, Barling 67, Berry 31; O'Reilly eight for 104). *Second innings:* One for 104 (Fishlock 93).

Umpires: E. J. Smith and A. Dolphin

HAMPSHIRE v AUSTRALIANS   157 (229)

At Southampton, May 25, 26, 27 [1938]. Drawn. Bradman made the match memorable by completing 1,000 runs for the second time in England before the first month of the season closed. He did not hit with the amazing freedom that marked his play when previously in England, but his share of a partnership with Fingleton yielding 242 was 145, scored in three and a half hours. He was not altogether sure when facing the slow spin bowling of Boyes, the left-hander, and of Hill. Strangely enough, when in 1930 Bradman made 1,000 runs in May, he reached that total at Southampton on the first day of the match just before rain delayed the completion of his innings until the Monday. On the present occasion the weather interfered seriously with the match. Rain prevented any cricket on the first day; it also caused a stoppage before Bradman reached a four-figure aggregate for the tour. ... Bradman [hit] twenty-two 4's.

Hampshire

†N. McCorkell, J. Arnold, *Mr C. G. A. Paris, W. L. Creese, Mr R. H. Moore, A. E. Pothecary, Rev. J. W. J. Steele, G. Hill, G. S. Boyes, Mr A. E. G. Baring and G. E. M. Heath.

First innings: 157 (O'Reilly six for 65).

Australians

J. H. Fingleton not out	123
W. A. Brown c Pothecary b Boyes	47
*D. G. Bradman not out	145
B 4, l-b 1	5
(one wkt dec)	**320**

L. Hassett, A. G. Chipperfield, E. S. White, W. J. O'Reilly, E. L. McCormick, S. J. McCabe, †C. W. Walker and L. O'B. Fleetwood-Smith did not bat.

Hampshire bowling: Baring 20–2–97–0; Heath 16–1–54–0; Steele 15–2–60–0; Boyes 17–5–39–1; Hill 19–4–45–0; Creese 9–5–20–0.

Umpires: W. Reeves and E. J. Smith

MIDDLESEX v AUSTRALIANS   158 (230, 231)

At Lord's, May 28, 30, 31 [1938]. Drawn. After continuous rain on Saturday and Sunday, the Australians did not show to advantage under strange conditions [when they batted on Monday]. ... The one stand on a pitch so soft that the ball often cut through realised 54. ... After arrears of 56 had been turned into a lead of 58 Bradman declared in order to give Edrich an opportunity to complete 1,000 runs before the end of May [which he accomplished in a not out innings of 20. All his 1,000 runs were scored at Lord's.] Bad light and showers interfered with the cricket on both days and the Australians were outplayed until a draw became inevitable. Several good catches were made. Compton, running from slip to short-leg, held a skier from Bradman. ...

Australians

J. H. Fingleton b Smith	2	–	c Edrich b Smith	32
C. L. Badcock c Human b Nevell	10	–	b Nevell	0
*D. G. Bradman c Compton b Nevell	5	–	not out	30
S. J. McCabe b Nevell	9	–	not out	48
A. L. Hassett lbw b Sims	27			
A. G. Chipperfield c Compton b Robins	36			
M. G. Waite b Sims	8			
†C. W. Walker not out	4			
W. J. O'Reilly lbw b Robins	0			
E. L. McCormick c Smith b Sims	12			
L. O'B. Fleetwood-Smith st Price b Sims	10			
B 2, l-b 6, n-b 1	9		W	4
	132		(two wkts dec)	**114**

Middlesex bowling: *First innings*—Smith 15–5–23–1; Nevell 12–1–38–3; Young 4–1–10–0; Sims 7.3–0–25–4; Robins 6–1–27–2. *Second innings*—Smith 12–4–26–1; Nevell 7–2–16–1; Young 5–2–7–0; Smith 5–0–23–0; Robins 4–0–10–0; Human 2–0–14–0; Compton 4–1–14–0.

Middlesex

W.J. Edrich, †W.F. Price, Mr W.H. Webster, D. Compton, J. Hulme, Mr J.H. Human, *Mr R.W. V. Robins, J. Sims, J. Smith, W. Nevell and J. A. Young.

First innings: 188 (Compton 65, Robins 43; McCormick six for 58, O'Reilly four for 56). *Second innings:* None for 21.

Umpires: F. Chester and F. Walden

ENGLAND v AUSTRALIA (FIRST TEST MATCH)

159 (232, 233)
34 (52, 53)

At Trent Bridge [Nottingham], June 10, 11, 13, 14 [1938]. Drawn. England, in a match memorable for the setting-up of many new records including seven individual hundreds, put together the highest innings total ever hit against Australia. Not until half-past three on the second day did Australia have an opportunity of batting, and with 151 scored half their wickets had fallen. McCabe then played an innings the equal of which has probably never been seen in the history of Test cricket; for the best part of four hours he maintained a merciless punishment of the bowling. Although his phenomenal effort did not save his side from the indignity of having to follow on, it broke the control of the play, which England had held from the outset, and by concentrating upon defence in their second innings Australia saved the game.

In a magnificent contest of skill, the excellence of the wicket always counted heavily in favour of batsmen. First innings conferred upon England a very important advantage. ... For the first time in a Test Match, four individual hundreds were registered in one innings for, following the successes of Barnett, Hutton and Compton, Paynter made the highest score against Australia in England and also shared with Compton in a record fifth-wicket partnership of 206. ... During the [England] innings four of Australia's bowlers each had a hundred runs hit off him.

No such inspiring start as had been given to England by the first-wicket pair [Hutton and Barnett put on 219] was enjoyed by Australia. Going on at 29, Wright, with his fourth ball in a Test Match, dismissed Fingleton, who played a long hop on to his wicket. By subdued and not altogether certain batting, Brown and Bradman raised the score to 111 and then Bradman, deceived in the flight of a ball, played it against his pads from which it glanced into the wicket-keeper's hands. ...

... Monday's play began with Australia's score 138 for three, McCabe being 19 not out, made in thirty-five minutes. A record of these facts is a necessary preliminary to a description of the amazing batting which followed from McCabe and gave such an epic turn to the game. Six wickets were down for 194 and then McCabe, assisted in turn by three left-hand batsmen – Barnett, O'Reilly and McCormick – altered the whole aspect of affairs. In a little less than four hours, McCabe scored 232 out of 300 – his highest score in a Test Match. His driving was tremendously hard, he hooked short balls with certainty and power, one off Farnes yielding a 6, and he showed real genius in beating Hammond's efforts to keep him away from the bowling. ... In the last ten overs bowled to him, McCabe took the strike in eight and hit sixteen of his thirty-four 4's, and in a last-wicket stand of 77 with Fleetwood-Smith he scored 72 in twenty-eight minutes. ['If I could play an innings like that,' said Bradman on McCabe's return to the pavilion, 'I'd be a proud man, Stan.'] ...

... When Australia followed on 247 behind, batting of a much different character was seen. Brown and Fingleton adopted 'stone-walling' tactics which called forth mild 'barracking' from some of the spectators and Fingleton followed the extraordinary procedure of stepping away from his wicket, taking off his gloves and laying down his bat. ... Tuesday's play was notable for a dour resistance by Brown and Bradman, who, making a hundred apiece, batted with grim patience and admirable skill. In view of the position of Australia they were of course justified in playing this type of game, and by adding 170 in three hours ten minutes they robbed England of practically all chance of winning. ... Troubled by a leg strain, Bradman was never seen as an attacking batsman, but he amazed everyone by the power of his concentration while batting the whole day. His second innings, begun twenty minutes before Monday's play closed, lasted six hours and there were only five 4's in his 144 not out, which, being his thirteenth hundred in England-Australia matches, allowed him to take the record from Jack Hobbs ... Annoyed by the wearisome cricket, spectators late in the day indulged in ironical cheering, whereupon Bradman showed disapproval of this slight demonstration by standing clear of his wicket until the noise subsided.

England

L. Hutton, C. J. Barnett, W. J. Edrich, *Mr W. R. Hammond, E. Paynter, D. Compton, †L. E. G. Ames, H. Verity, R. A. Sinfield, D. V. P. Wright and Mr K. Farnes.

First innings: Eight for 658 dec (Hutton 100, Barnett 126, Paynter 216 not out, Compton 102, Ames 46; O'Reilly three for 164, Fleetwood-Smith four for 153).

Australia

J. H. Fingleton b Wright	9	–	c Hammond b Edrich	40
W. A. Brown c Ames b Farnes	48	–	c Paynter b Verity	133
*D. G. Bradman c Ames b Sinfield	51	–	not out	144
S. J. McCabe c Compton b Verity	232	–	c Hammond b Verity	39
F. Ward b Farnes	2	–	not out	7
A. L. Hassett c Hammond b Wright	1	–	c Compton b Verity	2
C. L. Badcock b Wright	9	–	b Wright	5
†B. A. Barnett c Wright b Farnes	22	–	lbw b Sinfield	31
W. J. O'Reilly c Paynter b Farnes	9			
E. L. McCormick b Wright	2			
L. O'B. Fleetwood-Smith not out	5			
B 10, l-b 10, w 1	21		B 5, l-b 16, n-b 5	26
	411		(six wkts dec)	**427**

England bowling: *First innings*—Farnes 37–11–106–4; Hammond 19–6–44–0; Sinfield 28–8–51–1; Wright 39–6–153–4; Verity 7.3–0–36–1. *Second innings*—Farnes 24–2–78–0; Hammond 12–6–15–0; Sinfield 35–8–72–1; Wright 37–8–85–1; Verity 62–27–102–3; Edrich 13–2–39–1; Barnett 1–0–10–0.

Umpires: F. Chester and E. Robinson

GENTLEMEN OF ENGLAND v AUSTRALIANS 160 (234)

At Lord's, June 15, 16, 17 [1938]. Australians won by 282 runs. They held the upper hand practically throughout. McCabe ... scored with freedom on the first day, and the bowling suffered severe punishment from Bradman, who, in two hours, completed his seventh century of the tour without mistake, hitting thirteen splendid 4's. ... The Gentlemen ... lost six men for 109 with 139 required to avoid a follow-on, but the last four wickets realised 192 in two hours. ... So the Australians led by no more than 96. ... On the last day ... the Australians declared, leaving the Gentlemen three hours in which to get 432 to win. Aggressive methods against the spin bowling of Fleetwood-Smith brought disaster in their train and, the last five wickets falling for 24 runs, the innings ended in a trifle over two hours.

Australians

J. H. Fingleton c Gibb b Meyer	38	–	c Stephenson b Macindoe	121
W. A. Brown c Gibb b Meyer	30	–	c Valentine b Hammond	30
C. L. Badcock b Brown	31	–	not out	112
S. J. McCabe c Wilcox b Stephenson	79	–	c Meyer b Brown	5
A. G. Chipperfield b Stephenson	51	–	not out	20
*D. G. Bradman c Valentine b Meyer	104			
M. G. Waite b Brown	6	–	run out	32
†B. A. Barnett c Gibb b Brown	0			
E. S. White not out	42			
F. Ward b Meyer	1			
L. O'B. Fleetwood-Smith c Stephenson b Meyer	1			
B 8, l-b 6	14		B 7, l-b 6, n-b 2	15
	397		(four wkts dec)	**335**

Gentlemen of England bowling: *First innings*—Stephenson 25–5–94–2; Macindoe 22–7–57–0; Hammond 5–1–14–0; Brown 29–1–107–3; Meyer 26.2–4–66–5; Wyatt 10–0–45–0. *Second innings*—Stephenson 22–2–69–0; Macindoe 17–3–53–1; Hammond 11–1–27–1; Brown 20–0–97–1; Meyer 22–3–57–0; Wyatt 8–1–17–0.

Gentlemen of England

Mr D. R. Wilcox, †Mr P. A. Gibb, Capt. J. W. A. Stephenson, Mr R. E. S. Wyatt, Mr F. G. H. Chalk, *Mr W. R. Hammond, Mr N. W. D. Yardley, Mr B. H. Valentine, Mr F. R. Brown, Mr R. J. O. Meyer and Mr D. H. Macindoe.

First innings: 301 (Wilcox 50, Wyatt 37, Yardley 49, Valentine 49, Brown 88; Ward five for 108). *Second innings:* 149 (Gibb 67; Fleetwood-Smith seven for 44).

Umpires: F. Walden and W. Reeves

LANCASHIRE v AUSTRALIANS 161 (235, 236)

At Manchester, June 18, 20, 21 [1938]. Drawn. The game will be remembered chiefly for excellent bowling by Phillipson in the first innings and a brilliant hundred in seventy-three minutes by Bradman. Phillipson disturbed his opponents by his ability to make the ball run away to the slips and the Australians began so disastrously that three fell for 35 runs. ... With only an innings apiece completed by the last day, there was little hope of anything except a draw, but Fingleton and Brown rarely played attractive cricket, though making a stand of 153, and it was left to Bradman to give the spectators enjoyment. Scoring fluently all round the wicket, he reached 50 in thirty-eight minutes and the century in seventy-three minutes – the fastest hundred of the season to that date. Bradman obtained all but 30 of the runs added while he was in, and hit fifteen 4's. As, when he declared, only seventy minutes remained for play, Lancashire were in no danger of defeat.

Australians

J. H. Fingleton b Nutter	10	–	c Wilkinson b Phillipson	96
W. A. Brown c Farrimond b Phillipson	8	–	b Nutter	70
*D. G. Bradman c Pollard b Phillipson	12	–	not out	101
C. L. Badcock c Pollard b Phillipson	96	–	not out	14
A. L. Hassett b Nutter	118			
A. G. Chipperfield c Farrimond b Phillipson	5			
†B. A. Barnett c Pollard b Phillipson	9			
M. G. Waite lbw b Wilkinson	20			
E. S. White not out	12			
E. L. McCormick b Pollard	1			
L. O'B. Fleetwood-Smith absent ill	0			
B 2, l-b 7, n-b 3	12		B	3
	303		(two wkts dec)	**284**

Lancashire bowling: *First innings*—Phillipson 35–1–93–5; Pollard 30.5–5–82–1; Nutter 23–7–61–2; Wilkinson 16–0–55–1. *Second innings*—Phillipson 17–2–71–1; Pollard 13–4–27–0; Nutter 20–2–81–1; Wilkinson 22–4–63–0; Iddon 7–0–20–0; Hopwood 4–0–19–0.

Lancashire

C. Washbrook, E. Paynter, J. Iddon, N. Oldfield, J.L. Hopwood, A. Nutter, *Mr W.H.L. Lister, W. E. Phillipson, †W. Farrimond, R. Pollard and L. L. Wilkinson.

First innings: 289 (Iddon 44, Oldfield 69, Phillipson 52, Farrimond 49; McCormick four for 84). *Second innings:* Three for 80 (Oldfield 30 not out).

Umpires: A. Dolphin and G. M. Lee

ENGLAND v AUSTRALIA   162 (237, 238)
(SECOND TEST MATCH)   35 (54, 55)

At Lord's, June 24, 25, 27, 28 [1938]. Drawn. A match of many fluctuations and fine personal achievements ended with Australia needing 111 runs to win and with four wickets to fall. In the Nottingham game, the scoring of a double-hundred on each side had been unprecedented and yet in the very next Test Match the same thing was done again. Hammond … played an innings of 240 – the highest in England against Australia. Brown batted through the whole of Australia's first innings, scoring 206 not out and equalling the performances of Dr J.E. Barrett, Warren Bardsley and W.M. Woodfull by carrying his bat through a Test innings against England. … On the last day Bradman, as in each of his four previous Tests against England, hit a three-figure score and in doing so exceeded the highest individual aggregate in the series – the 3,636 runs made by Hobbs.

… After England's wonderful start in the previous Test, the events that followed success in the toss came as a rude shock. McCormick made the ball swing in to the batsmen and caused it to 'lift' awkwardly … Actually, excluding no-balls, McCormick in twenty-five deliveries took [the wickets of Hutton, Edrich and Barnett] for 15 runs … With England in this sorry position Hammond joined Paynter, the resolute cricket of the left-hander gave Hammond confidence to play his natural game, and this fourth-wicket pair set up a new record by adding 222. … So large was the crowd that the gates were closed before noon. Part of the record partnership between Hammond and Paynter was watched by His Majesty the King.

On Saturday, the cricket was seen by the largest crowd ever to assemble at headquarters – the attendance was officially returned as 33,800. The gates were closed before the start and, after hurried consultations between officials, spectators were permitted to retain positions they had taken up on the grass, the boundary ropes being moved forward a few yards, thus reducing the playing area. England definitely gained the upper hand before the close … [but] Hammond received a nasty blow on the left elbow and the injury, and also a pulled leg muscle, prevented him bowling in this match and for some time afterwards. …

It must be added that through an innings lasting seven hours and producing England's highest total at Lord's, the Australian fielding was maintained at a high standard.

By the call of time, Australia had lost half their wickets, but a fine, fighting innings by Brown checked England's progress. Bradman played on ... On Monday, the Englishmen lost little time in strengthening their grip on the game. Verity, put on first thing, disposed of Barnett and Chipperfield in eight deliveries and when O'Reilly went in seventh wicket down Australia needed 37 more runs to avoid a follow-on. O'Reilly promptly hit out at the slow bowling and a serious mistake occurred in the field. [O'Reilly when 11 was missed at long-on by Paynter.] ... Australia at this point required 17 more runs to save the follow-on and O'Reilly, pulling two successive deliveries from Verity for 6 and taking 16 off the over, soon settled that question. ... Soon after Farnes was brought back into the attack he not only bowled O'Reilly and had McCormick caught at short-leg off successive balls but was deprived of a 'hat-trick' owing to Compton missing a slip catch offered by Fleetwood-Smith. ... After three hours had been lost owing to rain Brown, at 184, was also missed by Paynter, this time at mid-on, and with Fleetwood-Smith showing surprisingly good defence, Brown was able to complete a double-hundred before the innings ended with a difference of 72 runs in England's favour. ...

The rain transformed an easy wicket into one soft on top and hard underneath, and England's opening pair fell for 28 ... half the England side were out for 76 when Hammond, who owing to his injury had a runner, tried a one-hand stroke at a ball outside his leg stump and skied it. ... In the hour of great need, however, Compton batted superbly for England ...

Hammond declared, with Compton not out after making 56 of his runs from boundaries, and left Australia an impossible task in the time available [315 in two and three-quarter hours]. Any thought of failure was soon dispelled by Bradman. After the tea interval the Australian captain batted in brisk style and he and Hassett added 64, short bowling by Farnes receiving instant punishment. It had long since become evident that the Test would be another case of stalemate and Bradman kept life in the cricket by hitting his fourteenth hundred against England as the outcome of less than two hours twenty minutes' batting; his 102 included fifteen 4's. ... An interesting point of the match was that Brown was on the field from the start of play until five o'clock on the fourth day. ... The total number of spectators admitted to the ground on payment was 100,933 – a record for Lord's – and the receipts were £28,164 11s. 9d.

England

L. Hutton, C.J. Barnett, W.J. Edrich, *Mr W.R. Hammond, E. Paynter, D. Compton, †L.E.G. Ames, H. Verity, A.W. Wellard, D.V.P. Wright and Mr K. Farnes.

First innings: 494 (Hammond 240, Paynter 99, Ames 83; McCormick four for 101, O'Reilly four for 93). *Second innings:* Eight for 242 dec (Paynter 43, Compton 76 not out, Wellard 38; McCormick three for 72).

Australia

J. H. Fingleton c Hammond b Wright	31	–	c Hammond b Wellard	4
W. A. Brown not out	206	–	b Verity	10
*D. G. Bradman b Verity	18	–	not out	102
S. J. McCabe c Verity b Farnes	38	–	c Hutton b Verity	21
A. L. Hassett lbw b Wellard	56	–	b Wright	42
C. L. Badcock b Wellard	0	–	c Wright b Edrich	0
†B. A. Barnett c Compton b Verity	8	–	c Paynter b Edrich	14
A. G. Chipperfield lbw b Verity	1			
W. J. O'Reilly b Farnes	42			
E. L. McCormick c Barnett b Farnes	0			
L. O'B. Fleetwood-Smith c Barnett b Verity	7			
B 1, l-b 8, n-b 6	15		B 5, l-b 3, w 2, n-b 1	11
	422		(six wkts)	**204**

England bowling: *First innings*—Farnes 43–6–135–3; Wellard 23–2–96–2; Wright 16–2–68–1; Verity 35.4–9–103–4; Edrich 4–2–5–0. *Second innings*—Farnes 13–3–51–0; Wellard 9–1–30–1; Wright 8–0–56–1; Verity 13–5–29–2; Edrich 5.2–0–27–2.

Umpires: E. J. Smith and F. Walden

YORKSHIRE v AUSTRALIANS   163 (239, 240)

At Sheffield, July 2, 4, 5 [1938]. Drawn. The Australians narrowly escaped defeat in a thrilling match that attracted about 60,000 spectators in the three days. Sellers, when winning the toss, put the Australians in upon a rain-affected pitch, and Yorkshire fought with such spirit that by lunch-time on the third day they stood within 67 of victory with seven wickets to fall. Then, unfortunately for the county's prospects of gaining their first victory over a team from the Commonwealth since 1902, rain put an end to the proceedings. Smailes, first with swingers and later with off-breaks, caused the Australians a lot of trouble on the first day even though, in the absence of much sunshine, the pitch did not become as difficult as Sellers had anticipated. Bradman and Hassett saved their side from disaster. Bradman shaped well at a trying time, driving and hitting to leg cleanly after an uncertain start, but Hassett took chief honours. … Waite, adopting similar tactics to those of Smailes, proved equally difficult to Yorkshire. … With a lead of 17, the Australians fared badly [in their second innings]. Hassett and Bradman, desperately ill at ease against Bowes and Verity, shared in a stand of 41, but the last six wickets fell in half an hour for 32 runs. Yorkshire required 150 to win and, with the whole of Tuesday available, made slow but sure progress until the weather baulked their efforts.

Australians

J. H. Fingleton b Smailes	2	–	lbw b Bowes	2
S. J. McCabe c Smailes b Bowes	13	–	lbw b Bowes	15
*D. G. Bradman st Wood b Smailes	59	–	c Barber b Smailes	42
C. L. Badcock c Turner b Robinson	11	–	lbw b Verity	22
A. L. Hassett lbw b Verity	94	–	lbw b Verity	17
S. Barnes c Wood b Leyland	10	–	c Sellers b Smailes	19
M. G. Waite lbw b Smailes	2	–	run out	0
†B. A. Barnett c Robinson b Smailes	12	–	c and b Smailes	1
E. S. White c Sutcliffe b Smailes	1	–	c Hutton b Smailes	2
E. L. McCormick c Leyland b Smailes	9	–	b Verity	0
L. O'B. Fleetwood-Smith not out	4	–	not out	7
B 3, l-b 1, n-b 1	5		L-b	5
	222			**132**

Yorkshire bowling: *First innings*—Bowes 12–4–15–1; Smailes 29–7–92–6; Robinson 12–5–39–1; Verity 17–1–69–1; Leyland 3–1–2–1. *Second innings*—Bowes 18–8–28–2; Smailes 19.2–4–45–4; Robinson 2–0–8–0; Verity 21–8–46–3.

Yorkshire

H. Sutcliffe, L. Hutton, W. Barber, M. Leyland, C. Turner, T. F. Smailes, *Mr A. B. Sellers, †A. Wood, E. P. Robinson, H. Verity and W. E. Bowes.

    First innings: 205 (Turner 34, Wood 41, Robinson 32; Waite seven for 101, White three for 26). *Second innings:* Three for 83 (Sutcliffe 36 not out).

Umpires: W. Reeves and A. Skelding

ENGLAND v AUSTRALIA
(THIRD TEST MATCH)

The third of the five matches arranged between England and Australia was to have been played at Old Trafford, Manchester, on July 8, 9, 11, 12 [1938], but owing to the persistent bad weather the game had to be abandoned without a ball being bowled. The captains did not toss and neither team was announced.

WARWICKSHIRE v AUSTRALIANS   164 (241)

At Birmingham, July 13, 14 [1938]. Australians won by an innings and 93 runs. Playing their first game for over a week, they thoroughly outclassed Warwickshire, who batted without resolution on turf which never became difficult. ... Owing to a slight head injury, Fingleton did not open the Australians' innings and McCabe, who deputised, left at 17. Warwickshire had to wait two and three-quarter hours for their next success and in that time Brown and Bradman added 206. Bradman, cautious at the start, afterwards hit with tremendous power and his last 85 runs came in an hour. The rest of the batsmen were tied down by the accurate leg-breaks of Hollies ... Going in a second time requiring 211 to save an innings defeat, Warwickshire again failed dismally. Four wickets went down for 28 and ... the county were all out in just over two hours.

Warwickshire

A. J. Croom, Mr J. R. Thompson, F. R. Santall, H. E. Dollery, J. S. Ord, †J. Buckingham, *Mr P. Cranmer, G. E. Paine, K. Wilmot, J. H. Mayer and E. Hollies.

    First innings: 179 (Dollery 31, Ord 61; O'Reilly three for 69, Ward four for 26). *Second innings:* 118 (Ord 30, Cranmer 37; Waite three for 33, O'Reilly four for 33).

Australians

S. J. McCabe b Wilmot	14	M. G. Waite not out	25
W. A. Brown b Hollies	101	E. S. White c Wilmot b Hollies	2
*D. G. Bradman c Wilmot b Mayer	135	W. J. O'Reilly b Paine	0
†S. Barnes c Cranmer b Hollies	24	F. Ward not out	13
A. G. Chipperfield c Buckingham b Hollies	46	B 4, l-b 4, w 1, n-b 2	11
J. H. Fingleton hit wkt b Hollies	9	(eight wkts dec)	**390**

E. L. McCormick did not bat.

Warwickshire bowling: Mayer 16–2–49–1; Wilmot 27–4–90–1; Hollies 42–8–130–5; Paine 30–7–65–1; Santall 3–0–28–0; Croom 3–0–17–0.

Umpires: G. Beet and C. V. Tarbox

NOTTINGHAMSHIRE v AUSTRALIANS   165 (242, 243)

At Nottingham, July 16, 18, 19 [1938]. Australians won by 412 runs. A weak Nottinghamshire XI gave an inexplicably poor display and, but for gallant efforts by Gunn and Hardstaff, the Australians would have won even more easily. Good pace bowling by Jepson and Voce helped to get rid of some of the more renowned Australian batsmen on the opening day, but Bradman and Barnes added 74 and the last five wickets put on 140. … [When the Australians batted again] Brown, Badcock, Bradman and Hassett completed Nottinghamshire's discomfiture. Hassett and Bradman shared in a third-wicket stand of 216 in two hours twenty minutes, Bradman becoming the first player during the season to reach 2,000 runs and equalling the record made by Trumper, during the 1902 tour, of hitting eleven centuries. Nottinghamshire should have saved the game without difficulty, but only Hardstaff offered serious resistance … Fleetwood-Smith bewildered the rest of the side.

Australians

W. A. Brown c Marshall b Voce	4	–	c Harris b Heane	63
C. L. Badcock c Wheat b Jepson	6	–	c Jepson b Voce	54
*D. G. Bradman lbw b Jepson	56	–	c Jepson b Marshall	144
A. L. Hassett lbw b Voce	2	–	c Wheat b Heane	124
S. Barnes lbw b Harris	58	–	not out	34
A. G. Chipperfield b Jepson	4	–	not out	27
M. G. Waite c Wheat b Harris	25			
†B. A. Barnett b Harris	3			
F. Ward not out	29			
W. J. O'Reilly lbw b Voce	33			
L. O'B. Fleetwood-Smith c Jepson b Harris	8			
B 8, l-b 5, n-b 2	15		B 4, l-b 1, n-b 2	7
	243		(four wkts dec)	**453**

Nottinghamshire bowling: *First innings*—Voce 30–3–72–3; Jepson 23–6–38–3; Harris 24.5–5–60–4; Gunn 11–0–38–0; Marshall 5–0–20–0. *Second innings*—Voce 21–2–80–1; Jepson 19–2–81–0; Harris 28–5–106–0; Gunn 9–0–44–0; Marshall 7–1–34–1; Heane 31–7–85–2; Hardstaff 3–0–16–0.

Nottinghamshire

W. W. Keeton, C. B. Harris, J. Knowles, J. Hardstaff, G. V. Gunn, *Mr G. F. H. Heane, G. Yates, Mr E. A. Marshall, W. Voce, †A. B. Wheat and A. Jepson.

    First innings: 147 (Gunn 75, Voce 32; O'Reilly five for 39, Fleetwood-Smith three for 35). *Second innings:* 137 (Hardstaff 67 not out; Fleetwood-Smith five for 39).

Umpires: J. Newman and D. Hendren

ENGLAND v AUSTRALIA
(FOURTH TEST MATCH)

166 (244, 245)
36 (56, 57)

At Leeds, July 22, 23, 25 [1938]. Australia won by five wickets. Their success enabled them to retain the Ashes. … A fine test of skill had many glorious moments, the cricket was often thrilling to watch, and the decision of the game about quarter-past four on the third day confounded all expectations. In contrast to what occurred at Trent Bridge and Lord's, only 695 runs were scored in the match; on each side the captain made top score, Bradman registering yet another three-figure innings.

    At no time was the wicket easy for batting and Australia won largely because they possessed better spin bowling. … Exactly why the pitch, even during the early stages of the game, played so queerly was hard to understand. A likely explanation was that it was kept on the damp side through moisture being drawn to the surface in the humid weather prevailing. At any rate bowlers were able to turn the ball and as the match progressed spin acted more quickly; by Monday the wicket had worn and O'Reilly took full advantage of this state of affairs. ... The decision to omit Goddard from the England XI suggested that the Selectors, despite a long and careful examination of the wicket before the toss, had no suspicions that the conditions were likely to be more favourable to spin bowlers than to Farnes and Bowes, both of whom appeared in the eleven.

To see England's batsmen struggling for runs after Hammond, for the third successive match, won the toss was at once unexpected and perplexing. In the course of five hours, and despite a splendid effort by Hammond, the innings was over. ...

When Wright, with the first ball he bowled in Australia's innings, got rid of Brown, B. A. Barnett was sent in to play out time with Fingleton and the outcome of this move far exceeded expectations. ... England bowled for nearly an hour and a half next morning before gaining further reward. ... The attack of Farnes and Bowes after lunch was accurate and full of danger; McCabe and Badcock in turn were clean bowled and Australia's first five wickets fell for 145. The light at this time was none too good but Bradman, as in each of the two previous Tests, did not let the occasion pass without placing to his name another three-figure score – his twelfth of the tour. Although a beautiful-length leg-break led to Hassett being caught at slip after helping to add 50, Waite stayed long enough to see Australia take innings lead. Shielding his successive partners, Bradman astutely 'nursed' the bowling and he made every possible run against high-class fielding. His strokeplay and his defence were alike admirable. Bowes, who rarely pitched short and made the ball swerve, had a great moment when he knocked Bradman's middle stump out of the ground. Only two runs were added after the Australian captain was eighth out – he batted a few minutes less than three hours and hit nine 4's. ...

Bad light once interrupted this innings and when England went in 19 runs behind an appeal was upheld. Barnett and Edrich survived an awkward fifty minutes prior to close of play and they put 60 runs on the board before being separated next morning. ... For the collapse which afterwards set in no one could have been prepared. O'Reilly, on a worn pitch, and ably supported by Fleetwood-Smith, finished off the innings before lunch-time, England's full ten wickets actually going down for the addition of 74 runs to the overnight score. ... With six men on the leg side close to the bat, and with no one in the long field, he demoralised the majority of the batsmen. ...

Left to get 105, Australia had to struggle hard for success. ... Intense excitement came into the cricket when Wright, after going on at 48, quickly sent back Bradman and McCabe. With the first four batsmen in the order all out, Australia had to contend with atrocious light but the batsmen refrained from appealing and, as Hassett began to drive and pull in an easy, confident style, England's chance of turning the tables gradually slipped away. ... Rain interrupted the play with nine runs needed but Australia got home without further loss, making the required runs in an hour and fifty minutes. ...

England

W. J. Edrich, C. J. Barnett, J. Hardstaff, *Mr W. R. Hammond, E. Paynter, D. Compton, †W. F. Price, H. Verity, D. V. P. Wright, Mr K. Farnes and W. E. Bowes.

First innings: 223 (Barnett 30, Hammond 76; O'Reilly five for 66, Fleetwood-Smith three for 73).
Second innings: 123 (O'Reilly five for 56, Fleetwood-Smith four for 34).

Australia

J. H. Fingleton b Verity	30	–	lbw b Verity	9
W. A. Brown b Wright	22	–	lbw b Farnes	9
†B. A. Barnett c Price b Farnes	57	–	not out	15
*D. G. Bradman b Bowes	103	–	c Verity b Wright	16
S. J. McCabe b Farnes	1	–	c Barnett b Wright	15
C. L. Badcock b Bowes	4	–	not out	5
A. L. Hassett c Hammond b Wright	13	–	c Edrich b Wright	33
M. G. Waite c Price b Farnes	3			
W. J. O'Reilly c Hammond b Farnes	2			
E. L. McCormick b Bowes	0			
L. O'B. Fleetwood-Smith not out	2			
B 2, l-b 3	5		B 4, n-b 1	5
	242		(five wkts)	**107**

England bowling: *First innings*—Farnes 26–3–77–4; Bowes 35.4–6–79–3; Wright 15–4–38–2; Verity 19–6–30–1; Edrich 3–0–13–0. *Second innings*—Farnes 11.3–4–17–1; Bowes 11–0–35–0; Wright 5–0–26–3; Verity 5–2–24–1.

Umpires: E. J. Smith and F. Chester

SOMERSET v AUSTRALIANS 167 (246)

At Taunton, July 27, 28, 29 [1938]. Australians won by an innings and 218 runs. Somerset cut a sorry figure and suffered defeat early on the last day. ... Bradman, putting together his thirteenth century of the tour, overshadowed everyone else. At first troubled by the swinging deliveries of Andrews, Bradman afterwards ran into his best form and he obtained nineteen of his thirty-two 4's in making his second hundred. He shared with Badcock, Hassett and McCabe in prolific stands ...

Somerset

Mr M. D. Lyon, F. S. Lee, H. T. F. Buse, Mr R. J. O. Meyer, *Mr E. F. Longrigg, H. Gimblett, W. H. R. Andrews, Mr C. J. P. Barnwell, A. W. Wellard, †W. T. Luckes and H. L. Hazell.

First innings: 110 (Fleetwood-Smith three for 40, White three for 8). *Second innings*: 136 (Buse 33; Fleetwood-Smith five for 30).

Australians

†C. W. Walker b Andrews	27	A. G. Chipperfield b Wellard	10
C. L. Badcock run out	110	S. J. McCabe not out	56
*D. G. Bradman b Andrews	202	E. S. White not out	2
S. Barnes lbw b Wellard	9	B 4, l-b 1, w 1, n-b 1	7
A. L. Hassett c Gimblett b Buse	31	(six wkts dec)	**464**

F. Ward, W. J. O'Reilly and L. O'B. Fleetwood-Smith did not bat.

Somerset bowling: Wellard 39–8–146–2; Andrews 24–2–108–2; Meyer 17–3–54–0; Buse 12–1–82–1; Hazell 11–1–57–0; Lyon 2–1–10–0.

Umpires: C. N. Woolley and E. Cooke

GLAMORGAN v AUSTRALIANS   168 (247)

At Swansea, July 30, August 1, 2 [1938]. Drawn. Welsh cricket lovers, of whom over 25,000 were present on the second day, when the 'gate' was a record, were bitterly disappointed, only five hours' play being possible in the match. When the county declared with five wickets down to enable the spectators to have an opportunity of seeing the Australians bat, the pitch was definitely unfit for cricket.

Glamorgan

A.H. Dyson, E. Davies, T.L. Brierley, T.H. Davies, *Mr M.J. Turnbull, C. Smart, Mr J.C. Clay, Mr W. Wooller, J. Mercer, E.C. Jones and H. Davies.

    First innings: Five for 148 dec (E. Davies 58; Waite four for 45).

Australians

W. A. Brown c Dyson b E. Davies		8	S. Barnes not out	5
J. H. Fingleton c H. Davies b Wooller		1	B 2, w 2	4
*D. G. Bradman st H. Davies b Clay		17	(three wkts)	**61**
A. L. Hassett not out		26		

A.G. Chipperfield, D. G. Waite, †C. W. Walker, E. S. White, F. Ward and E. L. McCormick did not bat.

Glamorgan bowling: Mercer 6–3–4–0; Wooller 10–6–9–1; Clay 10–4–15–1; E. Davies 4–0–21–1; Jones 2–0–8–0.

Umpires: J. Hardstaff and J. Smart

KENT v AUSTRALIANS   169 (248)

At Canterbury, August 13, 15, 16 [1938]. Australians won by ten wickets. For about two hours the pitch proved difficult, but this was sufficient to decide the whole course of the match. Facing a total of 479, Kent had to go in when, after weekend rain, strong sunshine was drying the wicket. Following on 371 behind, the county showed that there was nothing really wrong with their batting by averting an innings beating. On the first day consistent run-getting enabled the Australians to build up a big total. After the fall of two wickets for 38, Bradman and Badcock added 107. ... Bradman did not declare next morning, waiting for the pitch to become helpful to bowlers. His judgment proved correct for, following a foolish run-out [of Woolley] off the first ball of the innings, Kent collapsed ... Woolley [at the age of fifty-one and in his farewell season] touched his best form in the follow-on, hitting up 81, including a 6, a 5 and thirteen 4's, in an hour. ...

Australians

J. H. Fingleton lbw b Watt	23			
W. A. Brown lbw b Watt	4			
*D. G. Bradman c Todd b Watt	67			
C. L. Badcock c Davies b Todd	76			
S. Barnes c Todd b Woolley	94			
M. G. Waite c Chalk b Todd	18			
B. A. Barnett c Chalk b Todd	54			
†C. W. Walker c Fagg b Watt	42			
E. S. White c Todd b Wright	52	–	not out	0
F. Ward c Valentine b Todd	16			
L. O'B. Fleetwood-Smith not out	0	–	not out	6
B 24, l-b 7, n-b 2	33		N-b	1
	479		(no wkt)	**7**

Kent bowling: *First innings*—Watt 35–7–102–4; Todd 40–10–145–4; Davies 26–3–75–0; Wright 16.3–0–77–1; Woolley 14–1–47–1. *Second innings*—Levett 0.3–0–6–0.

Kent

F.E. Woolley, A. Fagg, L.E.G. Ames, Mr B.H. Valentine, *Mr F.G.H. Chalk, L.J. Todd, Mr C.H. Knott, Mr J.G.W. Davies, D.V.P. Wright, A.E. Watt and †Mr W.H.V. Levett.

First innings: 108 (Ames 30; Waite four for 43, White three for 35). *Second innings:* 377 (Woolley 81, Ames 139, Valentine 36, sundries 30; Waite five for 85, Ward three for 92).

Umpires: F. Chester and J. Smart

ENGLAND v AUSTRALIA   170
(FIFTH TEST MATCH)   37

Played at Kennington Oval, August 20, 22, 23, 24 [1938]. England won by an innings and 579 runs and each country having gained one victory the rubber was drawn. No more remarkable exhibition of concentration and endurance has ever been seen on the cricket field than that of Leonard Hutton, the Yorkshire opening batsman, in a match which culminated in the defeat of Australia by a margin more substantial than any associated with the series of matches between the two countries. Record after record went by the board as Hutton mastered the bowling in calm, methodical fashion for the best part of two and a half days. At the end of an innings which extended over thirteen hours twenty minutes, this batsman of only twenty-two years had placed the highest score in Test cricket to his name, and shared in two partnerships which surpassed previous figures. ... As a boy of fourteen, Hutton, at Leeds in 1930, had seen Bradman hit 334 – the record individual score in Test Matches between England and Australia. Now, on his third appearance in the series, the Yorkshireman left that figure behind by playing an innings of 364.

This Test will always be remembered as 'Hutton's Match', and also for the calamity which befell Australia while their opponents were putting together a mammoth total of 903. First of all Fingleton strained a muscle and Bradman injured his ankle so badly that he retired from the match and did not play again during the tour. Before this accident, England had established a supremacy which left little doubt about the result; indeed, Hammond probably would not have closed the innings during the tea interval on the third day but for the mishap to the opposing captain.

The moral effect of the loss of Bradman and Fingleton upon the other Australians was, of course, very great. After fielding out an innings lasting fifteen hours and a quarter, several of them batted – to all appearances – with very poor heart, but Brown, going in first, was last man out before a follow-on 702 runs in arrear. He played an heroic innings under the shadow of impending defeat ... but from a depressing start in each innings there was no real recovery. This came as an anti-climax after the batting mastery which obtained until the tea interval on Monday. It was not a case of England driving home the advantage but rather of Australia losing inspiration to make a braver struggle to put a better face on defeat.

Hammond's fourth consecutive success in the toss was, of course, one factor influencing the result. Another was the way in which the Australian team was chosen. The risks taken by Bradman in going into the match with only O'Reilly, Fleetwood-Smith and Waite to bowl seemed to be inviting trouble. ... Whether Bradman, as was suggested, gambled upon winning the toss after three failures and so being in a position to call upon his spin bowlers when the pitch had become worn will probably never be known. ...

With few bowlers of class at his call, Bradman had to conserve the energies of O'Reilly as much as possible. The field was set carefully for the saving of runs, and although [Hutton and Leyland] scored numerous singles on the off side Australia gave a superb display in the field, Bradman inspiring the team with his fast running and clean picking-up. ... A curiosity of the [first] day's cricket was that four times a no-ball led either to the wicket being hit or the ball being caught. ...

... Following [on Monday] the same steady lines as before, Hutton and Leyland carried on [their] magnificent batting until England had 411 runs up when the stand [worth 382 for the second wicket] ended through a wonderful piece of fielding. Hutton drove a ball from O'Reilly hard to the off side and Hassett fumbled it. Then he slung in a very fast return to the bowler's end and Bradman, sizing up the situation in an instant, dashed towards the wicket from mid-on, caught the throw-in and broke the wicket before Leyland could complete a second run.

[By stumps on the second day] Hutton claimed exactly 300 of the [634] runs scored at this point, and the 30,000 people who assembled at The Oval on Tuesday saw fresh cricket history made. The bowling and fielding of Australia looked more formidable than at any other time in the game and as Hutton carried his score nearer to the record Test innings, Bradman, the holder of it, brought several fieldsmen close in to the wicket for O'Reilly's bowling. Every run had to be fought for. … Hutton duly reached his objective and the scene at the ground, with the whole assembly rising to its feet, and every Australian player as well as Hardstaff congratulating Hutton, will be remembered for a long time by those who saw it. Hutton took nearly twice as long as Bradman did over as many runs eight years previously, but the Australian's big innings came during a Test limited in duration whereas Hutton played his innings on an occasion when time did not matter. …

England's total … reached 770 for the loss of six wickets and some spirited hitting by Wood came as a refreshing contrast to the stern batting which had gone before. [Wood added 106 with Hardstaff] and shortly after these batsmen were separated there occurred the tragic accident to Bradman, who when bowling caught his foot in a worn foot-hole, fell prone and was carried off the field by two of his colleagues. During the tea interval England's innings, which was the longest on record and produced the highest total for any Test Match innings and the highest for any first-class match in England, was declared closed. …

… [Towards the end of Australia's first innings] an unusual incident happened during the eighth and last stand, in which Fleetwood-Smith participated. When Brown cut the last ball of an over, intending to run a single, Hutton, with the idea of trying to give the less experienced batsman the strike, kicked the ball to the boundary. Instructions to umpires, however, provide for four runs to be added to the runs already made should a fieldsman wilfully cause the ball to reach the boundary, and as this meant the award to Brown of five runs he kept the bowling. … On the fourth day, the proceedings were so one-sided as to be almost farcical. The fact that Australia batted only nine men removed some of the honour and glory from England's triumph, but there was nothing in the condition of the wicket to excuse the poor resistance of so many Test batsmen. … The number of people who saw the game was 94,212, including 81,336 who paid for admission. …

England

L. Hutton, W. J. Edrich, M. Leyland, *Mr W. R. Hammond, E. Paynter, D. Compton, J. Hardstaff, †A. Wood, H. Verity; Mr K. Farnes and W. E. Bowes did not bat.

First innings: Seven for 903 dec (Hutton 364, Leyland 187, Hammond 59, Hardstaff 169 not out, Wood 53, sundries 50; O'Reilly three for 178, Bradman none for 6).

Australia

C. L. Badcock c Hardstaff b Bowes	0	–	b Bowes	9
W. A. Brown c Hammond b Leyland	69	–	c Edrich b Farnes	15
S. J. McCabe c Edrich b Farnes	14	–	c Wood b Farnes	2
A. L. Hassett c Compton b Edrich	42	–	lbw b Bowes	10
S. Barnes b Bowes	41	–	lbw b Verity	33
†B. A. Barnett c Wood b Bowes	2	–	b Farnes	46
M. G. Waite b Bowes	8	–	c Edrich b Verity	0
W. J. O'Reilly c Wood b Bowes	0	–	not out	7
L. O'B. Fleetwood-Smith not out	16	–	c Leyland b Farnes	0
*D. G. Bradman absent hurt	0	–	absent hurt	0
J. H. Fingleton absent hurt	0	–	absent hurt	0
B 4, l-b 2, n-b 3	9		B	1
	201			**123**

England bowling: *First innings*—Farnes 13–2–54–1; Bowes 19–3–49–5; Edrich 10–2–55–1; Verity 5–1–15–0; Leyland 3.1–0–11–1; Hammond 2–0–8–0. *Second innings*—Farnes 12.1–1–63–4; Bowes 10–3–25–2; Verity 7–3–15–2; Leyland 5–0–19–0.

Umpires: F. Chester and F. Walden

1938-39

Inspecting the pitch with England captain Walter Hammond, 1938.

1938-39

In a season notable for many fine individual performances, South Australia carried off the Sheffield Shield. Victoria, victims of the weather in a vital game with the ultimate champions, finished second, one point behind; Queensland, much improved, were third and New South Wales, suffering a sad fall from grace, last.

Fresh from his personal successes of the English tour, Bradman deserved the largest measure of praise for leading South Australia to triumph. Yet his gifts for captaincy were overshadowed by his remarkable batting. In six State matches he played six innings and averaged 160.20 for an aggregate of 801 runs. Bradman began the season with 118 in the Melbourne Club Centenary Match and followed with 143, 225, 107, 186 and 135 not out, so equalling the record of C. B. Fry, who in 1901 put together six successive centuries. After the game with New South Wales at Sydney, Bradman found himself with one more match for the opportunity of surpassing the famous England cricketer's achievement. Fifteen thousand people [actually seventeen thousand and more] attended the Adelaide Oval on the second day of the match with Victoria, eager to watch their favourite add another record to his name, but Bradman was out for five. Nothing more than has already been written can be said of Bradman. At the crease he was master and the bowler, servant.

From 'Cricket in Australia: Inter-State Matches, 1938-39'

D. G. BRADMAN'S TEAM v K. E. RIGG'S TEAM   171 (249)
(MELBOURNE CRICKET CLUB CENTENARY MATCH)

Played at Melbourne, December 9, 10, 12, 13 [1938]. Drawn. Bradman's side, composed of players back from the tour in England, showed superior strength. The Rest [Rigg's team] fared moderately against O'Reilly and Fleetwood-Smith in their first innings, during which play was stopped by a dust-storm of hurricane force. Bradman and McCabe made delightful centuries. They shared in a stand of 163 and Rigg's team batted again 211 behind. ...

K. E. Rigg's Team

*K. E. Rigg, I. S. Lee, R. G. Gregory, J. A. Ledward, S. G. Barnes, †D. Tallon, M. W. Sievers, E. H. Bromley, L. E. Nagel, G. Eyres and C. Christ.

First innings: 215 (Rigg 48, Barnes 63, Bromley 34; O'Reilly five for 75). *Second innings:* Eight for 324 (Rigg 71, Gregory 32, Ledward 85, Sievers 44 not out; Bradman one for none).

D.G. Bradman's Team

J. H. Fingleton c Sievers b Eyres	23	†B. A. Barnett lbw b Sievers	0
W. A. Brown c and b Christ	67	W. J. O'Reilly c Christ b Bromley	0
*D. G. Bradman b Nagel	118	L. O'B. Fleetwood-Smith b Sievers	2
S. J. McCabe c Lee b Nagel	105	E. L. McCormick c Gregory b Bromley	3
A. L. Hassett run out	12	B 11, l-b 6	17
C. L. Badcock not out	51		**426**
M. G. Waite b Sievers	28		

K. E. Rigg's Team bowling: Eyres 23–2–81–1; Sievers 15–3–53–3; Nagel 26–4–93–2; Christ 29–4–104–1; Bromley 11.7–0–53–2; Barnes 1–1–0–0; Gregory 3–0–25–0.

Umpires: A. N. Barlow and G. A. Browne

SOUTH AUSTRALIA v NEW SOUTH WALES   172 (250)

Played at Adelaide, December 16, 17, 19, 20 [1938]. South Australia won by an innings and 56 runs. [Some sources put the New South Wales first innings score as 390 and give the result as an innings and 55 runs.] Bradman made the second century of his record-equalling run, but in this match Badcock overshadowed him. They were associated in a stand of 175, and Hamence helped Badcock set up a South Australian fourth-wicket record with a partnership of 203 … South Australia declared at their highest total against New South Wales. … [When] New South Wales followed on, the wiles of Ward and Grimmett upset the whole side.

South Australia

K. Ridings b O'Reilly	31	M. G. Waite run out	2
R. S. Whitington c James b Murphy	0	F. A. Ward b Barnes	0
*D. G. Bradman b Murphy	143	C. V. Grimmett run out	35
C. L. Badcock not out	271	B 3, l-b 4, n-b 2	9
R. A. Hamence c Barnes b Fitzpatrick	90	(eight wkts dec)	**600**
†C. W. Walker lbw b O'Reilly —	0		

H. Cotton and J. Scott did not bat.

New South Wales bowling: Murphy 32–1–126–2; Cheetham 20–1–85–0; O'Reilly 36–9–99–2; White 28–1–103–0; Chipperfield 8–0–60–0; Barnes 15–2–62–1; James 1–0–13–0; Fitzpatrick 11–0–40–1; Fingleton 5–0–3–0.

New South Wales

J.H. Fitzpatrick, A.G. Cheetham, C.M. Solomon, S.G. Barnes, *J.H. Fingleton, A.G. Chipperfield, R. James, †F.A. Easton, E.S. White, W.J. O'Reilly and J. Murphy.
    First innings: 389 (Barnes 117, Chipperfield 154; Grimmett seven for 116). *Second innings:* 155 (James 42; Ward four for 40, Grimmett four for 59).

Umpires: J. D. Scott and A.G. Jenkins

SOUTH AUSTRALIA v QUEENSLAND   173 (251)

Played at Adelaide, December 24, 26, 27, 28 [1938]. South Australia won by an innings and 20 runs. Bradman and Badcock maintained their great batting form. In a stand of 202 they made brilliant strokes all round the wicket after the Queensland batsmen had failed dismally against Grimmett. The tricky slows completely nonplussed the batsmen in the first innings, but in Brown [who carried his bat] Grimmett found a worthy foeman when Queensland batted a second time 331 behind. …

Queensland

*W. A. Brown, R. Rogers, T. Allen, †D. Tallon, G. Baker, G.G. Cook, D. Hansen, M. Guttormsen, W. Tallon, J. Ellis and C. Christ.

First innings: 131 (Cook 34 not out; Grimmett six for 33). *Second innings:* 311 (Brown 174 not out, Baker 43, Cook 35; Grimmett three for 96, Ward three for 106).

South Australia

R. S. Whitington st D. Tallon b Cook	11	F. A. Ward run out	9
K. L. Ridings c D. Tallon b Ellis	7	C. V. Grimmett not out	0
*D. G. Bradman c Baker b Christ	225	H. J. Cotton b Baker	0
C. L. Badcock c W. Tallon b Ellis	100	J. Scott b Baker	0
R. A. Hamence c and b W. Tallon	17	B 5, l-b 3, w 1	9
M. G. Waite c Guttormsen b Cook	52		**462**
†C. W. Walker b Baker	32		

Queensland bowling: Ellis 26–0–87–2; Cook 25–2–85–2; Christ 33–3–102–1; Baker 8.5–0–36–3; W. Tallon 18–1–90–1; Rogers 8–1–42–0; Allen 2–0–11–0.

Umpires: J. D. Scott and A.G. Jenkins

VICTORIA v SOUTH AUSTRALIA 174 (252)

Played at Melbourne, December 30, 31 [1938], January 2, 3 [1939]. Drawn. Hassett played a masterly innings for Victoria but interest centred on Bradman. The South Australia captain gave another faultless exhibition and duly reached his fourth successive century. Whitington, who also scored a hundred, put on 150 with Bradman. ... Grimmett tore a leg muscle during the game and an attack of laryngitis troubled Bradman [who along with his opposing captain, Rigg, took no part in the final two days' play].

Victoria

*K. E. Rigg, I. S. Lee, R.G. Gregory, A. L. Hassett, J. A. Ledward, F. W. Sides, †B. A. Barnett, M. W. Sievers, D. Ring, E. L. McCormick and L. O'B. Fleetwood-Smith.

First innings: 499 (Gregory 71, Hassett 211 not out, Sides 44, Barnett 50, Ring 51, Fleetwood-Smith 43; Waite three for 123, Ward four for 125). *Second innings:* Seven for 283 dec (Lee 51, Hassett 54, Sides 61, Barnett 54; Ward five for 126).

South Australia

R. S. Whitington lbw b Sievers	100	–	not out	27
K. L. Ridings c Lee b Sievers	27	–	not out	18
*D. G. Bradman c Hassett b Sievers	107			
C. L. Badcock c and b McCormick	1			
†C. W. Walker b Sievers	14			
F. A. Ward c Barnett b Sievers	62			
R. A. Hamence b Sievers	84			
M. G. Waite lbw b Ring	0			
P. Ridings c and b Ring	33			
C. V. Grimmett st Barnett b Ring	34			
J. Scott not out	4			
B 5, l-b 15, n-b 2	22	B		5
	488	(no wkt)		**50**

Victoria bowling: *First innings*—McCormick 22–4–78–1; Sievers 43–11–95–6; Ring 31.1–2–116–3; Fleetwood-Smith 35–4–152–0; Gregory 4–0–25–0. *Second innings*—McCormick 3–1–13–0; Sievers 3–0–9–0; Ring 6–1–8–0; Fleetwood-Smith 3–1–2–0; Gregory 4–3–3–0; Hassett 2–0–10–0.

Umpires: A. N. Barlow and G. A. Browne

QUEENSLAND v SOUTH AUSTRALIA   175 (253)

Played at Brisbane, January 7, 9, 10, 11 [1939]. South Australia won by ten wickets. Bradman, recovered from his indisposition, gave another superlative exhibition in his fifth consecutive century [a record by an Australian batsman]. Ridings and Whitington paved the way for their captain with an opening partnership of 197. The three hundreds for South Australia followed one by Don Tallon, who, after his great wicket-keeping feat of the previous match [twelve dismissals, v New South Wales, to equal the world record], showed first-rate ability as a batsman. ...

Queensland

*W. A. Brown, G. G. Cook, T. Allen, R. Rogers, †D. Tallon, C. Stibe, G. Baker, W. Tallon, P. L. Dixon, J. Ellis and C. Christ.

First innings: 336 (D. Tallon 115, Stibe 58, Baker 78; Cotton five for 49). *Second innings:* 233 (Brown 81, Rogers 45, W. Tallon 40 not out; Ridings four for 26).

South Australia

K. L. Ridings b Ellis	122	–	not out	10
R. S. Whitington c D. Tallon b W. Tallon	125			
*D. G. Bradman c Christ b W. Tallon	186			
C. L. Badcock c Rogers b Christ	1	–	not out	4
R. A. Hamence c Stibe b Christ	13			
E. J. R. Moyle c Brown b Cook	46			
†C. W. Walker c and b W. Tallon	20			
F. A. Ward b Ellis	18			
H. J. Cotton st Brown b W. Tallon	2			
J. Scott not out	5			
M. W. Waite absent ill	0			
B 3, l-b 9, w 5, n-b 2	19			
	557		(no wkt)	**14**

Queensland bowling: *First innings*—Ellis 32.7–1–126–2; Cook 25–0–101–1; Dixon 19–2–93–0; Christ 43–9–110–2; W. Tallon 20–2–80–4; Allen 1–0–4–0; Baker 3–0–24–0. *Second innings*—Baker 1–1–0–0; Stibe 1–0–9–0; Rogers 0.7–0–5–0.

Umpires: K. Fagg and F. J. Bartlett

NEW SOUTH WALES v SOUTH AUSTRALIA   176 (254)

Played at Sydney, January 14, 16, 17, 18 [1939]. Drawn. Bradman held the stage and, after having to wait during two idle days caused by rain, he completed his sixth successive century, so equalling the world record held by C. B. Fry. [Including Bradman's two hundreds at the end of the 1937-38 season, this was his eighth successive hundred in matches in Australia.] Grimmett, fit again, helped most in the cheap dismissal of New South Wales on the first day and Bradman was 22 not out when stumps were drawn with South Australia 116 for two. The weather prevented a resumption until the last morning, when Bradman proceeded unperturbed but cautiously. He hit only seven 4's in an innings lasting five hours twenty minutes. He and Badcock put on 186. ... [Moyle kept wicket for South Australia in New South Wales' second innings, Bradman having kept in the first innings.]

New South Wales

A.G. Cheetham, B. McCauley, S.G. Barnes, *A.G. Chipperfield, C.M. Solomon, C. Pepper, V. McCaffrey, R. James, L.C. Hynes, †S. Sismey and J.L. O'Brien.

First innings: 246 (Solomon 34, James 45, Hynes 63 not out; Cotton three for 44, Grimmett four for 53).
Second innings: Five for 156 (McCauley 76, Barnes 33).

South Australia

K. L. Ridings lbw b Cheetham	28	C. L. Badcock c and b Hynes	98
R. S. Whitington lbw b Barnes	59	B 1, l-b 2, n-b 8	11
*†D. G. Bradman not out	135	(four wkts dec)	**349**
F. A. Ward c O'Brien b Hynes	18		

E. J. R. Moyle, P. Ridings, M. G. Waite, H. J. Cotton, C. V. Grimmett and R. A. Hamence did not bat.

New South Wales bowling: O'Brien 15–0–76–0; Hynes 16.3–0–86–2; Cheetham 23–0–104–1; Pepper 7–0–47–0; Barnes 8–2–25–1.

Umpires: G. Borwick and F. Lyons

SOUTH AUSTRALIA v VICTORIA   177 (255)

Played at Adelaide, February 24, 25, 27, 28 [1939]. Drawn. A catch by Fleetwood-Smith robbed Bradman of the chance of making fresh history, but rain probably deprived Victoria of the Shield and gave the trophy to their opponents. Hassett scored another century for Victoria [his fourth of the season] and on the second day [17,777] spectators assembled to see Bradman attempt to increase the sequence of his centuries to seven. They were disappointed, Thorn taking his wicket for five. ... The loss of the last two days through rain was cruel luck for Victoria, who needed only a win on the first innings to gain the championship.

Victoria

*K. E. Rigg, I. S. Lee, R. G. Gregory, A. L. Hassett, F. W. Sides, G. Tamblyn, †B. A. Barnett, R. B. Scott, E. L. McCormick, F. Thorn and L. O'B. Fleetwood-Smith.

First innings: 321 (Rigg 78, Gregory 33, Hassett 102, Barnett 51; Ward four for 57).

South Australia

R. S. Whitington b Scott	18	P. L. Ridings lbw b McCormick	12
K. L. Ridings lbw b Thorn	14	†J. A. J. Horsell lbw b Fleetwood-Smith	29
*D. G. Bradman c Fleetwood-Smith b Thorn	5	F. A. Ward not out	2
C. L. Badcock c Lee b Scott	14	B 6, l-b 2, n-b 7	15
R. A. Hamence lbw b Fleetwood-Smith	35	(seven wkts)	**207**
M. G. Waite not out	63		

C. V. Grimmett and H. J. Cotton did not bat.

Victoria bowling: McCormick 16–2–45–1; Scott 15–1–49–2; Thorn 16–2–51–2; Fleetwood-Smith 14–1–34–2; Gregory 2–0–13–0.

Umpires: J. D. Scott and A.G. Jenkins

1939-40

Waiting to bat for New South Wales, early 1930s.

1939-40

The outbreak of war in September 1939 cast a shadow over the Australian season then in prospect, but at the express wish of high Government officials the Sheffield Shield tournament was played to a finish. This effort to sustain the morale of the people, by taking their thoughts away from the serious international happenings for a few hours in the peaceful surroundings of the cricket field, earned so much public appreciation that crowds reached quite remarkable dimensions. The three home matches of New South Wales attracted aggregate attendances of 144,808, with receipts £9,115 9s. 9d. The gate for the match against South Australia totalled 75,765, with takings £4,915 1s. 6d. – figures which set up new records for Sheffield Shield matches at Sydney. Games in other States also were well patronised.

Cricket was particularly keen, the destination of the Shield not being settled until the last match of the series. The fortunes of the States underwent a dramatic change in the second half of the season. South Australia, having won their three matches at Adelaide, commenced their Eastern tour justifiably confident of retaining the Shield; but New South Wales, after early reverses, recovered splendidly and in an exciting finish to the competition deprived the holders of the trophy. Victoria, close contenders until the last, were placed third, and Queensland finished fourth. ...

O'Reilly's prominence as a bowler [he took 52 wickets for New South Wales in Shield matches at 13.55 runs apiece] was equalled, if not excelled, by the mastery of Don Bradman as leading batsman in the competition. The South Australia captain enjoyed another wonderful season, and for the first time in a Sheffield Shield season scored over 1,000 runs. His aggregate was 1,062, and his average 132.75, with 267 against Victoria at Melbourne and 251 and 90, both not out, v New South Wales at Adelaide the principal performances. Against Queensland, at Adelaide, Bradman scored 138, and outside Shield games he put together innings of 209 not out and 135 in two matches with Western Australia at Perth. Altogether in first-class cricket Bradman scored 1,475 runs for an average of 122.91, figures which render comment on the standard of his play superfluous.

From 'Cricket in Australia: Inter-State Matches, 1939-40'

SOUTH AUSTRALIA v VICTORIA   178 (256, 257)

At Adelaide, November 17, 18, 20, 21 [1939]. South Australia won by three wickets. The Shield holders showed a little superiority in batting over their opponents, who, however, did quite well after losing three men for 18 runs. ... South Australia, who began just as badly, gained a lead of 54, thanks to a century partnership between Bradman and Klose. Bradman, for the first time for many years [since December 1929, in fact], was run out. ... South Australia found themselves needing 310 to win, and it was just as well that Bradman was again in scoring vein. He stood firm, after early setbacks to his colleagues, and with Hamence hitting hard in an innings which fell one short of a hundred, the home State achieved their task.

Victoria

I.S. Lee, G.E. Tamblyn, A.L. Hassett, K.R. Miller, I.W. Johnson, D. Fothergill, *†B.A. Barnett, M.W. Sievers, D.T. Ring, R.B. Scott and L.O'B. Fleetwood-Smith.

First innings: 207 (Tamblyn 67, Johnson 33, Barnett 51; Cotton three for 78, Grimmett three for 67). *Second innings:* 363 (Lee 68, Hassett 89, Johnson 41, Sievers 56, Ring 31; Waite three for 76, Grimmett five for 118).

South Australia

R. S. Whitington c Fleetwood-Smith b Scott	0	–	b Fleetwood-Smith	27
K. L. Ridings c Sievers b Scott	6	–	c Ring b Sievers	1
*D. G. Bradman run out	76	–	lbw b Ring	64
R. A. Hamence lbw b Scott	6	–	c Sievers b Ring	99
C. L. Badcock lbw b Fleetwood-Smith	3	–	c Barnett b Scott	30
T. Klose c Hassett b Ring	80	–	lbw b Ring	0
F. A. Ward lbw b Fleetwood-Smith	1	–	not out	1
M. G. Waite c Miller b Sievers	67	–	not out	42
†C. W. Walker c and b Ring	4	–	b Ring	20
C. V. Grimmett c Sievers b Ring	9			
H. J. Cotton not out	1			
B 1, l-b 1, n-b 6	8		B 17, l-b 6, w 2, n-b 1	26
	261		(seven wkts)	**310**

Victoria bowling: *First innings*—Scott 11–0–55–3; Sievers 17–4–63–1; Fleetwood-Smith 14–0–59–2; Ring 18.4–1–76–3. *Second innings*—Scott 14–0–50–1; Sievers 14–3–40–1; Fleetwood-Smith 16–0–78–1; Ring 26–2–104–4; Johnson 4.7–0–12–0.

Umpires: J. D. Scott and A.G. Jenkins

SOUTH AUSTRALIA v NEW SOUTH WALES   179 (258, 259)

At Adelaide, December 15, 16, 18 [1939]. South Australia won by seven wickets. The superb batting of Bradman, who scored 341 without being dismissed, overshadowed everything else in a remarkable match. In his first innings of 251, scored at one run a minute, he included every possible stroke, and bowlers, with the exception of O'Reilly, were helpless. Bradman, who hit thirty-eight 4's and two 6's, often scored three times as fast as his partners, of whom Waite gave valuable support in a stand of 147. When South Australia wanted 155 for victory, Bradman dominated the cricket to such a degree that he almost reached three figures before the winning hit was made. ...

New South Wales

S. J. McCabe, *J. H. Fingleton, S.G. Barnes, C.M. Solomon, A.G. Chipperfield, A.G. Cheetham, C. Pepper, A. Roper, W. J. O'Reilly, †S. Sismey and J. Walsh.

First innings: 336 (McCabe 40, Solomon 131, Chipperfield 32, Cheetham 32; Grimmett three for 102, Klose four for 23). *Second innings:* 248 (McCabe 47, Barnes 33, Solomon 46, Chipperfield 57, Pepper 47; Grimmett six for 122).

South Australia

R. S. Whitington c Sismey b Roper	6			
K. L. Riding c Sismey b Walsh	29	–	b Cheetham	20
*D. G. Bradman not out	251	–	not out	90
R. A. Hamence lbw b Pepper	41	–	lbw b Pepper	12
M. G. Waite b Cheetham	46	–	not out	28
T. Klose c and b O'Reilly	4	–	b Roper	2
J. E. Tregoning b O'Reilly	0			
†C. W. Walker b O'Reilly	1			
F. A. Ward b O'Reilly	4			
C. V. Grimmett b O'Reilly	17			
H. J. Cotton absent hurt	0			
B 21, l-b 4, n-b 6	31		B 1, l-b 3	4
	430		(three wkts)	**156**

New South Wales bowling: *First innings*—Roper 14–0–83–1; Cheetham 15–1–80–1; O'Reilly 22.1–4–108–5; Pepper 9–0–56–1; Walsh 12–0–72–1. *Second innings*—Roper 3–0–26–1; Cheetham 7–0–33–1; O'Reilly 10–0–29–0; Pepper 8–0–31–1; Walsh 2.2–0–33–0.

Umpires: J. D. Scott and A.G. Jenkins. H.C. Newman last two days (Jenkins ill)

SOUTH AUSTRALIA v QUEENSLAND   180 (260)

At Adelaide, December 22, 23, 25, 26 [1939]. South Australia won by an innings and 222 runs. The power of their batsmen and the cunning bowling of Grimmett and Ward gave them overwhelming success. K.L. Ridings, Bradman, Badcock and Waite all reached three figures in helping to set up a record score for the Adelaide Oval. Ridings, a strong driver, shared with his captain in a second-wicket stand of 196. ...

South Australia

K. L. Ridings lbw b Baker	151	M. G. Waite c and b Dixon	137
T. Klose c Ellis b Cook	13	R. S. Whitington c Rogers b Christ	6
*D. G. Bradman c Hansen b Ellis	138	P. L. Ridings not out	44
R. A. Hamence lbw b Cook	6	B 10, l-b 17, n-b 2	29
C. L. Badcock b Dixon	236	(seven wkts dec)	**821**

C. V. Grimmett, F. A. Ward and †C. W. Walker did not bat.

Queensland bowling: Ellis 14–0–95–1; Cook 22–1–129–2; Dixon 24–0–142–2; Christ 27.1–3–144–1; Baker 22–0–127–1; Watt 14–1–135–0; Rogers 4–1–20–0.

Queensland

*W. A. Brown, G.G. Cook, T. Allen, R. Rogers, G. Baker, †D. Tallon, D. Hansen, D. Watt, C. Christ, P. L. Dixon and J. Ellis.

First innings: 222 (Allen 35, Rogers 49, Tallon 70; Grimmett four for 71, Ward five for 62). *Second innings:* 377 (Brown 156, Rogers 50, Baker 52; Grimmett six for 124, Ward four for 165).

Umpires: J. D. Scott and H.C. Newman

VICTORIA v SOUTH AUSTRALIA   181 (261)

At Melbourne, December 29, 30 [1939], January 1, 2 [1940]. Drawn. Insufficient time prevented South Australia hitting off the runs needed for victory. Another great innings by Bradman eclipsed everything else in the match. Ridings and Klose took the edge off the bowling in an opening stand of 108, and then their captain scored as he pleased. He used all the strokes in a masterly display which brought him 267 runs, including twenty-seven 4's, before Fleetwood-Smith, who received heavy punishment, took his wicket. ... [In their second innings] South Australia were set 179 to get. They were 118 behind with nine wickets left when the game ended.

Victoria

I.S. Lee, G.E. Tamblyn, A.L. Hassett, K.R. Miller, I.W. Johnson, P.J. Beames, *†B.A. Barnett, M.W. Sievers, D.T. Ring, R.B. Scott and L.O'B. Fleetwood-Smith.

    First innings: 475 (Lee 36, Tamblyn 38, Hassett 92, Miller 108, Beames 104, Ring 32; Burton five for 99). *Second innings:* 313 (Lee 39, Hassett 66, Beames 32, Barnett 46, Sievers 36, Ring 41 not out; Klose three for 43, Ward three for 102).

South Australia

K.L. Ridings c Johnson b Ring	56	–	not out	29
T. Klose b Scott	54	–	lbw b Ring	15
*D.G. Bradman c Johnson b Fleetwood-Smith	267			
C.L. Badcock lbw b Ring	58			
R.A. Hamence lbw b Fleetwood-Smith	20	–	not out	11
R.S. Whitington c Ring b Scott	41			
†C.W. Walker lbw b Scott	1			
M.G. Waite c Hassett b Ring	64			
F.A. Ward c and b Ring	26			
C.V. Grimmett c Sievers b Ring	6			
G. Burton not out	1			
B 6, l-b 9, w 1	16		B 3, l-b 1, n-b 1	5
	610		(one wkt)	**60**

Victoria bowling: *First innings*—Scott 25–0–135–3; Sievers 29–1–120–0; Ring 25.4–1–123–5; Fleetwood-Smith 27–0–156–2; Johnson 13–0–60–0. *Second innings*—Scott 3–0–9–0; Sievers 3–0–12–0; Ring 4–1–13–1; Johnson 5–2–14–0; Hassett 1–0–7–0.

Umpires: W.J. Craddock and A.N. Barlow

QUEENSLAND v SOUTH AUSTRALIA   182 (262, 263)

At Brisbane, January 6, 8, 9, 10 [1940]. Queensland won by two wickets. Following four successive defeats, their victory over the unbeaten South Australians was the sensation of the season. Victory was achieved after a first innings deficit of nearly 100. The introduction of Stackpoole, a fast bowler, played a big part in the surprising result. Stackpoole used pace which troubled everyone, including Bradman, who fell early in the match without scoring ... Grimmett took his 500th wicket in Shield cricket when beating Cook, and in keeping with Waite upset Queensland. Then, with Bradman finding his form in the second innings, South Australia left Queensland 350 to get ... and despite a spell when Grimmett took three wickets for four runs, the triumph was completed in an unfinished ninth-wicket stand.

South Australia

K. Ridings c Tallon b Stackpoole	35	–	b Stackpoole	1
T. Klose c Tallon b Stackpoole	27	–	st Tallon c Christ	31
*D. G. Bradman c Dixon b Stackpoole	0	–	c Tallon b Cook	97
R. S. Whitington b Gooma	38	–	b Stackpoole	0
R. A. Hamence c Stackpoole b Christ	26	–	c Brown b Christ	2
M. G. Waite c Christ b Stackpoole	13	–	b Dixon	62
E. J. R. Moyle b Stackpoole	32	–	b Dixon	6
†C. W. Walker b Stackpoole	37	–	b Christ	18
F. A. Ward c Tallon b Dixon	4	–	c Baker b Stackpoole	15
C. V. Grimmett b Dixon	12	–	not out	5
G. Burton not out	2	–	b Dixon	11
L-b 2, n-b 2	4		B 1, l-b 2, w 1	4
	230			**252**

Queensland bowling: *First innings*—Stackpoole 18.1–0–72–6; Cook 11–1–35–0; Dixon 16–5–33–2; Gooma 6–0–27–1; Christ 16–3–53–1; Baker 2–0–6–0. *Second innings*—Stackpoole 14–1–66–3; Cook 8–1–32–1; Dixon 10.3–2–33–3; Gooma 5–0–27–0; Christ 25–2–87–3; Baker 2–1–3–0.

Queensland

*W. A. Brown, G.G. Cook, R. Rogers, G. Baker, †D. Tallon, D. Watt, C. Bryce, G. Gooma, C. Christ, P.L. Dixon and J. Stackpoole.

First innings: 133 (Brown 37, Tallon 41; Waite three for 25, Grimmett four for 52). *Second innings:* Eight for 350 (Brown 111, Cook 54, Rogers 74, Watt 59 not out; Grimmett three for 116).

Umpires: S. Ryan and D. Given

NEW SOUTH WALES v SOUTH AUSTRALIA   183 (264, 265)

At Sydney, January 13, 15, 16, 17 [1940]. New South Wales won by 237 runs. By this magnificent performance they took a big step towards winning the Shield and at the same time practically extinguished their opponents' hope of retaining the trophy. The craft of Grimmett and the skill behind the stumps of Walker kept the New South Wales batsmen in check … [However] O'Reilly also found the conditions suitable for spin, and, with Bradman dismissed cheaply, South Australia finished 59 behind. Grimmett again bowled cleverly in the home side's second innings, but excellent batting … enabled New South Wales to set the visitors to get 371 for victory. Pepper and O'Reilly soon settled the issue. Including that of Bradman, caught by Carmody, a substitute, the fourth, fifth and sixth wickets fell at 85, and the end came quickly.

New South Wales

H. Mudge, M. B. Cohen, *S. J. McCabe, S.G. Barnes, A.G. Chipperfield, R. Saggers, A.G. Cheetham, C. Pepper, J.G. Lush, W. J. O'Reilly and †S. Sismey.

First innings: 270 (Cohen 74, McCabe 59, Barnes 34, Saggers 45; Grimmett six for 118, Klose three for 21). *Second innings:* 311 (Mudge 57, Cohen 70, McCabe 55, Saggers 57; Grimmett five for 111, Ward four for 120).

South Australia

K. L. Ridings b Lush	3	–	b Cheetham	1
T. Klose c Sismey b Lush	0	–	b Pepper	13
R. S. Whitington c Barnes b O'Reilly	37	–	c Chipperfield b Pepper	11
*D. G. Bradman lbw b O'Reilly	39	–	c sub b Pepper	40
C. L. Badcock c Mudge b O'Reilly	40	–	c Chipperfield b O'Reilly	20
R. A. Hamence c Mudge b O'Reilly	43	–	c Cohen b O'Reilly	0
M. G. Waite run out	9	–	c Mudge b Pepper	19
†C. W. Walker lbw b O'Reilly	1	–	c McCabe b Pepper	10
F. A. Ward b Pepper	17	–	b O'Reilly	1
C. V. Grimmett not out	7	–	b O'Reilly	6
G. Burton c McCabe b O'Reilly	7	–	not out	11
B 5, l-b 2, w 1	8		N-b	1
	211			**133**

New South Wales bowling: *First innings*—Lush 8–0–26–2; Cohen 5–2–9–0; O'Reilly 24.5–7–77–6; Pepper 27–3–85–1; Mudge 1–0–6–0. *Second innings*—Lush 4–0–13–0; O'Reilly 13.7–2–62–4; Pepper 12–1–49–5; Cheetham 5–1–8–1.

Umpires: G. Borwick and R. McGrath

WESTERN AUSTRALIA v SOUTH AUSTRALIA   184 (266, 267)

At Perth, February 10, 12, 13 [1940]. Drawn. Western Australia, who showed creditable form, found Bradman in brilliant mood. He was out just when seeming set in the first innings, but in the second he gave no chance in a great display. Driving, cutting, pulling and glancing, he was never at a loss for a stroke and put together a faultless double-century which occupied him little more than two and a half hours and included thirty 4's besides a 6. … Western Australia, with seven wickets in hand, were 158 behind when the game was given up.

South Australia

K. Ridings c Bandy b Halcombe	46			
T. Klose b MacGill	6			
R. A. Hamence c Lovelock b Eyres	3	–	b Eyres	14
*D. G. Bradman c Lovelock b MacGill	32	–	not out	209
L. Michael c Eyres b MacGill	5	–	not out	27
M. G. Waite lbw b MacGill	37			
V. R. Gibson c A. Jeffreys b Zimbulis	35			
J. Kierse c A. Jeffreys b Watt	23			
F. A. Ward c K. Jeffreys b Halcombe	15	–	b Eyres	12
C. V. Grimmett c Inverarity b Zimbulis	14			
†C. W. Walker not out	2	–	c Inverarity b Zimbulis	34
B 16, l-b 2, w 1, n-b 1	20		B 9, l-b 1	10
	248		(three wkts dec)	**306**

Western Australia bowling: *First innings*—Eyres 22–1–81–1; MacGill 18–1–49–4; Halcombe 13–0–51–2; Zimbulis 9–0–36–2; Watt 3–1–6–1; Barras 2–1–5–0. *Second innings*—Eyres 16–2–65–2; MacGill 15–3–66–0; Halcombe 9–0–59–0; Zimbulis 5–0–50–1; Barras 4–0–28–0; K. Jeffreys 2–0–28–0.

Western Australia

C. MacGill, A. Jeffreys, D. Watt, A. Barras, L. Bandy, K. Jeffreys, *M. Inverarity, †O. Lovelock, A. Zimbulis, G. Eyres and R. Halcombe.

First innings: 275 (MacGill 78, A. Jeffreys 36, Inverarity 57, Zimbulis 42 not out; Grimmett three for 94, Ward six for 105). *Second innings:* Three for 121 (Watt 52).

Umpires: J. P. Robbins and M. J. Troy

WESTERN AUSTRALIA v SOUTH AUSTRALIA   185 (268)

At Perth, February 16, 17, 19 [1940]. Drawn. Western Australia again gave a commendable exhibition, and received further object lessons in batting and bowling from Bradman and Grimmett. ... The Western Australia bowlers worked hard, but were allowed little encouragement. Klose and Ridings took the sting out of the attack and then Bradman scored easily all round the wicket in making 135. ...

Western Australia

C. MacGill, A. Read, D. Watt, A. Barras, *M. Inverarity, K. Jeffreys, L. Bandy, †O. Lovelock, A. Zimbulis, C. Puckett and G. Eyres.

First innings: 275 (Read 55, Inverarity 52, Bandy 30, Lovelock 45, Zimbulis 33; Grimmett five for 67). *Second innings:* 206 (Read 46, Eyres 39; Grimmett six for 57, Ward three for 81).

South Australia

K. L. Ridings c Barras b Zimbulis	34	V. R. Gibson c and b Puckett	21
T. Klose c Zimbulis b Eyres	60	†C. W. Walker b Puckett	3
*D. G. Bradman c Zimbulis b Eyres	135	F. A. Ward run out	8
R. A. Hamence run out	63	C. V. Grimmett not out	5
L. Michael c and b Zimbulis	10	B 4, l-b 6	10
F. Teisseire b MacGill	56		**429**
M. G. Waite c Eyres b Zimbulis	24		

Western Australia bowling: Eyres 23–3–79–2; MacGill 22–3–108–1; Puckett 24–4–89–2; Zimbulis 22–0–131–3; Bandy 1–0–12–0.

Umpires: J. P. Robbins and M. J. Troy

NEW SOUTH WALES v REST OF AUSTRLIA 186 (269, 270)
(PATRIOTIC MATCH)

At Sydney, March 8, 9, 11 [1940]. New South Wales won by two wickets. The match, which realised £1,471 15s. 9d. for patriotic funds [servicemen in uniform were admitted for half-price], produced grand batting displays by Hassett and McCabe, and some splendid bowling by Grimmett. ...

Rest of Australia

I. S. Lee c and b Cheetham	0	–	c Saggers b Cheetham	14
W. A. Brown c Saggers b Pepper	35	–	run out	97
*D. G. Bradman c Saggers b O'Reilly	25	–	c McCool b Cheetham	2
A. L. Hassett c Mudge b Cheetham	136	–	b Pepper	75
R. Rogers c O'Reilly b Lush	25	–	c and b McCool	17
M. G. Waite c McCabe b O'Reilly	5	–	c O'Reilly b Cohen	12
I. W. Johnson b Pepper	12	–	c McCool b Cheetham	8
†D. Tallon b Pepper	0	–	c and b Cohen	8
D. T. Ring c Mudge b O'Reilly	2	–	c McCool b Cohen	14
C. V. Grimmett c McCabe b Cheetham	27	–	c McCool b Cohen	0
R. Barry-Scott not out	13	–	not out	2
Extras	9		Extras	3
	289			**252**

New South Wales bowling: *First innings*—Lush 6–0–34–1; Cheetham 9–2–41–3; O'Reilly 18–4–78–3; Pepper 17–1–102–3; Cohen 2–0–25–0. *Second innings*—Cheetham 11–0–43–3; O'Reilly 8–0–49–0; Pepper 14–0–81–1; Cohen 7.7–1–25–4; McCool 9–1–51–1.

New South Wales

M. Cohen, H. Mudge, S.G. Barnes, *S.J. McCabe, C.M. Solomon, †R. Saggers, A.G. Cheetham, C. McCool, C. Pepper, J.G. Lush and W.J. O'Reilly.

First innings: 219 (McCabe 72, Cheetham 58; Waite three for 12, Grimmett five for 65). *Second innings:* Eight for 323 (Cohen 67, Barnes 46, McCabe 96, Saggers 32; Grimmett five for 130).

Umpires: G. Borwick and R. McGrath

1940–46

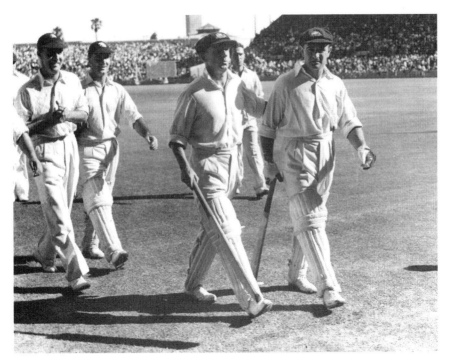

Barnes and Bradman walking in for tea in the Second Test against England at Sydney, December 1946. Both went on to score 234 and share a record fifth-wicket partnership of 405.

1940-41

Ten inter-State matches, and a game between teams captained by D.G. Bradman and S.J. McCabe, took the place of the Sheffield Shield tournament in the second war-time season in Australia. ...

D.G. Bradman, an Army lieutenant, played in only one match for South Australia, and his inability to turn out regularly had its effect on the side. Short of practice, Bradman failed in both innings against Victoria at Adelaide and on his other appearance against McCabe's team. Twice he was out first ball!

From 'Cricket in Australia 1940-41'

In Australia, inter-State matches have been played for charity. Don Bradman enlisted in the Australian Royal Air Force, but later was transferred to the Army School of Physical and Recreational Training. On Christmas Day 1940 he was bowled out first ball in a match at Adelaide. We have not found that secret.

From 'Notes on the 1940 Season', by R.C. Robertson-Glasgow,
Wisden 1941

SOUTH AUSTRALIA v VICTORIA 187 (271, 272)

At Adelaide, December 25, 26, 27, 28 [1940]. South Australia won by 175 runs. Bradman, given special Army leave to play, failed in both innings. On the opening day he was out first ball [the third ball of the innings], and Sievers, who made the catch, enjoyed the satisfaction of bowling Bradman cheaply in the second innings. ...

South Australia

K. Ridings run out	0	–	c Hassett b Seivers	17
C. L. Badcock c Sievers b Dempster	25	–	c Dudley b Sievers	172
*D. G. Bradman c Sievers b Dudley	0	–	b Sievers	6
R. A. Hamence c Baker b Dudley	85	–	c Baker b Dempster	62
B. H. Leak c Ring b Sievers	12	–	b Dudley	6
M. G. Waite lbw b Sievers	2	–	c Johnson b Dempster	20
P. Ridings lbw b Ring	2	–	lbw b Ring	90
†C. W. Walker c Baker b Johnson	40	–	c Meikle b Ring	4
C. V. Grimmett run out	2	–	c and b Johnson	31
F. A. Ward c Hassett b Sievers	10	–	c Baker b Dempster	4
H. J. Cotton not out	9	–	not out	2
Extras	4		Extras	7
	191			**421**

Victoria bowling: *First innings*—Dudley 7–0–34–2; Sievers 11.4–1–45–3; Ring 9–1–32–1; Johnson 3–0–8–1; Dempster 6–0–21–1; Meikle 8–0–47–0. *Second innings*—Dudley 11–2–38–1; Sievers 25–1–104–3; Ring 11–0–67–2; Johnson 8–0–66–1; Dempster 15–1–66–3; Meikle 4–0–26–0; Fothergill 6–0–40–0; Hassett 1–0–7–0.

Victoria

I.S. Lee, G. Tamblyn, D.T. Ring, R. Dempster, *A.L. Hassett, D. Fothergill, M.W. Sievers, G. Meikle, I.W. Johnson, †E.A. Baker and W. Dudley.

First innings: 172 (Ring 72; Cotton four for 39, Grimmett three for 54). *Second innings:* 265 (Hassett 113, Sievers 31; Grimmett four for 75, Ward three for 86).

Umpires: J.D. Scott and L.A. Smith

D.G. BRADMAN'S TEAM v S.J. McCABE'S TEAM 188 (273, 274)

At Melbourne, January 1, 2, 3, 4 [1941]. McCabe's Team won by an innings and 103 runs. The failure of Bradman, apparently out of practice, proved a great disappointment for the crowd. For the second match in succession he was out first ball. A mistimed stroke to backward-point cost him his wicket in the first innings and he played on in the second before he could settle down. ... Bradman's side, following on 244 behind, struggled on a rain-damaged wicket which O'Reilly and Grimmett fully exploited.

S.J. McCabe's Team

I.S. Lee, C.L. Badcock, S.G. Barnes, R. Rogers, *S.J. McCabe, †D. Tallon, K.R. Miller, M.W. Sievers, C.V. Grimmett, W.J. O'Reilly and J. Ellis.

First innings: Nine for 449 dec (Badcock 105, Barnes 137, Sievers 55 not out, sundries 36; Waite three for 84).

D.G. Bradman's Team

W.A. Brown c O'Reilly b Ellis	13	–	c Barnes b O'Reilly	16
K. Ridings lbw b Ellis	50	–	c Tallon b Miller	5
*D.G. Bradman c sub b Ellis	0	–	b O'Reilly	12
R.A. Hamence c Lee b O'Reilly	73	–	st Tallon b Grimmett	35
A.L. Hassett c Rogers b Grimmett	31	–	c Ellis b Grimmett	20
†R. Saggers not out	13	–	lbw b Grimmett	5
M.G. Waite c Miller b O'Reilly	15	–	c Barnes b O'Reilly	18
V. Jackson lbw b O'Reilly	0	–	c sub b Grimmett	14
C. Pepper c Badcock b O'Reilly	1	–	lbw b O'Reilly	10
R.B. Scott st Tallon b Grimmett	1	–	lbw b O'Reilly	0
V. Trumper lbw b Grimmett	0	–	not out	1
Extras	8		Extras	5
	205			**141**

S.J. McCabe's Team bowling: *First innings*—Ellis 10–2–23–3; McCabe 5–1–10–0; O'Reilly 14–2–41–4; Grimmett 22–1–100–3; Barnes 5–0–23–0. *Second innings*—Ellis 4–0–13–0; O'Reilly 10–1–53–5; Grimmett 8–0–46–4; Miller 6–0–24–1.

Umpires: A.N. Barlow and W.J. Craddock

1941–1945

Only one match in the 1941-42 Australian Inter-State Patriotic Competition took place before the war situation caused the abandonment of the tournament, Queensland beating New South Wales by 19 runs at Brisbane at the end of November. ...

From: 'Cricket in Australia: Inter-State Patriotic Competition, 1941-42'

Three two-day representative games at Christmas provided Australian enthusiasts with the first important cricket since Japan entered the war. Sponsored by the Services, the matches, which were played at Adelaide, Melbourne and Sydney, yielded excellent entertainment, and the public showed their appreciation of the opportunity to welcome back noted players now in uniform. Bradman, convalescing after fibrositis of the back muscles which caused his discharge from the Army in May 1941, did not play cricket, although he enjoyed some golf and tennis. ...

From 'Cricket in Australia 1942-43'

AN AUSTRALIAN APPRECIATION

By Don Bradman

Sent by Airgraph from Adelaide, November 23 [1943]

The present war has already taken heavy toll of gallant men who, after faithfully serving their countries on the cricket field in peace-time, have laid down their lives for a greater cause. Of those who have fallen, Hedley Verity was perhaps the most illustrious, and from the Dominion of Australia I feel it my sad duty to join with cricketers of the Motherland in expressing sorrow that we shall not again see him on our playing fields.

It could truthfully be claimed that Hedley Verity was one of the greatest if not THE greatest left-hand bowler of all time. Most certainly he could lay just claim to that honour during the 1918-1939 period. No doubt his Yorkshire environment was of great assistance for left-hand bowling seems to be in the blood of Yorkshiremen. It is one of their traditions and inalienable rights to possess the secrets of the art.

Although not a young man from a cricketing standpoint when the call came, Verity was little if any beyond the zenith of his powers. He was always such a keen student of the game, and his bowling was of such a type, that brains and experience played perhaps a greater part in his success than natural genius.

Although opposed to him in many Tests, I could never claim to have completely fathomed his strategy, for it was never static nor mechanical.

Naturally he achieved his most notable successes when wickets were damp. Nobody privileged to witness that famous Test at Lord's in 1934 (least of all the Australian batsmen) will forget a performance to which even the statistics could not do justice. But it would be ungenerous to suggest that he needed assistance from the wicket, as his successful Australian tours will confirm. The ordinary left-hander who lacks the vicious unorthodox finger-spin of the Fleetwood-Smith variety needs uncommon ability to achieve even moderate success in Australia, yet Verity was the foundation stone of England's bowling in both countries during his era.

Apart from his special department of the game, Verity could also claim to be a remarkably efficient fieldsman close to the wicket where safe hands and courage are greater attributes than agility. Add this to the fact that once he opened a Test Match innings for England, not without success, and we have a fairly general picture of a really fine player.

Those of us who played against this swarthy, capless champion (I never remember having seen him wear a cap) probably appreciated his indomitable fighting spirit even more than his own colleagues. We knew, when war came, that he would plainly see his duty in the same way as he regarded it his duty to win cricket matches for Yorkshire no less than England.

During our association together I cannot recall having heard Verity utter a word of complaint or criticism. If reports of his final sacrifice be correct, and I believe they are, he maintained this example right to the end.

His life, his skill, his service all merited the highest honour, and with great sorrow I unhesitatingly pay humble tribute to his memory.

[Captain Hedley Verity, the Green Howards, died a prisoner of war in Italy of wounds received in the Eighth Army's first attack on the German positions at Catania, in Sicily. He had been reported wounded and missing, and the news of his death, on July 31, 1943, was received on September 1, exactly four years after he had played his last match for Yorkshire and, at Hove, taken seven Sussex wickets for nine runs in one innings. Sir Donald Bradman's tribute appeared in the 1944 *Wisden* as part of a full obituary article by R. C. Robertson-Glasgow.]

Thus the present gives us little indication as to the future, except that there is every probability that batting gaps will be filled adequately – apart, of course, from Bradman. ... Bradman has not played cricket for a few years, and is not, I think, a prospect for the next tour. His back trouble, which caused his discharge from the Army, was symptomatic of a general breakdown in health, the result no doubt of extraordinary cricketing efforts, which so strained his nervous system and depleted his physical resources that his medical adviser forbade him to take part in strenuous activities, ordering complete rest.

At the same time, it can now be disclosed that he would not have toured England again as captain had there been no war. He told me this during our trip home in 1938, and no argument could move him. Even then, he was feeling the strain of making both centuries and speeches, and he was most definite that he would not be capable again of representing his country in such a capacity, either to his own satisfaction or in the manner expected of him.

Thus we must face the position that the greatest run-getter and amazing box-office attraction probably has made his last appearance on the Test Match stage. Cricket did much for Bradman, but he did much for cricket, and his going leaves a gap that will not easily be filled.

Whether he will play again for his club or State is a matter which cannot be determined now. Bradman himself does not feel that it is a time to talk of his cricketing future while the nation is fighting a 'life and death' war. He is, however, generally better in health though occasional setbacks are a worry. Evidently when he talked in 1938 of the future, he felt doubts about his health, doubts which would appear justified by events.

My mind goes back to 1926, when the [New South Wales] Selection Committee, of which I was a member, brought him to Sydney for a trial. He came to my office. I opened the door and a lad said: 'Are you Mr Moyes? I'm Don Bradman!' Twelve years later I listened to this country lad make speeches in England that were surely among the finest ever made by a cricketer. I saw him lead Australia, make centuries by the dozen, but the picture that remains is that of the lad who said so quietly: 'I'm Don Bradman.'

To me he has never changed. I believe that no one received more of his confidence in matters of cricket, and he was always the sportsman. Bradman was subjected to criticisms; that is inevitable with anyone who is great, but for the most part they were conceived in jealousy and nurtured in ignorance. Donald George Bradman was in the highest degree a 'cricketer'.

From 'Australian Survey: Bradman – Past, Present and Future', by Lieut. Col. A.G. Moyes, *Wisden 1945*

To those who seek to excuse laggard running [between the wickets] by the claim that it conserves a batsman's energy during a long innings I would quote the example of Bradman. He played long innings more consistently than any other batsman. Yet throughout them, in Test and lesser matches alike, he was an unsparing runner. His exceptional judgment, allied to speed between the wickets, gave him many runs which would have been missed by most other players. He … made the most of his own and his partner's strokes.

From 'Seeing Cricket After Four Years', by E. M. Wellings, *Wisden 1945*

1945-46

To many cricketers returning from various theatres of war, Australia's first post-war season presented early opportunity for inclusion in State sides alongside men of long experience. Although there were no Sheffield Shield matches, rivalry on the field was never lacking. The Australian Services, after their programme in England and India, kept together as a team and met the five States. They looked rather a tired combination and failed to win a match.

From 'Cricket in Australia 1945-46'

SOUTH AUSTRALIA v QUEENSLAND 189 (275, 276)

At Adelaide, December 24, 25, 26, 27 [1945]. Drawn. Complete indication of his all-round abilities was displayed by Colin McCool, who, after spinning out South Australia with figures of seven wickets for 106 [Tallon caught four and stumped one], scattered the field by carefree batting which brought him 172 runs, scored with a wide variety of strokes. ... Facing arrears of 208, South Australia improved at the second attempt and passed the century for the loss of one wicket before stumps were drawn.

South Australia: †R.J. Craig, C.R. Webb, R.A. Hamence, *D.G. Bradman, F.C. Bennett, T.E. Klose, G.R. Langley, M.G. Waite, P.L. Ridings, A.R.C. McLean and B. Dooland.

First innings: 365 (Craig 84, Webb 63, Hamence 37, Bradman c Tallon b McCool 68, Bennett 39; McCool seven for 106). *Second innings:* One for 110 (Webb 36 not out, Bradman 52 not out).

Queensland: *W.A. Brown, G.G. Cook, A. Carrigan, C. McCool, W. Morris, D. Watt, H. Pegg, V.N. Raymer, G.W. Lockie and P.L. Dixon.

First innings: Eight for 573 dec (Brown 98, Cook 76, Carrigan 67, McCool 172, Watt 40, Raymer 31 not out).

Umpires: J.D. Scott and L.A. Smith

SOUTH AUSTRALIA v AUSTRALIAN SERVICES 190 (277)

At Adelaide, December 29, 31 [1945], January 1 [1946]. Drawn. Thanks to Craig and Bradman, who between them contributed all but 66 of the total of 319, South Australia gained a narrow first innings lead of five runs. Hassett batted extremely well in the Services' second innings, and the State team, set to get 251 to win, finished 120 behind with nine wickets intact.

Australian Services: R.S. Whitington, D.K. Carmody, J.A. Workman, *A.L. Hassett, C.G. Pepper, A.G. Cheetham, D.R. Cristofani, R.M. Stanford, R.G. Williams, †S.G. Sismey and R.S. Ellis.

First innings: 314 (Whitington 77, Pepper 63, Stanford 59 not out, Sismey 35; Dooland five for 104). *Second innings:* 255 (Hassett 92, Cristofani 58, Stanford 57; Noblet three for 44).

South Australia: †R.J. Craig, C.R. Webb, R.A. Hamence, *D.G. Bradman, F.C. Bennett, L. Michael, T.E. Klose, M.G. Waite, B. Dooland, G. Noblet and J.L. Mann.

First innings: 319 (Craig 141, Bradman c Carmody b Williams 112; Pepper four for 100, Ellis five for 88). *Second innings:* One for 130 (Bennett 56 not out, Michael 54).

Umpires: J.D. Scott and L.A. Smith

1946-47

Donald Bradman receives three cheers at The Oval in 1948 on the occasion of his last Test match. It was also his last Test innings. Two balls later he was on his way back to the pavilion, bowled by Hollies's googly for a duck.

1946-47

Although the Sheffield Shield competition was dwarfed by the MCC tour, its revival, after six years' suspension through war, made inter-State rivalry keener than ever and the public following was equally stimulated. Victoria by all-round superiority were enabled to secure the trophy in impressive style, five matches being won outright and the other abandoned because of rain. ... Queensland created history by flying on their Southern tour; never before had a complete Sheffield Shield team travelled in this manner. ...

With Bradman playing only two State innings, one a century, South Australia fell away badly and failed to win a match. In Bradman's absence, P. L. Ridings led the side capably ...

From 'Overseas Cricket: Australian Inter-State Matches'

The MCC tour to Australia in 1946-47 resembled that of 1920-21, not a Test being won by England. In both cases English cricket had not recovered from the effects of world war. MCC were most reluctant to send out a team so soon after the cessation of hostilities, but so pressing was the invitation from the Australian Board of Control, backed in person by Dr H. V. Evatt, they gave way. To my mind MCC took the proper course. The presence of the English side not only revived cricket enthusiasm throughout Australia but, thanks to the great publicity given to the tour, cricket throughout the marvellous summer which followed in England received bigger public support than ever before. ...

Beyond question nothing went right for [England's captain] Hammond. Often when his men were battling hard and looked like establishing a promising position, an umpire's decision changed the whole complexion of the game. These incidents caused some friction and certainly bitter disappointment to the England team. Let me quote Ray Robinson, the Australian critic, writing in *The Cricketer*: 'More exasperating was the luck of the umpiring. Usually debatable decisions work out fairly evenly over a Test rubber, but weight of evidence suggests that the umpires were mistaken in giving Bradman not out caught for 28 in the First Test, Edrich out leg-before-wicket for 89 in the Third Test, and Washbrook out caught behind the wicket for 39 in the Fourth Test. These decisions came at such points in England's bids to gain an advantage that they could almost be termed turning-points of the three games. Dismissal of Bradman for 159 runs fewer – and four hours earlier – would have altered the course of the

First Test incalculably, and, perhaps, led to Australia having to play a second innings on the first of the sticky wickets. ...' I give his version because no one will accuse an Australian of possessing a disjointed view on decisions which meant so much to the victorious side as well as to the losers. ...

Whereas England brought seven players experienced in Tests against Australia, only Bradman and Hassett remained of the opposition. Yet they produced one of the best teams ever to represent them. For this happy state of affairs I am sure Australia were largely indebted to Bradman, their captain and one of their three Selectors. Early in the season Bradman looked far from well, but long days in the sun soon restored him to almost his old self. At first his batting, for Bradman, was uncertain. He has set such a high standard that one could not help being surprised at seeing him in difficulties; but, as in the past, his mammoth scores put Australia on top. Even more important was the way he moulded his men together, always encouraging them on the field and telling the bowlers what they should do. As a leader he clearly outshone Hammond, but I think Bradman would admit he was more fortunate than his rival in possessing so much talent at his command. ... There was no question as to which was the better side and, apart from Bradman, the Australians were a young team. They thoroughly deserved to retain the Ashes.

During the tour an MCC team travelled for the first time by air. The first flight, at night from Adelaide to Melbourne, was due to a railway strike. ...

From 'MCC Team in Australia', by Norman Preston

MCC TEAM v SOUTH AUSTRALIA   191 (278, 279)

At Adelaide, October 25, 26, 27, 29 [1946]. Drawn. By batting all the first day, Hutton and Washbrook gave MCC a grand start. The wicket was slow and neither batsman took the slightest risk. ... The Middlesex pair provided a contrast. Compton, hitting freely, outpaced Edrich in a stand of 111. Hammond ... closed the innings first thing on Monday morning. [Only Bradman and the wicket-keeper, Englefield, did not bowl in this innings.] South Australia naturally exercised care while facing such a formidable total. Bradman, looking rather frail, appeared in need of match practice during a stay of two and a half hours. After he was fourth out at 199 the side collapsed. Following on next day, the Australians found the MCC extremely smart in the field ... but Craig, a tall, slim batsman, saved his side by resisting the bowling for four hours and a quarter.

MCC Team

L. Hutton, C. Washbrook, W. J. Edrich, D. Compton, *W. R. Hammond, N. W. D. Yardley, J. T. Ikin, T. P. B. Smith, James Langridge, †T. G. Evans and R. Pollard.

First innings: Five for 506 dec (Hutton 136, Washbrook 113, Edrich 71, Compton 71, Yardley 54 not out, Ikin 35 not out; Dooland three for 142).

South Australia

R. J. Craig c Evans b Pollard	14	–	b Pollard	111
P. L. Ridings b Langridge	57	–	c Hammond b Compton	20
R. A. Hamence b Smith	0	–	st Evans b Compton	7
*D. G. Bradman c and b Smith	76	–	c Edrich b Pollard	3
R. James b Langridge	58	–	run out	15
K. Gogler b Smith	19	–	c Compton b Langridge	1
B. Dooland b Smith	12	–	c Hammond b Langridge	16
K. O'Neill c Evans b Smith	8	–	b Edrich	3
J. Mann b Langridge	3	–	not out	62
G. Noblet b Edrich	8	–	not out	25
†W. Englefield not out	6			
L-b 3, n-b 2	5		B 11, l-b 1, n-b 1	13
	266		(eight wkts)	**276**

MCC bowling: *First innings*—Pollard 26–8–66–1; Edrich 9.3–1–38–1; Smith 27–4–93–5; Langridge 20–2–60–3; Ikin 1–0–4–0. *Second innings*—Pollard 11–3–23–2; Edrich 10–1–37–1; Smith 19–1–70–0; Langridge 26–7–73–2; Compton 17–5–46–2; Hutton 1–0–6–0; Hammond 3–0–8–0.

Umpires: J. D. Scott and L. A. Smith

MCC TEAM v AN AUSTRALIAN XI 192 (280)

At Melbourne, November 8, 9, 11, 12, 13 [1946]. Drawn. This match, regarded as a Test trial for Australians, was spoiled by rain, which prevented any play on the first and fourth days. After the first blank day, MCC readily agreed to the game being extended to five days. As the wicket was always completely protected from the weather, it never became difficult. In his first outing against MCC, McCool showed his quality and made his Test place certain by dismissing the first six batsmen. With half the wickets down for 198 his analysis was five for 47. ... Saggers kept wicket magnificently, in contrast to Evans, who badly missed stumping Bradman off Compton when the Australian captain was 78. Bradman showed that he remained a master, and he inspired the young left-hander, Morris, who hit a century when first appearing against MCC. ...

MCC Team

L. Hutton, C. Washbrook, W. J. Edrich, D. Compton, *W. R. Hammond, N. W. D. Yardley, J. T. Ikin, †T. G. Evans, T. P. B. Smith, W. Voce and R. Pollard.

First innings: 314 (Hutton 71, Washbrook 57, Hammond 51; McCool seven for 106).

An Australian XI

M. Harvey c Ikin b Smith	22	J. Pettiford not out	27
A. Morris c Evans b Yardley	115	C. McCool not out	22
*D. G. Bradman c Pollard b Compton	106	B 1, l-b 1	2
A. L. Hassett c Hutton b Smith	28	(five wkts)	**327**
K. R. Miller c Evans b Smith	5		

J. Ellis, †R. Saggers, F. Freer and C. Puckett did not bat.

MCC bowling: Voce 27–2–98–0; Pollard 24–5–69–0; Smith 32–3–111–3; Ikin 3–0–13–0; Compton 14–3–26–1; Yardley 4–0–8–1.

Umpires: A. N. Barlow and R. Wright

SOUTH AUSTRALIA v VICTORIA   193 (281, 282)

At Adelaide, November 15, 16, 18, 19 [1946]. Victoria won by nine wickets. Miller, with one of the finest batting displays ever seen at Adelaide, and Tribe, who claimed thirteen wickets for 153, played themselves into the Test team. ... Troubled by a leg strain, Bradman did not field, but [in the second innings] he and Hamence put on 195 and helped to save the innings defeat. ...

South Australia

R. J. Craig b Tribe	36	–	c Hassett b Johnson	3
V. R. Gibson b Miller	5	–	b Tribe	1
P. L. Ridings lbw b Tribe	27	–	b Tribe	9
R. A. Hamence lbw b Tribe	2	–	c and b Freer	116
*D. G. Bradman st Baker b Johnson	43	–	st Baker b Tribe	119
R. James b Miller	73	–	c Meuleman b Ring	34
K. Gogler lbw b Tribe	36	–	b Tribe	33
J. L. Mann c and b Tribe	20	–	lbw b Tribe	5
B. Dooland c and b Tribe	2	–	not out	16
G. Noblet b Tribe	9	–	lbw b Tribe	1
†W. Englefield not out	4	–	b Ring	4
B 4, l-b 8, w 1	13		B 11, l-b 3, n-b 1	15
	270			**356**

Victoria bowling: *First innings*—Johnston 8–0–30–0; Freer 7–1–19–0; Miller 11–1–32–2; Johnson 20–4–55–1; Tribe 30.5–4–85–7; Ring 10–0–36–0. *Second innings*—Johnston 13–1–35–0; Freer 21–8–84–1; Miller 2–0–10–0; Johnson 14–3–43–1; Tribe 23–2–68–6; Ring 25–1–99–2; Hassett 1–0–2–0.

Victoria

G. E. Tamblyn, K. Meuleman, M. Harvey, K. R. Miller, *A. L. Hassett, I. Johnson, F. Freer, D. Ring, †E. A. Baker, G. Tribe and W. Johnston.

First innings: 548 (Tamblyn 75, Meuleman 87, Miller 188, Hassett 114; Dooland four for 229). *Second innings:* One for 79 (Miller 33, Hassett 36 not out).

Umpires: J. D. Scott and L. A. Smith

ENGLAND v AUSTRALIA   194 (283)
(FIRST TEST MATCH)   38 (58)

At Brisbane, November 29, 30, December 2, 3, 4 [1946]. Australia won by an innings and 332 runs. Whereas in past tours England enjoyed the good fortune of twice catching Australia on a sticky wicket at Brisbane, this time the tables were turned and England in each innings batted after a violent thunderstorm. So Australia gained her first Test victory in the Queensland city, and with confidence engendered from this initial success the Australians, under Bradman's vigilant leadership, went on to win the rubber. ... From the England team's point of view the whole course of the match balanced on an incident which occurred when Bradman was 28 and the total 74 for two wickets. Facing Voce, the Australian captain chopped the ball to second slip, where Ikin thought he made a perfectly good catch. Bradman survived the appeal, and not only went on to hit his first Test century against England at Brisbane but, with Hassett, he added 276 and established a new third-wicket record stand for these matches. Moreover, the Australians set up the highest Test total in their own country.

England began the match well enough after Bradman won the toss. From the third ball of Bedser's second over Morris was caught at first slip. Bradman entered, and immediately was in trouble against Bedser, edging the fifth ball of the same over to the slips and popping up the seventh to square-leg. Barnes, hooking brilliantly, did his best to shield Bradman from the bowling until at 46 he was splendidly caught at square-leg off a short ball. ... At this point Bradman had made only seven in forty minutes very shakily. There followed the Ikin incident. After lunch, taken with the total 77 for two wickets, Bradman and Hassett gradually wore down the bowling in the relentless heat. Bedser ... could not return after tea owing to stomach trouble ... Hassett always remained subdued, but Bradman found his true form, and the first day ended with Australia 292 for two – Bradman 162, Hassett 81.

Bedser reappeared next day, when Edrich broke the long stand by clean bowling Bradman with his fourth ball. Bradman [batting for around six and a half hours] hit nineteen 4's. ...

Rain and bad light limited cricket on Monday to ninety-nine minutes. Bradman did not have the pitch mown and Australia lost their five remaining wickets for 50 runs. ... England now faced Lindwall and Miller; both occasionally pitched short. During lunch the sky became overcast and thunder was heard when, with the second ball after the interval, Lindwall bowled Hutton playing back. Bad light and showers caused many stoppages, and the day ended with England 21 for one wicket. Late that evening a violent thunderstorm broke, and next day ... England on a nightmare pitch took their score to 117 for five wickets before another thunderstorm flooded the ground ... with hailstones as big as golf balls.

Contrary to expectations, the ground made a remarkable recovery next day in the brilliant sunshine, but the pitch proved more treacherous than ever, and, though England never gave up the unequal struggle, fifteen wickets fell in three and a half hours. So Australia won at ten minutes to five. An attack of chicken-pox robbed Australia of Lindwall, but Miller and Toshack were enough for England. The big shock was the fall of Hutton to the first ball of the second innings. He left to one of three catches by Barnes at short-leg. ... Toshack, the tall left-arm medium bowler, who was given plenty of advice by Bradman, responded so well that his figures were nine wickets for 99 runs. Except for the respite given by the rain, the heat was always stifling. ...

Australia

S. G. Barnes c Bedser b Wright	31		†D. Tallon lbw b Edrich	14
A. Morris c Hammond b Bedser	2		R. Lindwall c Voce b Wright	31
*D. G. Bradman b Edrich	187		G. Tribe c Gibb b Edrich	1
A. L. Hassett c Yardley b Bedser	128		E. Toshack not out	1
K. R. Miller lbw b Wright	79		B 5, l-b 11, w 2, n-b 11	29
C. McCool lbw b Wright	95			**645**
I. W. Johnson lbw b Wright	47			

England bowling: Voce 28–9–92–0; Bedser 41–4–159–2; Wright 43.6–4–167–5; Edrich 25–2–107–3; Yardley 13–1–47–0; Ikin 2–0–24–0; Compton 6–0–20–0.

England

L. Hutton, C. Washbrook, W. J. Edrich, D. Compton, *W. R. Hammond, J. T. Ikin, N. W. D. Yardley, †P. A. Gibb, W. Voce, A. V. Bedser and D. V. P. Wright.

First innings: 141 (Hammond 32; Miller seven for 60, Toshack three for 17). *Second innings:* 172 (Ikin 32; Toshack six for 82).

Umpires: J. D. Scott and G. Borwick

ENGLAND v AUSTRALIA
(SECOND TEST MATCH)

195 (284)

39 (59)

At Sydney, December 13, 14, 16, 17, 18, 19 [1946]. Australia won by an innings and 33 runs. ... When Hammond won the toss, most people expected a big score from England. The conditions were ideal, even if the pitch did prove responsive to spin. England's troubles commenced in the second over of the match, when Freer [in the Australian side for Lindwall] clean bowled Washbrook. Hutton and Edrich set out to repair the damage ... [but] with his third delivery Johnson got Hutton taken on the leg side by Tallon. That disaster occurred at twenty minutes to three, and in the next twenty-five minutes Australia virtually won the match when Tallon took two more catches off McCool which accounted for Compton and Hammond. So four England wickets were down for 99, McCool claiming two in less than three overs ... Johnson bowled his off-breaks so magnificently that at the end of seventy minutes, when given a well-earned rest, his analysis read eleven overs, eight maidens, three runs, one wicket. ...

Bradman, who limped badly the first day, did not field on Saturday, Hassett taking over the leadership. Within half an hour England were all out ... The Australian innings had been in progress only nine minutes when bad light, followed by an almost torrential downpour, held up the cricket for over three hours. ... Bradman preferred to rest his injured leg, and as soon as Johnson appeared Barnes repeatedly appealed against the light. At the fifth appeal the umpires gave way, and play ended for the day with the Australian total 27 for one wicket. ...

Brilliant sunshine on Sunday transformed the pitch, which rolled out perfectly on Monday when cricket took place in glorious weather. Biggest crowd of the match, 51,459, saw Barnes bat all day. ... Only three wickets fell this day, all to Edrich, as after Miller left at ten minutes to four, Bradman, without a runner, stayed with Barnes until the stumps were drawn with the total 252 for four wickets. Not before twenty minutes to six the following day did England break the Barnes-Bradman stand. Then, in successive overs, Bradman, who batted superbly despite a pronounced limp which must have been very painful, and Barnes were dismissed at the same total. Each hit 234, and they established a new fifth-wicket Test partnership record of 405. It was also a fifth-wicket world record for first-class cricket, and there was only one bigger in Test cricket, 451 by Bradman and Ponsford for the second wicket at Kennington Oval in 1934. Bradman batted for six and a half hours and hit twenty-four 4's. Barnes took ten hours forty minutes over his runs and hit seventeen 4's.

On the fifth day Australia forced the pace ... before Bradman declared, Australia again having made their highest Test total in their own country. The innings lasted eleven hours forty minutes. Twenty-four minutes remained before lunch, and in that time Hutton ... made 37 out of 49 before he unluckily hit his wicket when facing the last ball before lunch. ... The last day began with England 247 for three wickets, and Edrich went on to complete his first century against Australia. ... Apart from [Hammond and] Yardley, Australia encountered little more opposition and the match was all over by 3.15 pm ... Only once before had England been defeated twice by an innings in successive matches, and that was in 1897-98 when A. E. Stoddart's team toured Australia. The match drew an aggregate attendance of 196,253 ...

England

L. Hutton, C. Washbrook, W. J. Edrich, D. Compton, *W. R. Hammond, J. T. Ikin, N. W. D. Yardley, T. P. B. Smith, †T. G. Evans, A. V. Bedser and D. V. P. Wright.

First innings: 255 (Hutton 39, Edrich 71, Ikin 60; Johnson six for 42, McCool three for 73). *Second innings:* 371 (Hutton 37, Washbrook 41, Edrich 119, Compton 54, Hammond 37, Yardley 35; McCool five for 109).

Australia

S. G. Barnes c Ikin b Bedser	234	C. McCool c Hammond b Smith	12
A. Morris b Edrich	5	†D. Tallon c and b Wright	30
I. W. Johnson c Washbrook b Edrich	7	F. Freer not out	28
A. L. Hassett c Compton b Edrich	34	G. Tribe not out	25
K. R. Miller c Evans b Smith	40	L-b 7, w 1, n-b 2	10
*D. G. Bradman lbw b Yardley	234	(eight wkts dec)	**659**

E. Toshack did not bat.

England bowling: Bedser 46–7–153–1; Edrich 26–2–79–3; Wright 46–8–169–1; Smith 37–1–172–2; Ikin 3–0–15–0; Compton 6–0–38–0; Yardley 9–0–23–1.

Umpires: J. D. Scott and G. Borwick

ENGLAND v AUSTRALIA
(THIRD TEST MATCH)

196 (285, 286)
40 (60, 61)

At Melbourne, January 1, 2, 3, 4, 6, 7 [1947]. Drawn. England put up a much better show in this game, but experienced astonishing ill-luck. On the eve of the match James Langridge, who was among the twelve chosen men, strained a groin muscle while taking a catch at fielding practice. That mishap put him out for the rest of the tour excepting one game at Adelaide. Bradman won the toss and England suffered two tremendous handicaps. Within half an hour Edrich, fielding at short-leg, received a frightful blow on the shin from a fierce hook by Barnes, and he retired for the rest of the day. Soon after lunch Voce left the field with a pulled groin muscle. ... Despite the comparatively cheap dismissals of Barnes, Morris and Hassett, things looked bad for England when the total reached 188 for three wickets, Bradman again having lifted Australia out of trouble. Then with successive balls Yardley dismissed Bradman and Johnson. Bradman, feeling for an off-break, chopped the ball on to his stumps. So restrained was he during two hours fifty minutes that he hit only two 4's, a true indication of England's magnificent bowling in adversity. The next ball removed Johnson, leg-before, and with only four runs added Miller was smartly taken by the wicket-keeper. So in seventeen minutes the position changed to 192 for six wickets. Here McCool and Tallon gave an indication of Australia's immense all-round strength. [On the second day] McCool punished the bowling unmercifully ... [and] completed his first Test century ...

England began their innings just before three o'clock, and received an early shock when Hutton touched a beautiful ball from Lindwall ... into the hands of McCool, who made a very fine catch at first slip. ... The third morning [England resumed at one for 147] was the most vital of the match, and, to the bitter disappointment of the England team, they lost Edrich when he appeared to hit a ball from Lindwall hard on to his pads. Worse followed ... Compton, Hammond and Washbrook [also] being back in the pavilion for the addition of only 32 to the overnight score. ... Ikin and Yardley set about the task of retrieving England's fortunes and ... [in the end] Australia led by 14. ...

On the fourth day England captured only four wickets. ... The day brought new honours to Yardley, who in nineteen overs dismissed Barnes, Bradman and Miller. It was the second time in the match that Yardley removed Bradman and the third successive time in these Tests. Morris, the left-hander, batted all day while reaching 132, his first Test hundred ... [yet] when the seventh wicket fell at 341 England still stood a chance, but Tallon and Lindwall completely changed the situation with some of the best batting ever seen in a Test. The onslaught was violent, and in eighty-seven minutes they put on 154. ... Lindwall completed a magnificent century by going down the pitch and driving Bedser with tremendous power all along the ground to the sight-screen. ...

England wanted 551 in seven hours ... [but on the final day] rain caused four brief interruptions ... At times the light was extremely bad, but the England players never appealed, not even when Yardley and Bedser were struggling hard to save the game and rain was falling steadily. Twice Bradman suggested that they should go in before the players left the field. ... This was the first drawn Test in Australia for sixty-five years, but, although England averted defeat, failure to win meant that Australia retained the Ashes. The match proved a tremendous attraction. Vast crowds packed the large stadium. The official attendance aggregate was 343,675 and the receipts of £44,063 made a world record for a cricket match. ...

Australia

S. G. Barnes lbw b Bedser	45	–	c Evans b Yardley	32
A. Morris lbw b Bedser	21	–	b Bedser	155
*D. G. Bradman b Yardley	79	–	c and b Yardley	49
A. L. Hassett c Hammond b Wright	12	–	b Wright	9
K. R. Miller c Evans b Wright	33	–	c Hammond b Yardley	34
I. W. Johnson lbw b Yardley	0	–	run out	0
C. McCool not out	104	–	c Evans b Bedser	43
†D. Tallon c Evans b Edrich	35	–	c and b Wright	92
R. Lindwall b Bedser	9	–	c Washbrook b Bedser	100
B. Dooland c Hammond b Edrich	19	–	c Compton b Wright	1
E. Toshack c Hutton b Edrich	6	–	not out	2
N-b	2		B 14, l-b 2, n-b 3	19
	365			**536**

England bowling: *First innings*—Voce 10–2–40–0; Bedser 31–4–99–3; Wright 26–2–124–2; Yardley 20–4–50–2; Edrich 10.3–2–50–3. *Second innings*—Voce 6–1–29–0; Bedser 34.3–4–176–3; Wright 32–3–131–3; Yardley 20–0–67–3; Edrich 18–1–86–0; Hutton 3–0–28–0.

England

L. Hutton, C. Washbrook, W. J. Edrich, D. Compton, *W. R. Hammond, J. T. Ikin, N. W. D. Yardley, †T.G. Evans, W. Voce, A. V. Bedser and D. V. P. Wright.

First innings: 351 (Washbrook 62, Edrich 89, Ikin 48, Yardley 61; Dooland four for 69). *Second innings:* Seven for 310 (Hutton 40, Washbrook 112, Yardley 53 not out).

Umpires: J. D. Scott and G. Borwick

MCC TEAM v SOUTH AUSTRALIA   197 (287)

At Adelaide, January 24, 25, 27, 28 [1947]. Drawn. ... Hammond and Langridge put on 243 in four hours forty minutes. The return to form of both men, particularly Hammond on the eve of the Fourth Test, was most welcome ... and during his stay of six hours forty minutes he completed 50,000 runs in first-class cricket. ... A third-wicket stand of 203 by Ridings and Hamence ensured South Australia making a sound reply. ... Contributing to the weakness of the MCC was incessant no-balling. Nineteen times they were called – Voce nine, Wright seven and Pollard three – and the cost was 52 runs. ... The match was played in stifling heat with the temperature above 100.

MCC Team

L. Hutton, C. Washbrook, L. B. Fishlock, J. Hardstaff, *W. R. Hammond, J. T. Ikin, James Langridge, †T.G. Evans, W. Voce, R. Pollard and D. V. P. Wright

First innings: 577 (Hutton 88, Fishlock 57, Hammond 188, Ikin 35, Langridge 100; Dooland four for 67, Oswald three for 182). *Second innings:* Two for 152 (Hutton 77 not out, Hardstaff 40 not out).

South Australia

R. J. Craig lbw b Wright	10	†R. Vaughton c Evans b Voce	20
P. L. Ridings lbw b Voce	77	B. Dooland not out	23
*D. G. Bradman c Langridge b Wright	5	N. Oswald c Ikin b Voce	3
R. A. Hamence c Ikin b Wright	145	K. Webb b Voce	10
R. James b Hardstaff	85	B 12, l-b 3, w 1, n-b 14	30
R. M. Stanford b Hardstaff	31		**443**
V. R. Gibson b Hardstaff	4		

MCC bowling: Voce 26.7–2–125–4; Pollard 19–3–60–0; Wright 17–0–90–3; Ikin 13–0–60–0; Langridge 1–0–9–0; Hutton 8–1–45–0; Hardstaff 9–1–24–3.

Umpires: J. D. Scott and L. A. Smith

ENGLAND v AUSTRALIA
(FOURTH TEST MATCH)

198 (288, 289)
41 (62, 63)

At Adelaide, January 31, February 1, 3, 4, 5, 6 [1947]. Drawn. There were four extraordinary features about this Test. It was played in perpetual heat and dense humidity, with the temperature sometimes 105; Lindwall finished the England first innings by taking three wickets, all bowled, in four balls; and both Compton and Morris achieved the rare feat of hitting two separate hundreds. This was the first time for an Australian to accomplish this in his own country. ... In both innings Hutton and Washbrook gave England a splendid send-off with a three-figure stand, but after tea on the opening day Edrich, Hutton and Hammond were dismissed in a disastrous thirty-five minutes. ... Again England were upset by the slower bowlers, and it was not surprising that Bradman did not take the new ball at 200. ...

The second day provided plenty of thrills. ... [With England six for 455] Lindwall, after a rest and still using the old ball, held a sharp return catch from his first delivery [to end] Compton's finest display so far during the tour ... Lindwall then took the new ball, and in his next over bowled both Bedser and Evans off stump with successive deliveries; the next just missed the wicket and the fourth bowled Wright. ... Twenty-five minutes remained, and Bedser served England splendidly by causing Harvey to play on and then producing an almost unplayable ball that bowled Bradman for nought. Consequently Australia finished the day 24 for two wickets.

During the third day Australia made a complete recovery by adding 269 while losing only Morris – who hit his second Test century – and Hassett, who helped to put on 189 for the third partnership in nearly four hours. ... Miller and Johnson carried the score to 293 for four wickets before the close.

The heat was again almost overwhelming on the fourth day, when ... Australia went ahead. Miller, who offered three chances after passing three figures, remained unbeaten ... No sooner had Hutton and Washbrook opened England's second innings than a sharp thunderstorm accompanied by vivid flashes of lightning held up the game for twenty-three minutes. ...

On the fifth day, off the first three deliveries by Lindwall, Hutton and Washbrook got four runs needed to complete their second three-figure opening stand of the match ... then disaster occurred. Tallon, standing well back, held a snick from Washbrook. Some people thought the ball was scooped off the ground. ... [Next] Toshack caused such a collapse that by 5.15 pm eight wickets were down for 255. Compton alone of the recognised batsmen remained, and, shielding Evans from the bowling, he defied all Bradman's devices to remove him. At the close England were 274 for eight; Evans had not scored.

[On the final morning] Tallon failed to stump Evans off Dooland. Had this chance been accepted, Australia must have won, but, instead, England made such an excellent recovery that Hammond was able to declare ... [one ball] after lunch ... setting Australia to make 314 in three and a quarter hours. [Compton's unbeaten 103 was his fourth successive hundred in first-class innings.] Considering England's poor bowling resources and the experienced hitters at Australia's command, this was not an impossible task, but from the outset Bradman declined to accept the challenge. ...

England

L. Hutton, C. Washbrook, W. J. Edrich, *W. R. Hammond, D. Compton, J. Hardstaff, J. T. Ikin, N. W. D. Yardley, A. V. Bedser, †T. G. Evans and D. V. P. Wright.

First innings: 460 (Hutton 94, Washbrook 65, Compton 147, Hardstaff 67; Lindwall four for 52, Dooland three for 133). *Second innings:* Eight for 340 dec (Hutton 76, Washbrook 39, Edrich 46, Compton 103 not out; Toshack four for 76).

Australia

M. Harvey b Bedser	12	–	b Yardley	31
A. Morris c Evans b Bedser	122	–	not out	124
*D. G. Bradman b Bedser	0	–	not out	56
A. R. Hassett c Hammond b Wright	78			
K. R. Miller not out	141			
I. W. Johnson lbw b Wright	52			
C. McCool c Bedser b Yardley	2			
†D. Tallon b Wright	3			
R. Lindwall c Evans b Yardley	20			
B. Dooland c Bedser b Yardley	29			
E. Toshack run out	0			
B 16, l-b 6, w 2, n-b 4	28		B 2, n-b 2	4
	487		(one wkt)	**215**

England bowling: *First innings*—Bedser 30–6–97–3; Edrich 20–3–88–0; Wright 32.4–1–152–3; Yardley 31–7–101–3; Ikin 2–0–9–0; Compton 3–0–12–0. *Second innings*—Bedser 15–1–68–0; Edrich 7–2–25–0; Wright 9–0–49–0; Yardley 13–0–69–1.

Umpires: J. D. Scott and G. Borwick

ENGLAND v AUSTRALIA (FIFTH TEST MATCH)

199 (290, 291)
42 (64, 65)

At Sydney, February 28, March 1, 3, 4, 5 [1947]. Australia won by five wickets. So much rain fell before and during this final Test that it produced the best cricket of the whole series; because the pitch, without ever becoming treacherous, always encouraged bowlers. England could fairly claim that they experienced wretched luck. Hutton, after batting splendidly throughout the opening day while making his first Test century in Australia, was stricken down with tonsilitis that caused him to go to hospital. Rain prevented a ball being bowled on the second day; but Sunday was gloriously fine and the pitch, which had been under water – mushrooms sprang up in the outfield – dried quite firm. ... For the first time in the series England led on the first innings, but on the final day, at a most crucial point, Edrich, usually so dependable, dropped an easy catch off Wright offered by Bradman when only two and the total 47. Had that chance been accepted, victory might well have gone to England, for Bradman alone seemed able to establish any mastery over Wright and Bedser.

Following the blank Saturday, Hutton was taken ill, and on Monday ... Lindwall achieved a remarkable performance in taking seven wickets for only nine runs apiece. Undismayed by their moderate total, England bowled splendidly. The thermometer reached 102 [one degree less than Hutton's temperature when he went to hospital that same day], yet Bedser and Wright never spared themselves, and the fielding ... was also high-class. ... Wright came into his own by bowling Bradman and getting Miller taken at second slip. Bradman ran down the wicket and, misjudging the spin, missed the ball. ... Next day, while Bedser in eleven overs conceded only 15 runs and completely shut up his end, Wright carried all before him. In eleven overs he dismissed five men for 42 runs. ...

Batting a second time, England also broke down ... the day ended with six men out for 144 [and Hutton absent ill] ... The fifth day sufficed to bring about a finish. ... On a pitch so helpful to bowlers,

Australia's task of making 214 to win did not appear easy. ... Barnes and Morris ... understood the position and decided to get as many runs as possible while the effects of the roller remained good. Their progress was comparatively speedy, but at 45 Morris was surprisingly run out while going for a third run. ... Bradman scored two and then offered the shoulder-high catch which ... passed between Edrich's hands. In the next over Barnes [was out] and then Bradman and Hassett, with almost a day and a half before them, decided to tire out the bowlers. During their first fifty minutes together they made only 13, but when Wright and Bedser had to be rested Bradman promptly appreciated the change to Smith and Edrich. ... By the tea interval the total reached 110 for two, and Australia were almost safe ... and by sound batsmanship the third partnership took the total to 149 before Bradman lifted a drive into the hands of Compton at extra-cover. The Bradman-Hassett stand, by producing 98, turned the issue in Australia's favour ... [and they] won by five wickets just before six o'clock with a whole day to spare. ...

England

L. Hutton, C. Washbrook, W. J. Edrich, L. B. Fishlock, D. Compton, *N. W. D. Yardley, J. T. Ikin, †T. G. Evans, T. P. B. Smith, A. V. Bedser and D. V. P. Wright.

First innings: 280 (Hutton 122 retired ill, Edrich 60; Lindwall seven for 63). Second innings: 186 (Compton 76; McCool five for 44).

Australia

S. G. Barnes c Evans b Bedser	71	–	c Evans b Bedser	30
A. Morris lbw b Bedser	57	–	run out	17
*D. G. Bradman b Wright	12	–	c Compton b Bedser	63
A. L. Hassett c Ikin b Wright	24	–	c Ikin b Wright	47
K. R. Miller c Ikin b Wright	23	–	not out	34
R. A. Hamence not out	30	–	c Edrich b Wright	1
C. McCool c Yardley b Wright	3	–	not out	13
†D. Tallon c Compton b Wright	0			
R. Lindwall c Smith b Wright	0			
G. Tribe c Fishlock b Wright	9			
E. Toshack run out	5			
B 7, l-b 6, n-b 6	19		B 4, l-b 1, n-b 4	9
	253		(five wkts)	**214**

England bowling: First innings—Bedser 27–7–49–2; Edrich 7–0–34–0; Smith 8–0–38–0; Wright 29–4–105–7; Yardley 5–2–8–0. Second innings—Bedser 22–4–75–2; Edrich 2–0–14–0; Smith 2–0–8–0; Wright 22–1–93–2; Yardley 3–1–7–0; Compton 1.2–0–8–0.

Umpires: J. D. Scott and G. Borwick

1947-48

Bradman and King George VI at Balmoral at the end of Australia's unbeaten tour in 1948.

1947-48

A visit from India, the prospective tour of England by Bradman and his men, and Western Australia's achievement in winning the Sheffield Shield at the first attempt stimulated intense interest during the 1947-48 season in Australia. ... Bradman played only once for South Australia [in the Shield] and scored 100. ...

From 'Overseas Cricket: Australian Inter-State Matches'

SOUTH AUSTRALIA v INDIA   200 (292, 293)

At Adelaide, October 24, 25, 27, 28 [1947]. Drawn. The Indian bowling came in for severe punishment, but the batsmen acquitted themselves well, and the touring team came within 52 of victory with five wickets in hand. Niehuus and Craig, who each hit a hundred, opened with a stand of 226, and Bradman became the third successive man to reach three figures, but was lucky to escape at square-leg when 23. He completed a hundred at about a run a minute, and altogether hit twenty-two 4's in 156. ... When Bradman declared [a second time], India, wanting 287 to win, lost half their wickets for 60, but recovered splendidly, Mankad and Amarnath sharing in an unfinished stand of 175.

South Australia

R. D. Niehuus c Nayudu b Mankad	137	–	lbw b Phadkar	49
R. J. Craig b Sarwate	100	–	st Sen b Mankad	24
*D. G. Bradman c Sarwate b Mankad	156	–	st Sen b Mankad	12
R. A. Hamence c and b Mankad	31	–	b Phadkar	10
R. James c Mankad b Amarnath	3	–	c and b Phadkar	0
P. L. Ridings b Mankad	26	–	b Sarwate	17
†R. Vaughton not out	17	–	b Mankad	0
B. Dooland b Sarwate	14	–	b Phadkar	21
J. Noblet b Sarwate	1	–	not out	50
K. O'Neill not out	12	–	not out	23
B 16, l-b 5	21	–	B 9, l-b 4	13
(eight wkts dec)	**518**		(eight wkts dec)	**219**

N. Oswald did not bat.

India bowling: *First innings*—Phadkar 16–1–72–0; Amarnath 12–1–48–1; Mankad 36–1–127–4; Nayudu 9–0–62–0; Sarwate 16–1–83–3; Hazare 18–1–95–0; Sohoni 3–0–10–0. *Second innings*—Phadkar 15–0–59–4; Amarnath 2–0–7–0; Mankad 22–4–51–3; Nayudu 3–1–8–0; Sarwate 10–0–39–1; Hazare 7–0–26–0; Sohoni 6–1–16–0.

India

V. Mankad, H. R. Adhikari, G. Kishenchand, V. S. Hazare, Gul Mahomed, †P. Sen, *L. Amarnath, C. T. Sarwate, D.G. Phadkar, S. W. Sohoni and C.S. Nayudu.

First innings: 451 (Mankad 57, Hazare 95, Amarnath 144, Sarwate 47, sundries 31; Noblet three for 65). *Second innings:* Five for 235 (Mankad 116 not out, Amarnath 94 not out).

Umpires: G. S. Cooper and J. D. Scott

336

SOUTH AUSTRALIA v VICTORIA 201 (294)

At Adelaide, November 7, 8, 10, 11 [1947]. South Australia won by nine wickets. Bowlers were harshly treated on the first three days. Hassett batted delightfully for Victoria, his strokes in a faultless display including nine 4's and a hit for 6 which struck a woman spectator on the head. She escaped injury. … Victoria reached 440, to which South Australia's batsmen replied with scant respect. Bradman, scoring his ninety-ninth first-class century, made 173 with Craig for the second wicket …

Victoria

K. Meuleman, M. R. Harvey, *A. L. Hassett, R. N. Harvey, I. W. Johnson, S. J. Loxton, D. Fothergill, F. Freer, †E. A. Baker, D. Ring and W. A. Johnston.

First innings: 440 (Meuleman 30, M. Harvey 89, Hassett 118, Johnson 34, Fothergill 102; Ridings four for 66). *Second innings:* 182 (Fothergill 31; Noblet four for 19, Craig three for 37).

South Australia

R. D. Niehuus c Freer b Johnston	4			
R. J. Craig lbw b Ring	97			
*D. G. Bradman lbw b Johnson	100			
R. A. Hamence lbw b Ring	14	–	run out	27
R. James b Freer	27	–	not out	42
P. L. Ridings b Freer	151	–	not out	17
†R. Vaughton c Loxton b Johnson	14			
B. Dooland c and b Ring	62			
G. Noblet c Meuleman b Hassett	32			
N. Oswald not out	5			
K. O'Neill c Meuleman b Ring	4			
Extras	26		Extra	1
	536		(one wkt)	**87**

Victoria bowling: *First innings*—Johnston 33–5–94–1; Freer 34–4–87–2; Loxton 10–2–30–0; Johnson 34–7–89–2; Ring 46.3–3–176–4; Fothergill 2–0–11–0; Hassett 3–0–23–1. *Second innings*—Johnston 7–0–32–0; Freer 8–0–37–0; Ring 1.6–0–17–0.

Umpires: G. S. Cooper and J. D. Scott

AN AUSTRALIAN XI v INDIA 202 (295, 296)

At Sydney, November 14, 15, 17, 18 [1947]. India won by 47 runs, gaining their first victory of the tour over a side very little short of full Australian Test standard. The early stages went unfavourably, nine wickets falling for 229, but Kishenchand and Irani shared in a splendid partnership of 97. Bradman gave a glorious display in completing his 100th hundred in first-class cricket, but, although he made 172 and Miller showed good form, the last six wickets fell for 38 … Set to get 251 in two and a half hours, the Australians accepted the challenge, but could not cope with the clever left-arm spin bowling of Mankad …

India

V. Mankad, C. T. Sarwate, Gul Mahomed, V. S. Hazare, *L. Amarnath, H. R. Adhikari, K. M. Rangnekar, G. Kishenchand, W. S. Sohoni, C. S. Nayudu and †J. K. Irani.

First innings: 326 (Sarwate 32, Gul Mahomed 85, Hazare 38, Kishenchand 75 not out, Irani 43; Loxton three for 70). *Second innings:* Nine for 304 dec (Mankad 34, Sarwate 58, Adhikari 46, Kishenchand 63 not out, Sohoni 31; Johnston four for 71).

An Australian XI

R. Rogers run out	16	–	b Mankad	31
W. A. Brown c Hazare b Sohoni	8	–	run out	30
*D. G. Bradman c Amarnath b Hazare	172	–	c Sarwate b Mankad	26
K. R. Miller b Mankad	86	–	st Irani b Mankad	13
R. A. Hamence c Hazare b Sohoni	27	–	c Amarnath b Mankad	2
N. R. Harvey c Mankad b Hazare	32	–	not out	56
S. J. Loxton c Irani b Sohoni	0	–	lbw b Mankad	6
†R. A. Saggers c Irani b Sohoni	1	–	b Mankad	0
B. Dooland lbw b Mankad	5	–	c Kishenchand b Mankad	31
M. Herbert not out	26	–	c Gul Mahomed b Amarnath	1
W. A. Johnston c Irani b Amarnath	2	–	c Sohoni b Mankad	2
B 3, l-b 2	5		B	5
	380			**203**

India bowling: *First innings*—Sohoni 17–2–89–4; Amarnath 15.1–2–53–1; Mankad 24–2–93–2; Sarwate 16–0–51–0; Nayudu 4–0–19–0; Kishenchand 1–0–3–0; Hazare 14–1–67–2. *Second innings*—Sohoni 4–0–31–0; Amarnath 11–0–54–1; Mankada 12–0–84–8; Sarwate 2–0–24–0; Gul Mahomed 1–0–5–0.

Umpires: G. Borwick and W. J. Callum

AUSTRALIA v INDIA 203 (297)
(FIRST TEST MATCH) 43 (66)

At Brisbane, November 28, 29, December 1, 2, 3, 4 [1947]. Australia won by an innings and 226 runs. Unfortunate to be caught on a treacherous pitch, India collapsed twice, and the manner of their defeat must have resulted in loss of confidence for the remaining Tests. There was nothing wrong with the conditions when Australia batted first, and, after the early loss of Brown, Bradman gave one of his superb displays. He lost Morris at 97, but completely demoralised the bowlers by punishing methods which brought runs at a terrific rate. Not a ball could be bowled until five o'clock on the second day, but the surprising attendance of 11,000 watched the hour's cricket that took place. A further downpour saturated the pitch on the Sunday, but next day the sun appeared and India's task was hopeless. Realising the awkwardness of the conditions, the Australians soon declared. Bradman took four and three-quarter hours over 185, which contained twenty 4's.

With the ball doing all manner of unexpected tricks, India, used to the fast, hard pitches in their own country, were completely baffled. ... Toshack, with left-arm slow-medium deliveries, dismissed five men in nineteen balls for two runs. All out 58, India followed on 324 behind ... More rain restricted the fourth day to an hour, and nothing could be done next day, but conditions were not quite so difficult when play restarted on Thursday. ... Toshack, who again made the most of the pitch ... took eleven wickets [in the match] for 31 runs. ...

Australia

W. A. Brown c Irani b Amarnath	11	R. R. Lindwall st Irani b Mankad	7
A. R. Morris hit wkt b Sarwate	47	†D. Tallon not out	3
*D. G. Bradman hit wkt b Amarnath	185	I. W. Johnson c Rangnekar b Mankad	6
A. L. Hassett c Gul Mahomed b Mankad	48	E. R. H. Toshack not out	0
K. R. Miller c Mankad b Amarnath	58	B 5, l-b 1, w 1	7
C. L. McCool c Sohoni b Amarnath	10	(eight wkts dec)	**382**

W. A. Johnston did not bat.

India bowling: Sohoni 23–4–81–0; Amarnath 39–10–84–4; Mankad 34–3–113–3; Sarwate 5–1–16–1; Hazare 11–1–63–0; Nayudu 3–0–18–0.

India

V. Mankad, C.T. Sarwate, Gul Mahomed, H.R. Adhikari, G. Kishenchand, V.S. Hazare, K.M. Rangnekar, S.W. Sohoni, *L. Amarnath, C.S. Nayudu and †J.K. Irani.

First innings: 58 (Toshack five for 2). *Second innings:* 98 (Toshack six for 29).

Umpires: A.N. Barlow and G. Borwick

<table>
<tr><td>**AUSTRALIA v INDIA**</td><td>204 (298)</td></tr>
<tr><td>**(SECOND TEST MATCH)**</td><td>44 (67)</td></tr>
</table>

At Sydney, December 12, 13, 15, 16, 17, 18 [1947]. Drawn. The weather again proved unkind, less than ten hours' cricket being possible during six days. This meant there was little possibility of a definite result, although the Australians showed that they were equally as vulnerable as their opponents on a difficult pitch. ... [They] lost their first wicket in an unusual manner. In a previous match [at Sydney v An Australian XI] Mankad, the bowler, warned Brown about backing up too far, and when the batsman repeated this ran him out. [He also warned him in the Indians' match with Queensland immediately preceding the First Test.] This time Mankad gave no warning, and the first occasion Brown moved down the pitch too quickly the bowler whipped off the bails. The third and fourth days were blank through rain and, as could be expected, the saturated turf did not favour batsmen when the game restarted. Morris, Bradman and Hassett all fell cheaply, and despite brief resistance from Miller and Hamence ... the end came quickly, the last five batsmen being dismissed for 21 runs. Phadkar and Hazare made the most of the conditions and were almost unplayable.

Johnston (fast-medium left-arm) and Johnson (off-breaks) were just as effective when India batted again 81 ahead. Before play ended on the fifth day, seven wickets fell for 61 runs ... but all chances of a thrilling finish were dispelled when not a ball could be bowled on the last day.

India

V. Mankad, C.T. Sarwate, Gul Mahomed, V.S. Hazare, *L. Amarnath, G. Kishenchand, H.R. Adhikari, D.G. Phadkar, C.S. Nayudu, Amir Elahi and †J.K. Irani.

First innings: 188 (Kishenchand 44, Phadkar 51; McCool three for 71). *Second innings:* Seven for 61 (Johnston three for 15).

Australia

W.A. Brown run out	18	C.L. McCool b Phadkar	9
A.R. Morris lbw b Amarnath	10	R.R. Lindwall b Hazare	0
*D.G. Bradman b Hazare	13	†D. Tallon c Irani b Hazare	6
A.L. Hassett c Adhikari b Hazare	6	W.A. Johnston not out	0
K.R. Miller lbw b Phadkar	17	B 1, l-b 1	2
R.A. Hamence c Adhikari b Mankad	25		**107**
I.W. Johnson lbw b Phadkar	1		

India bowling: Phadkar 10–2–14–3; Amarnath 14–4–31–1; Mankad 9–0–31–1; Hazare 13.2–3–29–4.

Umpires: A.N. Barlow and G. Borwick

AUSTRALIA v INDIA
(THIRD TEST MATCH)

205 (299, 300)
45 (68, 69)

At Melbourne, January 1, 2, 3, 5 [1948]. Australia won by 233 runs. Bradman added to his long list of triumphs by hitting a hundred in each innings, the first time he had accomplished the feat in a Test Match. India fared reasonably well up to a point, but were again faced with ill-fortune with regard to the weather.

A third-wicket stand of 169 between Bradman and Hassett assured Australia of a good total. Hassett, missed in the slips off Hazare when 31, scored as fast as his partner, and at times runs came at two a minute. Bradman scored 132 out of 260, and on his departure the bowlers met with better reward, the last six wickets falling for 105.

When Mankad and Sarwate began India's reply with a stand of 124, the position was intriguing, but … rain overnight altered the state of the pitch, and when three of his batsmen fell cheaply Amarnath declared, although India were 103 behind. Bradman countered this move by sending in his tail-end men in the hope that conditions would ease. He must have been worried, however, when three of them fell for 13 and Barnes, one of his leading batsmen, followed at 32.

Any hopes India may have held of a complete collapse were soon dashed, for Morris and Bradman thoroughly mastered the attack and shared in an unbroken fifth partnership of 223. Bradman reached his hundred first and Morris followed suit just before the close of the day. Heavy overnight rain made the pitch responsive to spin, and Bradman, seizing his opportunity, declared. The India batsmen never looked like making a fight. Half the side fell for 60 and … the end was inevitable.

Australia

S. G. Barnes b Mankad	12	–	c Sen b Amarnath	15
A. R. Morris b Amarnath	45	–	not out	100
*D. G. Bradman lbw b Phadkar	132	–	not out	127
A. L. Hassett lbw b Mankad	80			
K. R. Miller lbw b Mankad	29			
R. A. Hamence st Sen b Amarnath	25			
R. R. Lindwall b Amarnath	26			
†D. Tallon c Mankad b Amarnath	2			
B. Dooland not out	21	–	lbw b Phadkar	6
I. W. Johnson lbw b Mankad	16	–	c Hazare b Amarnath	0
W. A. Johnston run out	5	–	lbw b Amarnath	3
Extras	1		B3, n-b1	4
	394		(four wkts dec)	**255**

India bowling: *First innings*—Phadkar 15–1–80–1; Amarnath 21–5–78–4; Hazare 16.1–0–62–0; Mankad 37–4–135–4; Sarwate 3–0–16–0; Nayudu 2–0–22–0. *Second innings*—Phadkar 10–1–28–1; Amarnath 20–3–52–3; Hazare 11–1–55–0; Mankad 18–4–74–0; Sarwate 5–0–41–0; Gul Mahomed 1–0–1–0.

India

V. Mankad, C. T. Sarwate, Gul Mahomed, V.S. Hazare, *L. Amarnath, D.G. Phadkar, H.R. Adhikari, Rai Singh, K. M. Rangnekar, †P. Sen and C.S. Nayudu.

First innings: Nine for 291 dec (Mankad 116, Sarwate 36, Phadkar 55 not out; Johnson four for 59). *Second innings:* 125 (Johnston four for 44, Johnson four for 35).

Umpires: A. N. Barlow and H. A. R. Elphinstone

AUSTRALIA v INDIA   206 (301)
(FOURTH TEST MATCH)   46 (70)

At Adelaide, January 23, 24, 26, 27, 28 [1948]. Australia won by an innings and 16 runs. Although they gained another overwhelming success ... the match was a personal triumph for Hazare, who followed Bradman's example in the Third Test and hit a hundred in each innings. Against such a powerful attack as that possessed by the Australians, this was a truly remarkable performance. To balance this, however, Bradman was once again in irresistible form, hitting a double-hundred. Hassett fell only two short of that figure and Barnes also completed a century.

Bradman gave Australia a big advantage when he won the toss for the third time; on a perfect pitch bowlers were helpless to check the flow of runs. Morris fell early, but Barnes and Bradman shared in a second-wicket stand of 236. ... Bradman, always the complete master, scored 201 out of 341 before leaving towards the close of the first day. ... An interesting race developed to see whether Hassett could complete 200, but he was just short, taking out his bat for an excellent 198. In reaching 674, Australia made the highest score ever recorded against India and also the biggest total for any Test Match in Australia.

India made a shocking start, losing two wickets for six runs, but they fought back well. Half the side fell for 133, but Hazare found a capable partner in Phadkar, 188 runs being added. ... Despite this gallant effort, India followed on 293 behind, and this time their start was even worse, two wickets falling without a run on the board. Six men were out for 139 and it looked as though India would capitulate easily, but Hazare again refused to be disturbed by the situation ... Six men failed to score in this innings, most of the batsmen finding the pace of Lindwall too much for them. ...

Australia

S. G. Barnes lbw b Mankad	112	I. W. Johnson b Rangachari	22
A. R. Morris b Phadkar	7	R. R. Lindwall b Rangachari	2
*D. G. Bradman b Hazare	201	†D. Tallon lbw b Mankad	1
A. L. Hassett not out	198	E. R. H. Toshack lbw b Hazare	8
K. R. Miller b Rangachari	67	B 8, l-b 6, n-b 2	16
R. N. Harvey lbw b Rangachari	13		**674**
C. L. McCool b Phadkar	27		

India bowling: Phadkar 15–0–74–2; Amarnath 9–0–42–0; Rangachari 41–5–141–4; Mankad 43–8–170–2; Sarwate 22–1–121–0; Hazare 21.3–1–110–2.

India

V. Mankad, C.T. Sarwate, †P. Sen, *L. Amarnath, V.S. Hazare, Gul Mahomed, D.G. Phadkar, G. Kishenchand, H.R. Adhikari, K.M. Rangnekar and C.R. Rangachari.

First innings: 381 (Mankad 49, Amarnath 46, Hazare 116, Phadkar 123; Johnson four for 64, Bradman none for 4). *Second innings:* 277 (Hazare 145, Gul Mahomed 34, Adhikari 51; Lindwall seven for 38).

Umpires: G. Borwick and R. Wright

AUSTRALIA v INDIA   207 (302)
(FIFTH TEST MATCH)   47 (71)

At Melbourne, February 6, 7, 9, 10 [1948]. Australia won by an innings and 177 runs. For the third time in the series they gained victory with an innings to spare. Bradman's luck with the coin continued, Australia batting first for the fourth occasion out of five, and once more the India bowling received scant respect.

Following the dismissal of Barnes ... Brown and Bradman were never in trouble until the Australian captain unfortunately tore a rib muscle and retired. ... Chief honours fell to Neil Harvey, a nineteen-year-old left-hander, playing in his second Test Match. He hit the first hundred of his career, showing the confidence of an experienced cricketer. ... Bradman declared attea-time on the second day.

Although India again lost the first wicket cheaply, they recovered well … [but none the less] followed on 244 behind. This time there was nobody to rescue them following the fall of the first wicket without a run scored, and a steady procession took place. … The last five wickets actually fell for 16 runs – a sorry end to the Test series for India, who could, with reason, complain of ill-fortune in most of the matches.

Australia

S. G. Barnes run out	33	†D. Tallon c Sen b Sarwate		37
W. A. Brown run out	99	L. Johnson not out		25
*D. G. Bradman retired hurt	57	D. Ring c Kishenchand b Hazare		11
K. R. Miller c Sen b Phadkar	14	W. A. Johnston not out		23
R. N. Harvey c Sen b Mankad	153	B 4, l-b 4		8
S. J. Loxton c Sen b Amarnath	80	(eight wkts dec)		**575**
R. R. Lindwall c Phadkar b Mankad	35			

India bowling: Phadkar 9–0–58–1; Amarnath 23–1–79–1; Rangachari 17–1–97–0; Hazare 14–1–63–1; Mankad 33–2–107–2; Sarwate 18–1–82–1; Nayudu 13–0–77–0; Adhikari 1–0–4–0.

India

V. Mankad, C. T. Sarwate, H. R. Adhikari, V. S. Hazare, *L. Amarnath, D.G. Phadkar, Gul Mahomed, G. Kishenchand, C. S. Nayudu, †P. Sen and C. R. Rangachari.

First innings: 331 (Mankad 111, Adhikari 38, Hazare 74, Phadkar 56 not out; Johnson three for 66, Ring three for 103). *Second innings:* 67 (Johnson three for 8, Ring three for 17).

Umpires: A. N. Barlow and G. S. Cooper

WESTERN AUSTRALIA v AUSTRALIAN TOURING TEAM
208 (303)

At Perth, March 13, 15, 16 [1948]. Drawn.

Western Australia: *D. K. Carmody, A. R. Edwards, T. M. Outridge, M. U. Herbert, A. D. Watt, C. W. Langdon, B. A. Rigg, †G. T. Kessey, T. E. O'Dwyer, C. W. Puckett and K. R. Cumming.

First innings: 348 (Edwards 57, Watt 32, Langdon 112, Rigg 65, O'Dwyer 31). *Second innings:* Three for 62.

Australian Touring Team: W. A. Brown, A. R. Morris, *D.G. Bradman, K. R. Miller, R. N. Harvey, R. A. Hamence, C. L. McCool, I. W. Johnson, †R. A. Saggers, W. A. Johnston and E. R. H. Toshack.

First innings: Seven for 442 dec (Morris 115, Bradman c Outridge b O'Dwyer 115, Miller 43, Harvey 79, Hamence 33 not out; O'Dwyer three for 99).

Umpires: J. P. Robbins and E. T. Tonkinson

1948

Losing the toss to England captain Norman Yardley at Trent Bridge before the opening match of the 1948 Ashes series. Not that it mattered: Bradman's Australians won by eight wickets.

1948

Replete with events that deserve permanent record in cricket history, last summer brought the most remarkable performance by any touring side, a close contest among the counties with the championship going to the youngest first-class county [Glamorgan], larger crowds than ever before assembling in England, and the biggest Benefits rewarding several of the professionals. All this despite much bad weather.

Beyond question the Australians took pride of place by going through the season unbeaten, and the honour of Knighthood bestowed upon their captain, now Sir Donald Bradman, came as a distinction never before awarded to a cricketer while still active in the game. In other parts of the book the tour is dealt with thoroughly, and the choice of five Australians as the Cricketers of the Year [Hassett, Johnston, Lindwall, Morris and Tallon], together with the special article on the captain detailing his career, conveys the wonderful way in which our guests dominated the proceedings. ...

These [previous] valuable references in the history of the long series of Tests between England and Australia are not meant in any way to belittle the doings of Bradman and his merry men, not only in the great representative encounters but in going through the season with a record unsullied by defeat. Truly the gallant captain proceeded from match to match with the happiest result no matter how the play seemed to be going against him. Surely he must have been born under a lucky star, with the most beautiful and effective sponsor in 'Dame Fortune'.

The tour might even have been stage-managed with Don Bradman the 'hero' and no 'villain' able to check his doings; he took his curtain after a century in the final first-class fixture and bowled the last over at Scarborough, where he received the honorary life membership of the Yorkshire County Club with a silver memento noting his wonderful Test Match performances at Leeds. And so to Scotland, where the King and Queen received him and the team – a truly great finale.

From 'Notes by the Editor' (Hubert Preston), *Wisden 1949*

When, announcing retirement from first-class cricket, D.G. Bradman claimed that the 1948 side bore comparison with any of its predecessors, he accurately reflected the majority of opinion on the nineteenth Australian team visiting England. In retaining the Ashes, held by Australia since 1934, these Australians enjoyed almost uninterrupted success, while becoming the first side to go unbeaten through an English tour: certainly they achieved all that could be expected of a combination entitled to the description great. Yet they gave cause for reservation of such sweeping judgment, as the Tests were by no means so one-sided as results suggested, and Yorkshire and Hampshire played themselves into positions arousing visions of the first Australian defeat by a county since Hampshire beat the 1912 team. Still, for the most part, victory followed victory so inevitably for the Australians that at times opponents took on an air of defeat almost before the match had been in progress more than an hour or two. Once or twice that impression extended even to the Tests.

A summary of their achievements proved the might of probably the most united Australian party sent to England. Not only did they win exactly half their thirty-four matches with an innings to spare, two by ten wickets, one by nine wickets, two by eight wickets and one by 409 runs, but eleven batsmen between them hit fifty centuries, and in first-class games seven of their seventeen players completed 1,000 runs, with Loxton only 27 short when he broke his nose while batting at Scarborough. Comparisons of totals reveal even more. The Australians made 350 or more in twenty-four innings whereas, apart from the Tests, the highest total against them was Nottinghamshire's 299 for eight. Twice the Australians failed to reach 200, but they dismissed opponents for less than that figure no fewer than thirty-seven times, and in seven innings for under 100.

After Bradman's team surpassed all records by winning four out of five Tests by a touring team in England, the theory that in international cricket winning the toss usually meant winning the match seemed to need the qualification that other matters should be equal, for Bradman guessed the spin of the coin correctly only once in the rubber. ...

For Bradman the tour provided the most fitting climax possible to an illustrious career. Apart from leading Australia to continued Test dominance, he made more hundreds than any batsman in the country and for the second time – he hit thirteen in 1938 – he emulated Trumper's performance of 1902 with eleven first-class centuries on a tour in England. In addition to this supreme batting ability, Bradman demonstrated his knowledge of the game in captaincy and generalship. Most pleasing to him must have been the warmth of the reception accorded him by crowds everywhere, particularly in his last two Tests, at Leeds and The Oval. The British public paid striking tribute to his popularity, and they made such big response to a newspaper fund for a Bradman testimonial that, after receiving a silver trophy, he asked that the surplus money should go towards the provision of concrete pitches similar to those on which he learned his cricket. ...

... To Bedser fell the unique distinction of dismissing Bradman in the first four Test innings, so making a sequence of five such successes – Bradman was out to Bedser in the final Test of the 1946-47 tour. On the first three occasions last season Bedser caused Bradman to send a catch to Hutton at short fine-leg, but after the Second Test Bradman could not again be lured into the trap when facing a late in-swinger pitched on the middle stump.

From 'Australians in England, 1948', by R. J. Hayter

WORCESTERSHIRE v AUSTRALIANS   209 (304)

At Worcester, April 28, 29, 30 [1948]. Australians won by an innings and 17 runs, with seventy minutes to spare. Despite cheerless, cold and sometimes showery weather, the visitors quickly settled down to English conditions. Lindwall took a wicket with the second ball of the match, but the pitch was more suitable to the slower men. ... Honours of the second day went to Bradman, who once again opened the tour with a century. These are his Worcester scores – 236 in 1930; 206 in 1934; 258 in 1938; and 107 in 1948. Following a stubborn first-wicket stand of 79, Bradman gave a fluent display, memorable for superb driving. He reached three figures in two and a quarter hours, and the second partnership added 186. Morris, the left-hander, enjoyed the distinction of scoring a century on his first appearance in England. ... Attendance 32,000 and receipts of over £4,000 were a record for Worcester.

Worcestershire

E. Cooper, D. Kenyon, C.H. Palmer, R.E.S. Wyatt, L. Outschoorn, *A.F.T. White, R. Jenkins, R. Howorth, R.T.D. Perks, †H. Yarnold and P.F. Jackson.

First innings: 233 (Cooper 51, Palmer 85, Howorth 37 not out; Johnson three for 52). Second innings: 212 (Palmer 34, Outschoorn 54; McCool four for 29, Johnson three for 75).

Australians

S. G. Barnes lbw b Howorth	44	A. L. Hassett c Wyatt b Jackson	35
A. R. Morris c Jenkins b Jackson	138	W. A. Brown st Yarnold b Howorth	25
*D. G. Bradman b Jackson	107	K. R. Miller not out	50
R. R. Lindwall lbw b Jackson	32	I. W. Johnson not out	12
C. L. McCool b Jackson	0	B 6, l-b 5, w 3	15
†D. Tallon b Jackson	4	(eight wkts dec)	**462**

E. R. H. Toshack did not bat.

Worcestershire bowling: Perks 26–3–95–0; Palmer 16–5–56–0; Wyatt 1–0–4–0; Jenkins 7–0–47–0; Jackson 39–4–135–6; Howorth 38–6–109–2; Outschoorn 1–0–1–0.

Umpires: F. Root and D. Davies

LEICESTERSHIRE v AUSTRALIANS   210 (305)

At Leicester, May 1, 3, 4 [1948]. Australians won by an innings and 171 runs. Miller, missed three times, hit the first double-century of the tour. He batted almost five and a half hours and shared in stands of 111 with Barnes and 159 with Bradman. The remaining batsmen did badly against Leicestershire's Australian slow bowlers, Jackson and Walsh. … Rain prevented play until 2.30 pm on the last day. Then the Australians took the last five wickets in an hour for 34.

Australians

S. G. Barnes lbw b Sperry	78	I. W. Johnson c Lester b Jackson	6
W. A. Brown b Jackson	26	†R. A. Saggers c Lester b Jackson	6
K. R. Miller not out	202	D. Ring run out	2
*D. G. Bradman c Corrall b Etherington	81	W. A. Johnston st Corrall b Jackson	12
R. N. Harvey lbw b Walsh	12	B 10, n-b 2	12
R. A. Hamence st Corrall b Walsh	7		**448**
S. J. Loxton lbw b Jackson	4		

Leicestershire bowling: Sperry 25–5–84–1; Etherington 26–2–94–1; Cornock 3–0–13–0; Jackson 37.2–3–91–5; Walsh 29–0–125–2; Lester 7–0–29–0.

Leicestershire

*L.G. Berry, G. Lester, F.T. Prentice, M. Tompkin, V.E. Jackson, W.B. Cornock, T.A. Chapman, J.E. Walsh, M.W. Etherington, †P. Corrall and J. Sperry.

First innings: 130 (J.E. Walsh 33; Ring five for 45). *Second innings:* 147 (Lester 40, Jackson 31 not out; Johnson seven for 42).

Umpires: A. Skelding and C.N. Woolley

SURREY v AUSTRALIANS   211 (306)

At [Kennington] Oval, May 8, 10, 11 [1948]. Australians won by an innings and 296 runs. … They were fortunate to win the toss, for, after being easy-paced on the first day, the pitch became fast and dusty; nevertheless, there was little excuse for Surrey's poor batting in the first innings. Barnes and Morris opened with a stand of 136 and Barnes and Bradman added 207. … Bradman, at his best, drove magnificently and made 146 in two and three-quarter hours. He hit fifteen 4's before being bowled by a fine ball. … With Lindwall quickly sending back Fletcher and Squires, Surrey were all out in three hours. Fishlock batted through the innings and never seemed in trouble …

Australians

S. G. Barnes lbw b Squires	176	†D. Tallon not out	50
A. R. Morris lbw b McMahon	65	D. Ring b McMahon	2
*D. G. Bradman b Bedser	146	W. A. Johnston lbw b Laker	6
A. L. Hassett b Bedser	110	E. R. H. Toshack c and b McMahon	8
R. N. Harvey b McMahon	7	B 6, l-b 5, n-b 1	12
I. W. Johnson c Fishlock b Bedser	46		**632**
R. R. Lindwall b Bedser	4		

Surrey bowling: Bedser 40–9–104–4; Surridge 26–4–86–0; Laker 37–4–137–1; Squires 10–0–62–1; McMahon 42.4–1–210–4; Holmes 4–0–21–0.

Surrey

L.B. Fishlock, D.G.W. Fletcher, H.S. Squires, T.H. Barling, M.R. Barton, †A.J. McIntyre, *E.R. T. Holmes, J.C. Laker, A.V. Bedser, W.S. Surridge and J.W. McMahon.

First innings: 141 (Fishlock 81 not out; Johnson five for 53, Ring three for 34). *Second innings:* 195 (Squires 54; Johnston four for 40, Johnson three for 40).

Umpires: H. Baldwin and A. Skelding

ESSEX v AUSTRALIANS 212 (307)

At Southend, May 15, 17 [1948]. Australians won by an innings and 451 runs. In light-hearted vein, they made history by putting together the highest total scored in a day of six hours in first-class cricket. Bradman led the run-getting revel on the Saturday. Complete master of the Essex bowlers on a fast pitch, he scored 187 in two hours five minutes, and by a wide variety of orthodox and unorthodox strokes hit thirty-two 4's and a 5. ... The biggest partnerships were 219 in ninety minutes between Brown and Bradman for the second wicket, 166 in sixty-five minutes by Loxton and Saggers for the sixth, and 145 in ninety-five minutes between Barnes and Brown for the first. Bailey dismissed Brown and Miller with successive balls, but generally the bowlers failed to stem the scoring. Because of injury Bailey did not bat in either innings [and] Essex [were] dismissed twice on Monday. ... The attendance and receipts – 32,000 and £3,482 – were ground records.

Australians

S. G. Barnes hit wkt b R. Smith	79	I. W. Johnson st Rist b P. Smith	9
W. A. Brown c Horsfall b Bailey	153	D. Ring c Vigar b P. Smith	1
*D. G. Bradman b P. Smith	187	W. A. Johnston b Vigar	9
K. R. Miller b Bailey	0	E. R. H. Toshack c Vigar b P. Smith	4
R. A. Hamence c P. Smith b R. Smith	46	B 7, n-b 2	9
S. J. Loxton c Rist b Vigar	120		**721**
†R. A. Saggers not out	104		

Essex bowling: Bailey 21–1–128–2; R. Smith 37–2–169–2; P. Smith 38–0–193–4; Price 20–0–156–0; Vigar 13–1–66–2.

Essex

T.C. Dodds, S.J. Cray, A.V. Avery, F.H. Vigar, R. Horsfall, *T.N. Pearce, R. Smith, T.P.B. Smith, †F. Rist, E. Price and T.E. Bailey.

First innings: 83 (Miller three for 14, Toshack five for 31). *Second innings:* 187 (Pearce 71, T.P.B. Smith 54; Johnson six for 37).

Umpires: W.H. Ashdown and D. Hendren

MCC TEAM v AUSTRALIANS 213 (308)

At Lord's, May 22, 24, 25 [1948]. Australians won by an innings and 158 runs, a most convincing victory against the strongest opposition met so far. They excelled in run-getting, and the bowling of Toshack and Miller, in the first innings, and of McCool and Johnson, in the second, proved too much for the MCC batsmen. The Australians lost Morris at 11, but Barnes, defying an attack of cramp, shared with Bradman in a stand of 160. ... Though at times subdued, Bradman obtained eleven 4's in two hours and a half before giving slip a catch. ... On the second morning, when rain deadened the pitch, Laker was punished for nine 6's over a short boundary. ... The total attendance was nearly 60,000, the gates being closed on the first day.

Australians

S. G. Barnes c Edrich b Cranston	81	C. L. McCool c Edrich b Young		0
A. R. Morris lbw b Edrich	5	†D. Tallon b Young		11
*D. G. Bradman c Edrich b Deighton	98	R. R. Lindwall not out		29
A. L. Hassett lbw b Young	51	E. R. H. Toshack c Compton b Young		2
K. R. Miller c Donnelly b Laker	163	B 4, l-b 2		6
W. A. Brown c Cranston b Laker	26			**552**
I. W. Johnson lbw b Laker	80			

MCC bowling: Edrich 23–1–110–1; Deighton 22–4–88–1; Cranston 26–6–69–1; Young 55.2–12–147–4; Laker 37–10–127–3; Compton 3–1–5–0.

MCC Team

L. Hutton, J.D. Robertson, W.J. Edrich, D.C.S. Compton, M.P. Donnelly, *N.W.D. Yardley, K. Cranston, †S.C. Griffith, Capt. J.H.G. Deighton, J.C. Laker and J.A. Young.

First innings: 189 (Hutton 52; Miller three for 28, Toshack six for 51). *Second innings:* 205 (Hutton 64; Johnson three for 37, McCool four for 35).

Umpires: F. Chester and D. Davies

LANCASHIRE v AUSTRALIANS   214 (309, 310)

At Manchester, May 26, 27, 28 [1948]. Drawn. After the loss of the first day through rain, Lancashire made a good fight for the first innings lead. In his third match for the county nineteen-year-old Hilton achieved distinction by dismissing Bradman twice. Cranston put the Australians in after winning the toss, and on a pitch drying under warm sunshine the Australians were seldom comfortable against Roberts and Hilton, both of whose natural left-arm breaks turned and sometimes lifted awkwardly ... In addition to beating Bradman, who deflected the ball on to the stumps, Hilton sent back Johnson and Barnes in one spell of twelve overs for 30 runs. ... The Australians batted brightly in the second innings, but Bradman was in difficulties against Hilton, who beat him with three successive balls immediately before getting him stumped. ...

Australians

S. G. Barnes c Cranston b Hilton	31	–	c Roberts b Cranston	31
A. R. Morris c E. Edrich b Pollard	22	–	c G. Edrich b Pollard	5
*D. G. Bradman b Hilton	11	–	st E. Edrich b Hilton	43
I. W. Johnson lbw b Hilton	5			
S. J. Loxton b Roberts	39	–	run out	52
R. N. Harvey b Roberts	36	–	not out	76
R. A. Hamence b Pollard	2	–	not out	49
†R. A. Saggers not out	22			
R. R. Lindwall c Lawton b Hilton	0			
W. A. Johnston b Pollard	24			
E. R. H. Toshack b Roberts	4			
B 6, l-b 2	8		B 1, l-b 2	3
	204		(four wkts)	**259**

Lancashire bowling: *First innings*—Pollard 20–8–37–3; Lawton 9–4–21–0; Hilton 19–4–81–4; Roberts 21.4–4–57–3. *Second innings*—Pollard 12–2–48–1; Lawton 8–1–43–0; Hilton 13–0–54–1; Roberts 14–3–35–0; Cranston 9–1–40–1; Wharton 7–1–20–0; Ikin 4–0–16–0.

Lancashire

C. Washbrook, W. Place, G. A. Edrich, J. T. Ikin, *K. Cranston, †E. H. Edrich, A. Wharton, R. Pollard, W. B. Roberts, W. Lawton and M. Hilton.

> *First innings:* 182 (Washbrook 33, G. Edrich 55; Lindwall three for 44, Johnston five for 49).

Umpires: H. Elliott and C. N. Woolley

NOTTINGHAMSHIRE v AUSTRALIANS   215 (311)

At Nottingham, May 29, 31, June 1 [1948]. Drawn. Nottinghamshire did well to escape defeat. They owed most to Simpson, who batted delightfully in both innings, and Hardstaff, who hit the first century of the tour against the Australians. ... [On the first day] Lindwall returned an analysis of six wickets for 14 runs in 15.1 overs. He was so accurate and quick off the pitch that batsmen managed to score from only ten of his deliveries. The Australians batted soundly but at times without enterprise. Brown, who rarely opened his shoulders, took three and three-quarter hours over 122, but Bradman, Miller and Hassett were more free. ...

Nottinghamshire

W. W. Keeton, H. Winrow, R. T. Simpson, J. Hardstaff, F. W. Stocks, P. Harvey, *W. A. Sime, H. J. Butler, A. Jepson, F.G. Woodhead and †E. A. Meads.

> *First innings:* 179 (Simpson 74, Hardstaff 48; Lindwall six for 14). *Second innings:* Eight for 299 (Winrow 31, Simpson 70, Hardstaff 107, Harvey 41; Johnson three for 78, Ring four for 104).

Australians

W. A. Brown lbw b Jepson	122	†D. Tallon b Winrow	27
A. R. Morris lbw b Jepson	16	R. R. Lindwall c Meads b Jepson	8
*D. G. Bradman b Woodhead	86	I. W. Johnson b Jepson	0
C. L. McCool b Winrow	17	D. Ring not out	9
A. L. Hassett b Woodhead	44	B 2, l-b 1, n-b 1	4
K. R. Miller b Woodhead	51		**400**
S. J. Loxton run out	16		

Nottinghamshire bowling: Butler 32–4–98–0; Jepson 43–7–109–4; Woodhead 32–3–92–3; Harvey 16–1–43–0; Winrow 13.2–2–54–2.

Umpires: G. M. Lee and T. J. Bartley

SUSSEX v AUSTRALIANS   216 (312)

At Hove, June 5, 7 [1948]. Australians won by an innings and 325 runs. In a match-winning bowling feat of eleven wickets for 59 runs, Lindwall worked himself into his best form at the right time – the last match before the First Test. In the first innings he hit the off stump five times. ... In contrast the Sussex attack presented few difficulties and, except when Brown pursued his customary solid course, runs flowed from the bat with hardly a pause. Brown and Morris shared in an opening stand of 153, followed by a partnership of 167 between Morris and Bradman, whose 109 took only two hours and contained eleven 4's. ... When Sussex batted again Lindwall bowled faster than on the opening day. In the first over he dismissed John Langridge and C. Oakes before a run was scored; Parks and James Langridge made a determined stand ... but Bradman recalled Lindwall and the end soon came.

Sussex

John Langridge, H. W. Parks, C. Oakes, G. Cox, James Langridge, J. Oakes, *H. T. Bartlett, †S. C. Griffith, P. A. D. Carey, A. E. James and J. Cornford.

First innings: 86 (Lindwall six for 34, Loxton three for 13). *Second innings:* 138 (Parks 61; Lindwall five for 25, Ring three for 42).

Australians

W. A. Brown lbw b C. Oakes	44	R. N. Harvey not out	100
A. R. Morris c and b James Langridge	184	R. A. Hamence lbw b C. Oakes	34
*D. G. Bradman b Cornford	109	B 10, l-b 10, n-b 1	21
R. R. Lindwall c Griffith b Cornford	57	(five wkts dec)	**549**

I. W. Johnson, †R. A. Saggers, S. J. Loxton, D. Ring and E. R. H. Toshack did not bat.

Sussex bowling: Carey 23–1–102–0; Cornford 31–6–122–2; James 26–6–90–0; Cox 16–3–54–0; C. Oakes 15–2–60–2; James Langridge 16–1–32–0; J. Oakes 3–0–32–0.

Umpires: B. Flint and J. J. Hills

ENGLAND v AUSTRALIA
(FIRST TEST MATCH)

217 (313, 314)

48 (72, 73)

At Nottingham, June 10, 11, 12, 14, 15 [1948]. Australia won by eight wickets. Bravely as England fought back, the result became nearly a foregone conclusion by the end of the first day after their disastrous batting against a fast attack of exceptionally high standard. ... Although only twenty minutes' play was possible before lunch on Thursday ... on a pitch affected sufficiently by a heavy downpour during the interval to make the ball skid through, England lost eight wickets before tea for 74. True, the light never became good and the bowling reached a high level, but England played poorly ... Australia suffered a handicap when Lindwall pulled a groin muscle midway through the innings and could not bowl again in the match. ...

Although a good spell by Laker gave England great encouragement at one period on the second day, Australia recovered and pressed home their advantage, but on a perfect pitch and in ideal weather conditions England deserved equal praise for limiting the batsmen to 276 runs in six hours. For the most part Yardley set a defensive field and, though lacking penetration, his bowlers performed their allotted tasks in concentrating on and just outside the leg stump. At one period Laker's off-breaks put the Australians into a position where they struggled for runs ... Then Yardley caused surprise by taking off Laker in order to use the new ball against Brown, normally an opening batsman accustomed to swing. The change in bowling provided Bradman with an opportunity to hit his first 4 after eighty-three minutes, but again he relapsed into long periods of defence and, as Brown followed suit, scoring became very slow with Australia fighting to restore their early superiority. They passed England's total without further loss, but at 184 Yardley ... [had] Brown leg-before with his fourth delivery. England met with no other success on Friday; an unbroken stand of 108 between Bradman and Hassett left Australia 128 ahead. Seldom had Bradman been so subdued in a big innings as he was over the twenty-eighth Test century of his career. He did not welcome Yardley's tactics in asking his bowlers to work to a packed leg-side field, and he spent over three hours and a half in reaching his hundred, the last 29 runs taking seventy minutes.

When play began on Saturday Bradman needed only two runs to become the first player to complete 1,000 for the season. These he obtained, but in the third over Hutton at short fine-leg held the first of his series of catches given by Bradman off Bedser's late in-swinger. Bradman's unusually subdued innings lasted four hours and three-quarters. For the most part he allowed himself no liberty. ...

[England batted again 344 behind.] Once more Australia gained the incentive of a fine start ... but Hutton showed sparkling form and Compton overcame an anxious start against Johnson. ... Miller [having bowled medium-pace off-breaks] turned again to fast deliveries and incurred the noisy displeasure of sections of the crowd when he bowled five bumpers to Hutton in his last eight balls, one of which struck the batsman high on the left arm. ... Before play began on Monday the Nottinghamshire Secretary, Mr H. A. Brown, broadcast an appeal to the crowd to leave the conduct of the game to the umpires and he deplored the barracking of Miller on Saturday. The not-out batsmen continued their good work, but the light became even worse than in the first innings. After an unsuccessful appeal, play was held up when the ground caught the edge of a thunderstorm. Almost immediately on the resumption Miller produced a fast break-back which beat Hutton completely in the still gathering gloom. Bad light interrupted the game soon afterwards and though the stoppage was brief, conditions became so bad again that the players retired a second time. On this occasion Compton wanted only three runs for his [third] century [in successive Tests at Trent Bridge]. ... Indeed, rarely can a Test Match have been played under such appalling conditions as on this day. ... England faced an almost hopeless task at the beginning of the last day when they stood only one run ahead with four wickets left, but hope remained as long as Compton was undefeated. He found another fine partner in Evans and in spite of two short breaks for rain they held out till ten minutes before lunch when Miller released a lightning bumper at Compton. The ball reared shoulder high; Compton shaped to hook then changed his mind and tried to get his head out of the way. As he ducked, Compton lost his balance on the muddy turf and tumbled into his wicket. ...

... Australia wanted only 98 to win. ... Bedser added interest to the last stages by bowling Morris at 38 and dismissing Bradman for his first 'duck' in a Test in England, caught in exactly the same manner as in the first innings ... The match ended humourously. After making a boundary stroke Barnes thought the game was over when the scores were level, and he snatched a stump before racing towards the pavilion. Barnes was halfway up the pavilion steps when the shouts of the crowd made him realise the error and he returned to the crease. When Hassett did make the winning hit, another scramble for souvenirs took place; and in this Barnes was unlucky. – R. J. H.

England

L. Hutton, C. Washbrook, W. J. Edrich, D. C. S. Compton, J. Hardstaff, C. J. Barnett, *N. W. D. Yardley, †T. G. Evans, J. C. Laker, A. V. Bedser and J. A. Young.

First innings: 165 (Laker 63; Miller three for 38, Johnston five for 36). *Second innings:* 441 (Hutton 74, Compton 184, Hardstaff 43, Evans 50, sundries 32; Miller four for 125, Johnston four for 147).

Australia

S. G. Barnes c Evans b Laker	62	–	not out	64
A. R. Morris b Laker	31	–	b Bedser	9
*D. G. Bradman c Hutton b Bedser	138	–	c Hutton b Bedser	0
K. R. Miller c Edrich b Laker	0			
W. A. Brown lbw b Yardley	17			
A. L. Hassett b Bedser	137	–	not out	21
I. W. Johnson b Laker	21			
†D. Tallon c and b Young	10			
R. R. Lindwall c Evans b Yardley	42			
W. A. Johnston not out	17			
E. R. H. Toshack lbw b Bedser	19			
B 9, l-b 4, w 1, n-b 1	15		L-b 2, w 1, n-b 1	4
	509		(two wkts)	**98**

England bowling: *First innings*—Edrich 18–1–72–0; Bedser 44.2–12–113–3; Barnett 17–5–36–0; Young 60–28–79–1; Laker 55–14–138–4; Compton 5–0–24–0; Yardley 17–6–32–2. *Second innings*—Edrich 4–0–20–0; Bedser 14.3–4–46–2; Young 10–3–28–0.

Umpires: F. Chester and E. Cooke.

YORKSHIRE v AUSTRALIANS   218 (315, 316)

At Sheffield, June 19, 21, 22 [1948]. Drawn. As the Australians would not risk further damage to their injured bowlers, Miller and Toshack, Bradman did not attempt to go all out for victory and a keen fight for first innings lead was the chief feature. In contrast to other fine work, Yorkshire dropped at least seven catches when the Australians were struggling in the first innings. The fall of Barnes to the third ball of the match made the Australians cautious, but, despite a second-wicket stand of 67 between Bradman and Brown, six men were out for 168. Hutton and Halliday opened with 56, but the rest of the Yorkshire batsmen did little against Toshack and Johnston, who, on the second day, bowled nearly four hours with only a brief break. Except when changing ends, Toshack sent down forty successive overs. The Australians again started badly on a drying pitch, but were helped by more dropped catches. Bradman and Brown put on 154 for the second wicket, and Bradman delayed his declaration till the side led by 328 with only seventy minutes left for play.

Australians

S. G. Barnes b Aspinall	0	–	b Smailes	6
W. A. Brown lbw b Wardle	19	–	b Yardley	113
*D. G. Bradman c Yardley b Wardle	54	–	c Hutton b Aspinall	86
K. R. Miller c Brennan b Coxon	20	–	b Aspinall	0
R. N. Harvey c and b Coxon	49	–	c Halliday b Yardley	56
R. A. Hamence c Brennan b Coxon	48	–	not out	6
C. L. McCool lbw b Coxon	4	–	not out	7
†R. A. Saggers c Yardley b Wardle	22			
D. Ring b Aspinall	3			
W. A. Johnston not out	15			
E. R. H. Toshack c Watson b Aspinall	4			
B 4, l-b 3, n-b 4	11		B 6, l-b 1, n-b 4	11
	249		(five wkts dec)	**285**

Yorkshire bowling: *First innings*—Aspinall 28.3–7–82–3; Coxon 26–5–66–4; Smailes 10–1–36–0; Wardle 20–8–37–3; Robinson 8–4–17–0. *Second innings*—Aspinall 12–1–53–2; Coxon 25–9–47–0; Smailes 24–8–57–1; Wardle 20–5–66–0; Robinson 5–0–17–0; Hutton 1–0–3–0; Yardley 7–2–9–2; Halliday 5–0–22–0.

Yorkshire

L. Hutton, H. Halliday, W. Watson, *N. W. D. Yardley, E. Lester, A. Coxon, R. Aspinall, T. F. Smailes, J. H. Wardle, †D. V. Brennan and E. P. Robinson.

   First innings: 206 (Hutton 39, Lester 31; Johnston three for 101, Toshack seven for 81). *Second innings:* Four for 85.

Umpires: J. T. Bell and K. McCanlis

ENGLAND v AUSTRALIA
(SECOND TEST MATCH)

219 (317, 318)

49 (74, 75)

At Lord's, June 24, 25, 26, 28, 29 [1948]. Australia won by 409 runs. ... Only on the first day did England provide comparable opposition, and their Selectors must have been very disappointed at the lack of determination by some of the batsmen against an attack again below full strength – this time because Miller was unable to bowl. ...

... Although the heavy atmosphere aided swing in the early stages on Thursday, that did not detract from the merit of England's performance in dismissing seven batsmen for 258 when Bradman won the toss for the only time in the series. The day began with excitement, Coxon in his second over of Test cricket dismissing Barnes, whose poor stroke to a short ball enabled Hutton at short fine-leg to bring off the first of three successive catches in that position. His next victim was Bradman, who fell to the Hutton-Bedser combination for the third consecutive time in Tests. Bradman, curiously uncertain and uncomfortable, might have been out in similar fashion when 13, though Hutton deserved more praise for getting his hands to the ball than blame for not holding it. ...

... [When England batted on the second day, they faced] a magnificent speed attack by Lindwall, ably supported by Johnston, left-arm medium-fast, and Johnson, off-breaks. Unfortunately for England the light was not good, but that did not wholly account for a collapse redeemed only partially by a defiant stand between Compton and Yardley. ... At the close of a one-sided day England stood 143 behind with only one wicket to fall.

Except for one thrilling over by Yardley, Australia's batsmen on Saturday revelled in the perfect pitch and glorious weather. Barnes, who should have been stumped when 18, and Morris consolidated Australia's 135 lead with a first-wicket stand of 122. ... Barnes and Bradman put on 174 for the second partnership. At first Barnes was content to leave most of the scoring to Bradman, but he quickened after reaching 50, and upon the completion of his big ambition of a Test century at Lord's he went over to vigorous attack. He took 21, including two successive 6's, in one over from Laker and fell to a catch on the boundary ... Yardley, the successful bowler, penetrated Hassett's defence first ball, and only a hurried jab by Miller prevented a hat-trick. Bradman looked destined to celebrate his farewell Test at Lord's with a century, but an acrobatic catch by Edrich, who dived full length and took the ball with one hand, brought about his dismissal 11 short of the hundred. This was the first ball of a new spell by Bedser, whose performance in disposing of Bradman in five consecutive Test innings – including the last of the 1946-47 series – earned a place in cricket history. When at the close Australia stood 478 ahead with six wickets to fall, Bradman was able to dictate the remaining course of the game.

A break in the weather during the weekend aggravated England's plight. Rain-clouds were again about when Australia resumed batting and three stoppages occurred while 117 runs were added in eighty-eight minutes ... No doubt in the hope that the conditions would improve sufficiently for his bowlers to use a dry ball, Bradman delayed closing the innings, but soon after England started batting with nine hours in which to get 596 for victory, rain caused the fourth hold-up of the day. Frequent showers put sufficient life into the pitch to enable Lindwall and Johnston to make the ball rear awkwardly, and the batsmen were soon in trouble. In contrast to Washbrook, who showed a welcome return to Test form, Hutton looked plainly uncomfortable. ... Bradman drew his fielders in for Edrich, posting two men at short-leg and himself at short mid-off. Both Edrich and Washbrook had to face a number of fast short-pitched deliveries ...

England entered the last day with seven wickets left, but her slender chance of saving the game practically disappeared with the second ball of the morning. Compton struck his toe in trying to drive and the edged stroke which resulted provided Miller with another opportunity to make a lightning low catch at second slip. ... [After that] the innings closed in 110 minutes for the addition of 80 runs. ... In addition to batting and bowling supremacy, Australia showed more agility and aggression in the field, with Barnes again a disturbing element to batsmen through his close attendance at forward short-leg.

The gross attendance of 132,000 and receipts of £43,000 beat all previous figures for a Test in England. – R.J.H.

Australia

S. G. Barnes c Hutton b Coxon	0	–	c Washbrook b Yardley	141
A. R. Morris c Hutton b Coxon	105	–	b Wright	62
*D. G. Bradman c Hutton b Bedser	38	–	c Edrich b Bedser	89
A. L. Hassett b Yardley	47	–	b Yardley	0
K. R. Miller lbw b Bedser	4	–	c Bedser b Laker	74
W. A. Brown lbw b Yardley	24	–	c Evans b Coxon	32
I. W. Johnson c Evans b Edrich	4	–	not out	9
†D. Tallon c Yardley b Bedser	53			
R. R. Lindwall b Bedser	15	–	st Evans b Laker	25
W. A. Johnston st Evans b Wright	29			
E. R. H. Toshack not out	20			
B 3, l-b 7, n-b 1	11		B 22, l-b 5, n-b 1	28
	350		(seven wkts dec)	**460**

England bowling: *First innings*—Bedser 43–14–100–4; Coxon 35–10–90–2; Edrich 8–0–43–1; Wright 21.3–8–54–1; Laker 7–3–17–0; Yardley 15–4–35–2. *Second innings*—Bedser 34–6–112–1; Coxon 28–3–82–1; Edrich 2–0–11–0; Wright 19–4–69–1; Laker 31.2–6–111–2; Yardley 13–4–36–2; Compton 3–0–11–0.

England

L. Hutton, C. Washbrook, W. J. Edrich, D. C. S. Compton, H. E. Dollery, *N. W. D. Yardley, A. Coxon, †T. G. Evans, J. C. Laker, A. V. Bedser and D. V. P. Wright.

First innings: 215 (Compton 53, Yardley 44; Lindwall five for 70, Johnson three for 72). *Second innings*: 186 (Washbrook 37, Dollery 37; Lindwall three for 61, Toshack five for 40).

Umpires: C. N. Woolley and D. Davies

SURREY v AUSTRALIANS   220 (319)

At [Kennington] Oval, June 30, July 1, 2 [1948]. Australians won by ten wickets. Bradman put Surrey in on winning the toss … [When their turn came] the Australians soon lost Hamence, who opened the innings because Brown split a finger while fielding, but Hassett and Bradman joined in a partnership of 231. Bradman (fifteen 4's) obtained his sixth century of the tour in two hours twenty minutes … [On the final day] the Australians needed 122 to win and Harvey and Loxton displayed such enterprise that they knocked off the runs in fifty-eight minutes. …

Surrey

L. B. Fishlock, D. G. W. Fletcher, H. S. Squires, M. R. Barton, J. F. Parker, †A. J. McIntyre, E. A. Bedser, *E. R. T. Holmes, B. Constable, E. A. Watts and W. S. Surridge.

First innings: 221 (Fishlock 31, Parker 76, Watts 30; Ring three for 51). *Second innings*: 289 (Fishlock 61, Parker 81, Holmes 54; McCool six for 113).

Australians

A. L. Hassett c Holmes b Watts	139			
R. A. Hamence c Parker b Watts	0			
*D. G. Bradman c Barton b Squires	128			
K. R. Miller c McIntyre b Surridge	9			
R. N. Harvey run out	43	–	not out	73
S. J. Loxton c Surridge b Parker	8	–	not out	47
C. L. McCool b Surridge	26			
†R. A. Saggers b Squires	12			
D. Ring not out	15			
E. R. H. Toshack lbw b Constable	1			
W. A. Brown absent hurt	0			
B 5, l-b 1, n-b 2	8		L-b 1, n-b 1	2
	389		(no wkt)	**122**

Surrey bowling: *First innings*—Surridge 22–0–123–2; Watts 10–0–64–2; Parker 25–5–62–1; E. A. Bedser 20–1–85–0; Constable 7.1–1–23–1; Squires 10–2–24–2. *Second innings*—Surridge 7–1–43–0; Parker 5–0–22–0; E. A. Bedser 5–0–23–0; Constable 3.1–0–32–0.

Umpires: G. M. Lee and F. S. Lee

ENGLAND v AUSTRALIA   221 (320, 321)
(THIRD TEST MATCH)   50 (76, 77)

At Manchester, July 8, 9, 10, 12, 13 [1948]. Drawn. Fate dealt its sharpest blow of the series to England by the breaking of the weather over the weekend at a time when defeat for Australia appeared more than a possibility. By the end of the third day England had recovered so well from another disastrous start that they stood 316 runs on with only three wickets down in the second innings, but visions of Australia struggling to avoid being beaten were dispelled by rain which made further play impossible till after lunch on the last day. Another interruption then meant that Australia needed to bat only two hours and a half, and on a pitch reduced to sluggishness by nearly two days of heavy rain they found little difficulty in saving the game. So the sequence of unfinished England-Australia Tests at Manchester since 1905 remained unbroken.

… Bradman, playing in his fiftieth Test, again lost the toss and England took first innings on a pitch lively for the first few overs. … [The openers soon went and with] Compton not settled down, Lindwall began a number of bouncers, one of which led to an accident to Compton. After being struck on the arm he took a big hit at a 'no-ball' bumper, but the ball flew off the edge of his bat on to his forehead. Compton staggered around and was led off the field with a cut head. Stitches were inserted and though he wanted to go back at the fall of the next wicket he was ordered to rest. … After a short knock at the nets, [he] resumed with five men out for 119. At once he introduced an air of confidence into the batting and … found a fine partner in Evans, whose bold hitting helped to bring 75 runs in seventy minutes. At the close England were 231 for seven …

Though the new ball was in use at the start of the second day Australia could not retain their grip, for Compton received splendid support from Bedser, who in two hours and a half shared in a stand of 121, only three short of England's eighth-wicket record against Australia. Bedser … looked capable of going on for a long time; unfortunately, he was run out through an error of judgment by Compton. Soon after Bedser's dismissal occurred a second distressing accident. Barnes, fielding in his usual position about five yards from the bat at short-leg, received a fierce blow under the ribs from a full-blooded pull by Pollard. After being carried off by four policemen Barnes was removed on a stretcher to hospital where examination showed that no bones were broken. Compton, who remained undefeated at the end of the innings, might have been caught at the wicket four times – three chances were very difficult – but he gave a grand display of skill and courage. …

Pollard unwittingly struck a big blow for England when he hit Barnes, because Australia, having dropped Brown after the Second Test, possessed only one recognised opening batsman. The necessary rearrangement no doubt played its part in Australia's only batting failure of the Tests ... A fine catch by Evans sent back Johnson ... and soon Bradman was leg-before to persistent Pollard. This was a great start for England on a slow, easy pitch ... At the fall of Miller's wicket Barnes, who had practised in the nets, where he collapsed after a few minutes, surprisingly went out to bat, but he was obviously in great pain and, after staying half an hour for a single, he sank to the ground and had to be assisted off. He was taken to hospital again and kept for ten days under observation. ... altogether on Saturday the last six wickets fell for 95.

... No play took place on Monday and cricket was not resumed till after lunch on Tuesday. Yardley declared first thing in the morning but more showers lessened the hope of victory. Although Young caused brief excitement when he got rid of Johnson with his second ball, the pitch was too lifeless to give bowlers help, and Morris and Bradman contented themselves with dead-bat tactics, each remaining at one end. In one spell of 100 minutes they did not change ends. Morris completed his fourth consecutive Test half-century and, like Bradman, showed adaptability to the conditions. The aggregate attendance of 133,740 was higher than that at Lord's a fortnight earlier. – R.J.H.

England

C. Washbrook, G.M. Emmett, W.J. Edrich, D.C.S. Compton, J.F. Crapp, H.E. Dollery, *N.W. D. Yardley, †T.G. Evans, A.V. Bedser, R. Pollard and J.A. Young.

First innings: 363 (Edrich 32, Compton 145 not out, Crapp 37, Evans 34, Bedser 37; Lindwall four for 99, Johnston three for 67). *Second innings:* Three for 174 dec (Washbrook 85 not out, Edrich 53).

Australia

A.R. Morris c Compton b Bedser	51	–	not out	54
I.W. Johnson c Evans b Bedser	1	–	c Crapp b Young	6
*D.G. Bradman lbw b Pollard	7	–	not out	30
A.L. Hassett c Washbrook b Young	38			
K.R. Miller lbw b Pollard	31			
S.G. Barnes retired hurt	1			
S.J. Loxton b Pollard	36			
†D. Tallon c Evans b Edrich	18			
R.R. Lindwall c Washbrook b Bedser	23			
W.A. Johnston c Crapp b Bedser	3			
E.R.H. Toshack not out	0			
B 5, l-b 4, n-b 3	12		N-b	2
	221		(one wkt)	**92**

England bowling: *First innings*—Bedser 36–12–81–4; Pollard 32–9–53–3; Edrich 7–3–27–1; Yardley 4–0–12–0; Young 14–5–36–1. *Second innings*—Bedser 19–12–27–0; Pollard 10–8–6–0; Edrich 2–0–8–0; Young 21–12–31–1; Compton 9–3–18–0.

Umpires: D. Davies and F. Chester

MIDDLESEX v AUSTRALIANS   222 (322)

At Lord's, July 17, 19, 20 [1948]. Australians won by ten wickets. A restrained display by Denis Compton saved Middlesex from complete collapse in the first innings. ... The Australians lost three wickets for 53, but recovered through a splendid fourth-wicket partnership of 172 lasting 115 minutes between Morris and Loxton ... Batting again 114 runs behind, Middlesex never recovered from the loss of four wickets for 27 coupled with the retirement of Robertson, struck in the face by a ball from Lindwall. ... The teams were introduced to Their Majesties the King and Queen during the tea interval on the second day.

Middlesex

J.D. Robertson, S.M. Brown, W.J. Edrich, D.C.S. Compton, J.G. Dewes, *F.G. Mann, †L.H. Compton, J. Sims, P.A. Whitcombe, J.A. Young and I. Bedford.

First innings: 203 (Brown 39, D.C.S. Compton 62; Johnston three for 43, Loxton three for 33). *Second innings:* 135 (Dewes 51, L.H. Compton 38; McCool three for 27).

Australians

W. A. Brown lbw b Whitcombe	8			
A. R. Morris c Brown b Young	109			
*D. G. Bradman c D. Compton b Whitcombe	6			
R. N. Harvey c Mann b Bedford	10			
S. J. Loxton c Edrich b Sims	123			
R. A. Hamence lbw b Sims	30			
C. L. McCool c Young b Sims	0	–	not out	7
R. R. Lindwall st L. Compton b Sims	1			
†D. Tallon b Sims	17			
D. Ring b Sims	2	–	not out	15
W. A. Johnston not out	6			
B 1, l-b 3, n-b 1	5			
	317		(no wkt)	22

Middlesex bowling: *First innings*—Whitcombe 13–2–43–2; Edrich 20–2–59–0; Bedford 11–3–44–1; Young 36–13–78–1; Sims 24–2–65–6; D. Compton 3–0–23–0. *Second innings*—Bedford 2–0–11–0; Sims 2–0–11–0.

Umpires: H.G. Baldwin and E. Cooke.

ENGLAND v AUSTRALIA   223 (323, 324)
(FOURTH TEST MATCH)   51 (78, 79)

At Leeds, July 22, 23, 24, 26, 27 [1948]. Australia won by seven wickets. By the astonishing feat of scoring 404 for three wickets on the fifth day of the match when the pitch took spin, Australia won the rubber. Until that fatal last stage England were on top, but a succession of blunders prevented them gaining full reward for good work on the first four days.

The biggest mistake occurred before the game started, for the Selectors decided to leave out Young, the slow left-arm bowler who had been invited to Leeds as one of the original party. Consequently England took the field with an unbalanced attack. Having only one slow bowler available, Yardley did not know what to do for the best on the last day, and he was forced to make Compton the spearhead and to employ Hutton, who to that point had bowled no more than twenty-two overs in the season. Even then England should have won. Evans, behind the wicket, fell a long way below his best form, and three catches were dropped in the field.

Australia put together the biggest fourth innings total in a Test Match between the two countries in England; also the aggregate of 1,723 runs was the highest for any match in England.

Handicapped through injuries to Barnes and Tallon, the Australians were forced to make two changes, Harvey and Saggers appearing for the first time against England. ... When Yardley won the toss for the third time in four matches, England gained first use of a perfect pitch. Without Barnes, Bradman did not place a fieldsman close in at forward short-leg and the batsmen welcomed their freedom. ... Hutton and Washbrook gave England a great send-off with an opening stand of 168, their best partnership in any Test Match. Hutton completely justified his recall to the side and Washbrook ... completed an almost faultless hundred out of 189 and fell in the last over of the day after batting five hours twenty minutes. His second stand with Edrich produced 100.

Bedser, sent in to play the last four balls overnight, proved such an efficient stop-gap that the third successive century partnership resulted. For the second day running the Australians met with no success before lunch, and the third wicket realised 155. ... [Both went in quick succession, however, and] from a total of 423 for two, England were all out 496.

Hassett and Morris opened the Australian innings, but did not shape confidently. Morris left at 13, and next morning Pollard, in his first over, sent back Hassett and Bradman in three balls, making Australia 68 for three. Then nineteen-year-old Neil Harvey joined Miller, and, delivering a terrific onslaught on the England attack, they rescued Australia from their precarious position. In just over an hour and a half they put on 121 by glorious strokeplay. Loxton carried on the big hitting [with five 6's in his 93] ... Harvey hit seventeen 4's while making 112 – his second successive Test century. ... Yet despite this punishment England held the upper hand, for with eight wickets down Australia were 141 behind. Then occurred a similar experience to that at Lord's, where Australia's tail-end batsmen could not be dislodged ... and England's lead was restricted to 38.

Hutton and Washbrook opened with a century stand for the second time in the match and created a new world record for Test cricket in accomplishing the feat twice. Both left at 129, but England consolidated their position by rapid scoring. ... At the close of the fourth day England led by 400 with two wickets left.

To most people Yardley's decision to continue batting for five minutes next day came as a surprise and the reason for it aroused plenty of comment. The main idea was to break up the pitch by use of the heavy roller. Three runs were added in two overs, and then Yardley declared, leaving Australia to score 404 in 345 minutes. The pitch took spin and the ball lifted and turned sharply. Unfortunately, Laker was erratic in length. Compton, bowling his left-hand off-breaks and googlies, baffled the batsmen several times, but without luck. Evans should have stumped Morris when 32, and Compton ought to have dismissed Bradman, Crapp dropping a catch at first slip. In half an hour before lunch Morris and Bradman put on 64, and after the interval, against a succession of full tosses and long hops, runs continued to flow. When 59 Bradman had another escape off Compton, and Yardley, in despair, called for the new ball even though the pitch favoured spin. Evans should have stumped Bradman when 108, and Laker at square-leg dropped Morris when 126. Not until 301 had been put on did England break the stand, and by that time the match was as good as won. ... Harvey made the winning stroke within fifteen minutes of time. No fewer than sixty-six 4's were hit in the innings, thirty-three by Morris and twenty-nine by Bradman.

The attendance figures of 158,000 created a record for any match in England. – L. S.

England

L. Hutton, C. Washbrook, W. J. Edrich, A. V. Bedser, D. C. S. Compton, J. F. Crapp, *N. W. D. Yardley, K. Cranston, †T.G. Evans, J.C. Laker and R. Pollard.

First innings: 496 (Hutton 81, Washbrook 143, Edrich 111, Bedser 79; Loxton three for 55). *Second innings:* Eight for 365 dec (Hutton 57, Washbrook 65, Edrich 54, Compton 66, Evans 47 not out; Johnston four for 95).

Australia

A. R. Morris c Cranston b Bedser	6	–	c Pollard b Yardley	182
A. L. Hassett c Crapp b Pollard	13	–	c and b Compton	17
*D. G. Bradman b Pollard	33	–	not out	173
K. R. Miller c Edrich b Yardley	58	–	lbw b Cranston	12
R. N. Harvey b Laker	112	–	not out	4
S. J. Loxton b Yardley	93			
I. W. Johnson c Cranston b Laker	10			
R. R. Lindwall c Crapp b Bedser	77			
†R. A. Saggers st Evans b Laker	5			
W. A. Johnston c Edrich b Bedser	13			
E. R. H. Toshack not out	12			
B 9, l-b 14, n-b 3	26		B 6, l-b 9, n-b 1	16
	458		(three wkts)	**404**

England bowling: *First innings*—Bedser 31.2–4–92–3; Pollard 38–6–104–2; Cranston 14–1–51–0; Edrich 3–0–19–0; Laker 30–8–113–3; Yardley 17–6–38–2; Compton 3–0–15–0. *Second innings*—Bedser 21–2–56–0; Pollard 22–6–55–0; Cranston 7.1–0–28–1; Laker 32–11–93–0; Yardley 13–1–44–1; Compton 15–3–82–1; Hutton 4–1–30–0.

Umpires: F. Chester and H.G. Baldwin

DERBYSHIRE v AUSTRALIANS   224 (325)

At Derby, July 28, 29, 30 [1948]. Australians won by an innings and 34 runs. Despite the absence through injury of Copson and Pope from Derbyshire's attack, the Australian scoring-rate was limited. Brown, who shared in century stands with Bradman and Miller, exercised such caution that his first 50 runs occupied three hours. ... Derbyshire followed on 216 behind, and left-hander Smith achieved distinction in making his county's highest individual score against an Australian team. The previous best was 81 by L.G. Wright in 1896. ... Barnes reappeared after injury in the Third Test, but did not field at forward short-leg. The attendance of 17,000 on the first day constituted a Derbyshire record.

Australians

S. G. Barnes b Gladwin	24	C. L. McCool c Smith b Rhodes	31
W. A. Brown c Gladwin b Gothard	140	†R. A. Saggers not out	6
*D. G. Bradman b Gothard	62	D. Ring b Jackson	4
K. R. Miller lbw b Jackson	57	W. A. Johnston b Jackson	0
R. N. Harvey c Elliott b Rhodes	32	B 21, l-b 5, w 1, n-b 1	28
R. A. Hamence st Dawkes b Gothard	21		**456**
S. J. Loxton c Revill b Jackson	51		

Derbyshire bowling: Jackson 34.4–4–103–4; Gladwin 33–6–107–1; Rhodes 30–2–99–2; Gothard 22–0–108–3; Smith 2–0–11–0; Marsh 1–1–0–0.

Derbyshire

C.S. Elliott, A. Townsend, D. Smith, A. Revill, P. Vaulkhard, E. Marsh, †G. Dawkes, *E.J. Gothard, C. Gladwin, A.E. Rhodes and L. Jackson.

   First innings: 240 (Elliott 57, Revill 41, Vaulkhard 36; Miller three for 31, Johnston three for 41, Ring three for 73). *Second innings:* 182 (Townsend 46, Smith 88; Loxton three for 16, McCool six for 77).

Umpires: J. Smart and A. Lockett

WARWICKSHIRE v AUSTRALIANS   225 (326, 327)

At Birmingham, August 4, 5, 6 [1948]. Australians won by nine wickets. Although the Australians won comfortably after Bradman put Warwickshire in on a wet pitch, the leg-break bowling of Hollies was the feature of the match. His eight for 107 in the first Australian innings surpassed anything done by an English bowler in an innings throughout the tour. During a prolonged spell he flighted and spun the ball splendidly and the performance earned him a place in the Fifth Test. Hollies kept the batsmen so much on the defensive that both the opening batsmen, Morris and Brown, 'hit wicket' playing back. ... Lindwall and Johnston made the ball lift awkwardly in Warwickshire's first innings. Lindwall began a collapse with three wickets in twelve balls ... In the second innings Johnston again showed great accuracy and clever variations of pace. With McCool turning leg-breaks sharply, the game finished by lunch-time on the Friday.

Warwickshire

K. A. Taylor, J. R. Thompson, J. S. Ord, M. P. Donnelly, H. E. Dollery, A. H. Kardar, *R. H. Maudsley, †R. T. Spooner, V. H. D. Cannings, T. L. Pritchard and W. E. Hollies.

First innings: 138 (Lindwall three for 27, Johnson three for 29). *Second innings:* 155 (Thompson 35; Johnston four for 32, McCool four for 56).

Australians

W. A. Brown hit wkt b Hollies	33	–	lbw b Hollies	7
A. R. Morris hit wkt b Hollies	32	–	not out	20
*D. G. Bradman b Hollies	31	–	not out	13
A. L. Hassett lbw b Hollies	68			
R. N. Harvey b Hollies	0			
S. J. Loxton lbw b Kardar	0			
C. L. McCool c Donnelly b Kardar	19			
R. R. Lindwall c Maudsley b Hollies	45			
I. W. Johnson not out	13			
†R. A. Saggers b Hollies	0			
W. A. Johnston b Hollies	6			
B 3, l-b 4	7		L-b	1
	254		(one wkt)	**41**

Warwickshire bowling: *First innings*—Pritchard 16–4–35–0; Hollies 43.5–8–107–8; Cannings 10–2–30–0; Kardar 32–11–75–2. *Second innings*—Pritchard 2–0–7–0; Hollies 4–0–17–1; Cannings 3–1–6–0; Kardar 2.4–0–10–0.

Umpires: H. Cruice and H.G. Baldwin

LANCASHIRE v AUSTRALIANS   226 (328, 329)
(C. WASHBROOK'S BENEFIT)

At Manchester, August 7, 9, 10 [1948]. Drawn. Instead of enforcing the follow-on when leading by 191, the Australians batted again, and Bradman delayed his declaration until lunch-time on the last day when only two hours and three-quarters remained for play. Bradman for his highest score at Old Trafford batted three hours thirty-five minutes and hit seventeen 4's. Lancashire seemed certain to play out time, but with the new ball Lindwall bowled Ikin, who was dismissed for 99 in the second consecutive match, and Pollard with following deliveries. Thus, Washbrook being unfit, only two wickets were left when Lindwall began his last and very fast over, but Roberts held out. Although financially a great success [his Benefit produced £14,000, a record at the time], the game brought misfortune to Washbrook, for he injured his right thumb when batting against Lindwall and withdrew from the England team for the Fifth Test. Roberts, the left-arm slow bowler, did good work on a drying pitch on the first day, when he bowled forty-one consecutive overs and took the first five wickets for 29 runs. ...

Australians

S. G. Barnes c Ikin b Roberts	67	–	c Wilson b Pollard	90
A. R. Morris c Wilson b Roberts	49	–	c Place b Pollard	16
*D. G. Bradman c Wilson b Roberts	28	–	not out	133
K. R. Miller lbw b Ikin	24	–	c Howard b Pollard	11
R. A. Hamence c and b Roberts	14	–	not out	10
S. J. Loxton c G. Edrich b Roberts	2			
R. R. Lindwall c Wilson b Roberts	17			
I. W. Johnson c and b Pollard	48			
†D. Tallon c Pollard b Greenwood	33			
D. Ring not out	17			
E. R. H. Toshack c Howard b Pollard	2			
B 16, l-b 3, w 1	20		B 4, l-b 1	5
	321		(three wkts)	**265**

Lancashire bowling: *First innings*—Pollard 27–6–58–2; Greenwood 19–4–62–1; Cranston 3–0–24–0; Wharton 1–0–4–0; Ikin 39–12–80–1; Roberts 42–14–73–6. *Second innings*—Pollard 27–8–58–3; Greenwood 13–2–53–0; Cranston 8–2–34–0; Ikin 15–3–51–0; Roberts 22–4–64–0.

Lancashire

C. Washbrook, W. Place, G. A. Edrich, J. T. Ikin, A. Wharton, N. D. Howard, *K. Cranston, P. Greenwood, R. Pollard, W. B. Roberts and †A. Wilson.

First innings: 130 (Washbrook 38; Lindwall three for 32, Johnson three for 5). *Second innings:* Seven for 199 (Ikin 99; Lindwall four for 27).

Umpires: T. J. Bartley and J. Smart

ENGLAND v AUSTRALIA   227 (330)
(FIFTH TEST MATCH)   52 (80)

At Kennington Oval, August 14, 16, 17, 18 [1948]. Australia won by an innings and 149 runs, so completing their triumph in the rubber with four victories and one draw. England having been placed in a humiliating position already, the Selectors tried further experiments which aroused strong condemnation ... and Australia met with little hindrance on the road to their most emphatic victory in this series of Tests.

Extraordinary cricket marked the opening day. So saturated was the ground by copious rain during the week that the groundsmen could not get the pitch into a reasonable shape for a punctual start. The captains agreed that play should begin at twelve o'clock, and Yardley, having won the toss, chose to bat – an inevitable decision with the conditions uncertain and the possibility of more rain. As it happened, apart from local showers early on Sunday morning, the weather proved fine until England fared badly for the second time. All things considered, the Australians found everything favourable for them, as was the case at Lord's. This does not explain the lamentable collapse of England for the lowest score by either side in a Test at The Oval, apart from the 44 for which Australia fell in 1896, the last occasion on which W. G. Grace led England to victory. ...

The sodden state of the pitch, with sawdust covering large patches of turf nearby, made one doubt its fitness for cricket. Bowlers and batsmen found much sawdust necessary for a foothold. This supposed handicap did not seem to trouble the Australians, and reasons for the downfall of England in two hours and a half for such a meagre score were the splendid attack maintained by Lindwall, Miller and Johnston in humid atmosphere against batsmen whose first error proved fatal. Hutton, the one exception to complete failure, batted in his customary stylish, masterful manner throughout the innings, being last out from a leg glance which Tallon held with the left hand close to the ground as he fell – a great finish to Australia's splendid performance. ... After lunch Lindwall bowled 8.1 overs, four maidens, and took five wickets at a cost of eight runs!

Everything became different when Australia batted. Barnes and Morris, with controlled assurance and perfect strokeplay, made 117, and shortly before six o'clock Bradman walked to the wicket amidst continued applause from the standing crowd. Yardley shook hands with Bradman and called on the England team for three cheers, in which the crowd joined. Evidently deeply touched by the enthusiastic reception, Bradman survived one ball, but, playing forward to the next, was clean bowled by a sharply turning break-back – possibly a googly. As if to avenge the fall of these two wickets in an over, Morris twice hooked Hollies to the boundary and the score rose to 153, while on Monday it reached 226 before Hassett left. … Morris missed the special distinction of making 200 through his own ill-judged call for a sharp run … He was eighth out …

Facing arrears of 337, England lost Dewes with 20 scored, but Hutton and Edrich raised the total to 54 before bad light stopped play. The conditions remained anything but good on Tuesday … [and after Hutton left] three wickets fell in deepening gloom for 25 runs. Evans, from the way he shaped without attempting a stroke, obviously could not see the ball which bowled him, Lindwall, with the pavilion behind him, sending down something like a yorker at express speed. The umpires immediately responded to the appeal against the light, and rain at four o'clock delayed the finish until Wednesday morning, when the remaining three wickets realised only 10 runs in a sad spectacle for England. The usual scramble for the stumps and bails as Morris held a lofted catch from Hollies marked the close; but much happened subsequently. Mr H. D.G. Leveson Gower on the players' balcony called for three cheers for Bradman and the victorious Australians. Responses over the microphone came in due course, the crowd of about 5,000 enthusiasts coming up to the pavilion to hear and see all that happened as a curtain to this series of Test Matches in which Australia completely outplayed and conquered England. – H.P.

England

L. Hutton, J.G. Dewes, W.J. Edrich, D.C.S. Compton, J.F. Crapp, *N.W.D. Yardley, A. Watkins, †T. G. Evans, A.V. Bedser, J.A. Young and W.E. Hollies.

First innings: 52 (Hutton 30; Lindwall six for 20). *Second innings:* 188 (Hutton 64, Compton 39; Lindwall three for 50, Johnston four for 40).

Australia

S. G. Barnes c Evans b Hollies	61	R. R. Lindwall c Edrich b Young	9
A. R. Morris run out	196	†D. Tallon c Crapp b Hollies	31
*D. G. Bradman b Hollies	0	D. Ring c Crapp b Bedser	9
A. L. Hassett lbw b Young	37	W. A. Johnston not out	0
K. R. Miller st Evans b Hollies	5	B 4, l-b 2, n-b 3	9
R. N. Harvey c Young b Hollies	17		**389**
S. J. Loxton c Evans b Edrich	15		

England bowling: Bedser 31.2–9–61–1; Watkins 4–1–19–0; Young 51–16–118–2; Hollies 56–14–131–5; Compton 2–0–6–0; Edrich 9–0–38–1; Yardley 5–1–7–0.

Umpires: D. Davies and H.G. Baldwin

KENT v AUSTRALIANS 228 (331)

At Canterbury, August 21, 23 [1948]. Australians won by an innings and 186 runs. The match produced two attendance records for Kent and the lowest score of the tour against the Australians – one fewer than England's 52 in the previous game. A painstaking innings by Brown and attractive displays by Morris, Bradman and Harvey contributed to the big Australian total. ... Despite cheerless weather, a record crowd of 19,000 on the first day was exceeded by 4,000 on Monday, when Kent took the last six wickets for 68 and themselves batted lamentably against Lindwall, Johnston and Loxton. Five wickets went for 16, and ... the innings lasted only eighty-five minutes. At the second attempt half the side fell for 45 ...

Australians

W. A. Brown c Evans b Ridgway	106	I. W. Johnson lbw b Todd	15
A. R. Morris c Evans b Dovey	43	R. R. Lindwall c Ames b Dovey	5
*D. G. Bradman c Valentine b Crush	65	†R. A. Saggers c Ridgway b Dovey	8
R. N. Harvey b Ridgway	60	W. A. Johnston not out	2
S. J. Loxton c Valentine b Dovey	16	B 1, l-b 2	3
R. A. Hamence c Ames b Ridgway	38		**361**
C. L. McCool b Crush	0		

Kent bowling: Ridgway 41–10–119–3; Crush 15–1–82–2; Todd 17–3–51–1; Dovey 50.3–13–90–4; Davies 10–5–16–0.

Kent

L. J. Todd, A. E. Fagg, L. E. G. Ames, H. A. Pawson, J. G. W. Davies, *B. H. Valentine, P. Hearn, †T. G. Evans, E. Crush, R. R. Dovey and F. Ridgway.

First innings: 51 (Johnston three for 10, Loxton three for 10). *Second innings:* 124 (Pawson 35, Evans 49; Lindwall four for 25).

Umpires: A. R. Coleman and A. Lockett

GENTLEMEN v AUSTRALIANS 229 (332)

At Lord's, August 25, 26, 27 [1948]. Australians won by an innings and 81 runs. Bradman celebrated his farewell appearance at Lord's with his ninth century of the tour, in the course of which he became the first overseas cricketer to score 2,000 runs during each of four visits to England. Once again the Australians' big total robbed the match of much competitive interest. Brown, who hit his eighth century in his most attractive innings of the season, showed even more freedom than Bradman, with whom he shared a second-wicket stand of 181. ... Bradman (nineteen 4's) threw away his wicket after reaching 150, but Hassett and Miller took part in the third century stand in succession, the Australians finishing the first day with 478 for three. ... [Next day] Hassett continued effortlessly and reached 200 in the last over before lunch, when Bradman declared. ... The Gentlemen's follow-on was notable for a free display by Edrich ... who hit twenty-two 4's [and] went from 72 to 100 in boundary strokes alone.

Australians

S. G. Barnes c Wooller b Bailey	19	S. J. Loxton c Griffith b Bailey	17
W. A. Brown c Bailey b Wooller	120	R. A. Hamence not out	24
*D. G. Bradman c Donnelly b Brown	150	B 6, l-b 4, w 1	11
A. L. Hassett not out	200	(five wkts dec)	**610**
K. R. Miller c Simpson b Wooller	69		

I. W. Johnson, R. R. Lindwall, †R. A. Saggers and D. Ring did not bat.

Gentlemen bowling: Bailey 27–4–112–2; Wooller 24–1–131–2; Palmer 21–3–58–0; Edrich 16–3–49–0; Yardley 24–5–88–0; Brown 27–0–121–1; Robins 4–0–22–0; Donnelly 6–0–18–0.

Gentlemen

R. T. Simpson, W. J. Edrich, C. H. Palmer, M. P. Donnelly, N. W. D. Yardley, F. G. Mann, *R. W. V. Robins, W. Wooller, T. E. Bailey, F. R. Brown and †S. C. Griffith.

First innings: 245 (Simpson 60, Robins 30; Johnson four for 60, Ring three for 74). *Second innings:* 284 (Edrich 128; Johnson three for 69, Ring five for 70).

Umpires: P. T. Mills and J. Smart

SOUTH OF ENGLAND v AUSTRALIANS 230 (333)

At Hastings, September 1, 2, 3 [1948]. Drawn. With his third century in successive innings, Hassett again played the leading part in a big score by the Australians, for whom Bradman and Harvey also completed three figures. Barnes gave a catch at the wicket off the first ball of the day and Brown went at 49, but Bradman and Hassett added 188 for the third wicket before Bradman fell to a good catch at mid-on. He did not offer a chance and hit a 6 and seventeen 4's. ... Rain stopped play shortly after tea [on the second day], and on the last day a series of heavy showers caused frequent delays. Compton led the way in bright batting with 82 out of 116 in under two hours, and Bradman rested his regular bowlers in the closing stages, during which Brown took four wickets ... in twenty-five deliveries.

Australians

S. G. Barnes c Griffith b Bailey	0	S. J. Loxton not out	67
W. A. Brown c Edrich b Mallett	13	C. L. McCool b Perks	5
*D. G. Bradman c Mann b Bailey	143	R. R. Lindwall not out	17
A. L. Hassett c Mallett b Perks	151	B 2, l-b 6, n-b 1	9
R. N. Harvey c Griffith b Perks	110	(seven wkts dec)	**522**
R. A. Hamence lbw b Mallett	7		

†D. Tallon and W. A. Johnston did not bat.

South of England bowling: Bailey 21–0–125–2; Perks 26–5–92–3; Mallett 35–5–102–2; Cook 31–5–97–0; Compton 7–0–43–0; Edrich 8–0–37–0; Barnett 3–0–17–0.

South of England

C. J. Barnett, W. J. Edrich, G. H. G. Doggart, D. C. S. Compton, T. E. Bailey, *F. G. Mann, B. H. Valentine, †S. C. Griffith, A. W. H. Mallett, R. T. D. Perks and C. Cook.

First innings: 298 (Barnett 35, Edrich 52, Compton 82, Mann 31; Brown four for 16).

Umpires: F. Chester and E. Cooke

H. D. G. LEVESON GOWER'S XI v AUSTRALIANS 231 (334)

At Scarborough, September 8, 9, 10 [1948]. Drawn. Rain seriously curtailed play on Wednesday and delayed the start on Thursday, but spectators assembled early each day and the ground was never more crowded than for this final match of Bradman in England. Probably the Australians were not handicapped when Bradman called wrongly to the coin spun by Robins, and their proviso that Mr Leveson Gower should not include more than six Test players in his eleven meant an easy match for the full strength of Australia. On a pitch completely covered by a tarpaulin before the match and whenever play ceased, the Australians were supreme. ... Barnes shared the batting honours with Bradman. Morris helped to wear down the attack in a stand of 102, and 225 runs were added before Barnes left to a catch on the boundary ... Bradman, having become highest scorer, skied a ball to cover-point. Batting three hours ten minutes, he hit two 6's and nineteen 4's. He began with 30 out of 38 on Thursday and made his 153 out of 305. Bradman did not declare until after tea; then, besides showing agility in fielding, he remained the personality of the match by bowling the last over. ...

H. D. G. Leveson Gower's XI

L. Hutton, L. B. Fishlock, W. J. Edrich, M. P. Donnelly, N. W. D. Yardley, *R. W. V. Robins, F. R. Brown, †T. G. Evans, A. V. Bedser, J. C. Laker and T. L. Pritchard.

First innings: 177 (Fishlock 38, Donnelly 36, Yardley 34; Lindwall six for 59, Johnson three for 45). *Second innings:* Two for 75.

Australians

S. G. Barnes c Yardley b Laker	151	I. W. Johnson c Hutton b Brown	38
A. R. Morris b Yardley	62	†D. Tallon c Edrich b Bedser	2
*D. G. Bradman c Hutton b Bedser	153	A. L. Hassett not out	7
S. J. Loxton retired hurt	12	W. A. Johnston not out	26
R. N. Harvey b Brown	23	L-b 7, w 1, n-b 1	9
R. R. Lindwall c Evans b Brown	5	(eight wkts dec)	**489**
K. R. Miller c Evans b Bedser	1		

H. D. G. Leveson Gower's XI bowling: Pritchard 19–4–60–0; Bedser 27–7–72–3; Laker 20–4–95–1; Brown 40–4–171–3; Robins 3–1–9–0; Yardley 13–2–56–1; Edrich 3–0–17–0.

Umpires: H. G. Baldwin and A. R. Coleman

SCOTLAND v AUSTRALIANS

At Edinburgh, September 13, 14 [1948]. Australians won by an innings and 40 runs. Another fine century by Morris and bright batting by McCool atoned for several Australian failures. Barnes, Miller, Bradman and Hamence fell for 91 before McCool joined Morris in a stand of 109. ... Scotland were dismissed twice in a day for 196 runs.

Australians

S. G. Barnes lbw b Youngson	5	D. Tallon c Laidlaw b Edwards	6
A. R. Morris b Laidlaw	112	†R. A. Saggers st Wykes b Laidlaw	8
K. R. Miller c Wykes b Colledge	6	D. Ring not out	3
*D. G. Bradman b Nicol	27	W. A. Johnston c Wykes b Laidlaw	0
R. A. Hamence c Laidlaw b Nicol	6	B 7, l-b 4	11
C. L. McCool lbw b Laidlaw	52		**236**
I. W. Johnson st Wykes b Laidlaw	0		

Scotland bowling: Youngson 21–2–62–1; Colledge 13–2–38–1; Nicol 17–1–55–2; Edwards 13–4–19–1; Laidlaw 12.2–1–51–5.

Scotland

G. L. Willatt, T. Crosskey, †J. C. Wykes, I. J. M. Lumsden, W. Nicol, B. G. W. Atkinson, J. Aitchison, W. A. Edwards, *W. K. Laidlaw, F. Colledge and G. W. Youngson.

First innings: 85 (Johnston six for 15, Johnson three for 18). *Second innings:* 111 (Crosskey 36; Ring four for 20, Morris five for 10).

Umpires: G. W. Lawson and R. Hollingdale

SCOTLAND v AUSTRALIANS

At Aberdeen, September 17, 18 [1948]. Australians won by an innings and 87 runs. Before a record crowd of 10,000 Bradman marked his last game in Britain with a brilliant innings which included seventeen 4's and two 6's. Scotland, sent in by Bradman, received a useful start from Crosskey and Willatt, and Aitchison and Nicol added 65 for the fifth wicket, but McCool and Johnson dismissed the remaining batsmen for 22. … Bradman's hard hitting delighted the crowd. In Scotland's second innings only Willatt batted confidently against an attack in which nine bowlers were used. Tallon took a turn with the ball, and Johnson, deputising behind the wicket, finished the game and the tour by stumping Laidlaw.

Scotland

G. L. Willatt, T. Crosskey, †J. C. Wykes, I. J. M. Lumsden, W. Nicol, J. Aitchison, B. G. W. Atkinson, W. A. Edwards, *W. K. Laidlaw, F. Colledge and G. W. Youngson.

First innings: 178 (Crosskey 49, Nicol 37, Aitchison 32; Johnson three for 26, Morris three for 17, McCool three for 31). *Second innings:* 142 (Willatt 52; Ring four for 30).

Australians

C. L. McCool c Lumsden b Edwards	108	*D. G. Bradman not out	123
R. A. Hamence lbw b Colledge	15	A. R. Morris c Aitchison b Youngson	10
R. N. Harvey c Aitchison b Youngson	4	W. A. Brown not out	24
R. R. Lindwall b Laidlaw	15	B 10, l-b 2, n-b 1	13
I. W. Johnson c Crosskey b Youngson	95	(six wkts dec)	**407**

W. A. Johnston, D. Ring and †D. Tallon did not bat.

Scotland bowling: Youngson 35–3–114–3; Colledge 27–4–93–1; Laidlaw 10–0–62–1; Nicol 15–5–56–0; Edwards 18–5–69–1.

Umpires: L. E. Tyson and W. Nelson

1948-49

Sir Donald Bradman leaves the SCG after his final innings there: February 26, 1949.

1948-49

In Australia, the brilliance of Trumper was succeeded by the equal brilliance of Macartney, and the brilliance of Macartney by the equal brilliance of Bradman. Yet Macartney's main successes in Test cricket were gained in England, and his early first-class cricket was marked rather by steadiness and slowness than by brilliance in batting, providing a complete contrast to the audacity of his maturer years. Curiously enough, it was much the same with Bradman, some of whose early innings in first-class cricket were extremely defensive in character.

The very mention of these few names tends to raise comparisons and inevitable controversies. During his amazing cricket career, Bradman was subjected to criticism because of his penchant for heavy scoring. It was a most extraordinary criticism because, as I think I have demonstrated previously in the pages of *Wisden*, the result, in almost every case, was of decisive importance to the success of his side.

From 'Cricket and the British Commonwealth', by The Right Hon.

Herbert V. Evatt, KC, MP, Deputy Prime Minister of Australia,

Wisden 1949

The farewell appearances of Sir Donald Bradman in first-class cricket and the selection of the Australian team to tour South Africa in 1949-50 were features of special importance in the Australian season of 1948-49. Bradman played in his own Testimonial match in Melbourne, scoring 123 – his 117th century in first-class cricket – and 10. In the A. F. Kippax–W. A. Oldfield Testimonial in Sydney he scored 53; and for South Australia against Victoria in Adelaide – this match was a Testimonial to A. J. Richardson – Bradman made 30 in his only innings, which was his last in big cricket. ... The Sydney match between combined teams (the Testimonial to Kippax and Oldfield) served as a special trial, and immediately afterwards the Selectors, Sir Donald Bradman, Mr E. A. Dwyer and Mr J. Ryder, chose the team to tour South Africa ...

From 'Australian Inter-State Matches', by T. L. Goodman

D.G. BRADMAN'S XI v A.L. HASSETT'S XI 232 (335, 336)
(BRADMAN'S TESTIMONIAL MATCH)

At Melbourne, December 3, 4, 6, 7 [1948]. The result was a tie. The match produced a magnificent farewell to Bradman by the Melbourne crowd. It also produced a riot of run-getting, 1,672 runs being scored in the four innings. Don Tallon, batting for Bradman's XI ... levelled the scores from the last ball of the match. Tallon made 91 of 100 runs scored in the last hour. Lindwall on the first day 'stole the show' with his 104 in eighty-six minutes. He and Saggers put on 160 in eighty-four minutes. The stage was set for Bradman on the Saturday. When 97 he was missed by McCool, off W. Johnston, in a manner that pleased the crowd of nearly 53,000. Bradman reached 123 – his 117th and final century in first-class cricket. ... Bradman received approximately £A10,000.

A.L. Hassett's XI

W. A. Brown, S. G. Barnes, *A. L. Hassett, N. Harvey, W. Langdon, C. L. McCool, R. R. Lindwall, †R. A. Saggers, L. Johnson, B. Dooland and W. A. Johnston.

First innings: 406 (Barnes 32, Hassett 35, Harvey 34, Langdon 60, McCool 35, Lindwall 104, Saggers 52; Loxton three for 39). *Second innings:* 430 (Brown 43, Barnes 89, Hassett 102, Langdon 42, Saggers 41, Johnson 53 not out; Ring three for 150, Bradman two for 12).

D.G. Bradman's XI

K. Meuleman c and b Johnson	100	–	c Johnson b Lindwall	3
A. R. Morris c and b McCool	25	–	c and b Barnes	108
R. A. Hamence st Saggers b McCool	58	–	b Lindwall	45
*D. G. Bradman c Harvey b Dooland	123	–	c Saggers b Johnston	10
K. R. Miller b Johnson	2	–	c Langdon b McCool	14
S. J. Loxton b Johnston	21	–	c Hassett b Lindwall	15
V. N. Raymer c Lindwall b McCool	40	–	b Johnson	11
I. W. Johnson c Johnson b McCool	22	–	c Johnson b Dooland	29
†D. Tallon lbw b McCool	11	–	not out	146
D. Ring c McCool b Johnston	17	–	b Dooland	6
G. Noblet not out	4	–	not out	9
Extras	11		Extras	6
	434		(nine wkts)	**402**

A. L. Hassett's XI bowling: *First innings*—Lindwall 15–3–41–0; Johnson 12–1–46–2; McCool 19.4–1–101–5; Johnston 21–4–92–2; Dooland 16–0–95–1; Langdon 4–1–17–0; Barnes 4–0–16–0; Hassett 1–0–2–0; Brown 1–0–13–0. *Second innings*—Lindwall 14–3–32–3; Johnson 14–0–53–1; McCool 8–0–74–1; Johnston 17–2–63–1; Dooland 16–1–105–2; Barnes 8–0–49–1; Brown 1–0–8–0; Harvey 3–0–12–0.

Umpires: A. N. Barlow and R. Wright

A.L. HASSETT'S XI v A.R. MORRIS' XI 233 (337)
(KIPPAX–OLDFIELD TESTIMONIAL)

At Sydney, February 25, 26, 28, March 1 [1949]. Morris' XI won by eight wickets. Besides providing A.F. Kippax and W.A. Oldfield with £A3,015 apiece, the fixture was of additional importance because it served as a trial for candidates for the tour to South Africa. On the first day rain restricted play to three hours ... On the second day (Saturday) the crowd of 41,575 people tumultuously welcomed back Sir Donald Bradman to the scene of many of his former triumphs. He responded by playing an attractive innings of 53 in sixty-five minutes. ...